COLOSSAL AMBITIONS

A Nation Divided: Studies in The Civil War Era

ORVILLE VERNON BURTON AND ELIZABETH R. VARON, *Editors*

Colossal Ambitions

Confederate Planning for a Post–Civil War World

Adrian Brettle

University of Virginia Press
Charlottesville and London

University of Virginia Press
© 2020 by the Rector and Visitors of the University of Virginia
All rights reserved
Printed in the United States of America on acid-free paper

First published 2020

1 3 5 7 9 8 6 4 2

Library of Congress Cataloging-in-Publication Data

Names: Brettle, Adrian, 1972– author.
Title: Colossal ambitions : Confederate planning for
a post–Civil War world / Adrian Brettle.
Other titles: Nation divided.
Description: Charlottesville : University of Virginia Press,
2020. | Series: A nation divided : studies in the Civil War
era | Includes bibliographical references and index.
Identifiers: LCCN 2020000762 (print) | LCCN 2020000763 (ebook) |
ISBN 9780813944371 (cloth) | ISBN 9780813944388 (ebook)
Subjects: LCSH: Confederate States of America—History. |
Confederate States of America—Politics and government. |
United States—History—Civil War, 1861–1865.
Classification: LCC E487 .B74 2020 (print) |
LCC E487 (ebook) | DDC 973.7/13—dc23
LC record available at https://lccn.loc.gov/2020000762
LC ebook record available at https://lccn.loc.gov/2020000763

Cover illustration: Windsor ruins, Port Gibson, Mississippi; photograph
by Marion Post Wolcott, August 1940 (Library of Congress,
Prints and Photographs Division, FSA/OWI Collection)

To the memory of Frank Johnson

CONTENTS

ACKNOWLEDGMENTS

THE DEBTS accumulated during the completion of this book are numerous. Family and friends have helped me enormously. Many years ago, the late Frank Johnson first started me thinking about writing and research. My parents, Harvey and Lindsay Brettle, backed my decision to choose an academic career without reserve, while both my brothers, Oliver and Linton Brettle, generously volunteered to serve as readers (and their offers were gratefully accepted). The late David Eisenberg was of great help and encouragement. Dick Crampton provided last-minute assistance on the dissertation, while Chris and Nadia Payne were instrumental in getting me to seriously think about going back to school. I am so grateful that Chris has gone on to be a loyal reader of various drafts of the book.

I have been fortunate to have had excellent teachers and mentors. Gary Gallagher has provided unstinting support from my choosing of the topic until the completion of the manuscript. I have also benefited from the time, advice, and encouragement of Michael Holt, Peter Onuf, and Elizabeth Varon. Other history department faculty at the University of Cambridge, the University of Virginia, and elsewhere have helped me understand the field and, whether they realize it or not, have contributed to this project. These people include Brian Balogh, Sir David Cannadine, Jon Parry, Brendan Simms, Paul Halliday, John Stagg, Joseph Kett, the late Clive Trebilcock, the late Mark Kaplanoff, Boyd Hilton, Andrew Roberts, Hywel Williams, Max Edelson, the late Elizabeth Brown Pryor, Joan Waugh, Philip Zelikow, and Paul and Adrienne Kershaw. Finally, I would like to thank Karen Chase of the English Department at University of Virginia and the members of her class on Charles Dickens; this course taught me the importance of ambition to the mid-nineteenth century mind.

Several aspects of this manuscript have been presented at various conferences and in other forums. I would like to thank Phil Williams, Barbara Wright, Mary Roy Dawson Edwards, Sandy von Thelen, Trice Taylor, Bryan Hagan, Robert May, Robert Bonner, Sir Richard Carwardine, Jay Sexton, Brian Schoen, Bruce Levine, Alan Taylor, Glenna Matthews, Adam Arenson, Daniel Lynch, Don Doyle, Pat Kelly,

Edward Rugemer, Matthew Karp, Thomas Schoonover, Howard Jones, Paul Quigley, Aaron Sheehan-Dean, Hugh Dubrelle, Niels Eichhorn, Amanda Foreman, C. Wyatt Evans, David Gleeson, Simon Keith Lewis, David Brown, Jeremy Black, and many others for their suggestions and encouragement.

The book could not have been completed without the fellowships, grants, and assistantships I have been lucky to be awarded. The Lee-Jackson Foundation awarded me an Archibald Craig Fellowship for my first year at the University of Virginia. Subsequently I have benefited from support from the University of Virginia history department and the Graduate School of Arts and Sciences, the Bradley Foundation, the International Center for Jefferson Studies, the Boston Athenaeum, the Virginia Historical Society, the Filson Historical Society, the Gilder Lehrman Institute, the Huntington Library, the Dolph Briscoe Center for American History at the University of Texas, Austin, and the North Caroliniana Society. Staff at these organizations and libraries have been of invaluable help to me in navigating their collections, especially Brenda Gunn and Margaret Schlankey at UT Austin; Mary Warnement at the Boston Athenaeum; Glenn Crothers at the Filson; Jason Tomberlin at North Carolininana; Steve Hindle at the Huntington; Tom Mullusky at the GLI; Frances Pollard and Kathleen Wilkins at the VHS; Andrew Jackson O'Shaughnessy, Christa Derksheide, Ann Berkes, and Jack Robertson at the ICJS.

Several colleagues at the University of Virginia assisted in this project, including Will Kurtz, Emily Seinfeld, and Rhonda Barlow, who have been willing readers and editors. I have also repeatedly profited from the vibrant discussion and constructive suggestions of attendees in meetings of both the Early American Seminar and Civil War Group at the University of Virginia. I would like to thank all of the many participants over the last six years, particularly Mike Caires, Jon Greenspan, Nic Wood, Whitney Martinko, Peter Luebke, David Flaherty, Randy Lewis Flaherty, Billy Wayson, and Adam Dean, all of whom have helped me on my way. Finally, I would like to thank the staff the Albert and Shirley Small Special Collections library for their unstinting support.

The department of history at Rowan University awarded me a teaching fellowship and allowed me to present chapters of the book at its faculty work-in-progress seminars. I would especially like to thank William Carrigan, Emily Blanck, James Heinzen, and Stephen Hague for their companionship, freewheeling discussions, and encouragement.

During 2017–18, I was lucky to be the beneficiary of a joint project between the John L. Nau III Center for Civil War History at the University of Virginia and the American Civil War Museum in Richmond. This enterprise was funded by a grant from the Andrew W. Mellon Foundation, which aims to bring new scholarship into the public sphere. Working as part of a team preparing an exhibit at the museum based on my book has been most rewarding, not least enabling me to sharpen and better communicate my arguments. John Coski at the museum has helped me with all manner of questions. My colleagues on the project, including Chris Graham, the guest curator, Ana Edwards, and Meika Downey, have my lasting gratitude; I thank Chris for reading through the manuscript.

In my present academic home, Arizona State University, I have received invaluable advice and last-minute guidance from Don Critchlow, Calvin Schermerhorn, Jon Barth, Daniel Strand, and Mark Power Smith. Lively meetings with the students of the Program for Political History and Leadership in ASU's School of Historical, Philosophical, and Religious Studies continually stimulate my thinking.

A number of other people have read the book through in its entirety, and I am deeply grateful to them all. Two readers for the University of Virginia Press—Robert E. May and one who remained anonymous—twice have offered critical advice, which I adopted wholesale in my revisions. Beverly Brown and Ann Horner not only provided me with somewhere to live in Richmond and Charlottesville, respectively, but have also read through the whole manuscript carefully and saved me from many mistakes. Dick Holway, my editor at the University of Virginia Press, has been a source of constant support and encouragement in the whole process.

COLOSSAL AMBITIONS

INTRODUCTION

The Vast World They Wanted

C OLOSSAL *AMBITIONS* recounts the Confederacy's ambitious plans
during the Civil War and places the Confederacy, and the war in a
broader sense, within a global context. It describes how the Confederate
war unfolded and what arguments were in play as Confederates imagined
victory and its aftermath. The overarching demands of war caused Confederate leaders to abandon or suspend many of the southern antebellum
dreams of territorial extension, for example, into the Caribbean and Latin
America. Nonetheless, Confederate policymakers and spokesmen engaged
in a surprising degree of sustained and often strikingly progressive planning to secure their nation's emergence as a world power. The experience
of four years of an intense war stimulated a constant cycle of imagining
and reimagining this Confederate future. What follows, therefore, is an attempt to reconceptualize Confederate war aims, to account for the surpris-
ingly resilient optimism at the heart of the Confederate war.

Confederates expected far more from their new polity than the defensive preservation of slavery from Federal assaults. Rather, patriotic Confederates remained convinced virtually to the end of the Civil War that
their nation would survive to implement the progressive commercial,
territorial, diplomatic, and racial programs they envisioned and debated
during the conflict. From the beginning, planners believed they were establishing a new great power on the global stage. At the war's outset, they
already boasted the fifth largest and fastest growing economy linked to
global markets, and with scope for apparently limitless commercial and
southward territorial expansion. These proposals and expectations ema-
nated from a variety of individuals, media, and settings and addressed
the themes of territorial acquisition, technology, trade, slavery, and postwar diplomacy with the United States.

Persistent Territorial Expansion

Although Jefferson Davis famously proclaimed "all we ask is to be let alone," his new nation swiftly embarked upon on a policy of expansion, one that would allow the Confederacy parity with the Union in carving up North America. "The North has wanted Canada and the South wants Cuba," he believed. In the past, as sections in one Union, "the expansion of both may have been restrained by the narrow views of each," Davis observed. Now, as separate entities, they would "be left freely to grow." Davis looked forward to the annexation of parts of Mexico and the rest of the West Indies. Territorial growth southward and westward was crucial if the Confederacy was to count as one of the great powers of the future; expanding the footprint of slavery across the tropics under Confederate stewardship would be the slaveholding republic's contribution to world development and progress, especially rescuing economies in the West Indies rendered stagnant, Confederate optimists believed, by emancipation. Expansion was crucial for domestic politics, too, so that nonslaveholders could access land and become slaveholders in the future. Davis remained committed to continental growth; indeed, he listened to proposals from frontiersmen to incorporate Arizona and New Mexico as territories into the Confederacy as late as the winter of 1864–65 and requested resources from the hard-pressed war department to support them.[1]

The Confederate press pushed territorial expansion in the context of grandiose ambition and optimism about the future once the war was over. In particular, James D. B. De Bow, editor of *De Bow's Review*, and Henry Hotze, editor of the *Index*, persistently predicted expansion. What underpinned their expectations for growth was a sense of entitlement based on Confederate exceptionalism. Anglo-American stewardship of an economy based on slavery demanded and necessitated expansion. Additionally, journalists in these papers and diplomats abroad articulated a vision that this large and growing Confederacy would serve not only a commercial function but also a diplomatic one: it would offset United States power and ambition by extending the European international system of the balance of power across the Atlantic. Over the course of the war, planners augmented the staple crop and slavery-based economy with access to the Pacific Ocean, together with dominance of the Mississippi-Missouri watershed.

It was not just the Confederate White House and the jingoistic press that were preoccupied with territorial growth—there were also constant debates in the Confederate Congress between 1862 and 1865 over such issues as the admission into the Confederacy of not only New Mexico and Arizona but also California and other Pacific coastal states. The midwestern states, especially Ohio, Illinois, and Indiana, Confederate leaders imagined, would either form an allied northwestern confederacy or join the Confederate states. Davis's supporters in Congress and his foes alike (such as Representative Henry S. Foote of Tennessee) expended much time and effort framing legislation to entice additional states to join the Confederacy, affirm claims to federal territories, and assert suzerainty over Native Americans across the continent. In their calculus, expansion would not be achieved by military conquest but by commercial penetration, the spread of slavery, and orderly constitutional processes.[2]

THE IMPORTANCE OF INTERNAL IMPROVEMENTS AND TECHNOLOGY

During the war, Southern state governments championed infrastructure development ("internal improvements") and endowed such enterprises with a global significance. According to wartime governor John Letcher of Virginia: the state's railroads "must soon be part of a network of roads reaching Kansas and fast progressing to Pacific." As a result, Virginia would be part of a "central belt" between the Atlantic and Pacific Oceans. For fellow Virginian and political rival Robert M. T. Hunter, successively U.S. senator, Confederate secretary of state, and Confederate senator, the completion of the James River and Kanawha Canal to the Ohio River would enable the future Richmond-Norfolk corridor to become "a great commanding center of credit and commerce," because it would link both the Atlantic and Midwest, controlling "the distribution of the commodities of the world over a vast area, filled with rich and profitable consumers." New York, perhaps even London, would be surpassed by the capital of the Confederacy.[3]

The southern commercial convention movement, which had called for economic development in the 1850s, did not suspend its program on the outbreak of hostilities between the Confederacy and the Union. Instead, meetings of wartime commercial conventions debated the consequences of communications technology. In February 1862, planters of the Mississippi Valley gathered in a convention at Memphis and summed up the changes technology was making: "The rapid increase of war steamers, the great number and length of railroads, and long lines of telegraphs are giving to the affairs of the world an accelerated motion." They folded their new nation into a discourse of progress toward civilization, declaring, "It is time the enlightened states and nations of the earth should cease political persecutions and war for the purpose of keeping each other down." The Confederate elite predicted that greater connectivity, by bringing nations together, would lead to slavery being accepted around the world. The Confederacy's prosperity, its spokesmen promised, "adds to the welfare of others."[4]

A few months after the Memphis convention, another wartime gathering of planters in convention, this time in Georgia, showed the direct potential of these tools of technology and communications for the Confederacy. Former treasury secretary, president of the provisional congress, and now General Howell Cobb presented to his colleagues a plan for a southern telegraph connecting together the slaveholders' global domain: Spain, West Africa, Brazil, Caribbean, and Confederacy. The Confederate commissioner in Brussels, Dudley Mann, wrote to the then secretary of state Judah Benjamin that the cable was part of something even grander: "a timely, well-matured policy" to make the Confederacy "the great telegraphic and traffic highway between the Old World and the West Indies, Mexico, Central and South America and the ports of the South Seas."[5]

FREE TRADE

Although they anticipated that the slavery-based economy would have potential to extend into mining and other resource extraction, Confederate planters, politicians, and merchants expected that the Southern economy would remain focused on staple crops harvested from an ever-growing area by enslaved people and then exported to the Union and Europe. The Confederacy would therefore be economically interdependent on other countries to provide the manufactured goods it needed. This mutual economic interdependence would make the Confederacy, once it had achieved political independence through war, a good ally and even a guarantor of global peace. It was "certain," Robert Hunter told the commissioners to Europe, that the Confederacy's "principles and interests" meant the new power would not be a "disturbing," but rather "a harmonizing influence amongst the nations of the earth."[6]

To the very end of the war, planners expected that the Confederacy would play a central role in the emerging world economy—and that global trade would help the new nation thrive. On January 30, 1865, Confederate House member Daniel Coleman De Jarnette told his fellow representatives that "commerce has been the great Archimedean lever which has moved the world. [. . .] The highest hopes and aspirations of all nations have been to possess and control it, because they know that no wealth can be acquired, nor power preserved, without it."[7]

SLAVERY AS THE FUTURE

Reading backward it is easy to see an inexorable trend toward abolition in the mid-nineteenth century, marked by British and French emancipation of enslaved people in the Caribbean and the emancipation of the serfs in 1861 by the Russian czar. Yet from the Confederates' perspective this retreat was not so clear, especially as they believed other nations, especially the British, were simply hypocrites who had swapped out one form of unfree labor for another; the British, Confederates noted, established unskilled indentured labor systems and planned to transport millions of Chinese and people from the Indian subcontinent to work in plantations. Moral disapproval of human bondage by British abolitionists was simply cover for their envy at the apparent success of American slavery under Confederate stewardship. Meanwhile Confederate commentators interpreted Russian emancipation as a self-interested bid by the czar to undermine the independence of the Russian nobility and centralize authority in his hands—a move toward tyranny and not freedom.[8]

The Confederates' planning underscores how central slavery was to the project of independence. White Southerners derived self-confidence from their staple crop production, and few could imagine an independent Confederacy as based on anything but slave labor. Even as the war delivered blows to the slave labor system, Confederates expected slavery to recover in peacetime and expected that their economy would continue to revolve around coercive labor. Paradoxically, Confederates found ways to conceive of themselves as more racially tolerant than Yankees were, especially regarding Native Americans and Hispanic Catholics in Mexico, and insisted that their version of white republicanism represented the world's best hope for future progress.

Far from regarding slavery as a labor system in decline, at the time of secession and the formation of the Confederacy, there were radical efforts to legalize the Atlantic slave trade. The decision of the provisional government not to proceed was less an attempt to appeal to international antislavery opinion and more an acceptance that reopening the trade was unnecessary. Commentators and planners were well aware of the population growth of enslaved people. Furthermore, secessionists in the Deep South knew that opinion in the states of the Upper South—especially Virginia—supported the continued prohibition of the trade on the grounds of its potential depressing effect on the lucrative domestic slave trade. To the end, planners considered the international abolition movement as evidence of foreigners' envy at the apparent economic success of African American slavery under Confederate stewardship. However, proslavery rhetoric encompassed more than economics, as Senator Robert M. T. Hunter of Virginia told a "mass meeting" in Richmond on February 9, 1865: "With our success we shall establish a system of government that shall challenge the respect of the world. We shall solve the problem of the extension of the Anglo-Saxon race to the country south of us, and show that the white and black races may be extended together." The promise of the slaveholders' republic included securing the future of the African race in the Western Hemisphere as well as the manifest destiny of the white.[9]

POSTWAR RELATIONS WITH THE UNITED STATES

Throughout 1864, Confederate planners thought that the United States would be the first nation to officially recognize the independence of their nation, once President Lincoln had failed in his bid to secure reelection. Confederates even debated during the Civil War's last year how magnanimous they should be to Federals in these circumstances. They also contemplated how to snatch victory from the jaws of defeat, in the event that the Confederate armies were forced to surrender. In preparing for postwar negotiations—in victory or defeat—with their erstwhile foes, planners considered the meaning of independence in a world where perhaps the resources the Confederacy possessed had proven insufficient. So they came up with their own plans for a reconstruction of the Union. Vice President Alexander H. Stephens imagined a reformed, shallower, Union committed to liberty and expansion and in which the Confederate states would retain slavery. Commercial agent and propagandist-in-chief in London Henry Hotze expected a reversion to the Articles of Confederation of the early republic, with the central authority as a guide rather than a government, as the basis of a modus operandi with the United States. Former U.S. representative, planter, and lawyer Henry Hilliard looked to the late Senator John Calhoun of South Carolina for inspiration with his idea of a dual presidency.[10]

While such reconstruction plans were a fallback position, Confederates' principal focus was on what sort of alliances they might form after independence. With a European great power conflict looking especially likely during 1863 and 1864, and precedent suggesting that it would merge with the American Civil War, planners increasingly examined European examples of how to coexist with a neighboring state that was also a rival. Representative John Adams Gilmer of North Carolina expected an international system, akin to the German Confederation, in North America that would also include Mexico and Canada, complete with a federal Diet and vetoes for member nations. Others wanted to integrate the political systems of Europe and North America in such a way as to secure Confederate independence in the same way as, for example, Belgium survived adjacent to France. Lucius Q. C. Lamar, once nominated to be Confederate minister to St. Petersburg, Russia, brought back from Europe and promoted in the Confederacy a vision for a federative league joining Europe and America in which stronger powers act as guardians of weaker ones. Remarkably, Confederates envisioned achieving a concert with their Yankee enemies in postwar world affairs, especially in upholding the Monroe Doctrine.[11]

The Ideological Underpinnings of Confederate Ambition

The persistence of grandiose ambition and optimism was rooted in Confederate ideology. In part, this belief system stemmed from their commitment to slavery as both an economic system and as a form of social control. The need to maintain slavery was tantamount to requiring its extension; slavery had to expand in order for southern society to persist and thrive. At the same time, the existence of slavery endowed Confederates with a sense of exceptionalism. The South, they believed, was the most successful slave society in history, and as a result, they concluded southerners were the inevitable leaders of the global defense of slavery in an envious, competitive world.

A commitment to slavery meant a future dominated by staple crop production for export. Planners therefore embraced the economic doctrine of comparative advantage in which national economies would specialize in an international division of labor. The Confederacy would be a producer of raw materials and reliant on other nations—Britain, France, even the United States—for supplies of manufactured goods. A social and economic necessity became an ideology of free trade for Confederates, who believed that this would underpin a system of international relations based on interdependent economies. At times, planners would complicate this vision with the need to protect infant industries at home and reward certain overseas countries with preferential terms of trade via commercial pacts and customs unions. The goal of a free trade interdependent future remained, for Confederates consistently believed that the more overseas customers they had, the more secure slavery would be.

As well as the central role of slavery, Confederate ideology was also driven by southern history, culture, and faith. Confederates looked back to what they conceived as the South's centrality during the Revolution and the republic's founding; they constantly recalled the section's domination of the Democrats, the majority party in the Second Party System, and southerners' confident use of federal power to further their agenda. These habits of power and influence at the national stage connected with what scholars, including Peter S. Carmichael and Stephen W. Berry II, have observed at the individual level: the instinctive southerner needs for a "certain grandeur" and "vague flamboyance," combined with an "impatience at being passed by" in an "age of progress." Faith sustained this ideology, in particular, the recent evangelical revivals to vindicate slavery, as southern churches copied northern successes and also cultivated their missions both to African Americans and abroad. Southerners increasingly regarded their social arrangements, including slavery, as sanctified; they subsequently injected a rhetoric of cleansing and purification into the Confederate national purpose and, above all, believed that the expansion of the Confederacy would be a sign of God's favor.[12]

Continuity and Change Over Time

While recent scholarship has emphasized the Confederates' aspirations to be empire builders and their appropriation of certain currents of modernization, historians have not fully recognized the breadth and tenacity of the Confederate vision of their own commercial and diplomatic might. The one consistent theme throughout the existence of the slaveholders' republic was that even when in a position of relative weakness, ambitious and optimistic Confederates continued to think of their future plans in global terms and to trumpet the worldwide significance of their slaveholding republic. To them, the bid to establish an independent nation was an event with global stakes. The course of the war exercised a profound influence on such plans, as Confederates adapted to new experiences and contingencies and sought to address weaknesses and exploit opportunities exposed by the conflict. As the war unfolded, Confederates, on balance, put more emphasis on internal development, self-sufficiency, and industrial independence and less on free trade, although there was no clear linear progression in Confederate planning. At times Confederate plans were vague and abstract and at other times they were well defined, pragmatic, and achievable within a clear time frame. What determined the nature of the plans at any given juncture of the war was Confederate estimates of the likelihood of an early or imminent peace. The future ambitions for the Confederacy did not include it becoming an armed camp fighting perpetual wars, but when Confederate military fortunes fell and the war appeared destined to last for many years, then the exact characteristics of the future nation in peacetime were open to change and revision. When Confederate fortunes rose, and planners expected the war to be over soon, then there could be more precision about the government's policy objectives and preparation for their achievement.

As Confederate schemes changed and adapted, so did the planners themselves. President Davis remained committed to the project of building a new nation from his nomination in February 1861 until his flight in late April 1865. The president's commitment to the expansion of the United States and then the Confederacy remained consistent to the end. According to his biographer William J. Cooper Jr., Davis "began setting forth ideas and themes that would mark his public life for a decade and a half" when he gave a speech about manifest destiny in February 1846. Davis declared that the secret of American expansion lay in "the energy and restless spirit of adventure" possessed by settlers. This individual spirit translated into geographical, racial, and cultural ambitions, which would continue "until our people shall sit down on the shores of the Pacific." These goals remained applicable to the Confederacy after secession. Many shared his determination and, despite being buffeted by grief and poverty, remained committed to the Confederate future. Others lost faith in their grandiose visions, often not because they had become disenchanted with the Confederate project, but because other priorities—private, local, state—took precedence and seemed no longer to be fulfilled by the securing of independence. Confederate constructions of the future were subject to bewildering change, and they reflected a broad range of emotions and dispositions—from despair and panic in moments of defeat to stubborn defiance in moments of victory. Woven throughout the Confederate story was a persistent and optimistic ambition, based on Southern whites' enduring belief in their providential entitlement to a prominent place in the world.[13]

Planners for the future of the nation in peacetime recognized and welcomed the expectation that their ambitions for the Confederacy would have global implications. The aspirations to dominate North America would have consequences beyond the continental mainland. This hope to change the world was not new. The earlier visions of confident leaders during secession and the early months of the Confederacy was for the nation to become the slaveholding superpower committed to producing the quantities of raw materials needed to fuel the industrial revolution in the Union and Western Europe. By 1862, however, planners and policymakers perceived this vision to be too complacent, and they then reverted to some interconnected policies that they had earlier pursued from within the federal government in the 1850s. These measures included the construction of a powerful fleet, the negotiation of commercial pacts, and the implementation of a proslavery foreign policy.

If the goal to be a significant force in the world remained for many Confederates, the preferred means to achieve this objective—how to build a new nation—continued to evolve. The adoption of a liberal-internationalist stance during 1863 contrasted with the assertiveness of 1862 and the quasi-imperialism of 1861, yet it still gave the Confederacy a wide-ranging albeit vaguer mission. In 1864, however, the apparent imminence of peace meant realism supplanted idealism for many individuals, convinced as they were that the new nation urgently required allies and probably would have to seek a compromise with the United States. Finally, by early 1865, the very idea of a national mission appeared to be less important for some Confederates. Laws of progress mattered less than laws of nature, and a cause necessary to extract further sacrifices from the people appeared more vital than nation building to deliver practical prosperity.

1

What Would an Independent South Mean for the World in 1861?

BETWEEN THE election of Lincoln in November 1860 and the onset of war in April 1861, optimistic nation builders charted the future of an independent South. They spoke about the South, rather than the Confederacy, as they expected all fifteen slave states to secede. Even if they feared that war would soon break out, these optimists did not consider that this prospect would dictate the future for southerners. They may have believed that Republicans and abolitionists had driven them out of the Union; but, as optimists, they also looked forward to the South having good relations with the United States. Commercial ties would take precedence over ideological differences between nations. Therefore, it was to their northern neighbor and Britain that the Confederate government first sent commissioners in February and March 1861, rather than to Brazil and Spanish Cuba, their fellow slave powers.

The diplomatic choices reflected the priorities of the incoming Davis administration. It considered that the Union and Britain would be the Confederacy's most important commercial partners and that this shared interest would be instrumental in preventing future armed conflict. Nevertheless, the Confederate future would be one that was emphatically proslavery, even if, after much consideration, the Confederate Provisional Congress chose not to reopen the Atlantic slave trade. That decision would not limit the ambition of the new nation. Its territorial growth would be determined by a rapidly increasing population, especially given the racial composition of the South, which meant a relatively large African American population had to urgently migrate westward and southward. Moreover, the future development of slavery required new lands to clear and cultivate. More broadly, planners of the new nation looked forward to securing it within a framework of competitive yet interdependent nation-states. New technologies—in particular steamships and railroads—stood ready to render areas of the tropics open to slavery and exploitation. Increases in staple crop production would enable the South to become a leading commercial power by being the center of an international trading economy dominated, at least in theory, by free trade. The South would not only be the leading exporter of raw materials but also the leading importer of manufactured goods. Confederate society broadly, its leaders imagined, would participate in the practical realization of this dream with every means at their disposal.

A National Mission Determined by People, Slavery, and God

In attempting the impossible task of predicting the future consequences of secession, leading white southerners drew on an interpretation of past events that suited them, then assumed these developments were both God-given and natural, and finally expected such trends to continue into the future. Moreover, they told themselves that there was no alternative, save ruin, to this course of action. The result was the anticipation of territorial expansion with a huge surge in wealth in the context of the establishment of a harmonious system of international relations—including the antislavery powers of the United States and Britain—based on increased commerce underpinned by the triumph of free trade principles.

Lewis Maxwell Stone, a prosperous Pickens County, Alabama, lawyer and state senator, seized upon continued expansion after secession as the vital condition to deliver individual prosperity and a collective advance of civilization. "Expansion seems to be the law and destiny of our institutions," he told the delegates to the Alabama secession convention on January 25, 1861. "To remain healthful and prosperous within, and to make sure our development and power," Stone explained, "it seems essential that we grow without." Prior to Lincoln's election, but looking forward to the event as certain, the author of a New Orleans newspaper editorial saw "such profitable expansion of [the South's] territory as the natural order of things." Southern expansion would be in the interests of virtue, civilization, and morality. Richard Thompson Archer, a wealthy cotton planter and slave owner who owned the Anchuca Plantation in

Claiborne County, Mississippi, linked expansion to acts of improvement by white southerners on a vast scale because "common sympathies common necessities common origin make us philanthropists."[1]

History taught that the conjunction of providential destiny, individual will, and institutional support, which together comprised civilization, not only gave momentum to expansion but also meant if the South failed to expand it would decline. "Civilization which has ceased to expand is doomed to perish," a journalist writing in the *Richmond Examiner* declared. "Stagnation is the precursor of disease and death." Progress placed great demands on the ambitions for the nation. "The idea of equilibrium is absurd," observed the Virginian-born George W. L. Bickley, president of the Knights of the Golden Circle, adding "society must advance or retrograde, and we shall do well not to try to stop."[2]

Lucius Q. C. Lamar, a member of Mississippi's secession convention, explained why merely maintaining slavery where it already existed was unacceptable to those who supported leaving the Union. To believe in slavery was tantamount to demanding its expansion. Mississippi's secession ordinance, drafted by Lamar, declared that the United States government "refuses the admission of new slave States into the Union, and seeks to extinguish [slavery] by confining it within its present limits, denying the power of expansion." It followed that the necessity of expansion of nations in general, so as to be on the right side of the dividing line between living and dying powers, was intensified by specific attributes of slavery. "Our social system," a Virginian journalist wrote, "must have *perfect security* in its present and future existence." Additionally, slavery "must have *perfect assurance* of its natural expansion and development. If it wants either it must ultimately perish" because slavery has inbuilt "within it the law of growth and expansion." Therefore, he agreed with the prominent South Carolinian Presbyterian clergyman, academic, and journalist James H. Thornwell that the Republicans "can circumscribe the area of slavery if they can surround it with a circle of non-slaveholding states and prevent it from expanding." If the Lincoln administration succeeded in its objective, slavery "will wither and decay under hostile influences." U.S. senator Robert M. T. Hunter of Virginia warned about the dire consequences if slavery was to be "penned in" and "localized" within a state's borders. Only membership of the Confederacy offered the Upper South continuation of the domestic slave trade and expansion of slavery.[3]

In 1860, Thornwell and others across the South propagated an ambitious agenda for the proposed nation to pursue, one that blended religion, proslavery thought, and economics. Clergymen, in their sermons and published pamphlets, carefully argued that secession was not an act of covetousness but instead could bring the people closer to God. According to historians Elizabeth Fox-Genovese and Eugene Genovese, Thornwell regarded continued submission to the United States government to be an act of voluntary surrender to sin. As a result, he wrote in a widely read pamphlet that southerners would not secede due to "ambition and avarice." In order to align the Confederacy with its providential mission, optimists had to persuade the rest that "good would spring from evil," "cast about for considerations to reconcile [the South] to her destiny," and think how the South "might be the gainer by the measure which the course of the [United States] government was forcing upon her." Thornwell regarded that not only duty to God but also the more secular pursuits of honor and fame were crucial for secessionists as "motives to reconcile the mind to its necessity." The threat of Republican Party tyranny had absolved secessionists of the charge of leaving the Union for the wicked reasons of vanity and pride; yet the ambitions of its citizens had to be realized in order to avoid a return to "enslavement" to the North.[4]

Benjamin M. Palmer, a close friend and protégé of Thornwell's and the pastor of the First Presbyterian Church of New Orleans, also strove to reconcile the future needs of the nation—peaceful southern expansion—with the demands of providence. He set out his position in the April 1861 edition of the *Southern Presbyterian Review*, the paper he cofounded with Thornwell and others in 1847, as "the premier scholarly religious journal in the south." The Presbyterian Church had split in 1857 over the issue of slavery, and southern clergy not only determined to vindicate slavery but also support its expansion. He wrote in response to an article in a rival quarterly by R. J. Breckinridge, a slaveholding Kentuckian cleric and another friend of Thornwell's, who accused secessionists of "ulterior motives" in leaving the United States. Secessionists wanted "a war," Breckinridge claimed, "which shall end when you shall have taken possession of the whole southern part of this continent down to the Isthmus of Darien [Panama]." Palmer dismissed the charge. "If we desire territory," he argued, "we shall not with school-boy greed pluck the apple when it is green, but will wait upon history till the time of ripeness, when it will fall into the lap." Far from abandoning the older American mission of spreading liberty through peaceful expansion, Palmer asserted the South would embrace it. Clergy were now convinced of the desirability of slavery and its growth, but they would not support the new nation legalizing filibustering as a means to that end. George W. L. Bickley—perhaps keen to obscure his own past record of involvement in such attempts to take over countries at peace with the United States via privately financed military expeditions—pointed out that it was important that "we do not go to Mexico as filibusters to rob, burn and devastate—but as colonists." He suggested southerners follow the earlier example of Texans instead and "go . . . in the character of a defensive colony," "become a center drawing to itself every good citizen," and "arrest this state of anarchy and misrule." The process to be followed would be gradual: "plant a southern colony with southern habits and southern institutions" and "not at once ask that states of Mexico be admitted" to the Confederacy. Instead the Knights of the Golden Circle would "Americanise it, plant our institutions there and build up a separate nationality" just as had happened in Texas.[5]

John B. Thrasher of Claiborne County, Mississippi, a lawyer, planter, and great slaveholder, echoed the clergymen in the adoption of a high moral tone to reinforce the need for the expansion of slavery. In the future, the slaveholding class would have a moral obligation to spread slavery where possible. Electioneering for southern Democratic presidential candidate John C. Breckinridge on November 5, 1860, Thrasher explained in a speech that it was a "duty to God, to ourselves and to posterity to perpetuate African slavery, and to extend it as a missionary duty." He regarded the Middle Passage and enslavement of Africans by white southerners as a "purely moral and religious act, and pleasing in the sight of God." While he believed God ordained the white race to rule the world, Thrasher contrasted the careful attributes of the southern slaveholders in 1860 with those of the reckless Revolutionary French in Haiti from 1790 to demonstrate how ownership of enslaved people was a privilege, which could be mismanaged. Slaveholders had to avoid complacency—hence the utility of expansion as requiring effort and vigilance on the part of slaveholders. Such restraint did not mean setting rigid limits to the growth of slavery. Coexistence with a hostile federal government would not only lead to a Haitian-style bloodbath, but it would also deny slaveholders the chance to realize the potential of slavery. Progress, geography, and economics apparently dictated that slavery would predominate as the labor force of the tropics. With that mentality in place, expansionists debated how far slavery should expand under the tutelage of southern slaveholders.[6]

Leonidas W. Spratt, a prominent South Carolinian journalist, claimed before the 1859 Vicksburg Commercial Convention that the slavery-based society of the South was ideally suited to move on with a measured dignity of power and progress. By the time of the formation of the Confederacy, Spratt had moved away from paternalism toward profits in a public letter addressed to John Perkins, a delegate from Louisiana to the provisional congress, who happened to be one of the largest slaveholders from that state. Spratt believed slavery had to remorselessly grow because of its potential as a labor force ideally suited to the cultivation of staple crops in the tropical and subtropical regions of the world—providing white southerners were there to manage it. "The system of domestic slavery, guided always by the best intelligence, directed always by the strictest economy," he insisted, "can underwork the world." Spratt portrayed slavery as an inexorable force because it was cost-effective, and he declared that "there is no other human labor that can stand against it." In this context, the role of the new nation was simply to allow slavery to expand of its own accord, provided slaveholders remained conservative in ideology and pursued ambitious individual and national programs. The language of Palmer was similar to that of Spratt. Both agreed that slavery connected the South to global commerce. The future of civilization and world progress depended on slavery's survival; it was threatened by "the decree of restriction and ultimate extinction" promised by the incoming Republican administration. "It is the duty of the south in the discharge of a great historic trust," Palmer preached, "to conserve and transmit the same." This duty meant allowing slavery to achieve its natural limits, a feat only achievable outside the United States.[7]

Once independence had been achieved, where these "natural limits" of slavery—under white southerners' auspices—extended was open to debate; but they agreed that forces beyond their control would drive the expansion of slavery in the future. An expert in tropical diseases, Dr. William H. Holcombe of Natchez, Mississippi, and Tensas Parish, Louisiana, based his calculation on the alleged immunity of African Americans to those endemic fevers of the lower latitudes. "It is the means," he predicted about slavery, "thereby the white man is to subdue the tropics all round the globe to order and beauty and to the wants and interests of an ever-expanding civilization." Southerners had "to succeed in establishing *as we shall* a vast opulent, happy and glorious slaveholding republic, throughout tropical America." It was important for optimists to identify providential, historical, even progressive, factors that would determine the extent of slavery; doing this enabled them to undermine the arguments of opponents while identifying themselves with a grand global vision and confirm slavery as an eternal institution. Palmer agreed that geography itself would dictate slavery's reach. "If African slavery exists at all, its limits must be determined by climate and soil," he considered, and he believed "that precisely where it ceases to be profitable there it will inevitably cease to exist." Joseph Eggleston Segar, a Virginian Whig politician who, in earlier years, had stressed the possibilities of internal improvements to foster a commercial revolution, nevertheless put the future of slavery on a more elevated basis. "No human legislation can prevent" its expansion, and "slavery *will* go wherever it is profitable just as sure as water finds its level," he insisted during a speech before the Virginia House of Delegates on March 30, 1861, "because the instincts of the human constitution and the laws of soil and climate are stronger than any law-giving of finite man."[8]

FINDING A PLACE FOR SURPLUS PEOPLE

The influential slaveholder and U.S. senator Robert Toombs of Georgia, with plantations across three states, believed it was the natural growth in numbers of enslaved people that had driven the rapid expansion of the South since the Revolution. Familiar with the arguments of the disasters that awaited societies suffering from overpopulation by Thomas Malthus via Harriet Martineau, he determined that continued territorial expansion would solve the problem. "What shall be done with them?" Toombs asked his fellow senators about African Americans—"We must expand or perish." Crucially, the Georgian then dismissed the argument made by his opponents that expansion was simply a means to obtain additional slave state votes in Congress, and furthermore, he insisted that expansion was vital whether or not the Atlantic slave trade was reopened. "Those who tell you that the territorial question is an abstraction, that you can never colonize another territory without the African slave trade, are both deaf and blind to the history of the past sixty years."[9]

Census data appeared to corroborate these arguments and pointed toward future acceleration in the rate of growth in numbers of enslaved people. The *Richmond Examiner* believed the population of enslaved people was doubling every twenty-five years; others put the period of increase at twenty. In this context, expansion enabled slaveholders to "diffuse" slavery southward and westward in order to disperse the apparently dangerous concentrations of numbers of enslaved people and indeed render that population growth an advantage rather than as something to be feared. Senator Robert Hunter, who owned over one hundred enslaved people in his home state, stressed the advantages for Virginia, and other Upper South and Border States, of joining an expansive southern confederacy. In a letter published in both the *Richmond Enquirer* (December 1860) and *De Bow's Review* (January 1861), he averred that independence would provide those states with "an outlet for their surplus population of slaves," who would go either into "these co-states," or "in whatever territory might be acquired by that Union."[10]

The mission to expand with its emphasis on providential destiny and individualism together with the impetus of population growth and increased mobility was something that southerners shared with other peoples, especially northerners and the British. What transformed this sentiment into something much more expansive for southerners was its interaction with race. Rather than panic about the precarious racial balance that would prevail once the southern states separated from the overwhelmingly white populated states of the North, the University of Virginia law professor James P. Holcombe, a prominent proslavery theorist, placed southern plans within the context of the global trend of imperialism. The expansion of empires led by the British—especially in India—combined territorial acquisitions with, Holcombe (according to Matthew Karp) averred, "the subjugation and in many places annihilation of aboriginal peoples." While relatively few Britons governed huge numbers of people in India, the peculiar circumstances of the South and slavery necessitated a constant process of adjustment and expansion. Holcombe argued at the Virginia Convention of 1861 that Deep South states "want future acquisition of territory" simply in order "that the normal relation of races may be preserved for all time"; otherwise, existing "southern territory . . . will not be adequate to the peaceful accommodation of the black race." Maryland author John H. Parkhill spoke for many in voicing his belief that the rate of growth of the African American population was higher than that of the white. He based his arguments about race relations on his study of Haiti. Parkhill claimed that Haiti's history demonstrated that "*the white and the black races cannot exist together as equals in the same community.*" Catastrophe would result if expansion did not take place. William Holcombe agreed with his brother James and Parkhill: "It is only thus that an inferior race can exist in contact with a superior one," and as a result, he anticipated "no terminus to the institution of slavery."[11]

The spread of slavery raised issues about the status of indigenous peoples, whose unwanted presence on coveted lands had arrested southerners' expansionist impulse during the Mexican War fifteen years earlier. Newspaper journalists and some politicians, using their selective reading of U.S. history as a guide, believed the native peoples would simply disappear before the advance of white slaveholders with African American enslaved people. Far from "Indians, Creoles, Spaniards [being] in the way," the *Daily Constitutionalist* of Augusta, Georgia, declared, "the case of Florida, Louisiana, New Mexico, California, and Missouri [show that] the dominant race will supplant all others, and slavery will expand South to Brazil and from her till stopped by snow." As a result, regarding "Arizona and Mexico, Central America and Cuba," Stone advised the Alabama convention, "all may yet be embraced within the limits of our southern republic."[12]

At the same time, the reservations expressed during the earlier debates of the 1840s reappeared. In January 1861, William L. Yancey warned his fellow delegates at the Alabama secession convention that a sudden expansion into Mexico would mean the inclusion in a southern confederacy of substantial numbers of Native American and Mestizo people. He had both racial and religious qualms about Mexicans becoming future fellow Confederate citizens. "It is, at least doubtful," Yancey declared, "whether we should wish an expansion in that direction that would bring with it the recognition of such a mass of ignorant and superstitious and demoralized population as Mexican states, if annexed, would necessarily bring." Nevertheless, this ambitious politician looked forward to the success of the new nation's diplomacy. Yancey had long been an advocate of territorial expansion, including during the Mexican War, and during the recent election campaign had stressed the commercial glory that awaited the southern republic even as he still professed unionism. His change of tone was because he wanted to present the South as the world's peacemaker, and he feared that an avowed program of expansion would undermine international support for the new nation. Others foresaw problems closer to home. "Even the slave would degenerate in Mexico . . . return to Africanism," the writer, journalist, lawyer, and politician William R. Smith of Alabama warned his fellow delegates. Imperialism would undermine the vitality and republicanism of white settlers because their

"American gravity would sink into Mexican frivolity." Smith gloomily predicted industrious commercial farmers and planters would change into impoverished soldiers and proprietors of inefficient haciendas and behave like petty tyrants.[13]

To obviate such concerns, James D. B. De Bow stressed, on moral, strategic, and racial grounds, slow and peaceful expansion, as opposed to rapid conquest. Although a vigorous expansionist, as editor, statistician, and leading light of the southern convention movement, De Bow now counseled that the Confederate states should adopt a gradual approach and not prematurely "conquer and annex territory that would destroy the homogeneousness of their population." More bluntly, U.S. representative Zebulon B. Vance reminded his constituents in Washington, North Carolina, that if a confederacy was to "take in the mongrel, cut-throat population of Mexico and Central America," its leaders should remember "the wisest and greatest of southern statesmen from Calhoun down have disapproved and argued against such a thing." The criticism was only against excessive expansion that involved the sudden acquisition of densely populated lands. After all, Calhoun had been a passionate expansionist, provided it was done "without subverting its constitution or destroying liberty." Even critics envisaged a realm larger than all the slave states together; Vance anticipated adding "cotton lands enough to employ one hundred million slaves."[14]

These projections of continued population increase of African Americans provided the context for proposals, offered up in early 1861, to reopen the African slave trade. Adopting such a policy would make territorial expansion more urgent and even more extensive. "The rapid increase of our slaves," Sidney Cherry Posey told the Alabamian Convention, "points to the necessity of acquiring more territory before we import more slaves from Africa." Many did not share Vance's opinion that the South had sufficient undeveloped lands to satisfy the future natural growth of the slave population, let alone enough for the resumption of imports of additional enslaved people. Above all, the South had to first secure its independence and freedom of action before considering the question of the international slave trade. "If our limits are to be circumscribed, and we are to have no territorial expansion or outlet," Posey's more fearful colleague Stone added, "then to increase the number of our slave population by importations from Africa would be disastrous."[15]

Advocates for the reopening of the international slave trade argued that such a policy would secure slavery where it existed and assumed that expansion would address the concerns about overpopulation. Former U.S. representative and now delegate to the Alabama Convention, James Ferguson Dowdell argued the availability of what he deemed to be vacant land in Central America would offset the concerns of his colleagues regarding the importation of additional enslaved people. There would be no problem arising from "a surplus of African slaves . . . [given] the advantage of our proximity to that country." With "a timely and judicious policy," Dowdell concluded, "we could settle the neighboring states and territories" in Mexico and Central America and thereby "secure safety to ourselves and security to our humane system of African slavery."[16]

South Carolinian journalists argued that reopening the international slave trade went beyond protecting slavery where it existed by pushing away hostile powers, but it would also increase the scope of ambitions possible for the future nation. Leonidas Spratt reported in De Bow's Review, at the 1858 Commercial Convention in Vicksburg and in speech in Jackson, Mississippi, that the reopened slave trade would be a "great progressive endeavor" as it promised to assist in the regeneration of Africa. R. Barnwell Rhett, editor of Spratt's rival newspaper the Charleston Mercury, considered benefits closer to home. Reopening the slave trade was a question that "might hereafter involve the development and expansion of our Confederate Empire?" For, the Mercury explained, southerners have "within our reach a large scope of fertile territory uncultivated in Texas, and may have ere long the silver mines of Arizona, and the teeming states of Mexico, to populate and reduce to agricultural productiveness . . ." Consequently, reopening the slave trade would assist in the growth and diversification of the southern economy, leading "to our successful competition with the hypocritical [regarding slavery] nations of Europe."[17]

The planners of the new nation considered the immediate spread of slavery and territorial growth essential to preempt similar plans by other powers. For example, some prominent southern politicians worried that the anticipated movement of millions of Chinese unskilled indentured laborers would provide the labor needed to revive Britain's moribund Caribbean plantation economy so as to compete with the South. However, this supposed migration was not treated as a nightmare to paralyze the planter class; instead it was treated as a sign that slavery was at the forefront of current trends in labor relations. The apparent conduct of competitor powers added urgency to the plans for expansion. Dowdell, in the Alabama convention, spoke of the need to preempt both British and French intentions to "plant their African apprentices in proximity to our borders, with a *purpose* to limit our expansion . . . under the plausible pretext of producing their own cotton, rice, and tobacco."[18]

The South would also export people it did not wish to keep at home. Racial attitudes blurred with prevailing notions of political economy in treating African Americans as examples of the deserving poor. Parkhill, who as a former sailor had probably worked with free African Americans in the U.S. Navy as well as encountering them in Baltimore, looked forward to Haiti being *"open to the immigration of our free blacks,"* although they would have to be removed on a compulsory basis. "The two classes of blacks, slaves and free, cannot remain together in the same community," he explained, "without producing pauperism and crime in one and discontent and insubordination in the other." Southern foreign policy would also benefit, as such a movement of people would offer the chance of "redeeming this fertile island from its present waste." Freed people "should be made the medium through which the reforming power of our civilization can be brought to bear on the social condition of Hayti [*sic*]." While many slaveholders feared a Haitian-style insurrection and race war in the South once Lincoln had undermined their local authority, they also considered present-day Haiti a failed economy and society now ripe for their regeneration efforts.[19]

Hunter expected the nonslaveholding white southerners—who were less able to migrate—to also benefit from the expansion of the Confederacy and movement of slaveholders and enslaved people. "With an outlet for emigration," Hunter stated, "the slave is first move under a decline in the rate of wages. The law of profit moves him to a theatre where he will earn more for his master, and yet more for himself." The mobility of slavery enabled by expansion would mean higher wages for those left behind as "the labor market which [the slave] leaves is thus gradually relieved from the pressure, and the white man remains in the land of his birth, to enjoy the profits of remunerating operations."[20]

The only tropical and subtropical regions in the Western Hemisphere not coveted by expansionists were those lands controlled by other slave powers. Southerners nonetheless expected to play a prominent role in improving the productivity and stability of these countries. In the 1850s, territory—meaning Cuba—that already had slavery was the first target of southern annexationists because the priority at that time was the immediate admission of new slave states into the Union, although the belief was not new that the labor system's international legitimacy would be aided by having other countries directly concerned with its continuance.

As Matthew Karp has shown, even as some politicians demanded the annexation of Cuba, other antebellum proslavery politicians had attempted to support slavery outside of the United States. Independence strengthened the case of the latter group. De Bow recommended the South, once independent, should negotiate both military "offensive and defensive" treaties and commercial pacts with both Spain—Cuba and Puerto Rico's colonial power—and Brazil, on the grounds that these countries were "neighbors and natural friends and customers of the South." As well as a shared interest in the perpetuation of slavery, Brazil imported flour from Virginia while exporting coffee. Coordination of the staple crop production of the slave powers offered the chance to boost the prosperity of all three, while enabling southerners to secure the future of slavery across the western hemisphere.[21]

"The Whole Continent ... to the South Pole"

Optimists had made their case in the wake of Lincoln's election, and now they sought to put a plan for an empire into action both indirectly and directly, as the Confederacy organized itself between January and April 1861. Indirectly, there were policy recommendations and actions that facilitated state power by increasing the federal government's revenue. Various organizations, at corporate, municipal, state, as well as federal levels, adopted pro-growth agendas in their attempts to protect key industries and accelerate internal improvements. Moreover, the personnel of the Davis administration possessed records that were unashamedly expansionist. The policy direction of the federal government—commercially, diplomatically, and territorially, especially in the admission of new states—then set the Confederacy firmly on an expansionist path before war intervened.

Even before the formation of the Confederacy, resolutions passed at state conventions asserted claims to federal territories. Hence the seemingly presumptuous behavior of the delegates in January at Alabama's secession convention when they debated sending envoys to Santa Fe in order to try to secure the application of the U.S. territory of New Mexico (including Arizona) to join the as yet unformed Confederacy as a new state. In addition, secessionists planned the expansion of the cotton economy into the Indian Territory. While formal policy on the territories would necessarily await the formation of a future confederacy, the delegates in the Alabama convention understood the prompt formation of a southern confederacy as an opportunity for the southern states to grab the share of the territories they believed was rightfully theirs and had been withheld by the Union.[22]

The delegates to the convention of the Confederate states in Montgomery had in Jefferson Davis, whom they nominated as president, a man presumed by observers to be intent on establishing a great power. Robert G. H. Kean, a Virginian lawyer, spoke for many in depicting the new Confederate president as an empire builder, in contrast to the provincial reputation of Lincoln: it was a case of "statesman versus stump speaker," or even, quoting Shakespeare, "Hyperion to a Satyr." Robert Bunch, the British consul in Charleston, warned his superior, Lord John Russell, the foreign secretary, that his government should be concerned about Davis's ambition, for he was a man of "impulsive character and advanced doctrines." Bunch attributed his characterization of the president to his record as a "warm advocate of the expeditions of Lopez, Walker and other filibusters." Bunch added that the new president was "a firm believer in the 'manifest destiny' of the South to overrun and convert into slaveholding states of a southern confederacy" numerous territories including "Mexico, Central America and Cuba." Bunch's assessment failed to consider Davis's recent shift from his earlier support of filibustering. The consul was, however, correct about his consistent record on territorial expansion. Historians tend to interpret the nomination of Davis as a moment of moderate triumph over the extremist fire-eaters—Yancey, Rhett, et al.—who had heretofore driven secession. While Davis had not been at the forefront of the secession of his native Mississippi, his credentials as an ambitious leader determined to grow the Confederacy were not in question.[23]

According to Bunch, Davis's cabinet and diplomatic appointments shared the president's vision of the Confederacy. Toombs, the secretary of state, was "a man of the most advanced opinions"—meaning an expansionist in the manner of Davis—and "a secessionist of the worst kind." Bunch probably had in mind, in the words of historians Freehling and Simpson, Toombs's "extravagant posturing and inconsistent programs" rather than any enthusiasm for secession. Toombs had looked forward to "the whole continent ... to the South Pole" being settled upon the "one ... rule of acknowledging slavery and protecting it." Along with his fellow senators John Slidell and Jefferson Davis, Toombs had been a passionate advocate for the purchase of Cuba. Such southern expansion, Toombs believed, would strengthen the Union by increasing markets for northern manufactures as well as the flow of southern raw materials northward.

As for William Yancey, the envoy to Britain, Bunch declared him "a rabid secessionist" and "a favourer of a revival of the slave trade, and a 'filibuster' of the extremist kind of manifest destiny." Bunch was sure about Yancey because the Alabamian had, recently, in both speeches and articles written for *De Bow's Review* and the *Montgomery Advertiser,* supported William Walker in Nicaragua, wished to reopen the Atlantic slave trade, and advocated expansion southward as far as Panama—even if he had recently expressed reservations about the inclusion of Mexicans in the new nation at the Alabama convention. Moreover, as with Toombs, Yancey's style of oratory was not to the taste of the Englishman, and he did not expect his abrasive manner to likewise appeal to the fastidious Russell.[24]

The attitude of Toombs and Yancey about the future of the Confederacy appeared, to the British consul Bunch, to be representative of the wider community of elite southerners from which they were drawn. Moreover, once he had been nominated president, Davis did not seek to change his reputation as an expansionist and appeared to vindicate Bunch's verdict. In early February, on his way to Montgomery for his inauguration, Davis assured an audience in Atlanta that territorial growth would commence for the South after independence. Under a Confederate regime, a journalist recorded that the president-elect "had no fears about Expansion; there were the West India Isles, which, under the old Union, were forbidden fruit to us, and there were the Northern parts of Mexico." Davis looked forward to the fact that the Republican Party, which had successfully blocked expansion since the Pierce administration in the mid-1850s, would no longer be there to perform the same function in the Confederacy.[25]

AN EMPIRE OF FREE TRADE

The consul drew the attention of the British Foreign Office to the new government's commercial aspirations. Yancey's colleague as commissioner, Dudley Mann, was a friend of Davis's and a former assistant secretary in the U.S. State Department. Bunch noted Mann's undoubted expansionist credentials, together with his earlier attempts to increase the size of the U.S. diplomatic corps. Most significant for the consul was Mann being "interested in the attempt to establish direct trade by steam between the southern states and Europe." Although judging through the prism of the aspirations of the leading citizens of Charleston, who were actively engaged in their own project for a steamship line between the port and

Liverpool, Bunch also detected what he construed to be an attitude of absurd presumption. "Their exaggerated idea of the importance of the southern states to Great Britain is really ludicrous." Nevertheless, this community had convinced itself of the legitimacy of their self-importance. Despite being "courteous of manner . . . that the better class of southerners are to foreign representatives," Bunch explained, "the exultation which they feel at having placed us in the position of dependents at their pleasure, cannot be concealed in their conversations with me." By March 1861, even friends of the consul seemed infected with this King Cotton propaganda, as "those with whom I am at all familiar openly tell me that we cannot live without them."[26]

If the shared interest of slavery connected the South with Cuba and Brazil, the common pursuit of commerce promised to involve many more nations in supporting the Confederacy. Writers in *De Bow's Review* and boosters in the southern commercial convention movement argued during the 1850s that free trade combined with greater production would protect slavery because it would increase the numbers of overseas customers of goods produced by enslaved people. In turn, the Confederacy would increase its imports from free labor economies. This commercial relationship—once conducted directly rather than via New York—would, over time, diminish antislavery sentiment in Europe. A virtuous circle would then ensue boosting commerce and reconciling more and more customers to the existence and expansion of slavery. William Henry Chase, the retired engineer and president of the Alabama and Florida Railroad Company, wrote in the January 1861 edition of *De Bow's Review*: "It is now not disputed by political economists that just as trade becomes free, and the intercommunications of nations and states are relieved of restrictions of all kinds—so its movement is extended and accelerated—the true equation of the world's interests rests."[27]

A southern confederacy stood to be the greatest beneficiary and the chief global champion of free trade economics. "There is but one commercial nation in the world," Chase added, which "could adopt the policy of free trade." Only a southern confederacy would be able to act in that capacity, "due exclusively to the possession of the cotton zone of the world." Secession would create a nation, which, owing to its cotton production, would have a government, whose policy would be able to get closest to zero import tariffs and export duties and, provided it also created a navy, become a force for world peace and commercial integration.[28]

For southerners, the relationship between free trade and empire was mutually supporting. This consensus was unlike in Britain, where there was an intense debate within the governing Whig-Liberal coalition. The idealist radicals, notably Richard Cobden and John Bright, believed adherence to free trade principles meant implementing a "scheme of universal dependence" between nations "by which the productive powers of the whole earth are brought into mutual cooperation," and this meant adherent countries adopting a most pacifist foreign policy. However, these radicals were confronted by the more realist moderates, led by the foreign secretary and prime minister, Lord Palmerston, who, while no less enthusiastic about free trade, nevertheless also agreed with southerners that in order to bring about such intimate economic relations a degree of political control would be necessary over at least the less developed areas of the globe and those points considered of strategic importance. They believed—in the words of De Bow, that "the march of empire and the course of trade" were mutually reinforcing, in a phrase that first came into use around this time, that "trade follows the flag." Chase and other commentators agreed with this opinion.[29]

In this context of free trade progress, Confederate production of cotton would soar, leading to the clearing of more land and territorial expansion. Consul Arthur Lynn in Galveston, geographically close to the undeveloped lands in Texas as well as familiar with secessionist arguments, explained what this theory would amount to in practice for the Confederacy and its British customers. "The profits of the plantations, instead of being absorbed as hitherto by the northern manufacturer, working under a protective tariff, will result more to the benefit of the planters." Lynn believed the flow of money to the planters would "enable them to bring into cultivation lands now idle. In [Texas] alone it is estimated there are lands capable of producing two million bales." Expansionists predicted the adoption of free trade principles would lead to a surge in exports from the seceded states. Such optimism about the future appeared to be justified by present performance. The British consul in New Orleans, Thomas Mure, reported to the foreign secretary, Lord John Russell, that cotton exports had in 1860 reached "the enormous sum" of one hundred and eighty-five million dollars.[30]

Two members of the U.S. Senate, Thomas L. Clingman of North Carolina and Louis Trezevant Wigfall of Texas, agreed on the grand prospects that beckoned for Confederate trade. The two politicians, according to historians Elizabeth Fox-Genovese and Eugene Genovese, had prevailed in their elections in 1860 against more moderate foes due to whipping up fears of slavery insurrections after John Brown's raid in October 1859. Clingman—already, in the words of historian Daniel W. Crofts, a "quasi-secessionist"—predicted the level of exports would be three hundred million in 1861. Once an anti-expansionist Whig, who had fought a duel with Yancey over Texas annexation, Clingman had by the late 1850s become a proslavery expansionist in both North America and the Caribbean with all the zeal of a convert. Meanwhile, Senator Wigfall forecasted exports going forward at "never again less than" two hundred and fifty million dollars. He may have wished to provoke northern senators with these numbers, but historian John Majeswki notes Wigfall's genuine interest in economic nationalism.[31]

Along with imports, living standards across the South would rise, once, as Rhett told Bunch, "free trade would form an integral portion of their scheme of government." The South Carolinian hoped to tempt the Briton with a promise of a future surge in demand for British manufactured products. Henry L. Benning, the prominent jurist and Georgia Convention member who possessed "kindred sentiments" with Rhett, quantified the domestic benefits of free trade: southern "consumers would gain eighty million [dollars] a year in clear money in the subsequent lower prices at which they could purchase their goods." Benning later became Georgia's commissioner to Virginia's convention. In his speech on February 18, 1861, to the delegates gathered in Richmond, he painted a "glowing picture of commercial and manufacturing prosperity" to be had and even a chance for Virginia to "recapture past grandeur" if it joined the Confederacy. Yet Virginians, for now, remained unpersuaded about free trade and secession. Nevertheless, advocates claimed free trade would in particular boost ports across the South. "Everybody can see," Clingman told the Senate, "how the bringing in of [$300 million of imports] would enliven business in our seaboard towns." Yancey had earlier predicted that southern ports would become "dynamos." Richer individuals would be ready and willing to undertake risky expansionist enterprises abroad.[32]

The first tentative diplomatic moves of the Confederate government aimed to promote a vision of reciprocal benefits arising from independence for the new nation and its customers. Politicians argued that their export-led slavery-based economy would benefit world trade and wealth. The revenue earned by the exportation of commodities would enable Confederates to increase their consumption of overseas manufactured goods, cheaper—they believed—than their equivalents from the North, the prices of which had been raised by protective tariffs. This commerce gave power. In their report on relations with the United States, the members of the Committee of Foreign Affairs in the provisional congress asked: "shall we not have the right to deal directly with those who in return can supply us with their cheaper manufactured commodities?" Commercial pacts would result with partner nations paying more for southern exports as part of the deal: "If foreign nations can sell us freely their manufactured commodities in consequence of their greater cheapness [than those of the United States] can they not afford to give us more for our cotton?" An unknown hand explained in the margin of the report that these nations would pay more because they were "the richer by the trade." The Confederacy would be a double winner in this transaction: "And if we pay less for their manufactured commodities—are we not so much the richer by the trade?" Confederates believed that the interdependent system of political economy between nations would work in their favor.[33]

As well as looking to opportunities across the oceans, visionaries also looked toward the states to the north as they planned their future, emphasizing the great conduits of commerce that might connect the regions economically. In the words of Dowdell, "the great Mississippi river insures friendly feelings." Some planners were equivocal about individual state secession. Nevertheless, these conditional Unionists hoped to construct a distinct commercial powerhouse on the basis of the slave states seceding together. Planter and canal operator Robert Ruffin Barrow, owner of seven hundred slaves and sixteen plantations in Louisiana and Texas, and hence one of the richest planters in the South, wrote a pamphlet from his main plantation near Houma in Terrebonne Parish. He sketched out the extent of southern commercial dominance. "All the produce etc. of the Ohio and Mississippi valleys must be brought to this city" of New Orleans. "The vast extent of southern territory yet unoccupied," Barrow opined, "must in time increase our wealth influence and importance among the nations of the earth beyond the most extravagant calculations of the present generation." This multimillionaire had built his personal empire on sugar and slavery in the 1850s boom and now sought to project his own achievements on the national stage.[34]

A writer for De Bow's Review translated Barrow's commercial vision into a territorial one. "Here in the great Mississippi valley," the journalist intoned, "is the possible future of a proud and august empire [extending from the] Ohio to the Mexican Gulf—Rockies to the Atlantic." As the river united commerce and wealth, within its valley "lie the germs of a civilization." The writer confidently asserted about southerners, "there is little reason to fear their capacity to meet the exigencies of a single and united empire." The journalist urged them to be ambitious, for with ambition would come power, and southerners "should embrace the destiny now beckoning them on to empire . . . and found a political authority, commensurate with the grandeur of Southern destiny."[35]

Once assured of the dominance of the Mississippi and Ohio river system, some of these southern free trade imperialists then looked toward the Pacific. Bickley regarded expansion into Mexico as vital for a Pacific Ocean outlet. He argued that Mexico would become "the natural channel" for the vast global trade between the markets of East Asia and the southern states. As "we contemplate a vast trade with China, Japan and all the Pacific isles," it is necessary "that an enormous trade must be established between the Gulf States and what is now the Mexican republic, the western or pacific states of America and the south of Asia and Polynesia."[36]

These target lands were mainly in the tropical and subtropical regions of the world. Boosters for the Confederacy planned in the context of a "global" south that was not a place of danger from and defense against international antislavery, as portrayed by historians Guterl and Karp, but a zone for southern commercial growth. Stone declared that the future southern confederacy would possess "the trade of all tropical America." De Bow predicted that the trade of the southern states "after disunion will easily and naturally supersede and exclude the Yankees and English in the Cuban and other West Indian, Mexican, and South American trade." A writer in De Bow's Review defined the global south as "The Mediterranean latitudes in Europe, Asia, and Africa, and the country south of the Mason and Dixon's line." He added that it "is the true and only seat of high civilization . . . France, Italy, Greece, Spain, Cuba, Brazil and our own Southern Confederacy, are in the ascendant." Although possessing a "Latin" theme and Francophile in orientation, the journalist was cautious about French leadership, and his idea of an international proslavery coalition was very different from the ambitions exhibited by French emperor Napoleon III in his later adventure to Mexico. The Confederacy and not France would lead this group with global ambitions against the antislavery alliance between Britain and the United States. The Confederacy's "unbounded" commercial power would extend further than even Napoleon's dreams, for it "will subdue and overrun the Chinese empire, and will ultimately civilize and Christianize benighted Africa, as well as every other inhabited portion of the globe" where slavery would flourish.[37]

Given that they had no significant domestic manufacturing industries to protect, the nation builders believed they could impose import duties to fund an effective government with ample revenue without violating free trade principles. Wishful thinking, overconfidence, and a sense of entitlement underpinned these sentiments. Senator Wigfall projected $250 million of imports, with a significant tariff of "forty percent ... puts into our treasury one hundred million." Echoing the arguments made two years earlier by a fellow senator, James H. Hammond of South Carolina, in his famous "King Cotton Speech," Wigfall explained the importance of his levy because "numbers constitute the strength of governments in this day. I tell you it is not blood; it is the military chest; it is the almighty dollar."[38]

Some ambitious individuals, including many former Whigs mainly from the Upper South who were still conditional Unionists, did not believe that the free trade policy endorsed by the Deep South, even when modified with an import duty, was sufficient to sustain the South's commercial ambitions. They also perceived the South to be an economic laggard, which had to catch up with the Industrial Revolution. The new nation needed a protected, thriving, industrial sector both to attract wavering upper and border South states and to achieve sufficient economic independence from the antislavery powers: Britain and the United States. "No nation on earth ever got rich that did not manufacture," the ex-Whig Vance told his constituents in his unionist address, "and manufactures cannot flourish without the protection of government." His fellow North Carolinian, Senator Clingman, tilting toward secession, believed the modified free trade policies proposed by Wigfall and others would be sufficient shelter for industry. "The result of only ten percent duties in excluding products from abroad," he told senators, "would give life and impetus to mechanical and manufacturing industry throughout the South."[39]

A growing manufacturing sector required a growing market. As historian John Majewski rightly points out, the "small market" offered by the seceded states would have been "disastrous" for the future of manufacturing in the upper and border South. This constraint explained the importance of expansion of markets, essential to fulfill the vision of what

Majewski describes as the "imagined economy" necessary to sustain a strong nation. In November, reflecting on Lincoln's election, Richmond lawyer, politician, and Thomas Jefferson's youngest grandson, George W. Randolph, told his secessionist niece of his wish to see Virginia being "put into connection with an immense southern market." These markets had to be big enough to "exchange the raw material for [Virginia's] manufactures," he continued, and enable his state to "advance in wealth and population with immense rapidity." Randolph's actions supported his correspondence, he was the lone secessionist among the three Richmond delegates to the state convention, and he also led attempts to boost the manufacturing of firearms in the Richmond armory. On March 16, 1861, Randolph challenged the Virginia convention with the glittering prospects to be had in the Confederacy, as otherwise the "imperial throne of southern commerce, now vacant for our occupancy, will be seized by some more enterprising rival."[40]

In order to fund nation-building efforts and attract the Upper South, the Confederate Congress listened to such concerns expressed by Randolph, William Massie, Vance, and others and chose to adopt a new, albeit lower, tariff rather than declare free trade. Having a "standard" tariff would also enable the new government to offer preferential terms to "most-favored" nations, including possibly the United States. Both the president and secretary of state insisted that this step would not violate the new nation's embrace of free trade in the future. Davis boasted that the tariff amounted to "the freest trade which our necessities will permit," and Toombs excused the tariff the Confederacy had to levy as "import duties for mere revenue purposes, so moderate as to closely approximate free trade." Implications of this amended policy of free trade would extend beyond the boundaries of the Confederacy.[41]

Massive exports of cotton would lead to a trade surplus, which would lead to a flow of specie from abroad into private and government pockets. As well as drawing in money, these direct commercial ties would over time lead to a decline in global antislavery sentiment. As a result, according to Majewski, "in simplifying complex matters of culture and political ideology into crude notions of economic interests, secessionists overestimated their ability to influence other nations and regions." Optimists did not believe they were dissembling or simplifying facts; instead they regarded antislavery sentiment in the same light as protectionism and mercantilism, as old-fashioned attempts to interrupt economic and international relations. They also believed that the coexistence of slavery and free societies in one nation had somehow distorted international attitudes toward the labor system to the detriment of the South. The future, these individuals contended, would be the era when the civilizing impulses of commerce dominated relations with other nations and other regions.[42]

Advocates for a southern confederacy did not wait for the new institutions to be established in order to begin work; instead they looked to states, municipal administrations, commercial conventions, corporations, and enterprising individuals to start the processes of economic expansion immediately. Steamship lines established on trade routes would connect regions of interest and open up new markets. In the midst of secession mania in South Carolina, oceanographer Matthew Fontaine Maury hoped to use the coming of an independent South to redirect the commercial convention movement toward a broader future goal than the narrower defense of slavery that had occupied meetings of commercial conventions in late years. Therefore, in late October 1860 he drew the attention of the Charleston Chamber of Commerce toward south Atlantic trade routes for the export of cotton, avoiding New York and instead connecting that port with southern Europe via Cuba, the Caribbean, and Brazil. These locations also happened to be areas where slavery existed or to be ripe locations for its expansion.[43]

The nation builders assumed that the antebellum plans for a program of internal improvements focusing on canals and railroads would be accelerated. These infrastructure projects would be developed in conjunction with establishing direct trade routes to destinations abroad. Nevertheless, even optimistic expansionists worried about the consequences of a panic arising from the political instability and that a subsequent period of hard times might jeopardize the construction of canals and railroads. For example, the eruption of the secession crisis after Lincoln's election meant that French investment from Paris firm Messieurs Bellot des Minieres Brothers and Company in a crucial Virginia canal hung in the balance. However, on December 29, 1860, "the officer of the James River & Kanawha Canal company" had good news for the Richmond-based commission merchant of the prominent "arch Whig" Nelson County planter William Massie. The agent reassured Massie not only "that the Frenchman would certainly comply if we have dissolution & a southern republic," but even "that he preferred this should be the case." A prompt admission of Virginia into the Confederacy would enable the improvement of its transportation system. De Bow saw wider significance in this project, for "a French company undertakes to connect, by canal, the waters of the Chesapeake with those of the Ohio." The Kanawha Canal would only be the first of many canals and improvements that would connect the Atlantic ports with "the valleys of the Mississippi, Missouri, Red River, the Rio Grande and the magnificent valleys of Mexico." Boosters expected their nation would become the transit point of international trade routes running east to west and south to north.[44]

Two prominent Virginia Democrats, rivals for the leadership of the state party, looked forward to railroads connecting the expanding South to the Pacific Ocean. In his January 7, 1861, address to the state's General Assembly, Governor John Letcher of Virginia—a storekeeper from Lexington in the valley—informed the delegates that Virginia would be part of a "central belt" from the Atlantic to Pacific, once the "system" was complete. "The state's railroads already point to the great North West," he explained, "and must soon be part of a network of roads reaching Kansas and fast progressing to the Pacific." Such a circumstance would give the state great leverage because it would possess "the power in or out of Union of this great interior and exterior trade." The governor, who was a recent supporter of Stephen A. Douglas's presidential bid and who had long placed the transcontinental railroad in the center of his strategy for preserving the Union, regarded the planned railroads (and canals, too, as he supported the "white elephant" James River and Kanawha Canal) as reinforcing his political vision of Virginia as the center of a reconstructed union. Robert M. T. Hunter deployed the same arguments, but in support of secession. In an independent South, Virginia would become the equivalent of the state of New York for the new nation, with its own counterparts for the Erie Canal and for the city of New York. "There would arise in and about the shores of the Chesapeake," Hunter predicted, "a great and commanding center of credit and commerce." This future metropolis "would enjoy immense and commanding advantages for ... the distribution to the world over a vast area, filled with rich and profitable consumers." Hunter and Letcher envisaged Virginia's urban centers of Norfolk and Richmond not to be primarily manufacturing cities, as had recently sprung up a across the North, but financial and trading hubs—looking to London and New York as their ultimate models.[45]

FUTURE RELATIONS WITH THE UNITED STATES

Although these same southerners viewed nations as rivals and were confident that they would ultimately surpass their northern neighbors in wealth and power, they also hoped that a policy of free trade would be the foundation of good relations with the United States. William Holcombe, who, in Elizabeth Fox-Genovese and Eugene Genovese's words, defined southerners on a "broader canvass" than slavery, considered that northerners would also benefit from the South's separation and expansion. "Each [section] has a separate mission to fill and a glorious destiny to accomplish," Holcombe predicted in a pamphlet. North and South could not expand in one union because "in our present relations, we incommode each other." The *New Orleans Picayune* agreed: "The sooner the divided confederacies begin their separate careers of progress—the easier they will get along." In Natchez, Mr. Lee—young Frank F. Winchester's tutor—told his assenting pupil that after southern secession, "the northern people will come to their senses and attend to their own business."[46]

As well as commercial amity, some commentators hoped that a foreign policy alliance might be made between the United States and the Confederacy to resist European interference in the Western Hemisphere. Such meddling appeared to be increasingly likely. According to Erika Pani, the losers in the Mexican War of Reform of 1858–60, the Conservatives, had already asked for French support, and the damage caused to foreign property in that civil war would lead to the planned debt-recovery expedition to Vera Cruz of Britain, France, and Spain later in 1861. Thornwell expected that the South would become joint guarantor with the United States of the 1823 Monroe Doctrine. The doctrine aimed to keep new European colonies, alliances, and monarchies out of the Americas. Thornwell therefore hoped that both republicanism and the American quest for hemispheric domination would benefit from an independent South. In a similar fashion to slavery benefiting from the presence of more than one slave power, two large republics would better further republicanism than one large. "Two governments may be able to work out the problem of human liberty better than one on this continent." The potency of the ideology of self-government would be boosted by military power with the two nations forming the "closest alliance against this foreign foe," in order to ensure that "no European power ever set foot on American soil," and no form of government would exist there other than republican. "Separation changes nothing but external relations of the section," Thornwell concluded and then asked a question: how else can southerners achieve "the fullest and freest development of our noble institutions?"[47]

As well as a shared interest in republicanism, North and South both wanted to expand, and this common impulse might also lead to a settlement. In January 1861, Virginian Robert M. T. Hunter told northern senators that they had to "trust in the good sense and in the instincts of empire," swallow their misgivings over the "hereafter clause," and accept the Crittenden Compromise as the necessary price for keeping the South in the United States. In the wake of agitation for secession, Vice President John C. Breckinridge had appointed fellow Kentuckian Senator John J. Crittenden to lead a senate committee of thirteen, which included Davis, charged with the task of devising a compromise. The Crittenden proposals of December 12, 1860, canceled both popular sovereignty and the Kansas-Nebraska Act and resurrected the 1820 Missouri Compromise line (thirty-six degrees, thirty minutes latitude as the northern boundary of new slaveholding states) to the eastern border of California as a way to settle the expansion of slavery. South of the line slavery would be protected by constitutional amendments rather than permitted; but, according to Robert May, it was slavery's protection in any territories subsequently annexed south of the line—the "hereafter acquired clause"—that "placed the topic of expansion in the center" of negotiations. On December 18, 1860, the committee formally submitted its proposals to the Senate. Debate centered on whether that zone of protection would extend from the portions of Arizona and New Mexico to any lands that might in the future be acquired from Mexico, the Caribbean, and elsewhere south of the parallel of thirty-six degrees, thirty minutes latitude. On December 31, Crittenden told the Senate that no agreement had been reached, but a few days later, on January 3, 1861, he called for his proposals to be submitted to the people to vote on in a plebiscite. Hunter's son-in-law and fellow Virginian, Representative Muscoe Russell Hunter Garnett, built upon his senior colleague's argument in his own speech to the House a few days later on January 16. The Virginia duo believed that the North, beset by a pending clash between capital and labor, needed expansion in order to survive. The Virginian then explained why the "hereafter clause" meant more than additional votes in the Senate. Any settlement had to "obtain [for the South] a fair share in the honors, the influence and the expansion of our empire." The future nation had to provide sufficient scope for the fulfillment of both individual and state ambition. "If Virginia could forget her material interests," Garnett declared, "she could never forgo, for her sons, the interests of empire [and] the possibility of playing their equal part in the drama of civilization." Any compromise had to have a great degree of sectional self-government because southerners were "ready to take our wanted place in the front line of the mighty march of human progress, and able and willing to play for the mastery in that game of nations where the prizes are power and empire."[48]

Hunter appeared divided over whether his home state's appetite for expansion would be better sated in an independent South or if it should remain in the Union. He had, after all, tried to run for president in 1860, and Matthew Karp draws attention to his record as an enthusiast for utilizing federal power in the antebellum era. However, Hunter had followed his mentor, Calhoun, in his move away from nationalism, even supporting nullification. Yet Representative Jabez Lamar Munroe Curry of Alabama understood the Virginian was not interested in joining a small, weak, confederacy. "The present temper of the South will enable us to construct a government that would endure for ages," Curry assured the senator. "The time is propitious and should not be permitted to pass away unimproved." Curry had adopted a very different tone as secession commissioner to Maryland the previous month when he had warned Governor Hicks about the risk of another Santo Domingo with massacres and race war, if the South remained in the Union. Perhaps the positive argument to Hunter reflected the advice of Curry's close friend, the novelist Augusta Jane Evans, who warned him that no confederacy could be established just on "hatred of Lincoln."[49]

Davis agreed with Evans and hoped for a twofold opportunity: first, possibly a bargain with the Union to achieve a mutually beneficial scenario of separate expansion to the north and south and, secondly, liberty for Confederates to look for areas in which to expand, which had earlier been denied to southerners when part of the Union. He hoped that peace with the Union would coexist with Confederate expansion. The interests of both North and South would be better served by separation, Davis believed, as jealousy would cease. On March 1, 1861, Davis wrote to a northern correspondent that "the North has wanted Canada and the South wants Cuba, the expansion of both may have been restrained by the narrow views of each, let them be left freely to grow."[50]

Observers regarded Davis's confident predictions of a mutually beneficial expansive relationship with the Union as heralding the future, while attempts to reconstruct the Union by compromise, such as championed by Crittenden, belonged to the past. On February 21, the editor of the *Charleston Mercury* wrote that Davis's remarks amounted to a vision of what the Confederacy would become. He wrote approvingly that Davis "spoke of the future of the Confederacy; that posterity should see a great nation ... stretching from the Atlantic to the Pacific, with the northern portions of Mexico forming portions of its broad domain." In contrast, according to the paper's Washington correspondent, the latest ongoing mediation attempt in the capital, the National Peace Conference, had simply wasted "a great deal of breath" talking about "the acquisition of future territory."[51]

On January 19, 1861, the moderate-controlled Virginia Assembly had invited all states to send representatives to a peace conference in Washington to be held beginning February 4. Over the next few weeks the conference became embroiled in issues of expansion. It adopted Crittenden's proposals but added what Cornelius Clark Baldwin, a supporter of the conference, called a "self protecting power," an effective sectional veto on any plans of expansion. Randolph, now a delegate to that state's convention, disagreed with his fellow Virginian; he called the compromise put forward "a most unreliable safeguard" because "this [Peace Conference] proposition, which requires the majorities of the Senators of each section to concur in the acquisition of territory, exposes us again to all the annoyances of controversy; and much worse than that, to the dangers of intrigue and infidelity." So a Virginia politician, Randolph, concurred with the *Charleston Mercury*, controlled by fire-eater Robert Barnwell Rhett, that "not one inch of soil will ever be added to this Union south of the Rio Grande. All expansion will be made by and for the southern confederacy." After the conference broke up without result, the Virginia Assembly continued to debate about expansion and compromise.[52]

While Virginia politicians debated, the new Confederate legislators acted on the immediate inclusion of all territories to which the South believed itself entitled as a result of the Crittenden proposals. The U.S. Senate's committee of thirteen had deliberated on the admission of New Mexico as a slave state, and even Lincoln had wavered on the question. Congress rapidly established separate committees on Indian Affairs and Territories. Legislators envisioned both New Mexico and Indian Territory within the Confederacy, at a time when Arkansas, sandwiched between the Mississippi and Indian Territory, had not yet seceded. Toombs sought congressional authorization to send an agent to the Indian

Territory at the same time as sending a commissioner to the Arkansas convention. By the time the Confederate Congress concluded its session on March 16, approval had been given, and appropriations granted, for the establishment of its own bureau for Indian Affairs. Congress stated its intention to expand the Confederacy by its extension of dominion over Native Americans. More importantly, the Provisional Congress established, after spending much time in debate, the process for admitting new states and new territories into the Confederacy.[53]

Nevertheless, some legislators considered that some states should be permanently excluded from admission to the Confederacy. The fear of a recurrence of antislavery agitation trumped, at least for the moment, notions of supplanting the United States. The Provisional Congress debated the merits of securing, in the Confederate Constitution, the effective disqualification of nonslaveholding states from joining the Confederacy. Eventually, delegates reached a compromise that majorities of two-thirds of both houses, in a future Confederate Congress, would have to approve the admission of nonslaveholding states. On March 30, Robert Smith of Alabama declared that in the immediate term "this provision secures us as amply against the admission of undesirable associates as language can."[54]

Smith and other expansive Confederates also looked forward to a time when these restrictions on the admittance of nonslaveholding states would be relaxed as a result of greater self-assurance among Confederate legislators and an ebbing of northern antislavery sentiment. Smith declared on March 30, 1861, that he was "looking to the future with full confidence that our domestic policy will justify itself and long outlive the puny assaults of maddened fanaticism, led on by ambitious politicians." He was more confident about the possibilities of commercially based territorial expansion even without slavery. "Sentiment in nations never long rules master of interest," Smith insisted, and he was sure "will the trouble be, not to have the west with us, but to keep it from us." He regarded this probability as something to welcome, not deplore, and he would "abide in confidence that some of the great North West States, watered by the Mississippi, will be drawn by the strong current of that mighty river and the laws of trade, to swell the number and power of this confederation." By admitting these states, including California, the South, according to Smith, would "grasp the power of empire on this continent and announce to the startled north that it has reached its western limit, and must spread, if spread it can, towards the frozen sea." Such sentiments overlapped with conditional unionists, who preferred a "wait-and-see" approach in the hope that agitation might die down and an acceptable plan of reunion might somehow reemerge.[55]

Vice President Alexander H. Stephens welcomed the chance that non-slaveholding states might join the Confederacy. The former Whig from Georgia had remained a Unionist until his state seceded. and then he sought to quell excitement and extremism by promoting measures to dilute the Deep South dominance of the Confederacy. In a speech delivered in the Savannah Athenaeum on March 21, 1861, Stephens declared that it was "not to be beyond the range of possibility or even probability that all the Great States of the North West shall gravitate this way." Stephens tried to navigate the sensitivity of the issue. "Our doors are wide enough to receive them," he added, "but not until they are ready to assimilate with us in principle." To Stephens, inclusion of free states was conditional on the acceptance of slavery, but he expected they would consent, given that the current Confederate states "are now the nucleus of a growing power, which ... will become the controlling power of this continent."[56]

The government backed Stephens's view that free navigation on the Mississippi would exert an attractive force on the Midwest. The state of Louisiana added to its ordinance of secession: "We the people recognize the right of free navigation of the Mississippi and tributaries—by all friendly States bordering thereon." On February 25, 1861, Davis signed into law a bill to declare the free navigation of the Mississippi. The river and its navigable tributaries were "hereby declared free to all citizens upon its borders."[57]

Some individuals wondered whether a closer arrangement would be either possible or desirable. De Bow and fellow expansionists debated about the future of states in what they referred to as the "North West"— meaning principally Ohio, Indiana, and Illinois. The alternatives for these northern and middle states were to "either claim to be admitted into the new confederacy of free trade states" or "in their independent condition, endeavor to recover their losses ... by the adoption of free trade principles." Planners did not doubt the power of commercial connections to surmount antislavery fanaticism would have at least the same result for the Midwest as for Britain. Fire-eaters wished for commercial relations only with free states. Even Yancey recommended the South "combat the fanaticism of the North West with the more enlarged and enlightened, and friendly commercial policy indicated in my resolution." The *Charleston Mercury* mused on the "altered relations to be established with the riparian states of the upper Mississippi." The newspaper speculated about a breakup of the Union into separate eastern and western pieces.[58]

Tempting the North with Canada was a recurring theme among politicians and pamphleteers boosting the new nation, and they also saw advantages encouraging the United States to confront Britain, while the Confederacy would remain friends with both powers. The efforts of Congress paralleled the economic and international policy of the government, which was peaceful commercial expansion. The initial diplomatic overtures made by the government were not toward those countries bound by a common interest in slavery, Brazil and Spain, but to the two nations with the biggest markets for the Confederacy. Davis announced missions to the Union on February 27 and Britain on March 16, with virtually identical language to "reestablish" and "establish" friendly relations, respectively. Davis dispatched commissioners from Montgomery, Alabama, to Washington D.C. on February 27, and all he suggested was that the mission was "animated by an earnest desire to unite and bind together our respective countries by friendly ties."[59]

By the spring of 1861, the future of the Confederacy appeared to be set. Extension of slavery and territorial expansion would be the national priorities for the new nation, with the aim of increasing production and exports of staple crops. In a worldview governed by free trade, the articulators of the new nation predicted that its success would foster international harmony. The relative increase of wealth and power in the South would be acceptable as the global economy as a whole would be growing. Therefore the arrival of a new entrant on the world stage would not be regarded as a disruptive event, but the overdue correction of internal flaws in the United States, which would enable southern planters to contribute more effectively to global prosperity. The planners of the Confederacy were at times wishful, inconsistent, and very vague; yet, at the same time, concrete steps with worked-out implications had also been undertaken. Nowhere were these contradictory traits more in evidence than with the planned relations with the United States. There was a juxtaposition of southerners' aspirations for harmony and collaboration with their former countrymen with avaricious plans for breaking up what remained of the Union and annexation of much of its territory; this suggests that observers then and historians now who believe that coexistence was possible between the Union and Confederacy and that war was therefore avoidable were wrong.

2

How War Changed
the Future Nation

APRIL 1861 TO FEBRUARY 1862

From the outbreak of war in April 1861 until February 1862, the expectations of a brief but intense conflict exercised a profound, albeit indirect, influence on Confederate planning. After all, by the end of the summer of 1861, an army of a million men had been authorized; but although half the soldiers volunteered to serve for three years and the other half for one year, these were conservative, precautionary terms of enlistment—especially compared with Lincoln's three months—for the expectation was that the fighting season of 1861 would conclude the contest. Only gradually, from the fall of 1861 onward and especially by February 1862, the time of both the formation of the permanent Confederate government and the start of the great Union military offensives in both western and eastern theaters, did events dispel any idea of an early peace.

Before then, the context of a brief unwanted war imposed more continuity than changes on postwar planning, especially arising from the need to impose war guilt on the United States government. Therefore, politicians and diplomats endeavored to prove both to opponents of the Lincoln administration in the Union and to the European great powers outside that the Confederate government harbored no designs on any part of the United States. In particular, the newly appointed commissioners to Europe reassured their audiences that the Davis administration had disavowed aggressive, immediate, wartime, southern and western expansion. Yet these individuals expected a suspension, not a termination of these ambitions. Confederate planners hoped that an early peace would ensue either with coexistence or, preferably, an alliance with the Union delivering benefits to both countries of commercial and territorial expansion. At the same time, a chance of rivalry with their northern neighbor suggested the need for initiative on the part of policymakers formulating foreign and domestic strategies for the new nation's security.

Wartime and planned postwar policies reflected that Confederates had to confront the possibility that their enemy might not only compete for influence in Latin America and the Caribbean but also use northern Mexico as a base to invade the Confederacy. As a result, the State Department determined to strengthen its supporters across this region as the government still wished to expand their nation southward in the future. In the immediate term, the State Department adopted a policy that was both proslavery and good neighbor. It strove to keep central governments in the region either weak or in slaveholder hands and in particular support the Spanish government's endeavor to reclaim its former colony of Santo Domingo and reintroduce slavery there. Confederates envisaged these steps as a temporary compromise and interim pledges toward claiming the whole of Latin America and the Caribbean as in its zone of influence.

Planners of the future Confederacy believed they were entitled to be ambitious given the proofs of strength offered by their new nation after the outbreak of war. The Confederate revolution appeared to claim a unity of support, which, in their eyes, more than compensated for the disparity in population between Confederates and Federals. Confidence remained in future growth in staple crop production in the context of free trade. They hoped the wartime events that damaged this economic growth, such as the wartime embargo on cotton exports, would be only temporary. By the summer of 1861, angered at Britain's acceptance of the U.S. government's announcement of a wartime blockade by presidential proclamation on April 19, spontaneous committees of correspondence had resolved to suspend any exports of cotton until Britain broke the blockade. Confederates believed in their ability to achieve their ambitions because what sustained them in their application was that the system of slavery had passed its crucial test of endurance with the outbreak of war and would remain in existence to support commercial and territorial expansion.

*   *   *

HISTORIANS DEEM the outbreak of war to be the decisive moment in the permanent renunciation of expansionist ambitions, to be resurrected in an opposite form when, after the war, ex-Confederates fled to seek the protection of the imperial regimes of Mexico and Brazil. Even as politicians established the new nation, scholars contend, fire-eaters and their preferred policies such as reopening the Atlantic slave trade had been sidelined. It was moderates, opposed to extremist measures of every sort, including expansion, who took charge. Yet, as evidenced by the reputation of Davis, the so-called moderates were as ambitious for the nation, if not more, than the men they supplanted. The act of renouncing the Atlantic slave trade was in pursuit of the expansion, not contraction, of the Confederacy. These moderates began early on to enact an expansionist agenda at the various levels of Confederate government. With this change of personnel leading the cause of the independent South, expansion became even more of a priority for the Confederacy. The moderates believed that a new nation needed a strong sense of ambition.[1]

War then reinforced the necessity that the Confederacy, when able, had to resume the expansive course set in motion during the two-month period of peace until April 1861. There may have been temporary expedients forced by war, such as the embargo and defensive military strategy, and when posted abroad, diplomats disavowed expansion in the quest for foreign recognition and intervention. These measures were transient wartime postures, which would not determine the nature of the future nation in a time of peace. The persistence of the foundation of race and slavery to the Confederacy's existence suggests why optimists clung to and extended their ambitions. As the historian Bruce C. Levine has observed, reflecting on the Confederate war effort, "the demand of racial ideology and race control trumped the call of military necessity." Paul Quigley adds that "sooner or later, though, everything comes back to the sine qua non of Confederate national identity: racial slavery." Planners expected that slavery and its requirements and consequences ensured that commercial and territorial growth would become more important as postwar objectives once the war broke out and then continued.[2]

It has been tempting for historians to look for "early portents" of Appomattox and for turning points marking the permanent reversal of Confederate fortunes. But only with the benefit of hindsight can it be seen that "the turning of the Border States to the Union" and creation of West Virginia were irreversible, and the tightening blockade and effective U.S. seaborne operations had sealed the Confederacy from the world. At the time, many individuals ascribed these events to "fortunes of war" and saw them either as temporary setbacks that would be corrected when peace came or as providentially useful lessons and trials in national development. Historian Robert Bonner is right to see Confederate politicians and even generals continuing to debate, even when the war was going poorly, "whether former free state allies" of the South "might be incorporated into the Confederacy."[3]

The way the Confederacy had to fight the war did not dictate how it intended to win the peace afterward. Although the events and experience of the war influenced priorities for the new nation, the relationship was complicated. Historians argue that the way Confederates fought the war determined the evolution of cultural nationalism, foreign policy, and approaches to the Border States and dictated their definite renunciation of expansion. Yet ideas about future peace mattered as well. As Emory Thomas makes clear, for example, Confederate financial policy remained geared to peacetime (to the detriment of its war effort) and that in turn was connected to postwar commercial and territorial ambitions.[4]

Given that the Confederacy fought the war defensively, scholars emphasize that the early phase of the war was for Confederates about defining the nation-state—setting the boundaries of citizenship and territory. Scholars contrast this behavior with that of the United States, with its military strategy of offense, and Lincoln's broad conviction that Unionist sentiment remained strong and only needed arousing across the Confederacy. But such a view misses the broad scope of Confederate aims: politicians and planners were not focused only on setting borders; instead they thought the Confederacy would become an empire. Legislators therefore broadly defined the meaning of citizenship and remained eager to pursue expansion, even if the present conflict with the United States postponed any active execution until a more opportune moment. Furthermore, as historians Bonner and Guterl make clear, fighting on land and naval strategy at sea revealed connections, ideas, and occasions that would at least enable preparations to be put in place for expansion at a later date.[5]

The start of the conflict also brought forth stresses and divisions, especially in a nation as unprepared for war as was the Confederacy. Historians have charged the Confederacy with being a mass of contradictions, which would only be reconciled, temporarily, with a vague call to patriotism as a lowest common denominator of sentiment. Instead, crucially, practical politics met patriotism in a celebration of future

Confederate national strength and dominance, for which the war was an interim period of preparation. Some scholars emphasize how Confederates highlighted either their role as victims of Lincoln's tyranny or as the last hope of republican self-government. Other historians, seeing the war as an event in a global conflict, note the prevalence of "King Cotton" coercion as part of the southern worldview. These wartime expedients mattered but were not the sum total of the Confederacy; instead they were often conceived of as initial wartime preparations or even transient interruptions on the road to peacetime empire.[6]

Assigning War Guilt, Rectitude at Present, and Increased Ambition in the Future

Confronted with a war they did not want, planners for the postwar nation disassociated their ambitions from war aims and insisted any war guilt lay with Lincoln and his supporters. The Confederate government resisted the United States with defensive goals in mind: it contrasted its war in defense of hearth and home with the Union's war of conquest. Those Confederates who seemed bent on territorial aggrandizement via war risked been censured, especially as they might complicate efforts to bring about a negotiated settlement. Hence on April 17, 1861, Catherine Edmondston, wife of a North Carolina planter, was "sorry to hear" reports that Leroy Pope Walker, the secretary of war and former associate of William Yancey in Alabama had, a few days before, pointed at "the Confederate Flag & said 'On to Washington & plant this there!'" She regarded Walker's gesture as vulgar and unrealistic, adding, "We do not intend to go & it seems an idle threat." From Washington, the Confederate commissioner John A. Campbell complained of the irritation in the North at what he called Walker's counterproductive "loose vaunts." There was a debate spelled out in newspapers, diaries, and correspondence about whether it was proper and appropriate to air such ideas at a time when soldiers were dying and increased resources had to be devoted to the war effort. President Davis considered that to articulate expansionist ambitions arising from war invited hubris, and he viewed such conduct as unchristian—hence he also reproved Walker for his outburst.[7]

These new moral arguments excited by the war reinforced older racial concerns that had inhibited expansionist ambitions for many Americans since the Mexican War. "Annexation would bring foreign and conflicting elements," wrote John M. Daniel, a former diplomat and secessionist in the *Richmond Examiner*, so "filibustering, conquest and annexation will be no part of the policy or practice of the southern Confederacy." There was no correlation between the level of ambition expressed and degree of mobilization demanded by Confederates; Daniel's early advocacy of conscription, as well as his Unitarianism, made his ambition unusual among his countrymen at this early stage of the war. Yet he was not alone in believing that a combination of African American slavery and Anglo-Saxon owners provided the only possible basis for an organic, harmonious, and—above all—improving society.[8]

For all this moral posturing, major slaveholders considered any constraints on ambition to be temporary. The executive committee of the Cotton Planters' Convention, which met in Macon, Georgia, on April 24, 1861, resolved that "in view of the troubled state of the country . . . the all absorbing war excitement and the dark uncertain future . . . [the committee] determined to postpone all further action" on topics such as direct trade with Europe, international steam packet lines, and preparation of exhibits for an upcoming world's fair to be held in London in 1862. This decision was temporary and reflected the confusion and uncertainty in the days following the shelling of Fort Sumter and Lincoln's call for volunteers. The mystery about when and how the war might end made short-term planning impossible as well as inappropriate, but it did not preclude activities focused on more distant horizons.[9]

In pursuit of postponing expansionist ambitions, politicians not only attempted to combine the virtue of restraint, suitable for a country in a defensive war, but they also enlarged the scope of their ambitions for the future nation. They achieved this feat and therefore kept their options open by studied vagueness about which peoples, territories, and states should be included within the Confederacy. This conduct was contrary to historians' insistence on Confederates' mania for definition. The debates of the second session of the Provisional Congress, which sat from April 29 to May 21, 1861, broadly defined the people of the Confederate states as being all who "will refuse to cooperate with the government of the United States in these acts of hostilities and wanton aggression."[10]

The ideological basis of the nation, its creed, demonstrated continuity with secessionists and then became more ambitious and expansive. The war revolutionized the Confederate revolution. Representatives in Congress believed citizens of other countries agreed about the magnitude of the event. Confederates "are looked upon as assailing the peace of the world," stated the *Report of the Committee on Foreign Affairs* in May, as rebels who "break up a long established government and effect thereby the interests of other nations." After all, it was a "contest for constitutional government in which the interests of mankind are concerned." Charles Tyler Botts of California, brother of prominent Virginia Whig politician John Minor Botts, believed what was at stake was the survival of the principles of at least "the founders of the Democratic Party thought, that men were best governed when they were least governed." For Botts, his vision of a commercial republic consisting of market-minded farmers and dynamic city systems required fostering, but not smothering, by government. The outcome of such an arrangement was that "the people were strong and rich in proportion as the government was weak and poor." The foundation of the Confederacy offered for Botts an apparent chance to realize this revolutionary ambition.[11]

Speakers across the Confederate states agreed that the combination of the inherited ideas of the American Revolution and the initial élan of the French Revolution gave the Confederacy immense power in utilizing the latent energies of the people to first resist the United States and then achieve their ambitions after the war had ended. James Headley, a Confederate supporter and attorney in Kansas, observed, "'Revolutions never go backward' but when begun they rush forward with the speed of the whirlwind." In his December 2, 1861, address, Governor John Letcher of Virginia approved—ironically—the sentiments in an early speech of Lincoln's about the 1848 revolutions in Europe. He also quoted, this time without apparent irony, the words of abolitionist Wendell Philips to cries of "hear hear" from the audience. "It is the quality of revolutions not to go by *old lines* or old laws; but to break up both and make *new ones*." Confederates "are a people," Yancey told a Livery Dinner in London that November, "a nation exhibiting elements of power that few states of the world possess." This popular unity would enable the Confederacy to win the war. Colonel William N. Bilbo of Tennessee, a prominent journalist, land speculator, and lawyer, assured his listeners in Nashville that "the true source of invincibility . . . is will." Lincoln had chosen war under a misapprehension. A Houston public meeting resolved on December 3: "The union sentiment in the south, which the federal administration relied so much upon for cooperation is conceded now not to exist." The assembly concluded emphatically about the Confederacy, "a nation thus conceived is simply invincible."[12]

SLAVERY AS THE BASIS FOR FUTURE EXPANSION

Far from struggling only to defend slavery where it existed, Confederates interpreted the events of the first months of the war with a sense of vindication and relief. These opinions led to a greater confidence in the future of the institution. According to its supporters, slavery had demonstrated a surprising resilience given the fears that pervaded during the secession crisis. On June 20, 1861, even the antislavery British consul in Charleston, South Carolina, Robert Bunch, reported to Lord John Russell, the foreign secretary: "no insurrection of the negroes is to be feared unless it be concocted and directed by white men." With no repetition of John Brown's raid on Harpers Ferry conceivable, the only possible scenario destabilizing slavery was an invasion by Union forces. When that eventuality began to become a reality, for example at Port Royal, South Carolina, slavery apparently did not collapse. Bunch observed on December 2, "no attempt has been made by the slaves to attach themselves to the U.S. forces. In some cases they have refused to move." Historians have drawn attention to the flight of enslaved people across the lines to Union-controlled enclaves, such as Fort Monroe, but such instances—for all their long-term significance for the process of emancipation—at the time only had local resonance in the Confederacy and no bearing on slaveholders' plans for the institution.[13]

Although Confederates recalled that both the War of 1812 and the Revolutionary War had harmed slavery, John M. Morehead, a railroad president and former governor of North Carolina, believed that this time the outcome would be different. The existence of large armed forces provided the means of controlling slaves more effectively and perhaps would render slavery more efficient. On November 23, Morehead told North Carolina Supreme Court judge Thomas Ruffin that he anticipated that "our southern republic is going to assume something of a military character. Our domestic institutions will require that those who rule shall be always prepared to control those under them." Given Ruffin's antebellum concern about how the rise of economic self-interest among slaveholders undermined what he hitherto had regarded as mild treatment of enslaved people, he probably welcomed the idea of a long-term military presence intervening and therefore moderating future relations between masters and enslaved people. During the same month, the provisional (Confederate) governor of Kentucky saw the advance of Confederate armies, slavery, and prosperity as mutually reinforcing, as "the presence of the negro races adds greatly to the military spirit and strength of the Confederate states. They till our grounds, whilst our sons fight our battles; and our ordinary pursuits are scarcely interrupted by the war."[14]

Slavery therefore became more important to these politicians during the early months of the war as the foundation not only of the war effort but also of the future nation. Given rumors that Britain and France would only recognize the Confederacy if it promised to adopt a plan for gradual emancipation, George W. Kendall, editor of the *New Orleans Picayune*, published a pamphlet in October by "an old citizen" of the city in order to provide Europe with a clearer idea of the "character of people, magnitude of resources and nature of institutions." Echoing Morehead, the writer believed "the crisis" would not harm slavery but instead "will materially advance our interest, facilitating our capacity to render slavery subservient to the wellbeing of our race, . . . prodigiously accelerate our progress in prosperity and national development."[15]

Proslavery arguments about climate and race continued to animate the New Orleans–based pamphleteer during wartime as he argued that because "slavery was the condition most conducive to the welfare of the negro," Confederates had a "duty" to "facilitate the extension of it." As he explained: "No well informed person will assume" that, with regard to white workers, "an adequate number be procured" on "wages low enough to render the cultivation of cotton renumerative." In any case, he doubted whites "could endure the intense heat of our climate, in the field." The writer insisted that cotton "must be raised by negroes or not at all." He anticipated that production would fall from over four million bales to under half a million in the event of emancipation. That alone should give the British reason to pause in their antislavery policy. "Slavery was designed to vindicate the wisdom and beneficence of God," the pamphleteer concluded, exhibiting evangelical faith in his vision of progress, so "the finite attempts to arrest its resistless career must prove as futile as would an effort to quench" the sun. Slavery's achievements were great to date as proven by its survival in war, "though to a very limited extent compared to its future availability."[16]

The war made postwar planners more conscious of what they thought the place of slavery was in the world. Specifically, they sought to explain why the European powers were withholding recognition of the Confederacy. The "old citizen" of New Orleans wished to persuade the British to ignore abolitionist propaganda about slavery, which he thought prejudiced them against the institution. Instead, they should follow the example of "leading minds" in Europe, who understood the codependency of "slavery and the mighty political institutions of Britain" and "no longer be content to accept the narrow and bigoted exeter-hall definition of slavery." Nevertheless, he agreed with Bilbo that this hope was unlikely to be fulfilled because they believed that hypocritical abolitionists planned, on the defeat of the Confederacy, to deploy competitor labor systems in the tropics. Evidence of the execution of these intentions apparently already existed in the Caribbean. "Having extinguished *natural* slavery," the journalist charged, England and France "resort to a system of *artificial* slavery." These countries practiced "dodging the name" with the "legalizing of the cooly [*sic*] slave trade." This strategy had limited success, since it was "attended with an even greater cruelty [yet] it did not prevent a material decline in the productiveness of the West Indies." Therefore, Confederate slavery had to be destroyed in order to render these inferior systems viable in world markets. Bilbo also considered slavery vital "in order to compete with pauper, abolition labor." Confederates remained in wartime as committed as their forebears in the 1850s to combat this perceived global antislavery challenge.[17]

The Confederate government expounded a world vision with the slaveholders' republic playing a key role. In his address to Congress at the beginning of the war, Davis had linked staple production and slavery with the world at large. He added that "the productions of the South in cotton, rice, sugar and tobacco . . . had become absolutely necessary to the wants of civilized man." The government saw the Confederacy as the symbol of the moral cause of minimal government; the promotion of free trade with its beneficial fruits of commerce; "for the full development and continuance of which the labor of African slaves was and is indispensable."[18]

PROMISING ECONOMICS

Planters, merchants, and speculators did not consider that a short war would disrupt longer-term plans for the economy. In December, Bilbo, who also speculated in coal mines, estimated that, but for the war, the entire commerce of the Confederacy, including industrial and mineral as well as agricultural productions, would be worth "today" $600 million, and "our advance will be marked by a unexampled rapidity of growth of arts and commerce, wealth and population." Planters believed cotton would continue to be the basis of this wealth, and promises of a bumper

1861 crop boosted expectations for the future. On July 4, the Convention of Cotton Planters gathered in the concert hall of Macon, Georgia, and the meeting predicted that the 1861 cotton crop would come in at or a little below the three-year average of four million bales.[19]

Long-term growth in production would come from Texas. According to Arthur J. Lynn, the British consul in Galveston, Texas had produced just four hundred thousand bales in 1860; but with railroad construction opening up new lands, he expected the production to rise to between two and six million bales. In the short term, the buoyancy of the agricultural sector was enhanced by the fact that both provision crops and other staples, such as rice and sugar, had all experienced exceptional yields due to the same benign weather conditions that benefited cotton. Hunt and James, consignment merchants in Richmond, replied to their client, Nelson County Virginia planter William Massie, on May 23, "we are glad to hear such good accounts of your crops all reports represent the wheat crop as very fine all over the state and the south." On July 8, Bunch observed, "the rice crop promises to be unusually abundant."[20]

It appeared during 1861 that the weather seemed to favor the Confederate cause and all the staple crops. The British consuls scattered across the Confederate ports confirmed these optimistic opinions. On July 1, Thomas Mure summed up the situation from his vantage point in New Orleans: "The weather in the Confederate States has been very propitious for the grain crops—there has been an increase of about 15–20% in the cultivation of wheat and corn—in Tex. and the southern sections of Ark. and Tenn. the wheat harvest is already finished and is reported to be abundant and of excellent quality. It is too early to give any definite report [regarding the] cotton crop the prospects are so far favorable." Abram Archer, Mississippi planter and University of Virginia graduate, boasted to his overseer Henry J. Hennington on August 7, that "crops around Port Gibson are very good to what they were last year and if we have a late fall we will make a large crop." Perfect fall weather then meant planters anticipated the harvest to be at the higher end of earlier estimates. From Savannah, the long-serving British consul, Edmund Molyneux, reported about the harvest to Russell on December 4 that the "weather during the last 3 months has been so propitious for maturing of the [cotton] plant that the total crop is est. at 4m bales which is a slight increase from last year's growth."[21]

Conditions appeared auspicious even for the fickle sugar cane. According to his annual review, Pierre Champomier, a New Orleans creole businessman and publisher, the situation in February 1861 augured well: "These gratifying prospects continued in a great measure throughout the spring and summer, and the planters of Louisiana were enabled to commence planting at a remarkably early period." He wrote, unlike 1860: "The season for grinding was most favorable and proved unusually propitious, and a very large crop was realized." Champomier criticized some planters for once being too cautious because, fearing an early frost, they "commenced grinding at an earlier period of the year than ever before known in Louisiana. Could the planters have foreseen so mild and pleasant a winter, so favorable a season for taking off their crops, a materially larger yield would have been produced," which he estimated to have been potentially double the size. The missed opportunity of 1861 inflated expectations for the future: "As usual a large crop is aimed at" for 1862.[22]

Although expectations of a short war disrupted the upward trajectory of the Confederate economy by suppressing demand for cotton, planters and journalists assumed the recession would be temporary and a postwar boom driven by rising prices would offset its effects. Depredations by the enemy would be transient. In October 1861, "an old citizen" of New Orleans believed that even if the Union forces were able to destroy half the estimated store of four million bales, such an action "would produce such a vacuum in the supply . . . that the remaining two million would attain a value, nearly equal to that which the four million would have represented." By this process, planters would be in the future "over and over again renumerated for their nominal sacrifice." Given the wealth stored in the staple, it should be stored in order to be later used in domestic and world markets. "To burn all the cotton as has been suggested by a Mississippi Planter," Dr. Peter Randolph, planter of Point Coupee Parish, Louisiana, told Archer, "would be to deprive our factories of what they require and consequently cut off the supply of a fabric in such universal demand throughout the slaveholding states and if the blockade is not broken will be in still greater demand." Most planters agreed it was premature to destroy the embargoed cotton crop.[23]

The effective cessation of cotton production for the 1862 crop in order to focus on the production of provisions did not mean that planters turned their back on a future of staple crop production. The Resolutions of the Tennessee Assembly declared that two cotton crops unexported would result in a glut and enable European customers to "dictate the price and terms of sale." Even if the 1862 crop was not raised, the store on hand would rise in value, and planters "holding a great staple, which is a *necessity* to them [the European powers, who] will not only be compelled to buy *but* also pay a remunerative price." The "iron" laws of supply and demand would enable the Confederate cotton industry to rapidly recover after the war, even if planters had switched to arable crops in the meantime.[24]

The stockpile of cotton would also serve as a guard against changes in the world cotton market after the war. Governor George W. Pickens of South Carolina accepted that the effects of the Union blockade and unofficial Confederate embargo on Britain "may result in forcing up new sources of supply for the raw material" in India and Australia, rather than the hoped-for intervention in the Civil War. Yet he believed the war would end soon and cotton exports would resume. In this contingency, "we should hold a large supply of cotton on hand, to . . . breakdown immediately any new sources of supply that may have been forced upon other countries under the artificial stimulus given to its production by blockade and our measures." Pickens did not consider himself to be complacent; rather he believed exporters would have to flood the market with cheap cotton to drive competitors out of business and so "secure the continued monopoly of the market Europe." Pickens believed in the lower prices and superior quality of products harvested by enslaved people. He also recognized the need to address the concerns of South Carolinians, as the Union's seaborne operations threatened them and their livelihoods, with visions of a magnificent future.[25]

Schemes to address war finance and inflation also informed postwar plans to boost the money supply into the Confederate economy and enrich planters and farmers. The report from the *Proceedings of the Convention of Cotton Planters* declared "the country having $200 million of vegetable gold almost ready to gather, had voluntarily placed it at the disposal of the government." Two prominent North Carolinians pondered the convertibility of cotton to gold and silver. "What we really want from foreign commerce," argued Henry K. Burgwyn, a planter of Thornbury, Northampton County, "is more gold and silver and a less, much less amount of costly foreign manufactures and wares." Duff Green, veteran politician, journalist, and speculator, in his address to the cotton planters called for a "regulation of foreign trade" by limiting inessential imports and obtaining specie in exchange for cotton exports. As a result, "we could by our exports so regulate our foreign exchange as to give us a money market undisturbed by continued fluctuations," by which he meant arresting the present depreciation of Confederate treasury notes by ensuring they would be convertible to specie.[26]

Green had long advocated running a trade surplus. Moreover, he had seen how the California gold rush had led to a boom as a result of the influx of specie into the U.S. economy during the 1850s, and he expected the postwar Confederacy would replicate these conditions. As he told the meeting, the basis of his system was faith in his mentor Calhoun's argument that historically the "excess of northern imports was paid for by the excess of southern exports." Now, with Confederate independence, a trade surplus was possible, which would bring in the specie "inasmuch as the products of the south constitute so large a part of the basis of the trade and industry of European nations" that the British and French would have no choice but to pay for Confederate exports in gold or silver, increasing the value of cotton and the prosperity of planters. With this wealth, Confederate consumers planned to purchase cheaper imported manufactured goods from Europe, in place of more expensive products from the Union. The planters also predicted they would be able to sell their cotton at higher prices because their European clients, by the working of the theory of comparative advantage, would consent to pay more because they had sold goods to the Confederacy. In the words of an official in the State Department, Confederates would, by selling cotton for more and buying manufactured goods for less, be twice "richer by the trade."[27]

THE PLACE OF THE NEW NATION IN THE WORLD

Forecasts of amassing wealth in the future had a practical purpose in that this money promised to pay down debt incurred during the war. The advocacy of free trade also defined the Confederate world. In the context of anticipated bumper crops, politicians sought to capitalize on the nation's anticipated commercial power by continuing to advocate free trade after the outbreak of war. Members of Congress made it their priority to pass the tariff bill after reconvening in Montgomery on April 30. The Confederacy stood for peaceful cooperative prosperity: what its proponents regarded as a modernizing vision of interconnected, interdependent nations.[28]

The war imposed immediate domestic pressures and international isolation on the Confederacy, and historians have exhaustively investigated these developments. The conflict also intensified the vision of free trade in the future as it promised, its advocates insisted, a route to both domestic and international harmony. On January 6, 1862, Davis explained to his cabinet why "he was for free trade and direct taxes after the war." With its inherent lack of discrimination, the president believed free trade treated everybody at home alike, and this situation would also be replicated abroad.[29]

The outbreak of the Civil War did not terminate but rather reinvigorated the commercial convention movement. On October 14, 1861, the Southern Commercial Convention, with four hundred delegates from nine different states, met in Macon, Georgia, for three days. Some of the delegates, and committee members in particular, promoted expansionist policies in Congress. Keen to demonstrate patriotism and suggest ways to pay for the war meant the convention dropped its late antebellum obsession with the reopening of the international slave trade and returned to focus on the "gospel of prosperity" that had characterized earlier gatherings. The convention's president, A. O. Andrews, said it was up to the Confederate states for the first time in world history to "test the practicality of an unfettered trade . . . [because] as a new Government, we have no old revenue system to unsettle—no class or business interests to be endangered, and if it succeeds, we shall have the glory of inaugurating it." As a new nation, the Confederacy alone had the chance to adopt an economic policy of pure free trade.[30]

As well as grandiose declarations, the convention also made two concrete recommendations for the postwar government to adopt: first, "in order to encourage the importation of articles necessary . . . return cargoes ought to be furnished to all vessels introducing commodities within the Confederate States"; second, the convention recommended that John H. Reagan, the Confederate postmaster general, "take such steps as at an early day as practicable as may lead to the establishment of postal relations between the Confederate States and European governments." Reagan was a familiar and moderate figure to the attendees, who had earlier opposed both the Montgomery Convention's endorsement of William Walker's enterprise to Nicaragua in 1858 and raids on Mexico from his home state of Texas. Nevertheless, he had, as postmaster general, just sanctioned service to the new Confederate territory of Arizona. As overseas services lay outside Reagan's remit, Davis had coincidentally just sent to Secretary of State Hunter, "for consideration and conference," a proposal to establish an "Ocean Penny Post Fortnight Express" to Europe.[31]

Far from turning inward with the outbreak of war with their embargo, Confederates and their supporters considered that any interruption of communications and diplomatic isolation would be temporary. The sheer interconnectedness of the southern economy and society with the rest of the world would soon become apparent to all and somehow hasten an end to the conflict. "So linked together are the commercial relations of civilized nations," Charles Botts declared in California in August, "that what redounds to the interest of one is immeasurably for the interest of all." Confederate certainty over domestic and international accord aris-ing from its economic policies arose because its advocates believed they were following the laws of nature as well as finding a way of addressing the crisis. As with the expansion of slavery, Confederates believed they were governed by natural laws of trade, which "are immutable, men will sell where they can sell highest [and] buy where they can buy lowest." Another commentator in Charleston added, "You cannot stop all the currents and eddies of commerce—any more than the Mississippi." These ideas of natural law accorded with notions of political economy prevailing in the Confederacy. Political economists, such as John Jacob Cardozo of South Carolina, espoused the importance of free trade; it was vital to accommodate the growing production of staple goods for export, which in turn enabled the import of cheaper goods and hence would increase real wages and profits even as prices fell.[32]

Diplomats expected free trade to deliver a system of international re-lations that would both deliver the new nation from its wartime isolation and in the future give an independent Confederacy not only security but also the central global role as its guarantor. In "the supply of this great staple [cotton] there is a worldwide interest," Hunter insisted in Sep-tember, and as "a single depository for such an interest, perhaps none could be found to act so impartially in that capacity as the Confederacy" because "it would be the greatest interest to such a government to pre-serve peace." The Confederacy would be an influence over other powers directly and indirectly toward this goal of perfection and peace because the Confederacy was a "harmonizing influence on human society," for "it would not only desire peace itself but to some extent become a bond of peace amongst others."[33]

Newspapers took these lofty goals and gave them a geographical ex-pression. The *Richmond Examiner* included both India and China within its future latitudinal trade system. Once both the Suez and Panama ca-nals had been dug, journalists considered that Confederate ports would be more accessible to shipping from these countries than the ports of the United States, so the paper expected New York to lose that carrying trade. Given the Richmond-based paper's desire to funnel commerce through Virginia, it was uninterested in a transpacific route; instead trade would go east, from the Chesapeake across the Atlantic, through the Mediterranean and the to-be-completed Suez Canal—construction of which had started in 1859, although it then took a decade to dig—across India and Thailand, via railways, to reach China. Most importantly, Confederate journalists debated whether China and India, along with Africa, Egypt, Turkey, and South America, would be developed as potential alternative cotton growing sites. This belief meant that these countries and regions became areas of interest, concern, and even as threats to the Confederacy. On May 13, the *Richmond Daily Dispatch* wrote that the British had tried everything in India—American seed, American gins, even American planters, "but all to no avail." Four months later, the *Examiner* also appraised, for the first time, both Indian and Chinese cotton capability. In the newspaper's opinion, population density and limited available land, together with high domestic demand for cotton goods, prevented any emulation of the Confederate paradigm of cotton surplus. Perhaps eager to rebut the antislavery British explorer David Livingstone's predictions, the journalist judged that potential cotton-growing regions in central Africa lacked the underlying "progressive" agricultural base necessary for cotton production.[34]

The leading southern periodical brought these discussions together with an integrated global southern view. "In all ages of the world," *De Bow's Review* claimed in May 1861, "those nations have become the most wealthy and enlightened that have carried on most Southern trade." Geography, slavery, and expansion together would enable the Confederacy to assume this commercially commanding position. "We of the slave states are admirably situated to trade with Mexico, the West Indies, and South America," the journalist continued, "and better situated than European countries for trade with southern Asia and the isles of the Pacific."[35]

VISIONS OF A NEW CONTINENTAL ORDER

Once war broke out, politicians sought continuity and agreed that, territorially, the country embraced not just all fifteen slave states, but also the territories of Arizona and New Mexico and the "Indian territory south of Kansas." However, with positive news from the military front, further discussions in Congress expanded theses territorial boundaries; the third session, which opened on July 28, just after reports reached Richmond about the Confederate Army's victory at First Bull Run, was particularly bullish. The former Virginia senator James M. Mason used a naturalization bill to extend the definition of Confederate citizenship to encompass the inhabitants of Washington, D.C. Mason, until recently a staunch advocate of the U.S. government's antebellum proslavery foreign policy—despite also being a quasi-secessionist—possibly hoped for an eventual reconstructed union under southern leadership.[36]

The State Department promoted an expansive vision abroad because the Confederacy, in order to obtain international recognition, had to project sufficient strength to convince the relevant audiences, principally in Britain and France, of Confederate capacity. This proof of capacity served two functions: to defend its independence now and to function as a great power in the future. Historians agree that diplomats disavowed expansion because a prospect of a disruptive new power would theoretically undermine efforts to win immediate international recognition of the independence of the new nation. At the same time, the message to the envoys was clear: the Confederacy had sufficient resources to be a powerful nation. In September 1861, Hunter, now secretary of state, instructed Mason to stress to the British both the Confederacy's "great but undeveloped capacities, and its developed strength." The eleven states, on their own, were "large enough to become the seat of an immense power" in which "nothing is wanted but time and peace for their development."[37]

Contrary to the insistence of diplomatic historians, individuals at the time contended that the Confederacy would not require European support and recognition in order to maintain an independent existence. To demonstrate this fact, Hunter presented the Confederate future as one of natural and orderly growth together with a hint about the expansionist ambitions of the new nation's leaders: "To these States there will probably be added hereafter Maryland, Missouri and Kentucky whose interests and sympathies must mind them to the South ... to say nothing of the once common territories west of these States which will probably fall into the new Confederacy." A vast area and now the war itself offered the chance to demonstrate Confederate potency. The new government believed its best diplomatic strategy was to project a power that would not require European support and recognition in order to maintain an independent existence. Rather, the Confederacy would be a useful, even necessary, military and commercial ally to have in the future. As Hunter instructed Henry Hotze, the future propagandist in Europe for the Confederacy, it was vital when communicating to overseas audiences "to convey a just idea of [the] ample resources and vast military strength" of the Confederate states and consequently "raise the character and government of the southerners in general estimation."[38]

Planning Postwar Relations with the Union

The war altered the expected future relations between the Union and Confederacy. The Confederate government insisted that it had no aggressive designs on any northern states. Historians have misconstrued this policy to mean Confederates renounced expansion as an objective of their nation-state. Instead, expansionist ambitions were an activity to be pursued during peacetime and not as war aims against the Union. In Davis's April 29, 1861, speech to Congress, when he stated "all we ask is to be let alone," he specifically prefaced that by observing: "we seek no conquest, no aggrandizement, no concession of any kind from the States with which we have lately confederated." The president hoped there would be an early peace with the United States. On May 28, Toombs quoted Davis's remarks in his dispatch to the Confederate commissioners in Europe with the following endorsement: "the object and desires of the government and people of the Confederate States cannot be better expressed than in the concluding paragraph of [Davis's] recent message to the congress." The day before Davis gave his speech, John A. Campbell, earlier a Confederate commissioner to Washington and still at that time a U.S. supreme court justice, wrote to him in the belief that peace with the Union was still possible. "We must consider with great care the effect of every measure upon our Northern antagonists and conciliate them if we can." Campbell and Davis hoped that a nonthreatening posture on the Confederacy's part would weaken the evident, to Campbell, northern resolve to prosecute the war after the fall of Fort Sumter.[39]

There were others who hoped that the Union would disintegrate. In such circumstances, the *Richmond Examiner* speculated on April 16, 1861, "We believe that in less than a year, the federal government will cease to exist. New Jersey and several of the North West states will be annexed to the Confederacy and New York will be erected into a great free port and independent city state." As well as Campbell's warning, the president also received encouraging reports of dissent in the Union. On April 15, a Jersey City merchant assured Davis of endemic pro-South sentiment in New York and New Jersey. New York City, strongly Democrat and pro free trade, appeared to some Confederates as a logical ally. Another Confederate commissioner to Washington, John Forsyth, editor and proprietor of the *Mobile Advertiser* and formerly Buchanan's minister to Mexico, had earlier told Davis about a move to declare New York a free city. The Alabamian probably wanted to block any compromise with the Lincoln administration and, as a former Douglas supporter, to demonstrate his fealty to the Confederate cause. In the vital weeks before and immediately after the decision to bombard Fort Sumter, expectations circulated that some northern free states would join the Confederacy.[40]

Henry A. Wise, a former governor of Virginia, wanted the Confederacy to supersede the United States. He insisted it was the Confederacy that was the true heir of the promise of 1776, and the Lincoln administration was a tyrannical aberration. It followed that a preemptive seizure of Washington, for example, would provoke the collapse of the Union and its reassembling under Confederate auspices with, perhaps, just the incorrigibly antislavery New England states excluded. The Virginia Presbyterian theologian Robert Lewis Dabney agreed and told northerners that the Union was where "the voice of justice and reason is no longer permitted to be heard." When Lincoln made his call for troops to suppress the rebellion on April 15, 1861, that gave proof of the president's selfishness and avarice. By declaring his intention to fight an aggressive war, Lincoln—Confederates believed—had violated the self-government of Federals as well as rebels. In such a situation, Dabney addressed northerners, Confederates "invite you, help us here to construct and defend another temple, where constitutional liberty may abide secure and untarnished."[41]

Wise hoped that a military offensive would forcefully deliver a reconstructed union he wanted, but many agreed with Dabney that such ambitions would be accomplished through peaceful means. On April 23, William Norwood, a resident of Georgetown near Washington, told Virginia politician James Lyons that an invasion of the Union made no sense, because "a peaceable separation & recognition of the S. Rep will be agreed to by the north." In this context, Norwood continued, "surely an attack on Washington City under such circumstances is not wise." Given that Lyons passionately believed in the "right and propriety" of secession, Norwood expected him to agree.[42]

Former conditional Unionists naturally hoped for a mutually advantageous settlement, provided peace came quickly. Governor Letcher worried about the loyalty of Virginia's northwest and how continued hostilities would also expose that region's military vulnerability. Therefore, he knew his state would benefit most from a rapid rapprochement with the Union, and a week later, on June 6, he told a group of northerners: "Let us part in peace, and you will gain more from it than by undertaking to whip us into the Union." At the same time, Letcher celebrated Virginia's heightened status as the dominant state of the Confederacy, so he welcomed Davis to the new Confederate capital on May 29, 1861, and resumed his focus on east-west railroad constructions in order to bring recalcitrant northwestern Virginia under control. An even more passionate Unionist supported a rapid rapprochement with the Union as the best possible policy for the Confederacy. Sam Houston, the recently removed Unionist governor of Texas, hoped that a speedy peace would avoid difficult choices for Texans, in their case relinquishing chances in the future to extend a protectorate over Mexico and put an end to Native American raids into Texas. In a speech on September 22, Houston declared "the sooner war is ended, the greater will be the probability of establishing friendly relations." He regretted that "the south can never reunite with the North," but a negotiation would "restore, to a great extent, the prosperity of the two sections." The onus was on Lincoln to agree to an armistice until "the meeting of Confederate and Federal congresses" can discuss terms.[43]

Many Confederates continued to expect the Union to surrender portions of federal assets and territories in what, on May 11, Hunt & James, William Massie's Richmond commission and forwarding merchants, anticipated would be "the great Back Down" on the part of the Lincoln administration. Even though they fired the first shots at Fort Sumter, Confederates believed in the superior moral strength of their position when it came to bargaining with their neighbor. On June 22, John E. Jones, an associate of Hunt & James, told Massie that the Confederate government must "insist an indemnity for being forced into a defensive war"; this would consist of an "immediate surrender of half the ships of war and all . . . fortresses, naval yards located in any southern state . . . and half of the territorial domain of the country." Confederate government policy, including a tariff, had created a chance for a compromise, and Jones recommended to the Davis administration that any "commercial treaties must be deferred to future negotiation." On May 17, in a public letter addressed to the editors of the *Church Journal* in Mobile, the prominent Alabamian educator William T. Walthall wrote that such terms should be expected by the Union because the Confederate government "offered a fair settlement of all undivided interests in public property, and an equal apportionment of the public debt." Therefore, the Reverend J. J. Nicolson commented in the same paper, "all that is necessary to restore peace and quiet to the land is for Lincoln to withdraw his war proclamation, his menacing ships and arms, and leave the south to its peaceful pursuits."[44]

Some supporters of an independent Confederacy continued to believe into the summer that the nation would prosper more in an alliance with the Union and hostility to overseas powers. These opinions tended to be held by individuals at a distance from the actual events. From his vantage point in California and possibly observing developments going on in nearby Mexico as well as further east, Charles Botts, in a speech delivered on August 10, looked forward to "the practical, desirable reconstruction" of a looser union. The relations between the Union and Confederacy would be governed in wholesome "emulating and rivaling" and, with an eye toward confronting the pending actions of creditor European nations seeking to recover their debts by force from the Mexican government, by "amity, allied offensively and defensively against the remainder of the world."[45]

A month earlier, Bunch dismissed any such concerns in London that the Union and Confederacy would be drawn together on account of the Mexican crisis. Across the Carolinas, the consul reported to Lord John Russell on July 22, "The hatred of the north is the most intense that can be imagined. I therefore treat any possibility of a future reconstruction of the Union as perfectly chimerical." The war had ruptured any hopes of Unionists that amity would eventually prevail, and Bunch believed Americans would remain divided for the foreseeable future and would not, "except under some very improbable contingency, be brought together for purposes of foreign aggression." Even in that scenario, the consul added, it was "much more likely that the one will become the ally of the enemies of the other in the event of a war between either and an European power."[46]

The eventual rapprochement between Britain and the United States after the Revolutionary War, symbolized by Jay's Treaty of 1794, offered a way forward even though that agreement had been very unpopular across the South. According to the May 1861 *Report of the Committee on Foreign Affairs* in the Provisional Congress, if the United States had been sensible, "they would have hastened to propose terms of friendly accommodation; and . . . they would have obtained such arrangements as might have made the south as valuable to them, as the United States proved to be to England after their separation." Perhaps it was already too late, former U.S. representative and proslavery poet William J. Grayson of South Carolina warned: "The season even for friendly commercial treaties is past already . . . every blow increases the mutual hatred." Grayson based his resolute optimism on seeing the South's mission of uplifting enslaved African Americans with both commerce and Christianity within the wider context of European and American imperialism. A conflict with the United States risked the interruption of this process.[47]

Confederates from the Upper South tended to be more conscious of the power of the United States and more mindful of the utility of European alliances. William Bilbo believed Confederates had to construct a nation-state both of sufficient power to negotiate with the Union on equal terms and able to expand; he also saw the future role of the Confederacy as blocking U.S. expansion. He envisaged the role of the Confederacy to "secure the liberty and consolidate the quiet of the two republics" by preventing "the United States from becoming the dictator of the western world by placing in the opposite scale the opinions, wealth, and maritime power of the new republic." Diplomats recognized the advantages of this approach, as it would rid the Confederacy of its isolation. Secretary of State Robert Hunter agreed on September 3 and, given his correspondent's recent advocacy of Cuban annexation and support of filibustering, perhaps considered it necessary to explain to the new commissioner to France, John Slidell of Louisiana, why he should tell the French that the Confederacy was now the status quo power. "By the establishment of a great Southern Confederacy," Hunter explained, "a balance of power is secured in North America, and schemes of conquest or annexation on the part of a great and overshadowing empire would probably no longer disturb the repose of neighboring nations." Slidell's manner rather than his beliefs fitted him for diplomacy. The narrative of "right" versus "might" suited diplomats in Europe; they wanted to present the Confederacy as a reliable ally in the future, one committed to defending interests greater than its own.[48]

CLAIMING A RIGHTFUL SHARE OF THE TERRITORIES

If politicians and diplomats had to adjust to the Union and the war by seeking a realignment across North America, other ambitions remained more constant. Before the war and even as their conventions debated secession in early 1861, the governors of Arkansas and Texas expected to control the future of the nearby Native American tribes. With the formation of the Confederacy and the outbreak of hostilities with the Union, efforts intensified both on the ground and in Richmond and Montgomery to embrace Native Americans within the new nation. Military, strategic, and commercial motives underpinned this plan, and as with the wider Confederate world vision, those individuals who looked to the future regarded Native American allegiance to the Confederacy as somehow natural and preordained. The third session of the Confederate Provisional Congress expected that self-interest would ensure Native American loyalty to the Confederacy, at least among settled tribes in the southern plains. Lawmakers continued to bring the Indian Territory into closer judicial and commercial relationship with the Confederate states.

Military personnel also hoped that war with the Union would solidify Native American loyalty—which had seemed hitherto to be wavering—to the Confederate cause. Immediately after the formation of the Confederacy, army officers stationed in Fort Smith, Arkansas, asked Native American tribes "if it is your intention to adhere to the United States Government during the pending conflict." In June, Brigadier General Ben McCulloch instructed Albert Pike, who was tasked with negotiations, to "say to the Indians that he sits between two stools." Only supporting the Confederacy offered the chance for slaveholding Native Americans to "keep them in full possession" of both "their lands" and "their negroes." McCulloch expected Native Americans to join the Confederacy for selfish reasons, because "nations like individuals are apt to be governed by their own interests . . . let them judge & choose between us." Privately, McCulloch added, the Confederate government "will never consent to see their country *settled or governed by abolitionists.*" His correspondent was skeptical that shared proslavery sentiment would be sufficient as an incentive to join the rebellion; Native Americans needed something more in exchange from the Confederate government so they "may not conclude that they are fighting for us only and not act equally for themselves." Hence Pike supported the move to secure their representation in Congress, even in the face of resistance by some in the cabinet who tended to take Indian support for granted.[49]

Far from opposing the establishment of an empire in the Southwest, as suggested by scholars, legislators promptly formalized control over the territory of New Mexico in a move they assumed would be accepted as a fait accompli by the United States. An August 1861 bill in Congress for the organization of the new territory of Arizona swiftly followed the news of a triumph by a former Knight of the Golden Circle, John R. Baylor, who had led an initial offensive composed of volunteers into New Mexico that July. Meanwhile Brigadier General Henry H. Sibley had already secured Davis's blessing for a more formal expedition. Sibley issued his own proclamation once he reached the border of New Mexico on December 20, and by the end of the year, reports of both the territory's aridity and mineral wealth began filtering back to Richmond. The mountains and the Mojave, Sonora, and Chihuahua deserts seemed unpropitious for the extension of staple crop agriculture, but mining offered the chance for employment of both white settlers and enslaved people. At the same time as these reports circulated in December, the bill's formal introduction in the fifth congressional session provoked a discussion on the proposed territory's northern boundary. The relevant member of the committee on territories, Judge Josiah A. P. Campbell of Mississippi, had proposed the thirty-six degrees, thirty minutes latitude line as Arizona's northern boundary. This boundary was rejected, and Congress agreed on a thirty-four degrees line instead. This decision was not a territorial concession, as the bill accorded the Confederacy the right to claim to both the remainder of New Mexico "or to any other territory north of the line of 34 degrees north." Leaving part of the territory unorganized left open the possibility that additional states would be carved out of the western territories and scope to achieve some kind of settlement with the United States.[50]

The expectation of a peace with the United States for now placed northern and western limits on the Confederacy. The official expansionist ambitions of the Confederate Congress did not yet extend to the admission of California, Oregon, and Washington Territory. As well as accommodating the assumed desires of the United States, De Bow and others undoubtedly conceived the region to be peripheral to the new nation's economy, as the future Confederacy would be centered on the labor of enslaved people in the Mississippi-Missouri river basin. There was neither a Confederate military presence nor evidence of proslavery

sentiment in California. Pressure to adopt an annexationist stance toward California came from Baylor and others most concerned with the
Southwest as it promised access to the Pacific and security for expansionist ambitions further south in Mexico. California might serve as a
buffer or a gateway, and slavery might spread into the southern parts of
the state. Texas delegate William P. Ochiltree, whose son was in Sibley's
expedition, got nowhere in his bid to extend Confederate citizenship to
Californians. Journalists, nevertheless, pressed for access to the Pacific
Ocean via Mexico, drew readers' attention to Confederate sympathizers
in Los Angeles, and then wondered if part or all of California would join
the Confederacy in an orderly manner. On July 11, the *Columbus (Georgia) Daily Sun* reported "intelligence" that in California, "the most formidable movement is on foot, on the part of rebels in that state, to proclaim
the southern part of it out of the Union, and to form a new state for
admission into the southern Confederacy"[51]

The Confederate press expected that while the Pacific slope would
break from the United States, it would not necessarily join the Confederacy. A belief in the establishment of a "European style geographic
frontier," defined by mountains and river watersheds, suggested that the
western border of the Confederacy lay along the continental divide. Beyond the Rocky Mountain ridge, a separate Pacific confederacy would
emerge. A multipolar North American continent looking increasingly
like Europe would in time emerge. This future Pacific confederacy was
approvingly, although vaguely, peopled with "European immigrants" and
would have a free trade policy; so, although not part of a formal Confederate empire, any Pacific confederacy would be clearly associated with the
Confederate economic "system" as an inferior and subordinate polity on
the American mainland.[52]

COMPLICATED EXPANSION INTO MEXICO

The Confederate government remained committed to the domination
of Mexico. However, the war imposed adjustments to how and when
that aspiration would be achieved. Confederates would have to compete
with European powers and the United States for influence, and with the
rapid imposition of the Union's naval blockade, Mexico would become an
important conduit for arms imported from Europe into the Confederacy.
Therefore, the government dropped the sense of entitlement that had
hitherto characterized southern intentions toward Mexico. Historians

mistake this restraint for a definitive renunciation of earlier ambitions in pursuit of recognition and a confession of weakness. Instead the change was more about timing than substance, as expansion would be postponed; in the meantime, preparations for a future control would be undertaken with professions of amity and the encouragement of commerce.[53]

The new measured tone toward Mexico adopted by the State Department combined the Confederacy's present wartime needs with its future promise as a great power. In drafting instructions for a Mexican mission to agent and former diplomat John T. Pickett, Secretary Toombs displayed a friendly manner, in contrast to his conduct as senator. He told Pickett to impress upon the Mexicans, "There are many reasons why Mexico should desire to . . . conclude a treaty of amity, commerce and navigation." The first reason was a shared interest in unfree labor. Proslavery theorists stressed how other countries—even the United States—were intent on developing labor systems modeled on their own. Far from being a despised corruption of slavery, Toombs argued that Mexico's peonage labor system was similar to it, so there was a "harmony of interests; which would lead to intimate trade relations as well as to cordial diplomatic cooperation." Additionally, geography mattered, as "Mexico being coterminous with the Confederate States renders the existence of a friendly alliance with the latter of the highest importance to the former." Mexico needed the Confederacy more than the Confederacy needed Mexico. Toombs wished to assert the Confederacy's status as the power most concerned in protecting Mexico against European, as well as American, intrigue, because the Confederacy would be able to "guarantee Mexico against foreign invasion . . . more promptly and effectively than any more distant nation." Again, rumors of intent of European powers to collect their debts mattered to this pledge. Finally, Toombs was conscious of the record of southern Democrats, such as James K. Polk and Davis himself, in Mexico. So he summed up the Confederate overture as a bipartisan effort with reference to his Whig background and suggested to Pickett that he should "remind [the Mexicans] that southern statesmen and diplomatists from the days of Henry Clay to the present . . . have always been fast friends of Mexico, and that she may always confidently rely upon the good will and friendly intervention of the Confederate States."[54]

Toombs qualified his Mexican guarantee on account of continued Indian raids, rumored U.S. intrigue, and residual antebellum southern aggression. Pickett had to impress upon the Mexicans that any "grant to

the United States of commercial, political or territorial advantages which
are not accorded to the Confederate States would be regarded [...] as
an evidence of an unfriendly disposition ... which [the Davis administra-
tion] would sincerely deplore and protest against in the promptest and
most decided manner." To deal with Indian raids across the Texan border, which so concerned Texans, Toombs instructed Pickett to communicate that "border feuds and forays must be put an end to by the forming
of an extradition treaty." In return, Pickett should tell the Mexicans that
the Confederacy "will undertake to enforce the clause (now absolute)
in the treaty of Guadeloupe Hidalgo restraining incursions of wild
tribes in consideration of certain commercial privileges and rights of
way across Mexican territory." Confident of their ability to control their
own Native American tribes, Confederates treated Mexican powerless-
ness to govern its Indians as a reason to intervene in its internal affairs.
The government had no interest in seeking Mexican recognition; instead,
Toombs told Pickett specifically to cultivate the mercantile community
and encourage Mexican privateering against United States vessels.[55]

By contrast, earlier scruples over the inclusion of Mexicans that had
hitherto restrained southern expansion for some individuals seemed
to matter less in wartime. Perhaps the experience of mobilization
while slavery survived increased Confederate confidence in controlling
subject peoples. The need for security through expansion in a dangerous world and anger over rumored collusion between the Lincoln and
Juárez administrations increased ambitions. Meanwhile developments in
Mexico itself resurrected calls from various Richmond newspapers—even
from the *Examiner*, which was strongly opposed to any distractions
until the war was safely won—for expansion at Mexico's expense. After
the First Battle of Bull Run in July, the tone of the Confederate press
became much more hostile and aggressive toward Mexico. Both the *Examiner* and the *Daily Dispatch* reacted violently to premature reports
about the Corwin Treaty negotiated between Mexico and the United
States. The U.S. minister Thomas Corwin had, in return for allowing
the Federal troops to cross Mexican territory, pledged that the United
States government would provide a loan to the Mexican government
to pay off those European creditors and in addition, according to one
version, promised to return Texas to Mexico. The prospect of postwar
revenge on Mexico aroused the press. On September 4, the *Daily Dispatch* warned that any provocation would "compel the Confederacy to
annex a portion of that Republic to our magnificent empire." Two days

later, the *Richmond Examiner* threatened that "the first account of the new nation will be settled with Mexico." A month later, the *Richmond Examiner* repeated its threats before stating that "the same southern race who aided the earlier conquest [in 1847] could not fail to do so again" and "teach a similar lesson when it becomes necessary." Mexico thus had to consider "the risk of thus losing two or three rich provinces." While the path of Mexico's "interest and safety" lay in peace, the paper concluded, if it provoked the Confederacy, then Mexico "can have war to her hearts content."[56]

Expansionist demands from newspapers aligned with Confederate government activity. Members of the State Department were also concerned with the activities of Corwin and sought to take advantage of recent events in Mexico. Its own civil war was only recently concluded, and the liberal administration of President Benito Juárez was just established since January 1861 in Mexico City. In particular, Confederate diplomats became interested in stirring up separatism in the provinces bordering the Confederacy and were encouraged by their impression that the provincial governors appeared friendlier to their cause than the pro-U.S. Juárez. In May, Toombs had sent the Cuban-born special agent Jose A. Quintero to Monterrey to wait on the provincial governor of Nuevo Leon, General Santiago Vidaurri. Two days before the *Daily Dispatch* article, William M. Browne, himself a former journalist and now the assistant secretary of state, composed instructions for Quintero, who was also a former journalist. As well as conducting diplomacy, Browne expected Quintero to "collect and transmit accurate and minute information" about "New Leon and adjacent friendly provinces of northern Mexico." Specifically, Quintero had to research "products and mineral resources," together with "the amount of population of each [province], divided into races and classes." Browne told Quintero to establish the land area and the economy of this part of Mexico, as well as the "general condition of the people; on a social, political and commercial point of view." The nature of these instructions suggests the State Department considered the future admission of these lands as Confederate territories and looked to plan future economic exploitation. The racial composition of Mexico had frustrated an earlier generation of expansionists during the 1846–48 war, but the northern provinces were believed to be lightly populated and underdeveloped. Quintero interpreted his instructions to include negotiations about a railroad connecting the Confederacy with Neuvo Leon.[57]

More immediately, Browne wanted Quintero to identity resources for the Confederate war effort, improve border security, and establish the veracity of rumors about the Corwin Treaty and to make known "the disastrous consequences which must necessarily ensue" of "so flagrant a violation of the neutrality of Mexico." In the immediate term, diplomats wished to play off the provinces against the central government in Mexico in order to pressure Juárez from adopting a pro-Union policy. "It is to be hoped," Browne advised Quintero on December 9, that Governor Vidaurri "will succeed in inducing Governor [Ignacio] Pesqueira [of Sonora] and the governors of the other frontier States of Mexico to unite with them in a protest to the Mexican Government." Vidaurri had once been a supporter of Juárez, but he had recently conquered the neighboring province of Coahuila to add to his own and therefore expected to be reined in by any restored central authority. Browne hoped that such a protest would either frighten the government in Mexico City to retreat from any agreement to admit U.S. troops or render the Corwin Treaty a dead letter by starting another Mexican civil war.[58]

Politicians looked beyond confronting Union intrigues in Mexico against the Confederacy toward preparations for dominating the Western Hemisphere. "Commissioners or other diplomatic agents should be sent at an early period to the independent American powers south of our confederacy," Davis declared on April 29, as "it is our interest and earnest wish to maintain the most cordial and friendly relations." Mexico, Central America, and South America mattered not least due to the cotton plant being indigenous in these regions: "All that is required by those countries is a strong and permanent government," a writer in De Bow's Review warned its readers the same month, "to make them serious competitors with us in supplying the world with cotton." The passive stance forced on Confederate policy in Latin America by the outbreak of war would, the journalist argued, easily be changed once independence had been secured. "The continual revolutions and civil wars that are occurring in Mexico and South America" provided opportunities for Confederate intervention at little cost, as "southern men may, with great propriety, ally themselves with one of the contending parties." Once "peace, quiet, stability and security" were restored, "it will be easy for the South to form good commercial treaties with these regenerated states."[59]

The Confederate policy toward Mexico would be conducted in accordance with "the duties of good neighbourhood." This policy meant an immediate end to filibustering and other unauthorized actions by private individuals in pursuit of Indians and profit. The new secretary of state Robert Hunter declared the era of filibustering to be over, as the Confederate government wished "to prevent border raids and lawless invasions of the soil of Mexico by our citizens." Instead of soldiers and adventurers, the Confederate presence there would be composed of merchants and traders because the State Department desired to promote between Confederates and Mexicans "those commercial relations which conduce so beneficially to their mutual welfare." The approach toward Mexico would then be extended to the rest of Latin America. The growth of trade would offer a much more solid basis for Confederate power and expansion in the future than military conquest, but the latter threat would always be held in reserve. "It is our interest and our purpose to cultivate peaceful relations with our neighbors," Hunter insisted. However, he added the caveat, "but our neighbors must evince a similar disposition towards us."[60]

Supporting the Status Quo in Cuba

Before the Civil War broke out, many members of the government—including Davis—thought about annexing Cuba; but once the fighting started, the conflict suggested other policies. Moreover, Confederates' attitudes to Cuba on account of its location and slavery reveal the aspirations these individuals had for their new nation. The Spanish colonial regime of the captain general, Count Serrano, had to be overtly supported due to a shared interest in slavery and to promote a growing "southern" Atlantic commercial network to compete with the "northern" Atlantic commerce between the United States and Britain. Both *De Bow's Review* in May and the *Examiner* in September suggested it would be better than annexation to instead guarantee Cuba as a possession of Spain. These articles matched evolving government policy as well as reviving a policy once advocated by some southerners, including Hunter, during the 1850s. In July, Toombs—still secretary of state—dispatched a special agent, Charles J. Helm, to Cuba to ensure that "the two countries may exist separately but are bound together in the firmest manner by the most friendly and unlimited commercial intercourse." In August 1861, Hunter extended the remit of the commissions to Europe from Britain and France to include, at Serrano's urging, an approach to Spain. As with Mexican governor Vidaurri, diplomats adopted a policy of propping up weak, decentralized regimes. Hunter's instructions to the envoys also included the argument that "of all the great powers in Europe, Spain alone is interested, through her colonies, [in slavery]. The close proximity of these colonies to our shores, and the great mutual dependence of social and commercial interests between them and our own states, seem to invite a close and intimate alliance between the two countries." As with Mexico, politicians and diplomats expected that geography, similarity of social structures, and sense of shared danger would bind the island close to the Confederacy.[61]

Confederates imagined that an international proslavery league was possible. As southern politicians before the war, they had tried to get the federal government to adopt this policy; but now as a result of their independence, it finally might come to pass. Newspapers suggested that the reach of this alliance might protect slavery in Brazil as well as Cuba. Hunter expressed that the Confederacy "would earnestly desire to see the nations thus bound together armed with the means to protect their common social system." On May 6, the *Richmond Dispatch* reported the visit by Don Felix de Castro, the envoy from Brazil to the then Confederate capital of Montgomery in Alabama. The minister expressed his "warm feeling for the Confederacy" and his confidence that Brazil "not only will sympathise with us but will . . . protest the United States blockade" of Confederate ports.[62]

A wish for a proslavery alliance meant the government of the Confederacy patronized expansionist ambitions of the other slaveholding powers. Both Spain's intervention in Santo Domingo, in which Serrano was closely involved, and its initial leadership of the debt-collecting expedition to Mexico provided evidence that the policy of the O'Donnell administration in Madrid was geared toward the reestablishment of Spain as a great power. The Confederacy, Hunter declared, "can never find any cause for jealousy or regret in the steady growth of the power and resources of Spain." Commentators welcomed the opportunities to increase trade with both Spain and its colonies. Yet there was no question as to any parity between Spain and the Confederacy. Given that the Confederacy would "be a great empire at no distant day," the Spanish needed to ensure it was "a great friendly power." Annexation of Cuba remained a possible long-term objective. In similar fashion to northern Mexico, diplomats understood their instructions to include cataloguing the resources of Cuba with both immediate wartime needs and longer-term commercial exploitation plans in mind. Mason assured Hunter in November 1861 that while waiting for transit to Nassau, he would spend his time fact-finding in Havana. Furthermore, by also blessing Spain's efforts in Santo Domingo, the Confederate government tried to develop a Caribbean policy dedicated to the parallel growth of slavery and commerce, one that Mason had earlier championed when chairman of the Senate Foreign Relations committee during the 1850s.[63]

Once he arrived in Havana in October 1861, having been delayed in starting his mission by an outbreak of yellow fever on the island, Helm obeyed his instructions and focused on cultivating this shared sense of interest with Cubans. He reported back success. Additionally, Toombs had appointed him special agent to the British and Danish West Indies. Toombs formally instructed Helm to just establish "friendly commercial relations" with these islands. But verbally, according to Helm, Toombs had additionally suggested that he establish, at least, a depot for the reshipping and storing of cargo at Nassau in the British Bahamas. As the war progressed, blockade running and commerce raiding indicated postwar Confederate interests to be developed in Latin America and the Caribbean. In early 1862, the *Examiner* studied the patterns of blockade-running because the newspaper believed the routes of the smugglers marked a preview of trade networks across the Atlantic and Caribbean that would be established in time of peace. The evidence of the appointment of Helm and the proposal by Toombs to establish a depot at Nassau suggested that the government endorsed such a project. The wartime establishment of trade routes across the Caribbean and the approach to Spain for alliance not only promised a future of commercial growth and the protection of slavery in the Caribbean but also reflected a Confederate vision of the world and their place in it.[64]

THE EXPERIENCE of war for a year meant both the press and government of the Confederacy asserted more vigorously the Confederate right to be a great power in the world. At the same time, the war deepened the Confederate sense of connection with overseas countries and territories—especially with those on Mediterranean and southward latitudes or areas of potential cotton production. These visions were not just dreams. Newspapers and both the executive and legislative branches of government continued to articulate the expansionist demands and security needs of the slavery economy. At the very least, for their neighbors, Confederates tolerated fragmented and sympathetic entities; for example, of Spanish colonies, a chaotic Mexico, and further secessions from the United States. If these conditions of weakness and friendliness were not met, outright annexation of territory was the logical alternative.

The conflict disrupted and postponed plans for the future of the nation, but planners predicted a resumption of its trajectory toward hemispheric and even global domination before long. The prospect of bumper crops cheered those who feared for the future of the plantation economy. The Confederate revolution endowed the nation with a sense of unity that compensated for weakness in numbers. The potential of slavery appeared to be enhanced as a result of its survival in circumstances of war, which in antebellum days—slaveholders feared—would have meant certain slave insurrection and racial war. Diplomats welcomed new encouraging signs of the survival and expansion of slavery under the aegis of foreign powers, which echoed the proslavery foreign policy of the federal government before the war. Yet at the same time, the war imposed change; the Union's blockade had the effect that some Confederates believed that their government's devotion to the principles of the political economy of free trade and interdependence of nations would have to be supplemented by other measures, such as using the stockpile of cotton as a means to force open markets, draw in specie, and crush competitors. However, away from its coasts and northwest Virginia, the sources of power of the Confederacy had not so far been seriously challenged by the Union. By February 1862, that situation changed, and the Union offensives drove a reappraisal of the strengths and weaknesses of the Confederacy, and that led Confederates to reconsider where and how their nation would expand in the future.

3

Self-Sufficiency at Home and Self-Assertion Abroad

CONFEDERATE AMBITIONS FOR THE REMAINDER OF 1862

THE CRUSHING experience of the early months of 1862 wrought a permanent change in the preoccupations of leading Confederates. Historians agree that by this time, the war consumed every moment and crowded out any philosophical thoughts about the future. "Who can give his whole mind to . . . abstract topics," asked South Carolina novelist William Gilmore Simms, in a letter dated September 20 to the readers of the *Southern Illustrated News*, "when the whole country is heaving with the throes of a mighty revolution?" This was a time when "all our thoughts resolve themselves into the war." The time was one of transformation, as well as a period of preoccupation. "The war, if it has not taken from us at once and entirely the habits of our whole existence in the past," wrote the *Southern Illustrated News's* editor and war correspondent, John Esten Cooke, who was also a historian and novelist, "has so altered and modified them that they are no longer the same."[1]

DURING 1862, while the outlook of optimistic Confederates changed dramatically, these individuals remained intensely ambitious for the future nation-state. Their preoccupation with immediate danger juxtaposed with plans for future opportunities because they became more conscious of a long-term need for sufficient national power to resist the United States after the conclusion of hostilities. The priority of planners was to achieve a secure position on the American continent. At the same time, wider ambitions to extend the territorial and commercial scope of the Confederacy suffered a momentary eclipse early in the year, but as the fortunes of war began to change after May 1862, these ambitions began once more to assume hemispheric, even global proportions. As a result, those individuals in a position to observe—whether from the vantage point of government or as soldiers, journalists, and planters—derived assurance from the developments and events of 1862, and supposed that these trends pointed toward a future of power and prosperity.

The foundation beneath this ambition was its protagonists' belief that the Confederacy became, during the second half of 1862, a leading military power and, in turn, their view of what this capability meant for the nation. The army, whatever its importance in the formation of wartime nationalism, would play little role in the future visions of the Confederacy. Earlier, the Confederacy had been projected to be a great commercial power on the basis of mass production of staple crops made possible by the slave-based labor system. While this commercial power remained, it was now augmented by the lessons of subsequent events, those components now deemed by planners as essential to a world power—an ironclad navy, an increasingly diversified economy, a dominant position in North American geopolitics, and an independent foreign policy based on self-assertion. These new facets of power supplemented the continuing Confederate strengths of staple crop production and slavery.[2]

The progress of the war determined the nature and scale of these resurgent national ambitions. The new secretary of state, Judah P. Benjamin, was one among many Confederates who obtained intelligence about the war from northern newspapers, especially the *New York Times* and *New York Herald*, as well as from the Confederate press. According to a later observation of Robert Kean, who in the spring of 1862 took up a post in the War Department, the secretary was too trusting of the reports he received. Confederate planners integrated their notions of northern public opinion on the war into their visions of the future Confederacy. Not only were ambitions driven by Confederate strengths and opportunities, but also by planners' wish to take advantage of weaknesses or counterthreats from the other side. There seemed to be ample evidence of divisions in the Union. The prospect of both secession and the peaceful admission of some northern states into the Confederacy leading to a more advantageous configuration of power relationships in North

America informed expectations of the country's dimensions and security. Finally, those planners who possessed a sense of history often chose to interpret the ordeal of the early months of 1862 as a vital stage in the rise of a nation.[3]

THE INDUSTRIALIZATION OF KING COTTON

Shifts in economic planning illustrated the changing ideas of what the nation would become in the world. Virginia commentators and diplomats believed that the development of an industrial sector would enhance the Confederacy's standing as a great power and ally. From its being a supplier of staple crops to other nations, experience had taught commentators that the Confederacy needed to also be a competitive industrializing nation. This development might deepen links with other nations. With the French economy's needs in mind, the *Richmond Examiner* on April 4 drew attention to the Confederacy's iron and coal resources. On February 8, Hunter had sent the same message to his commissioners and asked them to assure the French and British governments that the Confederacy's "commercial and industrial development will be unparalleled."[4]

This call for an industrial revolution did not mean an end to that global interdependency that had so marked the birth of the nation. Rather, politicians and business leaders in Richmond recognized the danger of falling victim to U.S. or European imperialism and welcomed industrialization as a means of ridding the Confederacy of the South's colonial taint—foreign-owned interests and undue dependency on foreign markets. On February 27, a railroad corporation convention met in Richmond. De Bow applauded the meeting and the several resolutions adopted because "it is of great importance . . . to the defence of the Confederacy that every facility be extended to the development of the mineral wealth of the Confederate States." Robert Rufus Bridgers of Edgecombe, North Carolina, railroad president and congressman, agreed, especially about iron; this interest was despite the fact that previously he was best known for his promotion of educational and agricultural development in his county. He understood that such industrial development would enable the Confederacy to prosecute the war more effectively, especially as a longer war was now in prospect. "Our only chance is to put up forges, foundries and rolling mills," Bridgers told Judge Thomas Ruffin on February 17; "there is but one rolling mill I understand in the Confederacy. It will with the proper engagement take six months to get under headway."[5]

Bridgers understood the new necessity, but plans for industrialization were long-term as well as an immediate response to the wartime shortages forced by the blockade. On June 6, in an article on "the productiveness of the South," John Forsyth, the editor and proprietor of the *Mobile Register* agreed with Bridgers and concluded in his paper, "the war is teaching us a lesson to subsist within ourselves, need industrial or material independence and in so doing cripple those whom the war will leave as our hereditary enemies." Forsyth clearly expected poor relations with the United States after the war; however, this did not preclude good relations with other nations. Historian Todd Wahlstrom notes how Forsyth, as an agent during the war, also sought to establish commercial relations with Mexico, including plans to build a transcontinental railroad between Texas and the port of Mazatlan on Mexico's Pacific Ocean coast.[6]

During his speeches in 1862, Davis used the rhetoric of industrialization, as well as the doctrine of self-sufficiency imposed by the blockade, to support an altered vision of a great future for the Confederacy. The blockade "is fast making us a self-supporting and an independent people," Davis boasted in his inaugural address on February 22, which would "only serve to divert our industry from the production of articles for export and employ it in supplying the commodities for domestic use." Look at "the immense resources which nature has lavished upon us," Davis directed the soldiers of the Army of Tennessee gathered at Murfreesboro on January 7, 1863. "Our mines have been made to yield up neglected wealth, and manufactories start up as if by magic. We are becoming independent in several ways. If the war continues, we shall only grow stronger and stronger as each year rolls on."[7]

For the president, the Confederacy's military resilience during 1862 amplified the importance of these resources for the future nation. Davis and his secretaries of state in their speeches and writings combined expansion and industrialization in a vision of the Confederacy that would be secure from Federal assaults. According to Hunter, an enlarged Confederacy would be able to "protect its own independence and interests" and therefore not require any allies against a vengeful Union. When Davis spoke of "immense resources," he oriented the focus of the nation toward protecting itself from the North as well as affirming expansion toward the west and south—in short, to aim to break-up the Union. The alternative to ambition was a continuance of hostilities between a rump Confederacy and the United States, which, in accordance with prevailing notions of political economy, would harm combatants and noncombatants alike. An enduring peace would follow only from Confederate strength, not weakness.[8]

THE LEADING AMERICAN POWER

During 1862, the most important goal for the Confederacy in securing this power was domination of the American continent. Leading Confederates planned two routes to achieve this objective. First, the government would admit new states on the Pacific coast and the whole Mississippi Valley; and second, less ambitiously, it would focus on internal dissent in the United States and foster secession of states from the Union to form new confederacies in the far West and Midwest. The Davis administration would then negotiate reciprocal commercial pacts with these entities, similar to those agreements Confederate diplomats were also, at the same time, attempting to broker with Britain, France, Spain, Russia, and Belgium—which in turn emulated trade treaties European countries were agreeing among themselves.[9]

To thrive in the postwar world, the Confederacy would need to be a Pacific Ocean power. Moreover, the government in Richmond believed leading Californians would help them achieve this ambition. Two such individuals had suffered arrest and detention in the North as a penalty for being pro-Confederate, and on January 15, Davis learned that former senator William M. Gwin and Joseph L. Brent would join the Confederacy as soon as possible. The former's advocacy of an independent California was well known. At the end of the year, the former Mississippi politician, soldier, and now diplomat Lucius Lamar communicated to Davis his belief of "a serious revolution in Southern California." Politicians and diplomats derived from anecdotal evidence and the arguments of exiles that the citizens of California demanded commercial relations with the Confederacy and resented the easterner-dominated, antislavery, protectionist policies of the Lincoln administration. In particular, according to refugees and informants, Californians resented war taxes to pay for a conflict in which they had little apparent stake.[10]

In recommending policies to the administration, Congress strove to take advantage of this supposed California discontent, and its plans extended to the rest of the West. Henry S. Foote of Tennessee, a former governor of Mississippi and local rival to Davis, had long been an advocate of American southern and western expansion, and as chairman of the House Committee on Foreign Affairs since February 1862, he now led the charge. On October 1, Foote introduced in the House of Representatives a joint resolution recognizing "the practical neutrality of the states of Oregon and California and the territories of Washington and Nevada." He argued that communication should be made "suggesting the advantages which result to the people thereof from an immediate assertion on their part of their independence of the United States." Foote explained how he saw the future relationship of the Pacific states and territories with the Confederacy; he proposed "the formation of a league offensive and defensive between the said States and territories and the Confederacy." The bill disappeared into the committee's deliberations and was not heard of again, but the House agreed in ordering it to be printed, a sign of politicians' support of the measure and that in due course it would become a postwar policy of the Confederacy.[11]

During the second half of 1862, the lands in the far West were secondary in importance to the main Confederate focus on the states of the Midwest. The debate over the status of these states went back to secession and the commercial convention movements. The discussions continued with increased emphasis in 1862 as the war hastened the time, optimists believed, that the Midwest would either join the Confederacy or at least secede from the Union, on account of the increasing exactions and onerous policies imposed by the Lincoln administration. In January, De Bow reviewed a pamphlet, which had been written in 1860 by an anonymous Virginian who suggested that a new confederation might be formed between the "Southern section and the Western agricultural States." De Bow disagreed, contending that the author "attributes to the freesoil people of the [old] Northwest a greater degree of conservative and of just feeling than they are entitled to be credited with." Nevertheless, De Bow set aside the antislavery sentiment of the inhabitants when he agreed that the nation's heart was the Mississippi basin and that, at the very least, there must be a free trade area encompassing that region. "It is, perhaps," he warily admitted, "conceivable that at some period we may safely and beneficially enter into some commercial relations with those States whose natural outlet is the Mississippi River."[12]

De Bow considered as axiomatic that the states of the watershed of the Mississippi-Missouri rivers would wish to enter into an arrangement with the Confederacy. He cheerfully believed the laws of geography and economics would ineluctably lead to a greater Confederacy dominating both the continent and global trade routes. "We will be more than half way on the route from Europe to China," De Bow wrote, "which is to

become the chief market." In pursuit of the commercial opportunities
to be had in the Manchu Empire, even New England would be attracted to
join some kind of pact. The whole continent will draw together, De Bow
predicted, as "the shipping interest of the East and the manufacturing
and agricultural interests of the Northwest will soon unite and give us a
peace." De Bow believed in a vibrant midwestern separatism based on a
combination of the desire for a reciprocal economic relationship with the
Confederacy, indifference to slavery, demand for peace, and opposition
the policies of the Federal government—ranging from infringement of
civil freedoms to the protectionist Morrill Tariff. If the Midwest would
only "be wise" and "become a separate government" and "[establish]
proper commercial relations with us," De Bow argued, "it will become
the seat of the richest manufacturing industry in the world." The Midwest would provide the manufacturing products needed by the Confederacy, in return "receiving their supplies of the raw material and tropical
products from the South." According, again, to comparative advantage,
the Confederate customers would be able to afford higher prices for the
goods provided by the states of the Midwest. These economic exchanges
between midwesterners and Confederates would therefore rapidly supplant any ideological attachment to other free states because "these two
peoples will be bound together by interests stronger even than the late
constitutional Union."[13]

To facilitate this realignment of power in North America, business
leaders and politicians advocated an interim commercial union with
the Midwest. At the 1862 Planters' Convention held in Memphis, Tennessee, J. B. Gladney chaired a committee that presented "new issues
before the people of the Western states." It called for the Confederate
government to foster divisions between the Midwest and New England.
Another supporter of an approach to the Midwest was Senator Hershel V. Johnson of Georgia, who wrote to the president on this topic on
March 26 and again, at length, to Hunter on August 27. Johnson, who
as the vice presidential candidate on the Douglas ticket in 1860, was an
expansionist—believer in the "regeneration" of Mexico—and he believed
in the "mission to spread American ideals to those thirsting for freedom
around the world." To that end, the Georgian insisted on the "need to
reforge the affective bonds that had united northerners and southerners
in a national community." In March 1862, with the permanent government in operation, he saw an opportunity to resume his pursuit of such

a goal to construct a new union. The senator believed the midwestern states were lukewarm in their support of the war and that the Confederate government, by timely concessions, would be able to take advantage of this situation. After all, Johnson observed, "western States have nothing to fight for, but the free navigation of the Mississippi River and advantageous commercial arrangements with the Confederate States." In these circumstances, "Let them be convinced that the Confederate States design no hostile policy toward them, in relation to these great interests," Johnson advised, "and I should have strong hope that they would rapidly abandon the federal Flag." Although the Provisional Congress at Montgomery had earlier announced a policy of freedom of the river, he considered the permanent government should do so again and loudly, as "the policy has not been made sufficiently prominent and notorious."[14]

The U.S. military successes all along the Mississippi River rendered moot both the February recommendations from the Planters' Convention and Johnson's approach a month later, as it looked likely that the Confederacy would soon have no presence on the river, let alone contact with the Midwest. Once the military situation had stabilized in the summer, planning resumed. Johnson asked Hunter in August 1862 to move the subject in the Senate; meanwhile, Gladney planned to get his Planters' Convention paper published in De Bow's Review and, that August, asked Davis to help spread the message. In the aftermath of the battle of Second Bull Run, it seemed opportune to the House of Representatives, Davis, and the military to make another approach to the Midwest. The military revival was a critical precondition; hopes for an invasion of Kentucky and even across the Ohio River became a reality to many.

While military advances catalyzed thinking, Confederate planners based their projections of the nation's future on more than hopes for a positive outcome of the Kentucky Campaign. Supporters of incorporating the Midwest into the Confederacy did not for a moment expect their armies to conquer these lands. Even though there were Confederate military offensives further east, the failure of Confederate General Earl Van Dorn to retake Corinth ensured that the Mississippi Valley remained largely in Union hands. Confederate future plans were based on assumptions of public support for secession north of the Ohio River; yet this opposition to Lincoln in the imminent off-year elections in the Union would also be stimulated by the performance of the armies in the field. Historian Robert Bonner notes that General P. G. T.

Beauregard's simultaneous proposal for a conference between governors of the Confederate and midwestern states "started a fascination with an exaggeration of the copperheads" among politicians and soldiers.[15]

The advancing Army of Tennessee carried a proposal of collaboration with the people of the Midwest. On September 7, providing material intended for inclusion in his generals' respective proclamations, Davis followed Johnson's advice and wrote to Robert E. Lee, Braxton Bragg, and Edmund Kirby Smith that they needed to remind the people there of the concessions already made and that "the Confederate Congress by public act, prior to the commencement of the war, enacted 'the peaceful navigation of the Mississippi River is hereby declared free to the citizens of the States upon its borders, or upon the borders of its navigational tributaries." Johnson had earlier argued that the Mississippi had to be understood, as Calhoun had once declared, as a shared asset, an "inland sea" for Americans. In drafting the proclamation, Davis drew on his belief in free trade fueling territorial expansion.[16]

Congressmen debated the wisdom of further concessions to the Midwest. On September 19, Foote, leading the majority of the House Foreign Affairs Committee, argued that Davis should supplement his proclamation declaring free navigation with the additional incentive of a commercial pact, or in shorthand: "the opening of the market of the South." Such a proclamation "would have a tendency greatly to strengthen the advocates of peace in the Northwest states," Foote and his supporters maintained, and even to "withdraw them ultimately altogether from their present injurious political connection." The expected continued Confederate military success and the prospect of access to the southern market should, Foote believed, be a sufficient inducement for the Midwest's withdrawing its support from the war effort.[17]

According to Foote and a majority of the Foreign Affairs Committee, the result of such midwestern behavior would be to force an end of the war on terms advantageous to the Confederacy; this would "enable us to dictate the terms of a just and honorable peace from the great commercial emporiums of that region." A peace settled in either Chicago or Cincinnati would inevitably lead to commercial domination of North America. Foote also requested that Davis, in addition to free navigation of the Mississippi and free trade, "make known, in said proclamation, the willingness of the government and the people of the Confederate States to enter hereafter into a reciprocity commercial treaty or treaties with one or more of [the seceded states]." European examples suggested that such pacts would solidify the peace. Davis omitted this clause on commercial treaties in his instructions to the generals, perhaps because it violated the president's free trade beliefs and, moreover, because Foote's committee disagreed on this issue of commercial treaties with midwestern states.[18]

Representative Ethelbert Barksdale of Mississippi and a minority within the Foreign Affairs Committee regarded Foote's resolution as a "recommendation that this government should tender to a portion of the citizens of the government with whom we are at war exclusive commercial privileges." The minority, the congressmen continued, "repel the suggestion that the people of the south are willing to purchase a peace by such a sacrifice and by so degrading a concession to northern cupidity." The consequence would be an "imputation of pussillanity ... a confession of conscious weakness, and its inevitable tendency would be to prolong the war." An offering of a commercial pact would be perceived as a desperate act on the part of the government. Besides, the minority considered that the majority was mistaken in the existence of a desire for peace in the Midwest; but if it did exist, then it was the result of the government's "manifestation of purpose to prosecute the war with vigor and effect." Barksdale argued that a degrading attempt to bribe commercial interests in the midwestern states would undermine Confederate resolve and send a signal to the Union of Confederate weakness.[19]

A vision of a *zollverein*, between the Confederacy and the Midwest, akin to that voiced by Foote, prevailed on the ground in place of Barksdale's rectitude. The advancing army broadcasted the government's message to the citizens and electorate of the Midwest. As well as including Davis's material, Bragg's September 26 proclamation to the people of the Midwest noted that as a result of Lincoln's recent preliminary emancipation proclamation, midwesterners would be used "to fight the battle of emancipation, a battle which, if successful, destroys our prosperity, and with it your best markets to buy and sell." General Bragg believed the freeing of enslaved people was much less popular in the Midwest than in New England and that destroying the Confederate economy would further harm midwestern interests. Addressing Barksdale's concerns about desperation, the proclamations of Bragg and other army commanders were addressed to the people of Kentucky only, but they still served a wider purpose, as Bragg told Davis on October 2, "I have deemed it best to issue my proclamation to the people of Ohio, and all the North West, before invading their country, and at a time when their elections are pending."[20]

After Bragg's retreat following the indecisive battle of Perryville on October 8, to the end of 1862, Davis believed in the need to appeal to the Midwest. Provided, the president believed, the Confederate army held Vicksburg and hence had the ability to block the Mississippi River, the Confederacy would eventually forge a commercial alliance with the Midwest. On his visit to Vicksburg on December 21, Davis warned General Theophilus Holmes, the army commander in Arkansas, that a United States capture of Vicksburg would enable the Lincoln administration to answer "the exigent demand of the North Western States for the restoration to them of the unrestricted use of that river, and by utilizing the heretofore fruitless possession of New Orleans." This eventuality must not arise. "By holding that section of the river between Port Hudson and Vicksburg," Davis told a crowd in Jackson, Mississippi, on December 26, the Confederacy would continue to apply economic pressure on the Midwest. "The people of the West, cut off from New Orleans," the president explained, "will be driven to the East to seek a market for their products, and will be compelled to pay so much in the way of freights that those products will be rendered almost valueless." Commercial needs would drive political behavior, and, Davis declared, "I should not be surprised if the first daybreak of peace were to dawn upon us from that quarter."[21]

CONFEDERATE AMBITIONS FOR A BALANCE OF POWER IN NORTH AMERICA

Diplomats agreed with generals and politicians that in order to be a credible partner to Britain and France, the Confederacy had to establish itself on a secure basis in North America. Far from acting in accordance with the constraints exercised on Confederate diplomacy on account of the pursuit of recognition, as scholars argue, the secretary of state wished to communicate his ambitions for the Confederacy to his European audience. "No treaty of peace can be accepted," Hunter informed his commissioners in a message for onward communication to the chancelleries of Europe, "which does not secure the independence of the Confederate States, including Maryland, Virginia, Kentucky and Missouri and the states south of them, and the territories of New Mexico and Arizona." Trade and internal improvements meant the Confederacy would incorporate territories further west and south because "streams of commerce will flow from sources far west of the Mississippi," Hunter added, and "if the Pacific and Atlantic shores of the North American continent are ever to be united by railroad its line will most probably run within [the Confederacy's] limit." The progress of the war both increased the size of what the Confederate nation needed to be and repositioned it as a power basing its claims to consideration in the world on its possessions across the American continent. Confederate planners therefore laid claim to the Indian Territory, Arizona, and New Mexico and envisaged the annexation of parts of Mexico.[22]

The Confederate definition of empire accommodated races other than whites and blacks. Unlike antebellum expansionists, planners for the Confederacy did not rely on the expected disappearance of Native Americans as a necessary precondition for the accomplishment of their objectives. Instead, Native Americans, especially those from what were deemed "settled" tribes, were to be coopted into the Confederate imperial enterprise. Throughout 1862, Confederates in Richmond continued to proclaim their suzerainty over the Indian Territory. In its last actions in early 1862, the Provisional Congress completed its legislation to organize, on January 8, the Superintendancy of Indian Affairs and, by February 14, judicial districts. On April 8, Davis approved and signed a bill into law "to provide for the organization of the Arkansas and Red River Superintendency of Indian Affairs to regulate trade and intercourse with the Indians therein and preserve peace on the frontiers." The reasons for this apparent tolerance of Native Americans were various. In part due to weakness, Confederates needed Indian military assistance. Additionally, planners of the future nation sought to differentiate the Confederacy from the United States and envisaged an empire that was global in scope. This worldview was based on racial gradation in the polity, and expansionists asserted Native American tribes instinctively looked to Confederates for leadership and would occupy intermediate places in an evolving racial hierarchy. This supposition was also based on Native Americans' slaveholding affinities on account of the Cherokee owning slaves, geographical proximity, and shared antipathy to the Union.[23]

The immediate Confederate need for Indian military help drove the inclusive approach. Three regiments of Native Americans fought as Confederates at the battle of Pea Ridge on the Arkansas-Missouri border in March 1862. The fact that the battle was a Confederate defeat rendered Native American support more important as Arkansas and Indian Territory were both now vulnerable to Union attack. By June 10, the Confederate envoy to the various Indian Nations, Albert Pike, could assure Davis: "This Indian Country is *wholly* in our possession I hope to keep it so." Benjamin noted in his diary on August 20 the *Richmond Dispatch* report that Pike had concluded treaties with—as well as the Cherokees—the Creeks, Choctaws, Chickasaws, Seminoles, Osages, Cadoes, Anodakas, and Wachitas and recently had effected treaties with the more difficult "nomadic" Comanches, Kiowas, and Apaches. Pike's success, historian Charles Hubbard explained, was due to his being able to identify a "community of interests" between Indians and Confederates.[24]

In return for their loyalty, the Davis administration granted Native Americans representation in government. "I am happy to inform you," Davis told Congress on August 18, 1862, "the Indian nations, within the Confederacy have remained firm in their loyalty and steadfast in their observance of their treaty engagements with this government." In return for military contributions and to cement their loyalty to the Confederacy, the government approved the admission of Native American representatives in Congress. On October 4, Representative Felix I. Batson of Arkansas announced the presence in the House of Native American lawyer and secretary of the Secession Convention of Arkansas, Elias Cornelius Boudinot, as delegate-elect from the Cherokee nation. A few days later, Davis approved Boudinot's election, and there were to be more delegates from those several nations in alliance with the government. If all of these tribes were to send delegates, their presence would have given the assembly a decided cosmopolitan air and an institutional manifestation of the government's ambitions to include Native Americans.[25]

Diplomats contrasted the success of their government's policy of collaboration and commerce with Native Americans with that of the Union, which they represented as one of extermination or to "improve them out of the world," as Mary Chesnut put it. On September 18 in London, Hotze informed the British readers of the *Index* about Davis's success with Indians as he "kept friendly relations and told them to stay neutral." By contrast, insisted Confederate propagandists, the U.S. government continued to persecute Native Americans and hence encountered distracting unrest among its tribes. That paper probably had in mind the Sioux rebellion in Minnesota, recorded also by Benjamin between the end of August and mid-September.[26]

This cooperative policy of the State Department, supported by its solitary eccentric agents, such as Pike—who combined this personal diplomacy with Native Americans with composing poetry on love and travel as he rode alone across the Navajo prairies and canyons—encountered opposition in 1862. Believers in clemency clashed with more orthodox expansionists from the Confederate southwest, who wished to continue the antebellum policies of formal annexation and coercion. On March 11, Hunter blocked, in the Senate, an attempt to annex the Indian Territory to Arkansas. The rise in importance of the army strengthened the hand of those who wanted coercion. In letters to Davis of August 25 and November 19, Pike complained that the command of the Department of the Trans-Mississippi had similar intentions toward the Indian Territory as those of the Arkansas politicians. Davis appeared divided; he praised the efforts of Pike, yet also instinctively wanted Native Americans, especially their troops, under more formal control. Over time, the structures of autonomy and Native American neutrality that Pike constructed gave way to more organization during the course of 1862, reflecting the changes across the Confederacy toward a more defined and assertive power.[27]

Preserving Native American loyalty remained crucial in the borderlands with Mexico. Davis stopped the actions of that "troublesome military independent agent," the governor of Arizona territory, John R. Baylor, when the latter apparently wished the "extermination of the Apache," whereas the basis of Confederate practice had been "to cultivate friendly relations even with the nomadic tribes." To make matters worse for the president, Baylor had then invaded Mexico and aroused the ire of the governor of Chihuahua province, Don Luiz Terrajas. Known as the "Caudillo," Terrajas was better as an ally than an enemy of the Confederacy, given he expropriated church lands, exploited cattle and mining, and built an "extensive economic empire" in his fiefdom. Moreover, the man who reported Baylor's activities to the president was Davis's friend, General Henry H. Sibley. The plight of the Indians had connections with Confederate policies toward Arizona, New Mexico, and Mexico.[28]

Arizona and New Mexico retained their importance to the Confederacy in 1862 because these territories provided the gateway to a route to the Pacific via northern Mexico. "The vast mineral resources of Arizona in addition to its affording an outlet to the Pacific," declared Baylor, "makes its acquisition a matter of some importance to our government." The inclusion of the Southwest in the nation would not be hostage to either the fortunes of the war or the unpredictable agenda of Baylor and his alleged atrocities, for Davis was confident that at the conclusion of a peace, these lands would be left to the Confederacy. Legislators in Richmond also wished to put distance between their nation and the hardscrabble adventurers of the frontier. The president approved an act for the organization of the territory on January 22, and Granville H. Oury took his seat as delegate-elect in the Provisional Congress. However, this former filibusterer from Texas, who had participated in the notorious Crabb Raid on the Mexican province of Sonora, was—despite Davis's support— "coolly received by his political colleagues and, although seated, was given no official status." Professionalism triumphed when Davis's own secretary, Robert Josselyn, resigned that post to become secretary to Baylor on March 13, 1862. Josselyn's later nomination as governor served as evidence of the government's continuing "tacit approval of at least the idea of recovering Arizona."[29]

Confederate long-term plans for the Southwest were not dependent on the fortunes of the Sibley expedition. At the same time, commentators and politicians as they reviewed the little army's progress would then talk about the future. The battle of Fort Craig made an impression in Richmond, out of proportion to its scale, and the news led to the passage in Congress of a joint resolution, proposed in the House by Representative John A. Wilcox of Texas, to congratulate Henry Hopkins Sibley and his command on April 10. Benjamin had judged it important enough to include in his report to his commissioners, declaring the "liberation of the territory from the presence of the federal forces." Texan politician and soldier Thomas P. Ochiltree—whose son, Tom, was Sibley's aide-de-camp—reported to Davis from San Antonio on April 27 that the Confederate flag was flying at Albuquerque and Santa Fe.[30]

Sibley had earlier convinced Davis that a military occupation of New Mexico was "essential." Earlier in the 1850s, when Davis was secretary of war, the future president got to know Sibley, and in July 1861 the latter traveled to Richmond and obtained Davis's approval for his plans to occupy New Mexico for the Confederacy. According to historian Donald Frazier, the president endorsed the "professional soldier with a plan." Baylor's initial success in New Mexico provided apparent evidence that "a single brigade of well-mounted troops" in a "self-sustained" and "inexpensive" campaign would be sufficient to secure the territory. Moreover, for the purposes of Davis's longer-term plans, Sibley "also had an ambitious vision which dovetailed into the southern empire" including both California and northwest Mexico. As a result, the president granted the brigadier general "latitude" to achieve the objective, and as late as June 7, 1862, Davis offered Sibley his congratulations "on the distinguished successes of your command" and sent two more regiments to him from Texas.[31]

Sibley stressed the reciprocal benefits to be had for those who would live in this nascent empire; he presented Confederate rule as a cosmopolitan and collaborative enterprise between Catholic and Hispanic New Mexicans, Confederate settlers, and Native Americans. According to Sibley's "Proclamation," announced in the Confederate press on February 10, the New Mexico territory belonged to the Confederacy for the same reasons as Cuba and Mexico, due to "geographical position, by similarity of institutions by commercial interests and by future destinies." Confederate administration, Sibley continued, would offer the citizens of New Mexico a "mutually advantageous governmental connection." He portrayed Union rule to be one of tyranny from which the Confederates had liberated the population. Therefore, he told the people to "follow your peaceful avocations"; Confederate rule meant "your religious, civil and political liberties will be reestablished." Protecting the rights of Hispanic and Catholic New Mexicans served as a possible blueprint for Mexicans also to be included within the Confederacy in the future. Their loyalty would support the war effort, and in return the extension of the Confederate government meant a reduction in the financial burdens on the people. Sibley announced simply: "I abolish the law of the United States levying taxes on New Mexico." The government of the Confederate empire promised to lay a lighter hand on the people.[32]

Yet the fighting to control these distant borderlands increased the burdens elsewhere in the Confederacy, especially for Texans. "Arizona & New Mexico would materially increase that frontier," the Rusk county pioneer farmer and physician, Peterson T. Richardson, wrote to Davis on March 6, at a time when Sibley still seemed successful in his possession of Albuquerque and Santa Fe. The Texan warned, "the expense of holding the same by a standing army, will in all probability cost more than the profits." The supply lines into an arid landscape, where troops would be unable to live off the land, worried those who would then have to supply the expedition. On May 1, 1862 Texas governor Francis R. Lubbock complained to Davis about the Brigade's current reliance on Texas "for troops and supplies" and suggested that if it was not reinforced from elsewhere, it should be withdrawn. Lubbock pointed out he had received a request from Sibley to send reinforcements and feared he could not send any.[33]

The audacious seizure of Galveston by Union forces in October 1862 dashed any hopes of a repeat of Sibley's expedition for the foreseeable future; even so, the claim of Confederates to New Mexico and

Arizona did not rest on the vicissitudes of war. As with other areas, soldiers and politicians deemed the loss of these territories to be temporary and anticipated they would be reabsorbed in peacetime. In the meantime, any military recovery revived hopes of a return to the Southwest. Once General John B. Magruder took command of the military forces in Texas on November 29, rumors began that lands lost would soon be recovered. "When I passed through Houston" on his way out of the Confederacy, the Confederate envoy to Russia, L. Q. C. Lamar, informed Davis on December 31 of a significant encounter. "I have just seen a Captain Skillman," Lamar told the president. "He says there are only fifty [Union] men at El Paso & that *they* are to leave in a short time, Arrizona [*sic*] to be abandoned. [U.S. General James H.] Carlton's force is moving on to New Mexico, for the purpose (so reported at El paso [*sic*]) of suppressing a formidable rebellion in the latter Territory." The man who had earlier called for "American liberty with southern institutions to be planted upon every inch of American soil" was cheered by this news. As 1862 closed, as far as this diplomat was concerned, the western territories remained in play and, once the Confederacy had achieved independence, would be included in the future nation.[34]

Expansion in Mexico

Ambitious planners believed that if the Confederacy were to be a viable counterweight to the United States in the future, it would have to either directly control or at least exercise preponderant influence over Mexico. The government attempted to keep up an interest and long-term claim in Mexico from a position of weakness. As a result, government policy aimed to keep the regimes of sympathetic border governors in place and the central administration weak. This objective explains Davis's anger over Baylor's incursion into Sonora, for nothing must remind the local strongmen of northern Mexico about antebellum southern transgressions of their sovereignty. Instead, the State Department looked to take long-term advantage of the deteriorating situation in the country. The government wanted to "form a clear idea of the complications that now exist in Mexican affairs," Assistant Secretary of State William M. Browne wrote to Quintero in Monterrey, Mexico, on January 14, together with "the power of that Republic to extricate itself from them." Santiago Vidaurri, the governor of Nuevo Leon, was in the process of shifting his allegiance away from the Juárez government. Perhaps to keep his options open, the "Lord of the North" had offered both his support and ammunition to the Confederacy, Quintero told Browne on January 25, but added that Vidaurri wanted money in return. Policymakers in Richmond were satisfied for the present with this cross-border relationship. "Quintero's services are highly appreciated by this department," the then secretary of war Benjamin observed to Wigfall, praising him for "his zeal . . . with which he has managed to maintain cordial relations with all the functionaries on the Mexican frontier."[35]

The Davis administration declined to subsidize Vidaurri and his colleagues; embroiling the Confederacy in a confrontation with the government in Mexico City while the Civil War continued was not an option. Instead, Confederate objectives would be met by the fostering of commercial ties, which, as historian Frank Owsley notes, had been Browne's policy priority all along. Immediate intervention would only occur if Juárez allowed Union troops to cross Mexican territory. Legislators hoped to permit cotton and tobacco exports via Mexico in defiance of the embargo and attempts to enforce the cultivation of provision crops. On April 17, in the House, Peter W. Gray of Texas amended "that this act shall not apply to the exportation of cotton or tobacco by loyal citizens overland to Mexico, a coterminous neutral country." Politicians hoped that their exclusion of Mexico from their embargo would contrast favorably for Mexicans with the Union's coercive blockade.[36]

The government soon changed Quintero's focus from the promotion of provincial separatism to the encouraging of trade across the border. Accordingly, he relocated from the provincial capital of Monterrey with its close proximity to Vidaurri. "Quinterro [sic], our commercial agent at Matamoras," Benjamin, now secretary of state, told Slidell on April 8. Just in time, Benjamin added, because he gave bad news to his superior, "not only is this blockade openly enforced, but that the [Union] naval officer, in command of the blockading sloop of war has declared that cotton *exported* from Matamoras is *contraband*." The State Department regarded the agent's role as promoter of cross-border trade in the long term as inseparable from the growing importance of circumventing the wartime Union blockade.[37]

Other individuals joined Quintero in promoting commercial connections between the Confederacy and northern Mexican provinces. From his base at El Paso, Judge Simeon Hart, a former secession convention commissioner from Texas to the territory of New Mexico, operated a transnational enterprise. He purchased cotton, operated mills, employed

Hispanic Americans and Mexicans, and traded through Mexico to obtain supplies for Sibley's army. Another agent, James P. Hickman, was based in Chihuahua. Lamar applauded this policy of engagement. "The sympathies of the Governments of the Northern departments of Mexico are in our favor," he optimistically summarized the Confederate effort at the end of the year; "nothing but wise & judicious conduct on the part of our officials is required to insure us against prejudice in that quarter." The policy was both straightforward and successful. "The plan of converting the cotton of Texas into means for carrying on the war," Lamar added, was "working admirably."³⁸

This combination of supporting an immediate military objective—in this case aiding Sibley's expedition—and taking steps to accomplish longer-term plans lay behind a concerted push by Confederates into northwestern Mexico in 1862. After the war, the Confederacy would require a secure port on the Pacific in order to compete with the United States and achieve even more ambitious goals. Sibley had dispatched Colonel James Reilly on a mission to the northwestern Mexican provinces of Chihuahua and Sonora with a series of diplomatic objectives on behalf of the Confederate government. Once he had established friendly relations between Confederates and Mexicans and "disabused the public mind about our filibustering proclivities," Reilly was to tell the governors to stop "all the negotiations with the federal govt." Reilly would then pursue a long-term plan, to negotiate "the free use of the port of Guaymas," on Sonora's Pacific coast, for Confederates. This matter "is of the greatest importance to us," newspaper proprietor and editor Edward H. Cushing of Houston, Texas, explained to his readers. "It opens to us the markets of the whole Pacific coast, and the eastern world," for "Guaymas is the best port on the Pacific south of San Francisco." Once in Confederate hands, it "will in future years be the metropolis of the whole coast." Finally, the city would be integrated into the Confederate market because the overland route from Guaymas to San Antonio, Texas, was "the only feasible railroad from the Mississippi to the Pacific and the route over which we have always prophesized the first railroad will be built."³⁹

The pursuit of transcontinental railroad schemes, Pacific Ocean ports, and annexations in a time of war would take scarce resources from more pressing priorities; yet boosters for expansion argued that the present fluid political situation in Mexico presented opportunities for Confederates that had to be seized now. Reilly's February 1862 mission to Chihuahua and Sonora coincided with the European tripartite debt-collecting expedition occupying Vera Cruz on Mexico's Atlantic coast. Expectations rose that the central government in Mexico City would collapse. A correspondent of Cushing's newspaper, who accompanied Reilly, anticipated that the negotiations between Mexico and France, Spain, and Britain "will lead in a few years to a revolution of Chihuahua, Sonora, Cinaolos, Durango and other northern Mexican states and perhaps their annexation to our Confederacy." With an initial success such as the Guaymas negotiation, a mood of expansionism would spread among the Confederate people as a whole as, Cushing speculated, "the old manifest destiny of our country will rise up again prominently in the perspective." The Confederacy had to be in a position to "take advantage of the changes in our neighboring republic and add to the Confederacy those rich states in Mexico so necessary for our future development."[40]

These Mexican provinces would voluntarily seek Confederate protection, whether from European creditors or the centralizing liberal policies of Juárez. Any Confederate attempt to conquer Mexico by armed force "would be to subvert the foundation of our government," De Bow warned, "founded as it is on the consent of the governed." Furthermore, the plunder from invasion "would bring with it such a chain of abuses and corruption that the [republican] government could not survive." Ambitious planners envisaged a program of gradual absorption via commercial expansion and elite collaboration. The *Index*—established in May 1862 as the Confederate propaganda newspaper in London with commercial agent Henry Hotze as editor—considered that any union between the Confederacy and Mexico would "have to be by the voluntary act of the people of the latter country and not by conquest."[41]

The setbacks in the war across the Confederate west in the spring and early summer of 1862, together with the fluid situation in Mexico itself, reinforced this gradualist approach. In terms of accomplishing the immediate need for a thriving contraband trade as well as the ultimate goal of absorption, the worst-case scenario for Confederates would be a resumption of the Mexican War of Reform and with it the risk of U.S. intrigue leading to a liberal alliance between Lincoln and Juárez against the Confederacy. Many individuals were suspicious of French emperor Napoleon III's evolving plan for the Americas, which started as a decision to remain in Vera Cruz when the Spanish and British left in the early spring of 1862, and some speculated it might ultimately lead to France recovering Louisiana. Nevertheless, observers of their southern neighbor regarded the limited French invasion of Mexico beginning in

April 1862 as potentially useful to them; French weakness, as demonstrated by their defeat at Puebla the following month, meant the emperor
needed Confederate help. According to the *Index*, the French should be
materially assisted. In addition to duty-free tobacco and cotton promised in a commercial agreement with France, the Confederacy would be
able to offer the struggling French expedition "an abundance of men,"
the *Index* promised, adding "and the [just] enterprise will be exceedingly
popular." The paper looked forward to an eventual partition of the country with France, which would leave the Confederacy in sole control after
the French withdrew. The *Index* saw no issue in an enlarged Confederacy having a mulatto minority along with a tolerant attitude to Native
Americans.[42]

The U.S. assault on Texas in October 1862, especially the occupations of both Galveston and Brownsville, meant even diehard Texan annexationists of Mexican provinces, despite their misgivings, reconciled
themselves to a French presence on their southern border, even as some
individuals, including former governor Sam Houston, rued that the
chance to grab Mexican territory had permanently passed. Lamar no-
ticed this shift in mood as he traveled through Texas in late 1862 en route
to Europe. "The probability of [the French] occupying Matamoras is discussed by some of the intelligent men of this place [San Antonio]," he advised Davis, and "I do not think the interests of your Govt. would suffer.
The occupation of that part [of Mexico] by the French would bring us,
to the opposite side of the Rio Grande, supplies for our troops." The
short-term imperative of the pacification brought by the French, which
enabled resumption of contraband, coexisted with Confederate ambitions to be the predominant power in Mexico after the war.[43]

GLOBAL AMBITIONS

Ambitions to make a mark in the world remained among Confederates
during 1862; nevertheless there was a change in emphasis. Looking back at
what was now perceived as the complacent optimism of the first months
of independence, the nation builders reverted to some interconnected
policies, some of which they had earlier pursued from within the federal
government during the 1850s. An ocean-going fleet would be needed to
project power, protect commerce, and open markets. The government
would seek to leverage this commercial strength to enrich the country,
break its diplomatic isolation through reciprocal trade pacts with other

nations, and deploy its cotton surplus strategically to ensure other nations would be unable to develop competitive cotton supplies. Finally,
the government supplemented its policy of expansion of slavery with a
proslavery foreign policy geared toward protecting slavery abroad, and at
the same time it tried to prevent other powers from introducing competing immigrant labor into the Western Hemisphere. Taken together, the
exponents of this vision recognized the world as more competitive than
collaborative; in coming to that conclusion ambitious planners believed
realism had replaced idealism in their outlook. This shift in sentiment
reflected an appreciation of Confederate strengths, not weaknesses arising from the war.

A Steam-Powered Fleet

While wars tend not to initiate invention, they do ensure the rapid dissemination of new technologies. For a newcomer nation such as the
Confederacy, this development was beneficial as it diminished the existing advantages of established powers with their large investments in
old technologies. Historians overlook this circumstance when they stress
that in naval terms the Confederacy was spectacularly weak, with its
citizens doomed to watch as the Union fleets tightened their grip on the
ports. With only commerce raiding as a tonic, according to this narrative,
merchants impotently saw what little remained of their commerce pass
into the hands of unscrupulous blockade runners from overseas, intent
on delivering wasteful luxury goods and encouraging immoral speculation. More importantly for the future, owing to developments in technology, politicians and planters believed that the Confederacy would soon
be a naval power. Confederates drew on a perceived present-day opportunity and their memory of prewar southern championship of a strong
navy needed to both confront the abolitionist empire of Britain and project power overseas. Postwar commercial ambitions of the Confederacy
needed a powerful navy.[44]

A timely technological breakthrough enabled planters to believe they
could quickly develop a navy of the first rank. "The rapid increase of war
steamers," a select committee reported to the Cotton Planters' Convention in Memphis in February, "are giving to the affairs of the world an
accelerated motion." On hearing the news of the naval action in Hampton Roads, where the CSS *Virginia* sank both the USS *Cumberland* and
USS *Congress* on March 8, 1862, Benjamin observed, "the battle was a

demonstration for the first time in naval warfare that wooden vessels however wellbuilt or powerfully armed are helpless against ironclad vessels properly constructed." The secretary's interest in naval matters had been clear during his earlier conversations with William Howard Russell about the blockade. Moreover, this "cosmopolitan" and "globally orientated" New Orleans citizen doubtless also knew that a navy would be vital to realize the nation's tropical destiny. Given the Union's overwhelming superiority in wooden ships blockading the ports, Dudley Mann, the Confederate commissioner to Brussels, agreed with Benjamin and told him: "Steam is steadily superseding the wooden. This is most fortunate for the Confederate States."[45]

The secretary of the navy, Stephen R. Mallory, had already translated this belief in the importance of ironclads into policy. The Floridian politician had earlier, as Senate Navy Committee chairman in the 1850s, been associated with efforts to build a stronger U.S. navy, probably because he also demanded the forcible annexation of Cuba. As early as May 9, 1861, according to historian Frank Owsley, Mallory had obtained congressional funding to send the "talented and resourceful" James Dunwoody Bulloch to Europe in order to create a Confederate fleet by a combination of private purchase and construction. Before the war, Bulloch had operated a steamship line between New Orleans and New York and was an expert in maritime and international law. Therefore, he had the requisite skills to circumvent the restrictions on building warships imposed by the neutrality proclamations issued by the rulers of Britain and France.[46]

A fleet was needed in the home ports. The Confederacy "cannot compete with the United States in terms of numbers," Mallory told Davis on February 27, 1862; therefore the government "must concentrate on plated or ironclad ships." Legislators responded to the call. A few days later on March 6, the House passed a resolution asking the president what additional means would be required for naval operations in 1862. On March 18, Mallory assured Charles Magill Conrad of the House's Navy Committee: "I presume the importance of iron plated vessels to us cannot be underestimated." And the secretary telegraphed Captain Duncan N. Ingraham in Charleston to build ships there "at any expense." Conrad, formerly a Whig senator from Louisiana, had been President Millard Fillmore's secretary of war in the early 1850s and was, moreover, receiving telegraphs about the situation in New Orleans. Mallory informed Davis that the navy would need fifty light draft ironclad steamers and four ironclad frigates. Davis's response to the House showed that he agreed with his navy secretary on the need for the fifty shallow-water ironclads, but he raised the estimate on the ocean deep-water ironclads to ten. Mr. P. M. Eachin of Melrose P.O., Robeson County, North Carolina, grudgingly told his representative, Thomas David Smith McDowell, that these naval estimates were evidence that at last "the government is going into the construction of a navy on a scale somewhat proportionate to the exigencies of the circumstances under which we are situated." Being in the timber business, Eachin looked forward to the orders from new government navy yards at Georgetown, South Carolina, and Wilmington, North Carolina. Appropriation bills followed through Congress during the two 1862 sessions. Given the Royal Navy had just eight inferior ocean-going ironclads, Confederates certainly wished to project their power on the high seas.[47]

Once in possession of a powerful navy, national planners anticipated first breaking the blockade and hence persuading the Union to recognize Confederate independence and then fighting future wars the way they wished. Naval conflicts would arise from the government's policy of free-trade enforcement, meaning the protection of a growing merchant marine and the forcible securing of markets for the exports of the Confederacy's staple crops. "It is of vital importance," De Bow wrote in March, "that we look for and get a navy at least to insure us an outlet for our productions." Furthermore, a navy was also the preferred way of carrying on the struggle with the United States if that proved necessary. "If we had a navy we could conveniently fight the United States for years," he added. De Bow believed such warfare was less detrimental to slavery, republicanism, and the Confederate economy; he insisted, "and a navy we *must* have." As well as guaranteeing commercial autonomy, according to De Bow, a navy would also assist in securing the Confederacy's republican foundations by obviating the need for a standing army, for "nothing will so soon open a prospect of peace and rid us of a standing army as a navy."[48]

A Confederate navy would protect returning merchantmen and their cargoes, not only of manufactured goods, but also of gold and silver. "As we can get the specie only in exchange for our productions," De Bow reasoned, therefore only a navy would offer what John Esten Cooke called "Commercial Enfranchisement." In the meantime, "until we can secure a navy," Cooke argued, "our products and the markets we offer for foreign commodities must buy for us and our interests protection." Cooke was therefore pleased that "there is an increasing taste with our people for commerce and navigation." The historian and novelist was wistful in his descriptions of the land war, "If I get thro' this war, I will have much to write of—if," but he was practical about the consequences for the future arising from building a navy. Anticipating capital shortages in the Confederacy after the war, both Liverpool businessman James Spence and London-based shipowner and politician William Schaw Lindsay submitted plans to the State Department for outside-supported steamship lines to connect the Confederacy directly with European markets.[49]

COMMERCIAL AND INDUSTRIAL ASPIRATION

The navy would help protect slavery and sustain Confederate commercial and industrial ambition. Commentators believed the fact that the enslaved people had not yet risen up had vindicated the institution and especially undermined the European variant of abolitionist thought. In January, De Bow predicted "one of the happy results of the present war will be the proofs afforded it, that *neither slavery nor slaves, in the European sense of these terms, have any existence at all in the Confederate States of America.*" According to De Bow, African American slavery was "natural" and destined to survive the stresses of war. Slavery's endurance of the intensification of the war in 1862 would correct the European misunderstanding of an enslaved person as someone "deprived of some of his most essential natural rights and privileges."[50]

Davis agreed that slavery's resilience demonstrated by the war meant it could be applied to tasks beyond planting. When in October Mallory suggested coal miners needed to be exempt from conscription, Davis believed slavery would solve the problem. "Why not use slave labor?" he suggested, which would keep white miners in the ranks. During 1862, slavery became vital for the government in order to support the demands of conscription. In this context, journalists and politicians continued to treat the instances of flight of enslaved people to Union lines as a minor and temporary irritation; personal losses did not mean the institution as a whole was in decline. Population growth of enslaved people would offset the departure of individuals to the Union armies. De Bow looked forward to a future census that would give "the slaveholding states, including New Mexico and the Indian territory west of Arkansas nearly one hundred million [people], of whom twenty-four million will be slaves, enabling the South to furnish twenty-four million bales of cotton." Slavery's growth would support the diversified economy of the evolving Confederacy as well as continue to boost staple crop production.[51]

Cotton exports remained central to Confederates' visions of their future in spite of the present restrictions of production arising from the experiment with the embargo, the increasing constraints of the Union's blockade, and the switch in plantations across the Confederacy to provision crop production. In his inaugural speech as wartime president on February 22, 1862, Davis stressed the likelihood of a speedy resumption of cotton exports once there was peace. "By the character of their productions [the Confederate people] are too deeply interested in foreign commerce wantonly to disturb it." He reassured the world that planters did not wish to cease being staple crop producers, "nor would the constancy of these supplies be likely to be disturbed by war." De Bow, by now a cotton agent, explained the president's thinking in more detail the following month. "It is clearly in our interest," he argued in March, "to supply the general demand, at a fair and remunerative price. So long as we do this, we defy competition and hold all Europe at our feet . . . [for] Commercial reciprocity is the surest base of permanent peace and national prosperity." Even though a temporary move by planters to grow provision crops was necessary, he held that it was vital for the infrastructure of cotton production to be retained and to remain in readiness to resume cultivation and surpass prewar levels. "If such a course . . . be carried out," he continued, "we shall then be in a position in 1863 to raise such a crop of cotton as the wants of the world may demand: the independence of the Confederacy and unrestricted trade with Europe being considered a foregone conclusion."[52]

The military reverses sustained by the Confederacy during the spring of 1862—with their promise of a longer, more destructive war—challenged this sanguine expectation of a speedy and painless reversion by planters and farmers to their prewar occupations. On May 13, after the fall of New Orleans, the Cotton Planters' Convention met in Americus, Georgia, and envisaged long-term changes to agricultural production in the Confederacy. "I deem it a reasonable conjecture," Howell Cobb told the gathering, "that the [cotton] crop has been reduced 5/8 . . . for cotton planters are universally, turning their attention to the production of provisions." Bunch agreed as he noted the great planting families of South Carolina, "the Hamptons, Mannings and Prestons," had also ceased cotton planting and "will not make one bale this year." The effects of such a transformation may be permanent because, Cobb predicted, "it may reasonably be supposed that the war has created such a revolution in the farming interest of the cotton states," that new habits of cultivation will persist. "Many years at least," Cobb warned, "will elapse before we shall fall into the [former] mode of business." Given his earlier embrace, as chairman of the convention at Montgomery, of continuity between the economies of the southern United States and the Confederacy, the meaning of independence had now changed for the new nation. As far as Georgia planter-politician was concerned, the Confederacy—in order to be truly independent—would never again be solely the staple crop producer it had been before the war.[53]

By the early summer of 1862, the Union's military offensives in the West and General George B. McClellan's advance to within fifteen miles of Richmond promised greater consequences than forcing planters to temporarily change their crops. The stored cotton, whether warehoused in the Confederate capital and in the major ports or kept in sheds on the plantations of the Mississippi Valley, was now in danger of destruction in the event of a military collapse. This situation meant more than the loss of wealth—it would end Confederate hopes of a rapid return to world markets. The crushing of new rival sources of cotton production overseas depended on the dumping of huge qualities of the staple at the exchanges in Liverpool and New York, thereby ruining competitors with low prices. Postwar cotton scarcity would ruin this calculation. On June 17, as he notified Earl Russell of the fall of Memphis, Consul Bunch also warned him, "It is calculated that one million bales [of cotton] have been destroyed already."[54]

However, these fears of a general destruction of the stored cotton soon appeared groundless, with the Confederate armies in both main theaters apparently stabilizing the military situation over the following months. By the late summer, it became clear that not only would the Confederacy succeed in saving the bulk of its stored cotton, but also there would be a sufficient 1862 crop to offset the destruction of warehoused cotton in the lower Mississippi Valley. The consuls computed a store of between three and a half and four million bales. Betting on higher prices, Benjamin priced a bale at $200 in specie in the northern markets, which meant a value of $800 million. Cotton continued its central role in future domestic government finance and as collateral in attempts to raise money abroad. "Why not send it out and buy ships?" asked Mary Chesnut.[55]

Individuals around Davis considered using the stored cotton in a more instrumental fashion than simply storing it in readiness for peace, when planters would be able to intervene in world markets. The secretary of state agreed with the consuls that planters had this growing reserve of stored cotton, which would also be used to support diplomatic efforts to facilitate international trade and broker commercial agreements with European powers. Benjamin hoped to use the cotton to forcefully obtain future allies, as well as to bribe advocates for immediate recognition and, according to historian Don Doyle, "chain" creditors to the fortunes of the Confederacy. "We have to offer the cotton, tobacco and naval stores accumulated in the Confederacy," Benjamin wrote to his commissioners in Europe at the end of 1862 that even with huge discounts for postwar conditions, "I feel confident that at one third the present European prices for our staple, we have exchangeable value for the whole $300m." If European customers paid even these bargain prices for the crops, Confederates would demand European manufactured goods at a premium, and Benjamin instructed his envoys to spread this meaning behind the message of the government's "assured conviction of an early renewal of commerce with the Confederate States." He recommended that the European governments should get ready in advance by the establishment, "in their West Indies colonies[,] of large depots of the supplies known to be needed there, ready for immediate introduction to the Confederacy."[56]

In a shift in emphasis during 1862, the cotton mountain would serve Confederate interests in the future, as well as facilitate a free-trade utopia of international harmony and interdependence. It would provide, in the words of historian John Majewski, when he discusses "war socialism," an economic rationale for southern independence. The priority of the economy would now be to "repatriate" gold by running a trade surplus. "We cannot hope to exist as a people long by *mere sufferance*," De Bow declared. It was not enough for the Confederacy just to be tolerated as a people—that would be to lose national self-respect. Instead, he continued, "let us move onward in peace, and with an unfettered commerce, we will export three hundred million dollars" worth of cotton. If Confederate consumers "buy $100m say $200m," De Bow concluded, "how long before the specie basis of trade and commerce of Europe would be transferred to the Confederate States?"[57]

As well as this more noticeable assertion of a vision for a national economy, the primary mission of the Confederacy remained increasing staple crop production underpinned by the spread of slavery. Diplomats reconciled the two goals by means of proposing commercial pacts with industrializing European powers. The State Department presented to the French a strong and expansive Confederacy in the future, sustained by growing cotton production and slavery extension. Hunter understood that the Confederacy had to be in a position to convincingly offer inducements. "It must be the matter of deepest interest to Britain not only to increase and cheapen the supply of cotton and sugar," Hunter reasoned to his commissioners in Europe, "but also to enlarge the market and multiply the productions." The Confederate government's promise of increased staple crop production from a growing territory under cultivation would strengthen the proposed commercial agreement. Comparative advantage "should enlarge the area in which agriculture would be the principal employment, and increase greatly the number of customers who would desire to purchase [British] manufactures." Confederate territorial expansion would result from the growth of the economies of the industrial powers, for "if this trade is likely to be valuable to [Britain] then it is her interest to increase it as much as possible and to enlarge the area from which she draws tribute."[58]

A WORLD WAR FOR SLAVERY

For ambitious planners for a postwar Confederacy, a friendly attitude to Cuba and its colonial master, Spain, was dictated by the continued need to grow slavery in the Western Hemisphere. The increasing commitment of the Spanish government to recover control of its former colony of Santo Domingo provided evidence for optimistic Confederates that the retreat of slavery from the Americas was over, even though Madrid had also assured the British that slavery would not accompany recolonization. "On the question of slavery," De Bow declared, "the Spaniards are our natural allies and this consideration may . . . override every other." Commissioner Pierre Rost echoed De Bow when he assured the Spanish foreign minister, Calderon Collantes, that the Confederate government "deem it its interest that a great country like Spain should continue a slave power. The two, together with Brazil, would have a monopoly of the system of labor, which alone can make intertropical America and the regions adjoining it available to the uses of man." Brazil and Cuba would be junior partners in this proslavery enterprise because of the "slave in Brazil," the *Southern Illustrated News* opined, "where his condition is infinitely worse than it is here, or in Cuba, where it is worse even than in Brazil." As Rost made clear to the Spanish government, safeguarding slavery in Cuba was not solely a defensive move to protect the labor system. It was part of more ambitious plans to expand slavery across the

tropics and ensure that slavery would continue to monopolize the production of other staple crops, sugar and coffee, in addition to cotton.[59]

Historian and diplomat William H. Trescot of South Carolina had
been a prominent antebellum advocate of sustaining slavery in Cuba by
any means possible; either by backing Spain's continued colonial rule
or having the United States government act as external guarantor of
the independence of a "kindred and slaveholding republic." In 1862, he
emerged from retirement and pressed the State Department to adopt
its own proslavery foreign policy. "The question of what is to become
of the negroes now in possession of the enemies is a very important one,"
Trescot told Benjamin on August 5, "to those of us" who have plantations "in the invaded sections of the country." He thought that it was
"mistaken pride" for Americans before the war to stand "apart from the
world" on matters relating to slavery. As a result of the U.S. government's
decision to not openly resist Britain's worldwide efforts to undermine
slavery, Trescot meant, the Atlantic slave trade had been strangled and
the international cause of emancipation advanced. With the Union's war
becoming an antislavery crusade, he insisted that the Confederacy had
to fight a proslavery war in response. This conflict would be a world war
fought overseas, as well as on the battlefields of Virginia and Tennessee. Slavery and the Confederacy would be strengthened by such a contest, Trescot argued, for progress in history was "made by antagonism"
between nations.[60]

The opening salvo in this long-term "game of power" over the control of sources of unfree labor around the world was the colonization
schemes of the Lincoln administration. Trescot understood Lincoln's
tentative moves to promote African American migration to Haiti to be
part of a wider conspiracy to take all African Americans from Union-
controlled North America and settle them overseas, spreading U.S.
power and influence in the process. In particular, he wished to draw
Benjamin's attention to U.S. plans to transplant freed slaves as "the various propositions to make settlements in Liberia, in central America, in
Mexico confirm that intention." When assistant secretary of state in the
late 1850s, Trescot had been approached with a proposal from Denmark
to settle Africans freed from illegal slave traders in the Danish Virgin
Islands. He interpreted the Danish move as part of a conspiracy against
slavery. The war had provided an opportunity for these plotters, and
Trescot predicted that an abolitionist alliance between the United States,
Britain, and France would bring people from the contraband camps to

all the European Caribbean colonies. American proslavery theorists, as well as critics of imperial policy in Britain including Thomas Carlyle, had long argued that the post-emancipation Caribbean colonies were both economically defunct and depopulated. With such demand for "trained" and "docile" labor, Trescot believed there would be an attempt to settle formerly enslaved people from the Confederacy in the Caribbean, especially those who fled to freedom following the U.S. capture of the South Carolina Sea Islands in late 1861. He expected that advocates of colonization were "satisfied that nothing would be more desirable for those islands than just such an importation of labour as would be furnished by the confiscated negroes now in possession of the United States forces." According to Trescot, the Sea Island freed people would provide "a supply of educated and docile laborers far superior to the African and peculiarly adapted to the agricultural wants of the islands."[61]

Trescot assumed that European powers would eagerly collaborate with the United States in undermining slavery in the Confederacy. He had been familiar with antislavery sentiment when he had earlier served as an attaché in the London legation. When British journalist William Howard Russell visited the South Carolinian just after the outbreak of war, he had noted Trescot's blend of "anti-British jealousies and even antipathies" juxtaposed with his courtesies as host. The South Carolina planter-politician-diplomat therefore considered European colonial authorities complicit in these Union activities to introduce former Confederate slaves as a supply of forced labor into the Caribbean. This included a resurrection of "the agreement with Denmark to receive all Africans, taken by United States slavers, as apprentices at St. Croix." The United States "may possibly attempt to deport our own slaves captured on the frontier," Benjamin promptly agreed; he planned to write "a dispatch on the subject calling the attention of the Danish government to our own view of our rights," he added, in order to "defeat any attempt of the Yankees to palm off southern slaves for captured Africans." Immediately on August 14, Benjamin ordered Dudley Mann to proceed to Copenhagen and warn the Danes. By October, Mann reported on a mission accomplished and assured Benjamin that in their meeting the Danish foreign minister "justly appreciate the solicitude of the Government of the Confederate States in relation to the matter."[62]

Diplomats welcomed the broader conception of the Civil War as a global struggle over racial hierarchy, as that cause would—they believed—win new allies for the Confederacy. These individuals considered that the rumors of Lincoln's embrace of African American equality and colonization were sufficient to bring Central American regimes previously hostile to the slaveholders' republic on account of the legacy of filibustering into adopting pro-Confederate positions. A correspondent of Mann's from Chinandega in Nicaragua confirmed what Mann wanted to hear and that the government of President Tomás Martinez regarded "Lincoln's recent speech to the delegation of free negroes . . . as an insult." Mann hoped that the Creole elites in Latin America would see their own position atop an Amerindian and Mestizo majority as much threatened as that of slaveholders by the evolution of U.S. policy during 1862. Lincoln "is prepared to colonize the free negroes of the United States in Central America under the protection of the U.S. flag," the Martinez administration allegedly understood, and "he intends to make them not only the equals of the people of this country but the equals of the best of them." At once, according to Mann's contact, this rumor "has changed the sympathies of those who were not with the South before in favor of the South now." Martinez "conferred with all of the Central American Governments, and that they are united in their opposition to the introduction of free negroes."[63]

Mann and Trescot, as experienced diplomats, believed and transmitted such reports to Richmond because they and other Confederates suspected individuals, corporations, and governments from the United States and Europe planned to reintroduce or expand variants of forced labor systems around the tropical world. These enterprises would be achieved via involuntary migration of what whites in both Europe and America deemed to be inferior races. They also made sense if one wanted to thrive in a global order where for nations, ambitious Confederate planners believed—in the words of De Bow—"the productive industry of a people is the true source of their wealth." To proslavery theorists, this belief had long underpinned their worldview. What was especially exciting to them now was that recent world events appeared to demonstrate that, along with the United States, other great powers were moving in the same direction. For example, in the Treaty of Nanking that ended the Second Opium War, fought between the European powers and China between 1857 and 1860, Britain and France not only "made it a condition of peace with China that they should be permitted to introduce their manufactures into China," De Bow alleged, but also "to take Chinese coolies, as laborers, to Australia and Algeria." This development posed a threat to slavery because, he explained, this clause was agreed with "the purpose being to use them as *slaves* in the culture of cotton." In making this agreement, De Bow argued, the British and French governments demonstrated that they now concurred with the "King Cotton" thesis. In particular, "these facts," he asserted, "show the relation which the growth and manufacture of cotton have on the progress and civilization of the age in which we live."[64]

Central America would be one of the crucial tropical areas where these competing plantings of people would be carried out. Confederate planners expected their nation to outperform its rivals in this contest because its slaveholders would accompany their enslaved people. As well as U.S. colonization schemes, on June 23, Mann warned Benjamin that Napoleon III had by then realized that "Algeria is a profitless colony" and "to get rid of the redundant population ever hostile to orderly government, a more promising field for adventure must be presented." Such a field was Mexico. The threat that Napoleon's Grand Design of the Americas potentially posed to Confederate interests was profound; in the words of a Houston newspaper editor, it would "confine slave territory within a boundary that will shut us out of three quarters of the undeveloped territory of the continent adapted to slavery." The Confederacy had the inestimable opening advantage in this competition arising from its stewardship of African American slavery. On racial grounds, this form of slavery was also apparently better suited to the exploitation of the tropics than any of its alternatives, provided whites accompanied the enslaved people. Pamphleteer Joseph C. Addington of North Carolina termed the latitudes between thirty-five north and thirty-five south "the black man's natural belt," and when African Americans labored under Confederate control this tract of land would become a "garden" that was "enlarging daily its boundaries." He anticipated the aspirations of 1890s imperialists who, according to historian Paul Kramer, understood that "racial difference made empire possible." Addington hoped that empire would sustain and deepen this racial difference—in this case determined by slavery—rather than change it.[65]

The Planters' Convention believed advances in communications as well as growth of commerce and slavery expansion would facilitate slaveholders' control of this southern world. Howell Cobb stated in May 1862: "There is not now nor will there probably soon be, in the commercial world so interesting a question as the laying of a telegraph cable across the Atlantic." Cobb reminded the planters of his earlier October 1860 correspondence—in the wake of the snapping of the first (1858) transatlantic cable—with Senator Alfred Iverson of North Carolina and the oceanographer Matthew Fontaine Maury and how he, Cobb, was "impressed with the importance of this work and the impracticality of its performance from Cape Race [Newfoundland] and Cape Clear [Ireland]." Cobb read out Maury's letter to the planters: "You will be gratified to learn that you are not alone in your opinion as to the advantages of your route. The idea was broached pending the famous Atlantic Telegraph, that the best route would be from England, via Spain and Portugal, thence to Madeira, thence to Cape Verd [sic] islands, thence to the Penede de San Pedro, thence to Brazil, and overland to the Cuayanes [sic] thence along the windward and leeward islands and Cuba, to the United States." Maury added that the southern route was "not without its strong advocates on the other [European] side." Cobb had earlier accepted that "all questions of this kind were necessarily postponed—hoping that our difficulties would not be of long continuance." However, by May 1862, as "the country is involved in a war of indefinite continuance," Cobb feared the delay had become open-ended.[66]

The State Department hoped funds were in place to construct this oceanic cable from private sources. On May 5, Dudley Mann told Benjamin: "It is in contemplation to lay a cable and a company is in embryo for the accomplishment of the object." The southern trans-Atlantic telegraph was "regarded by scientific men as practicable, and it is estimated that 1,000,000 will perfect the undertaking." Mann concluded with the cable, "a timely, well-matured policy we may make our country the great telegraphic and traffic highway between the Old World and the West Indies, Mexico, Central and South America, and the ports of the South Seas."[67]

By THE end of 1862, the military disasters of the late winter and spring seemed a distant memory to planners of the new nation, even though they bitterly regretted the failure in Kentucky, much more so than Lee's setback in Maryland, which barely registered in their calculations. Yet, buoyed at year-end by Lee's victory at Fredericksburg and premature reports of Bragg's encouraging first day at Murfreesboro, Confederate optimists confidently assumed they had made progress toward independence and then an expansive, prosperous future. They believed that such a destiny had now been constructed on more solid foundations than had existed in 1861. The estimate they placed on the resources of the nation—military strength on land and sea, the value of the cotton store, and a growing industrial base—had advanced. Diplomats believed that the developing war policy of the United States government, with its inclusion of emancipation, colonization, and a harder war, had alienated world opinion. As a result, they considered that the numbers of their supporters had increased in the Midwest, throughout Latin America, the Caribbean, and Europe. Members of the State Department interpreted the behavior of European powers and the U.S. as symptomatic of an evolving competition for a new world order. This system of international relations would be based on possession both of land and sources of labor, and this belief that the Confederacy would be able to secure these resources validated their worldview. Planners' expected a secure, powerful future nation-state once the war had been concluded. However, the continuing vast scale of the Union's war effort, demonstrated by its winter campaigns in both the eastern and western theaters, showed that much more work remained to be done in 1863 in order to achieve these ambitions.

4

Renewal through Adversity

CONFEDERATES REBOOT
THEIR AMBITIONS IN 1863

IN 1863, Confederate planners recognized that the United States government now prosecuted a war for emancipation. Given they had believed the Lincoln administration intended this policy all along, one might assume the advent of emancipation had little effect on planning. However, the evolution of the war due to the military failures that occurred from the summer onward—the Tullahoma campaign in Tennessee, Gettysburg, and, especially, in the wake of Vicksburg when the Confederacy broke in two, divided by the Mississippi—led to profound changes in what optimists believed the future of the Confederacy to be. The paradox of a weaker power in the world that stood for broader, more universal objectives emerged. Confederate planners expected to ally with other countries and peoples after the war. In order to prepare for that eventuality, these individuals embraced abstract ideals, some of which echoed Enlightenment thought and included individualism, natural law, and a reinvigorated advocacy of free trade, together with other notions, such as "scientific" racial thinking, which were of a more recent vintage. At the same time, the outcome of these universal appeals would be practical—the erection of barriers to what politicians, planters, and journalists regarded as U.S. aggression. As the Federals were focused on overturning these ideals, optimists argued, more was at stake for the world than the survival of the Confederacy.

Being leaders of a future great power remained important to Confederates in 1863. The Confederacy's survival as a government into the third year of the war enhanced ambitious optimists' sense that the nation was entitled to a prosperous future. Many Confederates still believed their nation represented the last hope of republican self-government on earth. Given what a broader cross section of Confederates regarded as the Union's definitive surrender to tyranny by the majority, many of the slaveholding republic's leaders considered their nation had a responsibility and duty to expand against the hostile status quo.

Planners deemed postwar economic and territorial expansion a necessity in order to offset current weakness during 1863 by evidence of future strength. As individuals, they did not regard expansion as either a delusion or escapism; instead, they understood it as a necessity in order to avoid incapacitating themselves by self-questioning that outcome of despondency. Optimists regarded future growth as the necessary hope of better times just ahead to cherish in the context of times of gloom. Their ambitions counterbalanced the growing numbers of pessimists' fear of subjugation. This latter apprehension arose intermittently during 1863; for instance, in the early spring, when the Confederacy's "Gibraltar" on the Mississippi, Vicksburg, appeared bound to fall, and General Joseph Hooker began his offensive in Virginia. Briefly banished by Lee's costly triumph over Hooker at Chancellorsville in May, despondency returned among Confederates when Vicksburg surrendered on July 4, although Gettysburg made a much smaller impression. It returned a third time in November after the Union's victory at Chattanooga, Tennessee.

Reunion with the United States, even if under Confederate leadership, remained impossible for planners; therefore, their vision of a powerful nation-state depended on the recovery of lands then under Union control. Popular support in such "occupied" localities and not military conquest, they imagined, would deliver these lands. To this end, leaders of the Confederacy needed to ensure a popular vote for delegates who supported them in the expected postwar elections to conventions in the occupied states. However, after two years of war, with U.S. military occupation of large tracts of former Confederate lands, advocates of an independent South had to work harder in their task of persuasion. Evidence abounded that citizens of these regions, plied with Union propaganda and rendered apathetic by disappointment, would be very difficult to motivate to return to the Confederacy. In order to influence opinion, members of the government had to present a compelling vision of opportunity arising from a commercially and territorially expanding Confederacy—one that the Davis administration hoped the oppressed population of the lands under the transient government of the U.S. military would see as the fulfillment of their dreams. Meanwhile, northerners would be welcome to associate their states within the free trade international economy the government championed. Notwithstanding the damage inflicted to slavery and cotton production, planners still believed in the resiliency of both the labor system and the export of staple crops that depended on it to rapidly redeem the physical and financial debt of war.

Believers in a Confederate future remained committed to sustaining what they believed to be a racially hierarchical, growing, and socially stable republic. Those adventurers who lobbied for expansion from the periphery of the Confederacy increased in relative power compared with decision-makers in Richmond. Especially after the fall of Vicksburg had completed the Trans-Mississippi Department's isolation from the rest of the Confederacy, western and southern plans for expansion had to rely on the championship of agents in the localities, including from outside the Confederacy such as sympathizers in California.[1]

Meanwhile, in Richmond, the government dedicated its foreign policy, which still aspired to hemispheric dominance, to three complementary objectives: first, neutralizing the Union's Monroe Doctrine and colonization efforts; second, promotion of free trade; and, third, adherence to the law of nations. In 1863, politicians stressed moral superiority because, given the war was not likely to end soon, any concrete ambitions would have to be postponed further into the future. At the same time, expansionists' assertion of their national virtue revealed their continued confidence in the nation's strength; they based its power on the government's inherently sound cotton-backed finances, in view of the slaveholders' republic as the best governed society on earth, and the State Department's dedication through commerce to be the force for peace in international relations.

General Henry A. Wise grasped this paradox of renewal through adversity in both personal and national terms. Stationed near Charleston during November 1863 and writing to his wife at midnight—sleep rendered impossible on account of the noise of the U.S. Navy's continuous bombardment of nearby Fort Sumter—the former governor of Virginia did not believe himself to be witnessing a turning point of the war. Rather, a sense of a revival, and not only in an evangelical sense, seemed to prevail in these unpromising circumstances. Wise was only too well aware that it was the "eleventh month of the 3rd. year of a still continuing depressing war." The conflict "divides, separates, despoils, and destroys," he continued, "until it seems as if all old things are passing away and as if the Nations, North & South, and all things in them were becoming new." In response to this situation, planners echoed the ambitions of the Founding Fathers and sought not just diplomatic recognition but also the exercise of a claim of rights that other nations would respect. Politicians and planners who believed in a new beginning during 1863 considered that they had inherited a place in the international community, and they drew strength from their notion of a domestic compact between sovereign polities.[2]

We Shall Have to Start Afresh

Throughout 1863, members of the government continued to regard peace, not as an abstract and nostalgic dream, but as a concrete, albeit transformed, reality that required planning and preparation. "War is but temporary," President Davis reminded legislators in December, while "we desire that peace shall be permanent." Nevertheless, peace would not only be very different from wartime but would also not resemble the prewar past. "I expect we shall have to start afresh," stated South Carolina planter and soldier Eldred J. Simkins, "when Peace Glorious Peace shall restore quiet to our land & us to our homes." For leading Confederates, preparations for this new beginning had to commence during the war.[3]

Given the sufferings inflicted by the war, it made sense for Confederate leaders to emphasize that the future would be different. This need was especially the case in the beleaguered Trans-Mississippi Department, once it had been entirely cut off from the rest of the Confederacy. Colonel Joseph Lancaster Brent wrote an August 27 memorandum for General Richard Taylor, which detailed the mood in and around Alexandria, Louisiana. "Unless some change takes place," Brent concluded, "the dark portents that shadows the future of this department will in a few months burst in an overwhelming & fatal storm." The change, akin to Simkins's "start afresh," had to be a departure, and Brent knew what function it had to perform. "The remedy is to be found in instilling hope into the soldiers and people, now almost despairing of our cause." To achieve this goal, Confederate leaders pointed out that their nation would be the center of a new world order, in which other countries and peoples would assist it to achieve its goals.[4]

Optimists believed that somehow the experience of the war compressed time and meant the Confederacy had developed into a great power at a faster rate than had seemed possible before. "One single month now is worth an ordinary age," the *Southern Illustrated News* observed in August. The war rendered future greatness more realistic and necessary. Adopting the new language of social evolution, Senator Benjamin H. Hill saw the war as accelerating the rise of a nation at an astonishing pace. The Georgia politician had once been a reluctant Confederate despite his championship of the expansion of slavery. The nation's survival over two years of conflict had removed his doubts. "We began in weakness," he declared on January 7, yet "in the very struggle for life we are growing strong." Wise understood the transformation in terms of individual character and self-reliance; these would be necessary attributes as "we must be able to maintain ourselves after the war ends," he explained in a letter to a South Carolina politician published in November, and so "become the strong men of America." Wise adhered to his belief since 1861 that the Confederacy would be the heir of the United States.[5]

The government had to motivate people to fight the war and that would be helped if the future prospect of peace, with all its commercial and territorial possibilities, would be wonderful and worth striving for. "The question is very simple," the *Southern Illustrated News* editorialized on March 14: "We are to be exterminated or made the slaves of the most loathsome of the human species, or we are to conquer and become the wealthiest and best of modern nations." In a speech in August, Vice President Stephens warned the citizens of Charlotte, North Carolina, that they "would be the veriest fools in the world to sit down and nurse our depression until it grew into despair." Instead, "come life or death, weal or woe, they will be free. Take care that we do not use the fact of our recent reverses and its consequent depression as an excuse for a want of inclination to go to work and help in the cause of the Confederacy." Stephens, given the humiliating rejection of his recent request for an interview with the Lincoln administration in order to "have the war carried on in a more Christian & humane manner," believed it necessary to reaffirm his faith in the Confederate future.[6]

The Reverend Calvin Henderson Wiley, superintendent of public schools in North Carolina as well as prominent clergyman, insisted Confederates were not helpless victims of adverse divine providence, and they had to solve their predicament. His countrymen had to make an effort in the present in order to achieve a great future; they also, Wiley continued, had to avoid the equal and opposite debilitating sense of entitlement of rewards in the future for present-day sufferings. "Coming glories do not . . . account for past inflictions which were never heeded." He called for reform of any abuses of slavery and justified this task's urgency in wartime by expressing his disdain for, in historian Nicholas Guyatt's phrasing, "self-serving . . . providentialism." After all, Wiley concluded, "the future state of the world does not furnish a satisfactory solution for the wars which its inhabitants have already endured." Skeptical of rosy visions of expansionism and a cosmopolitan future, he insisted that the destiny for Confederates lay in their hands.[7]

Meanwhile, for other individuals, achievements in the war provided evidence of the promise of greater accomplishments in the future. Senator Albert G. Brown of Mississippi had started his career as a leading advocate of the establishment of state universities across the Deep South and then evolved into a demagogic champion of poor white equality sustained by unlimited slavery expansion, filibustering, and a southern homestead act. Now in 1863, he saw the effects of the war entering its third year as to time to meld his expansionist and improving impulses. It was time, he declared, for Confederates to "act upon more enlarged principles." As 1863 wore on, the sense of awe at the scale of the war and its implications grew. The question arose how the future nation would be worthy of a memory filled with growing numbers of casualties. Furthermore, deeds of individual heroism on the battlefield needed to be vindicated by the Confederacy on the world stage. "All the records of the many campaigns have demonstrated that we have carved for ourselves an historic name," Colonel George A. Gordon told an audience in Savannah, Georgia, that November. Yet this circumstance posed "a question for nations no less than for individuals," Gordon continued as he asked the crowd, "What will he do . . . with the liberty purchased at the price of so much blood?" For citizens, Gordon argued, each day of surviving the epic war added to their increased sense of national purpose, so that "the question assumes an awful magnitude, as the circle of responsibility enlarges and it embraces the nation at large . . . tomorrow and tomorrow will add to the weight of responsibility and we cannot refuse to say what we will do with it."[8]

The growing sense of responsibility was compounded by a rereading of the causes of the war as Confederates saw them: the survival of republican self-government; slavery as the only system that reconciled capital and labor; the Confederacy at the forefront of the "new thinking" of scientific racism. Historians notice that Confederates generally placed their revolution in a wider context, especially the 1848 failed European revolutions and thwarted quest for national self-determination in Hungary, Italy, and Germany. In 1863, expansionists distinguished their cause in two significant ways: first, they were of the Anglo-Saxon race, and hence their revolution was, in terms of progress, ideologically well ahead of the ongoing upheavals in continental Europe; second, the Confederacy presented to the world a new nation infinitely more powerful than the new countries created, thus far, by nationalism in Europe.[9]

As well as continuing to fight for slavery and republican self-government, expansionists sensed the new power unleashed by the centralization of their state. President Davis saw a virtuous circle between the present experience of war and future national power. It was necessary that the Confederacy "should be tried in this severe erucible [sic] in which we are being tested," he declared on January 5, "in order to cement us together." Moreover, "when peace and prosperity shall come to us," Davis continued, "we will go on assisting each other to develop the great political ideas upon which our government is based and the immense resources which nature has lavished upon us." Davis looked to the war as both creating new strength and transforming existing sources of power into something greater. "We are awakening to an appreciation of their deep significance," he observed in reference to political ideas. The president then turned to exploitation of resources and concluded: "In the latter direction we are displaying unexampled energy."[10]

In his tour of the threatened southeastern states in October and early November, during the aftermath of the successful battle of Chickamauga, Davis tried to reveal the significance of the new united nation. "With a resolute purpose and united effort we would regain all that we had lost," he promised, "and accomplish all that we have proposed." Once that foundation had been achieved, "the Confederate States would spring forward in a career of happiness and prosperity surpassing the dreams of the most sanguine." Senator Brown, although a foe of the president, agreed that the demands of war would transform the population and its prospects: "The times in which we live call for the exercise of all our faculties, and the unreserved use of our resources. We must liberalize our views," Brown begged, in order that Confederates would be able to "cultivate a more comprehensive patriotism."[11]

Wiley believed that Confederates' experience of secession and fighting a war to defend that right made them the leaders of the revolutionary right to self-determination, which in turn made them the patrons of a future of international harmony—at least in the Western Hemisphere. Wiley explained this sense of ethical leadership, which inevitably fell to Confederates. The government "believes that the existence of other distinct nations on the continent is not inconsistent with its own rights and interests," the North Carolinian educator wrote. Moreover, "it is willing to accord to others what it claims for itself, the privilege of living under a government and laws of their choice." Such a stance contrasted with the assertiveness of 1862 and the quasi-imperialism of 1861; yet it also gave the Confederacy an important and wide-ranging, albeit vague, mission: that of safeguarding the "interests of humanity and advancing civilization." Wiley did more than preach—he sought in his state wartime Whiggish educational improvements, especially provisions for teacher training. Politicians agreed with Wiley's analysis; Secretary of State Benjamin told Alabama senator Clement C. Clay that Confederate power rested on "superiority of reason and intellect over raw strength." It was more than simply aspiring to be members of a transatlantic community of advanced ideas; diplomats considered moral liberal internationalism as the basis of practical government policy after independence.[12]

The Confederacy's vital dynamism, its advocates argued, arose from its particular system of government that gave full voice to individual ambitions and aspiration. Everywhere else in the world, planners of the new nation believed, forces threatened this freedom of the individual. The legacy of the French Revolution and triumph of Lincoln meant the dictatorship of the mob threatened in parts of Europe and the United States where the demagogue did not yet rule and in Europe aristocratic oppression still held sway; most dangerous of all, however, especially in Britain, the mechanization of the Industrial Revolution promised an even harsher denial of personal liberty. Shortly after her arrival in Britain on September 13, Confederate spy and diplomat Rose Greenhow visited Thomas Carlyle at his London home. She wished to meet the leading portrayer of the Industrial Revolution as the destroyer of man's dignity and individualism and wanted him to write another article to follow one that had been published in *MacMillan's Magazine* that August. In the article, Carlyle had equated plantation slavery with wage labor in factories. He posited an imaginary conversation from "Peter of the North to Paul of the South." The essayist concluded the dialogue that summarized what he thought distinguished the work systems: "Paul, you unaccountable scoundrel, I find that you hire your servants for life, not by the month or year as I do!" Diplomats in Europe attempted to conceive the new nation as a project confronting the unbridled individualism of the era. Without going as far as to embrace new theories of socialism, they argued that a sense of solidarity underpinned its claim to nationhood. The Confederacy had to be understood as "a community of men and interests whose existence is fully established," Slidell explained to Napoleon III, "and who should be as responsible as a single individual."[13]

Those who looked forward to the triumph of the Confederate nation believed it would mean not only the fulfillment of collective aspiration but also the assumption of the great responsibility of virtuous government. "The duty of states is to a certain extent the duty of individuals," the anonymous writer Juridicus declared, agreeing with Slidell, and as a result, "the position which the Confederate States truly occupy [is to] acknowledge the obligations of moral rules." In the Union, this duty "may be neglected: insane passion or insatiate ambition may for a time seem to crush beneath the car of conquest the right of the weak and the duty of the strong." The journalist showed the lingering effects of the "Second Great Awakening." Postmillennialism thrived in the North, with the belief that individual effort was required to bring about God's work, while premillennialism, dominant in the South, taught society as a whole to wait for God's sign. "That a great God directs the conduct of men in their individual relations all admit," Juridicus concluded, and in the Confederacy "that the same power directs men in their aggregated communities all may in like manner admit."[14]

Diplomats confidently assumed that the Confederacy's place in the world rested on morality as well as inherited strengths, especially the stability of institutions, which continued to be provided by slavery and staple crops. On this foundation, Dudley Mann believed the Confederacy's "power for repelling aggression becomes more manifest as the contest is lengthened." Due to its ability to withstand Union pressure, "the government of the Confederate States has been as stable as any government within the confines of civilization." Although Mann used abstract language, he told Europeans that the Confederacy was not committed to exporting its revolution. Unlike Lincoln, the Davis administration "entertains no Utopian theories" about the world. "In its intercourse with foreign governments," Mann explained, "its steady policy will be the maintenance of cordially harmonious relations." In the face of Union aggression and European appeasement, Confederate leaders would bide their time and by so doing elevate their nation by their forbearance. As he expected the war to close soon, "we will not be long in forcing our way to a higher position as relates to the maintenance of the probity of international law, and the just observance of the principles which should obtain in international intercourse, than the mightiest of European powers." This conduct would bring future respect. As Davis told Congress on December 7: "To forego our undeniable right to the exercise of those [belligerent] pretensions is a policy higher, worthier of us and our cause, than to revoke the adherence to principles that we approve"; as a result, "[we will] awaken a great people . . . by our forebearance [*sic*]."[15]

GOVERNMENT POLICIES FOR THE FUTURE GREAT NATION

Given this combination of growing strength and the absence of constraints, policymakers began to consider measures promoting individual self-development. Nothing better illustrates the self-conscious transformation of the Confederacy than the fact that the Congress debated a homestead bill in spring 1863, discarding the measure's earlier antislavery reputation in the hands of the Republicans, who promoted the independence of nonslaveholding whites. In April, a special committee recommended that the bill pass the House. The measure had a practical postwar purpose, as representatives grappled with how soldiers would be paid.[16]

As well as providing land-as-pensions for soldiers, a postwar Confederacy would have to possess sufficient resources to rebuild a devastated economy and pay off a huge national debt. Representative John Brown Baldwin of Virginia, a moderate Shenandoah Valley politician, spoke for many in expressing his belief that the future prosperity of the Confederacy would render such a debt affordable. In a speech to Congress on January 16, Baldwin declared that within eight months, "it is not beyond the capacities of our people," if all parts of the Confederacy invested on the scale of his fellow citizens of Augusta County, that the nation "would [be able to] fund $700 million" of debt. Baldwin, a wealthy slaveholder and "champion" of his district, earlier told Mary Chesnut, "I was always true to my country," when she challenged him on his tardy conversion from unionism to the Confederacy. Such conduct replicated nationally would both sustain the social order and develop for the Confederacy a reputation for probity. "It is believed that once we have established our independence," Baldwin concluded, "we shall be entitled by our resources to take a position of high credit among the nations, and that we could make loans at much lower rates of interest." Since they needed to know how much taxation could realistically be raised to meet long- and short-term debt obligations, various Confederates embarked upon a series of computations of expected government revenues, line item expenditures, and amounts of inward investment.[17]

In estimates of the likely resources the country would possess, a picture of the future Confederacy began to emerge. The currency crisis of 1863 and its attendant congressional debates stimulated production of financial plans that—for their assumptions—included predictions about future peacetime Confederate government policy. Pamphlets circulated, including "A Plan of Financial Relief" by political economist Jacob N. Cardozo, and Charles P. Culver's "A Scheme for the Relief of the Financial Embarrassments." The commentators and members of the government did not necessarily agree. Phillip Clayton of Georgia, the assistant treasury secretary, predicted the civil expenditures of the peacetime Confederate government would be just thirty-five million dollars per annum, a figure that presumably was a slightly adjusted pro rata share of the 1860 United States government budget of sixty-three million dollars. Given that Clayton had held the same post in the Buchanan administration, this thinking should not be a surprise. Moreover, according to Mary Chesnut, Clayton had worried about excessive government expenditure since at least August 1861, when it was already running at two million dollars a week. Culver assumed that postwar commerce would also require greater government action and expense. "Clayton overlooked the fact that we will have a navy to build and equip, lands to purchase and dockyards and forts to build and supply," Culver complained. "I agree with him that a large standing army will not be necessary but an efficient navy will be our arm of defense both at home and abroad." Such a complaint revealed Culver's ideas about the Confederacy's strategic blue-water needs.[18]

Other individuals agreed with Culver that, given the expansion of the Confederate navy would be crucial to the growth of seaborne commerce, work on it had to be ratcheted up now. The progress of the war encouraged the planning of a fleet. In early 1863, naval successes on the Mississippi and in Charleston harbor restimulated visions of a naval destiny, to be realized in the short term by commerce raiding on both the Atlantic and Pacific oceans. By the summer, Catherine Edmondston celebrated the successes of the *Alabama* and *Florida*. "Our little navy has carried dismay and destruction into the heart of Abolition Commerce." She looked forward to similar results from the ironclad *Albemarle*, then being constructed two miles from her home in North Carolina. Steamboats continued to represent modernity and progress for visionaries and, for the planners of the new nation, promised to defend and expand both slavery and the far-flung commerce of the future nation. With Davis's encouragement, the bill to establish a volunteer navy passed the House on April 18—a start, the bill's proponents hoped, toward a great maritime future. "The laws of success, in all enterprises," the preamble stipulated, "is that you must commence, make progress and succeed . . . each step of progress facilitating every succeeding step."[19]

Legislators expected each state to establish its own navy in addition to that of the Richmond government. Proponents of a navy hoped that competition between the states would stimulate the development of a significant naval capability collectively. In January, Joseph Seawell told Governor John Letcher of Virginia: "I understand that the North Carolina governor has sent to Europe officers to purchase and equip a vessel of war and then to command and officer her, to cruise against the merchant vessels of the enemy." Reports of the successes of the *Alabama* at the end of 1862, together with the simultaneous capture and conversion of Union vessel *Harriet Lane* into another commerce raider at Galveston, rendered such expectations credible to many observers. Governor Zebulon B. Vance of North Carolina desired to establish a state navy in order to export cotton. The reaction was swift. "If North Carolina can do this," Seawell reasoned, "why not Virginia and every other Confederate State?"[20]

The slow establishment of state navies during wartime frustrated diplomats and sailors. By September, the Virginia Volunteer Navy had been organized, and Captain Edward C. Stiles had purchased on account the steamer *Hawk*. Slidell concurred, "We have to say we think it very important that the *Hawk* should proceed with as little delay as possible on her cruise against the commerce of the enemy." The young and enthusiastic Edward Archer, son of a director at the Tredegar Ironworks, received his appointment from Secretary of War James A. Seddon as assistant engineer for the Virginia Volunteer Navy Company on September 26, 1863. Delays, chiefly caused by financing difficulties, meant the new navy only got underway in 1864. Meanwhile, other states began to make their own preparations. In his message to the State Assembly on November 23, 1863, Governor Milledge Luke Bonham of South Carolina urged the "favorable consideration of the legislature ... [regarding] the establishment under act of congress of a 'volunteer navy.'" This "succeeding in the organization of a navy," a Georgian navalist claimed, would be "necessary to our social independence after peace." For Confederates, nationhood encompassed commercial independence, achieved by the export of staple crops.[21]

The navy was important because optimists planned the Confederacy to be a main participant in an interdependent global economy by means of maximum staple production. Trade and slavery both needed to be protected. According to John Schley, a prominent Georgia planter, central to this Confederate strength was the increase of staple products that will bring "wealth, prosperity independence and power," based on the "preservation, increase and perpetuity" of slavery. Confidence in the institution of slavery had increased in 1863 due to its apparent resilience in the face of the continued war and sustained what historian Robert Bonner termed the slaveholders' "imaginative vision." Enslaved people remained the Confederacy's main asset and slavery the basis of that country's power.[22]

Confederate ambitions were underpinned by the belief that the nation's economy would revert after the war to one predominantly agricultural and based on slavery. Some individuals welcomed wartime industrialization, but with the possible exception of mining, they viewed these occupations as temporary necessities. Nevertheless even the most resolute of optimists—such as the secretary of state—recognized, as Howell Cobb had seen two year before, that the period of transition back to staple crop production would be protracted. "After the war," Benjamin predicted, "the supply of cotton for some years must be less than in the past, owing to the diminished quantity of labor resulting not only from the ravages of the war but [also] from the diversion of much slave labor to mining and other pursuits." Although the immediate postwar years would be an era of austerity, as the country recovered from the wartime devastation and loss of markets, optimists believed the succeeding recovery must be swift due to two reasons: an anticipated surge of foreign investment and a quicker peacetime expansion of the Confederacy's agricultural economy than the more industrialized Union's economy.[23]

Above all, rapid growth would be possible because planners for the new nation continued to believe that they were still sitting on an enormous stockpile of cotton built up since 1861; this crop would then be quickly sold, leading to an infusion of cash into the economy and—with an export duty—revenues to the government. On the basis of this cotton reserve, planters and their allies dismissed the long-term viability of possible alternative sources of cotton supply. A "most experienced cotton broker" assured the British consul in Mobile that even taking into account wastage, burning by Confederates, and seizure by Union forces, some 4.5 million bales remained in store in the Confederacy. Such a supply, once roped and bagged, could be immediately exported on peace and be subject to a duty of five cents per pound.[24]

British consuls based in the Confederacy believed their superiors in the Foreign Office back in London ought to be concerned about the risk of a postwar glut in cotton. The development of a profitable cotton industry in India might be jeopardized. Hotze, as newspaper editor as well as commercial agent, endeavored to fan these fears in London as a way to rally support there for the Confederate war effort. He predicted in January that "peace and the reopening of southern ports would liberate a year's crop," calculating that plans to grow cotton in alternative sites, such as India or Egypt, were "based on high prices continuing so this risk could wreck the viability of such plans." He remained confident throughout the year; in August, Hotze reviewed in his newspaper a pamphlet by British millowner Samuel Smith, The Cotton Trade of India, and liked what he read. He concluded that due to the inferiority of the quality of Indian cotton as well as its price, on Confederate independence New Orleans "will again take the highest position" as cotton entrepôt. The propagandist believed his British readers were slowly grasping that only the Confederacy would be able to provide good-quality cheap cotton. Nevertheless, "every day peace is postponed adds to the difficulty of resuming the culture on an adequate scale," Hotze warned, "and at best many years must elapse before we can get cotton at the same price and quantity as before the war." In September, Hotze reported with satisfaction that from "India the accounts of the cotton crop are very discouraging to those who believed that that country could supply the place of the Confederate States."[25]

The foundation of international commercial growth remained free trade, at least as a long-term objective. The president continued to believe that protectionism was socially divisive, as well as economically unsound. Although the 1862 cabinet decision to modify free trade in order to meet the demands of war remained in place, there was something of a revival in free-trade sentiment among planners of the nation. Observers noted a surge in blockade running during the first half of 1863 and how shipping volumes exceeded peacetime trade levels in both Charleston and Wilmington. Commodore Matthew F. Maury believed such developments amounted to a "transatlantic revolution." This evidence meant that once peace was declared, diplomats and agents expected that such commerce, especially with Britain, would be set to grow to unprecedented levels.[26]

Confederates believed this prospect portended a community of interest and mutual obligations between the Confederacy and the European powers. In Lancashire, England, on September 2, Maury declared that the proliferation of blockade running between the Confederacy and Europe provided the basis for "the present position and future prospects" of the Confederacy. Not only were the "fleets of the Confederacy and neutral steamships engaged in regular trade between neutral countries and the Confederate ports," Benjamin informed Mason on June 6, but also, "this trade is daily increasing." Some of the expected peacetime operations of the State Department appeared to be already in operation. "It is entirely safe and much more prompt to send [dispatches] by closed British mail to our agents at Nassau or Bermuda whence they are forwarded by our government steamers," he told Slidell on June 22, as these ships were "now run with the regularity of packets." Notwithstanding the difficult diplomatic irritations between Britain and the Confederacy during 1863, Benjamin envisaged that after the war it would be "England, with which nation our commercial relations will be very extensive."[27]

Diplomats conceived these preparations as interrelated and developed a worldview to support their actions and their future power. The Confederacy was to take part in what its citizens regarded as a new interdependent system of foreign relations based on political economy. The priority for planners was then to work out how to incorporate the United States into this framework.[28]

NEW WAYS TO CONTAIN THE UNITED STATES

Given there was little likelihood of an early peace with the United States, optimistic Confederates stressed that the war's expanding scope would enable a new modus operandi with their northern neighbor. In February, Schley appropriated as his theme in a pamphlet that all past axioms were null because the war "alters the case." In the same way that individuals had changed, so had the continent. "It seems as if all old things are passing away," Wise told his wife, "as if the nations, North & South, and all things in them were becoming new." This sense of novelty extended to national boundaries. "The new map of America is as yet a blank," wrote a former U.S. diplomat living in exile in Richmond, William J. Buchanan of Maryland. "New issues, new facts, other principles are springing to the surface."[29]

The political map of the entire continent of North America was destined for upheaval, and in that context, politicians and journalists asserted their right to fluid boundaries and therefore to expansive land claims. "The recognition of the Confederate States is not an admission or a guarantee of the right to a certain specified and defined territory," the anonymous South Carolinian writer Juridicus insisted in April. "It is the admission of the existence of an independent government, the territorial possessions of which may be affected by the chances of war, or the other circumstances which tend to enlarge or contract territorial limits." Mindful of the consequences of possible British and French mediation, Tennessee representative William G. Swan agreed with Juridicus: let no European power "trace *our* boundaries, measure *our* domains and limit *our* institutions," he told the House in February. Fixed boundaries meant the confinement of slavery, which was intolerable to expansionists. Swan, a former Whig, also believed Confederate sovereignty was further threatened as the British consuls in the Confederacy continued to report to Washington. Historian Charles Hubbard suggests that Swan's campaign to expel the consuls and recall Mason from London was motivated by a wish to embarrass Davis and Benjamin; but Swan also believed the standing of the Confederacy as an equal nation in the world was jeopardized by tolerating this state of affairs.[30]

The sovereignty sought by Swan was equality with the great powers of Europe. With an aim to become the dominant power on the North American continent, State Department strategists hoped for "a first among equals" status in a multipolar Western Hemisphere; this position would, in turn, enable their nation's commercial and slavery expansion into the less developed areas of the tropics. Diplomats envisaged in North America a map looking like that of Europe. Once possessed of a secure northern border and settled relations with the Union, the Confederacy would be able to pursue imperial interests toward the south. "In a comparatively short time," the commissioner to Brussels, Dudley Mann, told Benjamin, "we shall develop a republic that will exercise in its dignified administration of affairs as controlling an influence upon the destinies of the American continent as France exercises in Europe."

France's entente with its northern neighbor, Britain, enabled Napoleon III to pursue his ambitions and recover his country's prestige.[31]

The encouraging example of the entente meant politicians and Congress sought to improve future relations with the United States. Throughout early 1863, the Committee on Foreign Affairs chaired by Foote considered resolutions on conditions for peace with the Union. He also publicly urged Davis to accept any peace terms offered by Lincoln. At the same time, the Southern Carolina writer William M. Bobo—presumably with Foote's concurrence—anonymously publicized these secret deliberations in Congress to a wider audience and set out what implications the resolutions had for the extent of the Confederacy. In exchange for peace and a commercial agreement with the Union, perhaps encompassing the whole of North America, "the integrity of the Confederacy territorially must be preserved intact," meaning the inclusion of Maryland and of a continued northern boundary stretching from the "Ohio [River] to the north of Missouri and thence west" as far as the Pacific Ocean. Representative William W. Boyce of South Carolina, Foote's colleague and ally, also wished to extend any free-trade treaty to Canada. He had long been an opponent of territorial expansion on the grounds that it was unnecessary: "if it be possible for a nation to have territory enough, we certainly have it, and whatever else we may need, we do not need any more space," he noted, adding that the pursuit of expansion had alienated potential allies in the past. Squabbles over land should not be allowed to disrupt relations with the United States. Nevertheless, for Boyce that restraint did not preclude commercial growth.[32]

As part of coexistence with the Union, believers in a great nation expected that a recognized independent Confederate government would lead to withdrawal of all Union forces occupying the large swaths of territory within these enlarged boundaries. Senator Brown—whose state of Mississippi had been largely occupied by Union forces by the end of 1863—disputed the likelihood of such compliance if Union armies advanced even further into the Confederacy. "One year ago, Mississippi was as secure as you think yourselves to be," Brown warned his colleagues in December as politicians digested the implications of the defeat at Chattanooga. "If we lose the country," he continued, "personal liberty, habeas corpus, and the Constitution go with it." These setbacks would be permanent. "We can never wrest these things from Yankee hands if once our country is conquered." Brown hoped the loss of territory could be reversed, but "if it be not, I drop the curtain and refuse even a glimpse into the future." Most Confederates believed that these states would be recovered after peace on account of their people represented in state conventions deciding to return to the Confederacy. Moreover, Robert Kean from his vantage point in the War Department critiqued members of Congress—especially Brown—for being overly pessimistic about the approaching 1864 campaign.[33]

In any event, the war would not determine the Confederacy's geographic extent; only peacetime developments would. Confederates still expected that popular votes would be held for conventions in all the Border States to determine whether they remain in the Union or ratify their admission into Confederacy. Future status would be predicated on the affiliations of the elected delegates, the most important questions being who would be qualified to vote and how demoralized the population had been rendered by Union rule. According to optimistic planners, public opinion in the Border States, up to this point suppressed by Republican Party tyranny, would vote for delegates who wished their states to join the Confederacy. However, in contrast to 1862, the task of readmitting the Border States would be more difficult. On April 16, John Warren Grigsby of Danville, Kentucky, a former consul to France, a leader in education affairs in his locality, and then serving in the Army of Tennessee, told his friend Governor John Letcher of Virginia: "We Kentuckians still hope that we will be permitted to make one more effort to redeem our old commonwealth." The job had got harder however: "But if the Yanks are permitted to fill the state with troops, the chances of accomplishing much seems to me be rather slim." The Unionist populations in the occupied states would either have to submit to secession or leave. "All the Union population are conscious of the severe retribution that will await them," J. Marshall McCue advised his colleagues in the Virginia Assembly of Delegates. He used the same mixture of "revival and revolution rhetoric," with which he roused mass meetings back in his district when he demanded present sacrifices for future reward, and promised his colleagues that these unionists "will flee out of Kentucky, Missouri, North West Virginia into Kansas, Iowa, Illinois, Ohio, and Pennsylvania."[34]

In a manner reminiscent of their earlier efforts to acquire Cuba and parts of Mexico by purchase in the 1850s, some Confederates wondered whether bribes might be necessary in order to persuade the Union to surrender the strong points it had occupied in the Confederacy. "Our army as yet does not (nor is it likely to) hold any possessions within the federal government that would [be] an equivalent exchange for New Orleans," Culver wrote to Hershel V. Johnson on October 27. He expected that "the federal government will not yield up its present positions within the Confederate States without a valuable consideration." Culver therefore advised Johnson that the government needed to budget for future payments to the Union for the surrender of its forts in the Confederacy. Financial strength making up for military weakness reflected the Confederate hope for the enlightened diplomacy of arbitration dictated by the civilizing impulses of commerce. "Money is one the greatest levers of the world," the writer of a Petersburg broadside reasoned, and "if so use it properly to buy a peace." Johnson supported Hunter's efforts at financial reform in the Senate and believed that northerners would respond to such a bribe. As a Swedenborgian, Johnson understood that money, together with other material objects, could and should be used to accomplish divine will. Planners for the Confederacy expected their booming slavery-based economy would afford to pay for those parts of the South then controlled by the United States.[35]

Wealth and a booming economy would mean more than the slave states would wish to join the Confederacy. However, with emancipation now U.S. government policy, greater differences arose between politicians over the question of the formal admission of free states into the Confederacy. Foote, profoundly proslavery and keen to unite Confederates against enemies, both internal and external, believed that "to admit any free or partly free state in the Confederate States would be suicidal." Governor John Milton of Florida agreed with Foote. "An effort is being made to organize a political party," he warned Davis, "which will prove troublesome—if not dangerous to the permanency of the Confederate States." Milton forwarded a circular written anonymously by "Confederate," which had been sent to the governor, calling for "the admission of Ohio, Illinois, and Indiana into the Confederacy." "Confederate" insisted the inclusion of these states would "broaden and strengthen the nation and free it from its old dependence on slavery and cotton." Given that slavery and cotton were to be the central focus of Confederate power, Milton and Davis suspected that this pamphlet was intended to divide Confederates.[36]

Optimists, especially early in 1863, continued to encourage the fragmentation of the Union with promotion of Midwest and Pacific confederacies. The Emancipation Proclamation, as well as the campaigns for approaching elections in the Confederacy, did change some attitudes, especially toward the Midwest, whose inhabitants had earlier been deemed by Confederate observers to be hostile to abolition. With these states' apparent acquiescence in the United States government's policy of emancipation, any notion of free states joining their nation became less attractive to Confederate planners or even to be allies.

Davis still assumed his nation would profit from divisions within the United States; but rather than attempting to entice midwesterners to secede and form a commercial association with the Confederacy, he hoped they would undermine the Union from within. He looked forward to "first separation of the North West from the Eastern States," predicting "the discord among them which will paralyze the power of both," as he told Richmond citizens on January 5. Next would follow "for us future peace and prosperity." A month later, Kenneth Rayner, a lawyer in Raleigh, North Carolina, and former Whig U.S. representative from Hertford County, echoed Davis. "You notice the news from the North West," he told Judge Thomas Ruffin, "There is no doubt great agitations and excitement there, which I hope will [rebound] to our benefit."[37]

In 1863, especially whenever the war news appeared encouraging, some politicians, pamphleteers, and newspaper editors continued to recommend the alternative idea of a southern-led Union. At the beginning of the year when Murfreesboro was still believed to be a victory and Fredericksburg a recent memory, Anthony M. Keiley wrote to Benjamin that when peace comes "we can dictate to the returning States [excluding New England] the terms of admission to Our Union." Keiley, a Virginian Catholic who was serving in the Army of Northern Virginia and anxious to get a post in the State Department, had been active in the antebellum Democratic Party. In June 1863, as Lee's offensive northward began to get underway and Confederates still held Vicksburg, such ideas resurfaced. Henry Hotze presented to his English readers of the *Index* a vision of a "southern dominated Union, excluding New England" resulting from Confederates closing "with the offer the Northern Democrats are only too ready to make." Congress, as well as Hotze, preferred that commercial power would be the means to exercise Confederate dominance as opposed to the formal admission of the nonslaveholding states into the Confederacy.[38]

Confederate expansionist ambitions would be achieved by negotiating commercial treaties with all states outside New England. Pacts would not only lower tariffs on a reciprocal basis but also carve out spheres of influence. Foote stressed the economic benefits both in terms of commerce and resources that would accrue to the Confederacy as a result of access to the Pacific Ocean and its coast. Therefore any commercial agreement had to ensure the Confederacy and allied States would both share "the exclusive use of all the rich mineral lands stretching along the slopes of the Pacific," Foote insisted, together with "free trade with all the nations of the earth and the future maritime growth and power that has no parallel and lastly a monopoly of the trade of the Pacific Ocean." The government had clear ambitions both of mining in the West and expanding commerce and trade with China and Japan, as well as with Europe.[39]

ASSEMBLING A COALITION AGAINST THE UNION

Poor military news inevitably upset Confederate plans for domination of the continent. This failure meant that allies would have to assist in the task of containing the power of the United States on which Confederate independence rested. Therefore, planters, politicians, and journalists presented the goals of the future nation in universal terms designed to also encompass those of other nations and peoples in order to encourage their collaboration in that enterprise. These potential partners included Native Americans, adventurers in the far West, the French and other allies in Mexico, and, finally, the other slave powers. As the Union presented its struggle against slavery and for reunion in the universal terms of freedom, equality, and self-government, so the Confederacy portrayed its bid for future independence in a similar fashion.

Toward that long-term end, it was vital to achieve three interrelated objectives in 1863: first, keep alive the claim to New Mexico territory including Arizona; second, end the anarchy in Mexico that interrupted trade and the security of foreign residents, thereby preventing the establishment of a lasting Confederate presence there; and third, prevent the United States from occupying any "empty" country. However, with the exception of dealing with Native Americans, the attention of the government to these objectives was only sporadic during much of 1863. The exercise of these ambitions to the west and south relied chiefly on the efforts of agents on the ground to petition for aid and mobilize scarce resources with at best verbal encouragement from Richmond. This inattention was not because the government had turned cold on expansion; at the end of the year, the State Department sensed an opportunity with the establishment of a conservative regency in Mexico, after the French army marched into Mexico City in July, to actively engage in Mexican affairs and formulate a distinct foreign policy.[40]

WORKING WITH THE INDIANS

Planners for the Confederacy conceived of Native Americans as natural, albeit inferior and dependent, members of what they regarded as a complex and advanced polity organized around a racial hierarchy. Their possession of Indian Territory remained integral to the optimists' mission to manage what they deemed to be backward races. This racial policy would then form the basis of expansion, in particular politicians' intention to increase trade with, settle, and, in the long term, occupy portions of Mexico.[41]

The government hoped that a future of mutual advantage beckoned in its relations with Native Americans. In his report sent to Congress on January 12, the acting Indian commissioner, Sutton S. Scott of Kentucky, confirmed that he had assured the Cherokees, Choctaws, Chickasaws, Creeks, and Seminoles that the Confederate government was much friendlier and more reliable in its dealings with them the United States had been. Scott believed the Native Americans received this news with enthusiasm. President Davis "loves you," Scott told the Native leaders and offered, as proof, that "the treaties were about extending rights and privileges which had been denied by the old government." Moreover, because they were not enslaved, Native Americans would occupy an advantageous position in the racial hierarchy of the Confederacy, in contrast to the Union where, without significant populations of African Americans, Scott believed the Indians were effectively at the bottom of society. In the Confederacy "you are made to occupy a high and exalted position," the commissioner assured them, "one adapted to your civilization and advancement and suited to your pride and independence of character."[42]

In their hierarchy of races, the leaders of the slaveholders' republic deemed most Native Americans to be in a category above that of African Americans. Historian Robert Bonner argues that Confederates intended to exercise "racial stewardship," as opposed to enslavement, over Native Americans. "They are not some kind of wild negro," Hotze bluntly explained as he reviewed Scott's report in the April 23 edition of the *Index*, and "with the exception of a few tribes are a high-spirited and superior race." Therefore, Scott has had "no trouble confirming their loyalty" because, according to Hotze, at least the settled tribes' "sympathies with the

South and [possessing] similar institutions being slaveholders." It was up to Native Americans to make the most of their profitable position in the future. The Davis administration would place "facilities for advancement" within their reach, and if they were properly used, Scott believed it would be "easy" for Native Americans, within a few years, to "become powerful and prosperous nations."[43]

Native Americans would not have their own state in the Confederacy, but they would have representation in the institutions of government. The Indian Territory "was a magnificent country," Pike attested in order to demonstrate the importance of his work, "equal in extent, fertility, beauty and resources to any one of the States—nay, superior to any." At the end of the year, Representative Thomas B. Hanley of Arkansas, a member of the House's Indian Affairs Committee, introduced resolutions confirming that Indian delegates from the five nations be seated in the House. Once the resolution was passed, Native American legislators would be able to introduce legislation relative to their nation, and one of them would become a nonvoting member of the House committee. The Confederate policy on Indians had oscillated between coercion and conciliation in 1862 but appeared to be conciliatory during 1863. As well as recognizing that any Confederate power in Indian Territory depended on Native American consent, this attitude also reflected the government's policy of the primacy of commercial relations and presenting itself as the champion of humanity.[44]

A campaign launched by the Confederate agent to Indian Territory discredited the military-led policy of coercion of the Native Americans. In an article circulated in spring 1863, Albert Pike argued that the army officers on the ground in 1862 acted with "conduct calculated to incite our Indian allies to revolt" by "stoppage of their supplies." Regarding the larger consequences of the soldiers' actions, "so far as they related to our Indian allies," Pike explained, "I notice them here because if we lose the Indian Country, as we are almost certain to do, Arkansas and Texas are ruined." Pike's argument clearly persuaded the government; on April 29, Congress requested him to examine and approve the quartermaster's accounts relating to payment of Indian troops. Davis shared this prevailing sensibility about Native American welfare; if Governor Baylor of Arizona had, as rumored, exterminated the Apache in Arizona, he observed on March 28, it would indeed be "an infamous crime."[45]

WORKING WITH LOCAL BOOSTERS

Members of the Davis administration continued to claim the territory of New Mexico, including Arizona, as an integral part of their future nation. With no resources being available for a repeat of Sibley's expedition, whose surviving soldiers had been redeployed to Louisiana, the government relied on individuals on the frontier to maintain the Confederacy's presence in the Southwest. There seemed to be sufficient numbers to effect this ambition. As historian Donald Frazier notes, "San Antonio [Texas] remained a hotbed of Arizonan and far western plotters," while the Richmond government itself "in tacit approval of at least the idea of regaining Arizona, sent Mississippian Robert Josselyn to act as governor." Josselyn, a close friend and former secretary of Davis's, and three other "territorial officials" drew salaries. Specifically, the territory served as the gateway to both Mexico and the Pacific Ocean. Many Confederates earlier believed New Mexico had been awarded to the South—as it lay south of the old Missouri Compromise line—in various attempts at sectional compromise championed by Crittenden and Buchanan and even allegedly endorsed by Lincoln. Moreover, the favored route of the Southern Pacific Railroad would run through the southern edge of the territory, before heading south along the Yaqui valley into Mexico to the province of Sonora's port of Guaymas on the Gulf of California.[46]

The president enthusiastically—albeit verbally—supported proposals of those who demanded wartime moves to secure these lands. He actively considered renewed moves into New Mexico and Arizona in both March and December 1863. Malcolm H. MacWillie, the territorial delegate of Arizona and protégé and former attorney general of the expansionist governor John R. Baylor, persistently tried to prompt action in Richmond and justified his requests with the lure of mines and the railroad. However, time was of the essence, MacWillie warned, because apparently New Mexico was in a state of revolution against Union authorities and, on June 8, recommended that Davis move swiftly to establish governments in both New Mexico and Arizona while popular support remained. If the Confederate government did nothing, MacWillie feared, these territories might be awarded to the Union in any peace treaty because only the U.S. had official presence there.[47]

Davis forwarded MacWillie's request to the attorney general for his legal opinion. Optimists remained confident that they would secure this territory, even if, as with other large parts of the Confederacy, it remained under temporary Union control. After the war, they believed, the territorial legislatures would proceed to organize as Confederate states. Nevertheless, the Davis administration also endeavored to support adventurers' wartime activities. On December 16, Lansford W. Hastings, then a major in the Confederate Army and a pioneer of the far west who had devised the infamous cutoff bearing his name that shortened the overland route to California, wrote to and then saw Davis and presented a proposal to raise between three thousand and five thousand troops in California, seize Arizona and New Mexico for the Confederacy, and thus maintain communication with the Pacific. According to Frazier, Hastings was one of those individuals who suffered from "imperial delusions" due to the exaggerated reports he believed of Confederate sympathy in California and Colorado; nevertheless, Davis not only found the time to see him but also requested a conference with Secretary of War Seddon to discuss the topic.[48]

WORKING WITH THE FRENCH IN MEXICO

Opponents and supporters of the Davis administration agreed that Mexico lay within the Confederacy's exclusive sphere of influence. However, even journalists most ambitious for the future Confederacy conceded that Mexico lay beyond direct control and hence, in the short term, the government had to rely on others to act as Confederate proxies. In the meantime, "Mexico in her chronic anarchy was bound to fall under the overmastering influence of either Britain, the United States or France." In those circumstances, the *Richmond Enquirer* opined that because France was the weakest of the three alternatives, it was "the only one we could tolerate on our southern border." Any pacification was better than none. At least the French would not discriminate against Confederates and would offer a regime "which should assure security for foreign residents and hold out some hope of order, development and rational freedom."[49]

Ambitious individuals hoped that with formal Confederate action impossible, colonies of sympathizers would perform multiple functions: support the French; maintain the slaveholder republic's interest and say in ongoing developments; and facilitate increased cross-border trade in contraband. "Napoleon III steps forward to grasp the prize which is beyond our reach," Sam Houston wistfully declared in a speech on March 18, 1863, "and we who are the most interested have but to make the best of it." The government did exactly that and expected any future settlement and development of mining in Mexico to be done by Confederate supporters from California, once French troops had conquered the country and the Archduke Maximilian's imperial regime was established in Mexico City. In April, with the French army still outside Puebla, it was rumored in Richmond that "large numbers" of southern men were immigrating to Mazatlan, a port on Mexico's Pacific coast. In the summer of 1863, Colonel Andrew Jackson Grayson, one of these colonists, stressed to Davis the advantages of such a movement for the Confederacy; but he added that the migrants needed protection from the region's endemic violence if they were to thrive. The president subsequently raised the proposal with Benjamin. The commissioner in Paris hoped the French troops would guard the colonists. The French minister of marine had accordingly been made aware of "the necessity of the occupation of Guaymas with a small corps sustained by a squadron," Slidell notified Benjamin on December 15, as "this force may be made the point d'appui of an extensive emigration from California of natives of the southern states."[50]

Confederates presented their objectives for Mexico in terms calculated to have the widest possible appeal. To facilitate future colonization, government policy toward Mexico was dictated by "an overriding interest in law and order," for "the Confederate States is the natural ally of a re-generated Mexico." Due to their shared border, Texans especially stressed the importance of expansion of trade with Mexico as the agent of this regeneration. In his March speech, Houston attributed his support for French efforts to pacify the country to "our interest that the condition [of Mexico] should be changed and that she may be opened to our trade under peaceful auspices." Now stationed back in Monterrey, Quintero agreed; he saw in the French an authority in Mexico less susceptible than either the liberal party of Juárez or the provincial governors to U.S. pressure to stop contraband trade with Confederates. "As soon as the French shall occupy Matamoras," he assured Benjamin, "the necessary steps will be taken to have the free use of the port. Under their rule most of the obnoxious duties on cotton will be repealed." By restoring order, the French occupation would aid in the strengthening of commercial ties across the border. The government sought to reciprocate by encouraging cross-border trade. In April, Senator Williamson S. Oldham from the Commerce Committee confirmed that Davis had revoked the cotton orders across the Rio Grande.[51]

Confederates reluctantly accepted French activities because, of the three powers—Britain and the United States being the others—at present possessing the means and motive to intervene in Mexico, France was the weakest and would need their help in maintaining the Mexican regime. Napoleon III would move toward recognition of the Confederacy, Hershel V. Johnson told Davis in August, since he could not maintain his foothold in Mexico in the event that the Confederacy reunited with the United States. Johnson believed the Mexican empire Napoleon envisaged would be dependent on Confederate independence and support. Francophone opinion, centered in Louisiana, welcomed the chance to take advantage of cooperation with France in Mexico in order to deepen a political, cultural, and economic affinity they believed they had with the French. Historian Don Doyle stresses a strong bond between the Confederacy and Napoleon's schemes, going so far as the State Department developing a "Latin Strategy" subservient to the emperor's vision. There is some evidence for this contention. On February 21, Alfred G. Haley of Louisiana wrote to Davis and suggested an alliance with France, guaranteeing part of Mexico and in return for this aid allowing Confederate emigration; as a result, the Southerner will mingle with the "gallant Gaul in Mexico."[52]

However, while politicians welcomed a French-dominated southern neighbor in the short term, once the war was over this situation would change. Diplomats expected that a combination of their power and Napoleon's fickleness would mean the Confederacy would control Mexico in the future. On January 9, Keiley wrote to Benjamin that he believed Napoleon III desired "a great American friend to be the present defence of this colony [in Mexico]." This alliance would be temporary, and Keiley predicted that within five years, "we can purchase the supremacy of the western world at the cost of our friendship with the master of the Eastern." They had no doubt that the French opposed slavery. Even the Catholic Keiley, who probably approved of the religious motives of the French in their occupation of Mexico driving out secular liberals, had little emotional and long-term tie to Napoleon's "Grand Design for the Americas."[53]

A New World War against the Monroe Doctrine

In 1863, politicians cast the Confederate government's commercial and foreign policy in the broadest possible terms: it was committed to the promotion of free trade, competitive exploitation of undeveloped areas, and the consequent condemnation of nations protecting their own

spheres of interest. If the French occupation of Mexico temporarily supported Confederate objectives, U.S. intentions both at home and abroad
had the opposite effect. The State Department denounced the record of
U.S. policy in Latin America in general and in Mexico in particular. During 1863, the cornerstone of Confederate foreign policy became opposition to the Monroe Doctrine. Diplomats defined this policy as the U.S.
interdiction of European attempts to revive Latin American economies,
the blocking of free trade, and the imposition of inappropriate forms of
republican self-government on what planners deemed to be backward
peoples. The result, according to Confederate understanding, was that
successive U.S. administrations had consigned Latin American nations
to successive corrupt and anarchic regimes.[54]

Confederate optimists regarded U.S. adhesion to the Monroe Doctrine in the context of the latest apparent triumph of free trade—the
opening up of the China market in the aftermath of the Second Opium
War that had ended in 1860. "The Chinese walls of exclusiveness are falling in the extreme east amid the applause of all enlightened nations," the
Index's Paris correspondent boasted. However, the Lincoln administration's assertion of the Monroe Doctrine would mean the imposition of
U.S. commercial privileges across Latin America, the journalist added,
as "the American Democracy seeks to rebuild [barriers to free trade] in
the New World!" The correspondent believed the future of international
harmony, the world economy, and the political development of individual
nations were at stake. "Whilst the spirit of liberty and progress tends to
build together and unify modern societies," he continued, the "American
Republics seek to segregate them in savage isolation." Those planters and
politicians who believed in free trade found common ground with diplomats and clergy who resented the arrogant exceptionalism and providentialism in both manifest destiny and the Monroe Doctrine. Both groups
preferred the Confederacy to trade more with other nations, and slavery,
as well as commerce, would be safeguarded. The Monroe Doctrine was
an act of "delusive hope," Wiley declared, and Confederates "therefore
must repudiate the doctrine of one dominion for America, not simply
because we are no longer interested in it: we must repent of the sin of
having aided [when part of the Union] in nourishing this unholy lust
of Universal Control." Wiley considered religious-based expansionism to
be a movement of questionable morality.[55]

In December, the State Department's instructions for a commissioner
to Mexico City set out a commercial and political critique of the Monroe

Doctrine. Benjamin castigated the U.S. guarantee of republican governments in the Americas as tantamount to "assist the anarchists." He professed no interest in any interference in the mode of government to be chosen by the peoples of the Latin American nations and believed that international trade, if left to flourish, would bring the various polities of the Western Hemisphere into close cooperation. In the same month, Davis declared in his message to Congress: "Although preferring our own Government and institutions to those of other countries," Confederates had "no disposition to contest the exercise by them of the same right of self-government which we assert for ourselves." A "sincere and friendly interest in their prosperity" was all that his administration sought for Mexicans, Davis concluded; this outcome would be best achieved by "the continuance of those peaceful relations . . . on the frontier." Present conditions offered hope for the future, Davis insisted, noting "even a large development of the commerce already existing to the mutual advantage of the two countries."[56]

In 1863, political as well as commercial developments in Mexico appeared to be pointing toward a closer realignment between that country and the Confederacy. After the French army had entered Mexico City in July and Juárez fled, together with his liberal administration, Mexican conservatives established a regency pending the decision of the archduke whether to accept the crown. The regency made approaches to Richmond, and it was expected the future Emperor Maximilian would follow suit with Slidell in Paris, after the Austrian had consulted Napoleon III. In December, as a result of these promising expectations, the Confederate government secretly recommended to the Senate the appointment of an envoy to Mexico. The need for secrecy, according to Benjamin, was because of the "great danger that the U.S. would endeavor to defeat the object of the mission if known." As the instructions to the envoy make clear about the situation of the Confederacy and Mexico, "both states [are] united by a community of danger and interest."[57]

The Confederate government kept the appointment of its envoy secret because it wanted to keep its options open. Policymakers expected any revelation of Confederate friendship with the Mexican regime to be balanced by Union hostility, and Benjamin did not want to embarrass the regents. At the same time, members of the Davis administration did not want to preclude a negotiated peace with the United States. Looking forward to the result of what they were convinced would be the final 1864 campaign; Davis and Benjamin believed the United States "will be anxious to enter into a peace with the Confederacy on the basis of the Monroe Doctrine as one of the stipulations." A hostile Mexican-Union relationship served Confederate interests and improved the Confederacy's strategic position vis-à-vis the United States. If Mexico gravitated toward the Union, that would not only doom the chance to expand slavery southward but also would block Confederate access to the Pacific. With an eye on a Southern Pacific Railroad, Arizona delegate and would-be acquirer of Mexican and Indian lands, Malcolm Mac-Willie warned Davis that any alliance between Mexico and the United States would be "inimical to the interests of the Conf. States." Above all, "An imperative necessity will shortly exist for some such port in the Pacific," a Californian, Cameron Erskine Thom, spelled out in January, "to be occupied by another power than that of Lincoln."[58]

Working with Other Slaveholding Powers

The preservation and growth of slavery remained the objective of those who expected to migrate west and south after the war. The production and export of staple crops, dependent on slavery, continued to be integral to the foreign and economic policies of the government. Although mindful of the losses inflicted on slavery, especially in the lower Mississippi Valley, proslavery optimists maintained their confidence that it would survive and recover. They also hoped that in time slavery would resume its expansion and, to that end, were very concerned about Union plans for freed people to colonize Latin America. Expansionists remained fearful that not only the United States but also Britain and France were poised to impose their own unfree labor systems on the tropics. If taken, these steps would prevent the reintroduction of slavery into these regions. Slavery had to outcompete these alternative labor systems. The final element of Confederate proslavery policy was an effort to support the Spanish colonial regime in Cuba, believed to be vulnerable both to governmental instability in Madrid and pressure from the United States to emancipate its enslaved people.

J. Marshall McCue believed all other countries envied the Confederacy's perfection of a forced labor model. After all, not only was slavery competitive, but it also had sustained a war effort lasting two and half years. The war, the delegate told the Virginia assembly, amounted to a *"preservation of the institution of slavery,"* and Britain, France, and New England had been "disappointed in finding the institution [not as] an element of our weakness, as they hoped, but of our strength as they discovered." Therefore, these countries would make it their business both to undermine slavery and establish competitor forced-labor economies in the tropics. McCue was fond of asking for sacrifices from fellow Confederates, but there was no question, at least yet, of sacrificing slavery.[59]

Sustaining slavery abroad remained a desire for Confederates, as it had for southerners before the war. Hotze hoped to take advantage of a row between Britain and Brazil. He heard that the Brazilian minister had withdrawn from London "in consequence of the gross outrage perpetrated at Rio by the British Admiral under instructions from Lord Russell." As a result, he continued, "this suspension of diplomatic relations affords us a golden opportunity for establishing with the slave power of the southern hemisphere such relations as will bear most important fruit in the future." For now, however, Brazil remained unimportant as expansionists deemed slavery to be secure there—they had always wanted Brazil to be a "stable self generating slave society," and this policy objective remained that of the Confederacy.[60]

Diplomats considered slavery more vulnerable in Cuba and Puerto Rico than Brazil due to United States pressure on these Spanish colonies and signs of governmental instability in Madrid. Furthermore, the State Department still harbored hopes that Spain would reintroduce slavery into Santo Domingo, which, according to historian Wayne Bowen, was a belief shared by the Dominican rebels resisting the ongoing Spanish recolonization effort. These factors combined to render the support of Spain an important foreign policy objective. An opportunity for diplomats to increase their influence in Madrid and protect slavery in those islands arose with the January appointment of the pro-Confederacy captain general of Cuba as Spanish foreign minister. The agent in Havana, Charles Helm, reminded General Serrano about "the community of interests between the Confederacy and the Spanish possessions in the West Indies." Spain needed to act as the Confederacy's de facto representative among the Courts of Europe because "the interest of the south requires a slave power in Europe to cooperate with her in the protection of the peculiar institutions of the Confederate States, Cuba, Porto [sic] Rico, Cuba and Santo Domingo." In exchange for Spanish diplomatic support for the Confederacy in London and Paris, the Davis administration would protect slavery in the islands, as "our people will be as jealous of your rights in the West Indies as of their own at home." Diplomats deemed it essential to sustain slavery in the Spanish colonies in order to both have slavery existing under a foreign regime and have an advocate in Europe on behalf of the "slaveholding-interest."[61]

Support of Spain comprised part of a broader government objective of presenting the Confederacy as a partner with other nations in pursuit of joint interests, promoter of international commerce, and guarantor of global peace. In Benjamin's instructions to Slidell to serve as commissioner to Madrid in addition to his job in Paris, he argued that a close alliance made sense because, due to commerce and slavery, "relations are destined to be so intimate." Benjamin argued that the reciprocal action of Spain should be to recognize the independence of the Confederacy, not only on the basis of the shared interests of slavery and commerce, but also on the "gratitude and respect of mankind" and the "interests of a common humanity." The ending of "the war of extermination" and the creation of "cordial amity" with a Confederacy devoted to the peaceful development of its own natural resources would redound to Spain's glory, as well as that of the Confederacy.[62]

The secretary of state considered that the paramount interest of the Confederacy was to prevent Cuba from falling into the hands of the United States. Benjamin wrote that the Confederate government "cannot fail to foresee attempts by [the United States government] to seek elsewhere for acquisitions it has failed to receive from us." Benjamin cited as evidence for this Union covetousness the 1852 refusal of the United States secretary of state, Edward Everett, to add the signature of the United States to a proposed Tripartite Convention with Britain and France guaranteeing Spain's possession of Cuba. He hoped Slidell's presentation of an aggressive destabilizing United States would render Confederate friendship essential for Spanish policy in the Western Hemisphere. For its part, according to historian Wayne H. Bowen, the Spanish government chose neither to encourage nor discourage these overtures because it not only feared the United States but also expected—not without reason—that the Confederacy, if successful in the Civil War, would also seize Cuba.[63]

In 1863, Confederate ambitions had a greater reliance for their fulfillment on commercial growth and moral values, as opposed to military strength and territorial annexation. This recognition resulted from the circumstances at this juncture of the war, when the Confederacy's military weakness vis-à-vis the Union seemed to be ever more pronounced. These planning objectives, chosen as they were to garner allies, also made

sense. However, planners continued to be very confident both in the imminent prospect of peace and the accomplishment of their independence.
Not only these visions of the future of the Confederacy tied to what they
saw as the progress of civilization but also their expectations of commercial growth, moral uplift, and—when and where possible—territorial
expansion provided, they calculated, the true basis for an enduring national power.

Nevertheless, the pursuit of these expansive programs risked drawing
attention from the primary objective of supporting the war effort. As
a result of these competing pressures, expansionist ambitions remained
in place, especially to the West and South, but they became somewhat
less important as practical policy objectives. Serious military reverses in
Tennessee led to the U.S. Army of the Tennessee pressing into northern Georgia. At the same time, a growing financial crisis caused intense
problems for the government in Richmond. Decision-makers recognized
that the containment of the United States required more than appeals to
abstract goals and future prosperity, especially when the latter seemed
a very distant reality. On December 14, the old Whig North Carolina
politician Kenneth Rayner asked Judge Thomas Ruffin: "How can the
country stand the scarcity of this winter and next spring?" He did not expect Ruffin to answer the question because he added, "all knowledge on
the subject is experimental." A future worthy of such resilience might be
possible, but in order to achieve it the citizens of the Confederacy would
have to demonstrate a greater sense of purpose in 1864.[64]

5

A Conservative Future

JANUARY TO THE FALL OF 1864

DURING 1864, leading Confederates portrayed their nation as the bulwark of stability confronting destructive upheaval promised by a Union victory in the Civil War. They argued that the military deadlock in both Virginia and Georgia would lead to Lincoln's electoral defeat in November. These circumstances remained in place until November when U.S. General William T. Sherman commenced his advance from Atlanta, which coincided with the reelection of Lincoln. Until then, the solid immovable Confederate armies appeared to contrast with what Confederates regarded as the recklessly improvident, in terms of lives and money, and militarily incompetent offensives launched at the urging of the mob democracy of the Union.

The continued survival of the government into the fourth year of the war further elevated the meaning of their nation to leading Confederates. The institutions of the government represented a reassuring continuity all the way back to the promise of the Founding Fathers. During 1864, optimistic individuals maintained the government's role was to unleash the energies of the people—repudiating the course of the United States government, which had succumbed to despotism. At the same time, the strength of the future Confederacy was still based on the power of slavery and fortified by the stockpile of cotton.

Money, or lack thereof, mattered more than ever in 1864. The prior experience of rampant inflation together with serious privations that winter led to intense debates over two currency bills in Congress in May and June; this, in turn, amended thinking about the postwar Confederacy. Sound finances had to be the priority for the government, and planners for the new nation expressed remorse over the memory of the 1840s debt defaults by southern states. Diplomats tracked the performance of the Cotton Loan in London and Paris and compared it with the dollar—gold convertibility prices in New York. Such present-day preoccupations had future consequences for what planners wished the Confederate economy to become. They had to adjust their preferred vision of a world with nations connected by free trade and cooperative economies devoted to comparative advantage. Instead, with a more mercantilist way of thinking about the economy, the Confederacy aimed for a trade surplus, and hence a flow of gold and silver into Confederate coffers. Imports would be limited by the establishment of a significant manufacturing sector—economic planners not only sought to import goods and knowhow in order to boost wartime munitions production; they also consciously set about the development of new advanced industries.[1]

Electoral and military issues had to be resolved before any clarification of the future relations between the Confederacy and the United States. In terms of any territorial settlement, leading Confederates continued to resist any idea of *uti possidetis* (what you have you hold); aiming instead to recover lost land via postwar state conventions and even by military reconquest. At the same time, the imminence of the U.S. presidential elections meant the defeat of Lincoln would quickly deliver peace. Would-be Confederate negotiators reacted to this situation by debating the extent to which they should be magnanimous toward the Union in the context of what they believed to be a victory. Tactically, they wondered if they should try and help secure this outcome by actively seeking to boost the electoral fortunes of northern Democrats with offers of commercial and even military alliance. However, Davis knew that the biggest factor in the terms of any settlement with the United States government would be the fortunes of war delivered on the battlefield. If the armies held firm to their positions outside Atlanta and Petersburg, any outcome seemed possible.

The prospect of an early peace, together with a concurrent lowering of their ambition, meant planners dropped their lofty idealism and replaced it with what they believed to be practical realism as their guiding principle governing policy. The new sense of realism extended to what diplomats expected to be the nation's future foreign policy. Pragmatism characterized diplomats' behavior. They toyed with cooperating with the Union in dividing the Western Hemisphere through a joint sponsorship of the Monroe Doctrine. At the same time, however, politicians and diplomats also looked for chances to form coalitions against the United States. The approach by the Mexican regency at the end of 1863 raised hopes of a new ally, especially as evidence came in of apparent Union hostility to the regime of Emperor Maximilian. Regarding Cuba and other Latin American countries, as well as Mexico, politicians and diplomats sought to put in place alliances with the elites of European descent and then looked forward to additional support from migrating slaveholders once they had established colonies with their enslaved people across the hemisphere. Diplomats insisted these arrangements would be necessary to counter a United States government committed to the overthrow of these regimes. They claimed that not only did U.S. congressmen talk about their duties to export republicanism, but also into 1864 the Lincoln administration continued to approach these Latin American societies about the colonization of freed people—a more threatening prospect after the Union had committed for emancipation. These U.S. goals were to be apparently imposed in place of the carefully calibrated racial hierarchies of both Confederate and Latin American regimes.

The Confederacy represented a world vision profoundly at odds with those historians who argue the mid-nineteenth century witnessed the coming of "globalization." This period was a time when, according to world historian Chris Bayly, the birth of the "modern world" was well underway; a world of free and mobile labor, nations industrializing under protective trade barriers, and international relations managed by alliances between centralized nation-states dominated by cities. Confederates proposed instead a world order determined by the balance of power and where nations of a different sort played an important role in world affairs. These countries were characterized by rural and decentralized societies, dominated by commercial agriculture sustained by forced labor growing crops for export. Such polities were complementary to, rather than competing with, industrialized nations with whom they had reciprocal commercial relations dictated by the creed of free trade.[2]

The fact that diplomats both praised and excoriated the Monroe Doctrine suggested desperation characterized Confederate thinking about foreign policy. Nevertheless, a flexible approach perhaps suited a world then just becoming acquainted with Prussian prime minister Count Otto von Bismarck's ruthless exercise of realpolitik. Opportunism seemed to be the fashion for international relations. Confederates criticized U.S. policy in Latin America in part because of its incompetence; they argued that the Lincoln administration's support of republican oppositions in Mexico and elsewhere undermined the economies of those countries. At the same time, planners for the new nation also upheld certain principles as they charted a course for the future. Confederate foreign policymakers looked toward protection of vulnerable, "kindred," regimes in the Western Hemisphere, such as Maximilian's fragile empire in Mexico. This support would specifically apply to the slaveholding societies both in Brazil and—increasingly beleaguered, it appeared—Spain's colonial administrations of Cuba, Puerto Rico, and Santo Domingo. Diplomats had no doubt that slavery would be finished everywhere in the Western Hemisphere if the Union prevailed in the Civil War. They anticipated that proslavery thinking would then fit into a wider worldview. The State Department hoped that in the long term, the Confederacy would emerge from its present isolation as a member of an extended transatlantic entente with Britain, France, and Austria—a league that was committed to preserving the status quo in international relations, restoring the balance of power in Europe, and extending it to North America. Arrayed against this alliance would be those countries intent on changing the global order: Prussia, Russia, and the United States. In a world governed by national self-interest, it would be natural for countries with little in common domestically to act together in foreign policy.[3]

SLAVERY REMAINS THE FOUNDATION OF CONFEDERATE AMBITIONS

Historians tend to regard slavery as doomed by 1864 for three reasons: first, the inroads of the Union armies facilitating the mass escape of enslaved people; second, the loss of control over plantations by mistresses devoid of the necessary forces of coercion—namely white men of military age; and finally, the "go-slow" resistance and "silent sabotage" among even apparently loyal enslaved people. Yet slavery remained the foundation of optimists' ambitions for the postwar years, as the source of their power and their revolution. "The great State institution of the South was the true basis for such a government," Davis declared on September 30 in Columbus, Georgia. "A great law of nature pointed out a menial class, distinct from the governing class," and as a result of slavery's existence, "here then, and here only, every white man is truly, socially and politically equal to every other." Despite the beginning of debates over the enlistment of enslaved people, optimists remained confident that slavery would resume its growth after the war. At times and especially in places near to or under occupation by Union troops, some Confederates—for example, planters in the lower Mississippi Valley—considered adapting themselves to a postslavery society. Nevertheless, they also contradicted themselves in their attitudes and at other times were optimistic about slavery's future because they continued to believe in African Americans' loyalty, that the northern alternative of factory work was much worse, and that slavery must remain the basis of staple crop production.[4]

The Confederacy's strength was based, its advocates believed, on a superior system of labor. The contention that slavery attended to the welfare as well as the output of its workers meant proslavery theorists believed that patriarchal slavery worked better than factory systems, at least for staple crop production in hot and unhealthy climates. With the world apparently devolving into one governed by competition rather than cooperation among the powers, all advanced, ambitious civilizations, including the United States, would need some form of forced labor system. Otherwise free labor powers would be unable to participate in the contest over which nation or nations would control the extraction of staple crops in the subtropics and tropics. The conduct of northerners in occupied areas appeared to confirm this hypothesis. In March 1864, Confederate cavalry under Texan brigadier general Lawrence Sullivan Ross retook Yazoo City and other parts of the Yazoo Valley as far as Washington County, Mississippi. According to the acting British consul in Mobile, the cavalrymen discovered that after the fall of Vicksburg the previous summer, "the plantations were devastated and abandoned by the Confederates and the slaves were carried off by the U.S. troops." However, with neither planters nor slaves, northern speculators had arrived and reverted to neo-slavery work practices as they cultivated the "most productive" plantations with "slaves, stolen from various planters on the first invasion."[5]

Optimists believed slavery would thrive in the future. Confederate-managed slavery was the most effective form of labor system in the region because, as the New Orleans correspondent of the *Index* insisted, the northern speculators were too exploitative of the slaves and careless of the working environment, especially about disease. "The condition of the slaves on the United States Government Plantations is sad beyond expression," the journalist reported, adding that in "contrast to the mild paternal government of the planters—the negro is disappearing like the Indian . . . the smallpox is raging on the plantations of Bayou lafourche [sic]." Prominent journalist John Tyler Jr., writing in February 1864 for *De Bow's Review*, saw this situation as reflecting the war aims of New Englanders. He had long singled out Yankees for their apparent Puritan intolerance, hypocrisy, and willingness to countenance social subversion. Tyler charged that these wartime speculators planned "emancipation and the apprentice system of negro labor" thereby "leading to the reopening of the slave trade disguised as apprentice trade." Charles S. Morehead, a former governor of Kentucky, contended that northern abolitionists were devoid of any genuine feeling of sympathy for African Americans, whom they simply wished to conscript into their new, more oppressive, but also inefficient labor model.[6]

Morehead also argued that African Americans were known to be incapable of thriving in free labor conditions, and therefore he accused Federals of intending the eventual extermination of the African race in the Americas. Meanwhile, the success of the slavery-based Confederate economy would demonstrate to the French and British how wrong their governments were to emancipate the slaves in the West Indies. According to historian Matthew Karp, antebellum southerners frequently referred to the decline of the economies of the European colonies in the West Indies as proof of the failure of Africans to successfully transition from slavery to freedom. As a result, colonial authorities were looking for fresh supplies of labor and even considering the reintroduction of coerced systems of control.[7]

Confederate credit and commerce both rested on slavery because of the security provided by possession of the stockpile of cotton the slaves had produced. Once the war was over, this store would be exported, easily displacing from overseas markets what Tyler termed the "coarser material from India." Price as well as quality underpinned Confederate cotton's market superiority. "If the American war has proved anything," Hotze observed, "it certainly has proved that no cotton country can compete with America." Consequently, "peace in America will produce a genuine and well-founded panic amongst non American growers . . . the supplies from India etc., will be instantly checked, they depend on high prices." Hotze expected that the Confederate cotton growers would resume their domination of the market after the war. As much as Hotze approved of British rule in India on racial grounds, it was important to

Confederate observers of the Raj that Confederate cotton production prevailed over that of India as a vindication of slavery around the world over "the abolitionist empire."[8]

In 1864, planners of the Confederate nation remained in awe of the power of their commerce. Free trade in the future was the way this commerce would serve the Confederate people. Davis was a vigorous proponent of government legislation in wartime, but he looked forward to laissez-faire as underpinning the future commercial relations of the Confederacy. "With peace and freedom a glorious career opens for these Confederate States," he told a crowd in Augusta, Georgia, on October 3. For the people would be free of tariffs and so "Relieved from class legislation," Davis continued, "free from taxes—indirect it is true, but imposed by your rulers for twenty years past." The Jacksonian Democrat claimed it was the economic and social policies of the Whig administration of 1840 that began the oppression of the South. "No longer subject to Northern speculators, grinders in the faces of the poor, and deniers of the rights of men," the president assured the citizens, "you will start forward in the brightest of futures." The removal of the burdens imposed by tariffs and the absence of subsidized northern capitalist competition would lead to a prosperous outcome for the Confederacy.[9]

Such a future was dependent on cotton production. The staple crop remained what its proponents regarded as the tangible gift of the Confederacy to the world. It was a "true and remarkable" fact, Hotze wrote, still in uncritical loyalty to King Cotton, "that all the productions of the southern states conduce to the moral and physical well being of man." As a result, the "interests of the world coincide with the dictates of law, justice and humanity." Confederates believed any relations they were to have with other powers were to be determined by the primacy of economic self-interest combined with lingering antislavery prejudice and distrust of the Confederate republican mission; therefore, cotton exports, which promised to better the human condition, would offset international distrust and jealousy of the Confederacy's global mission.[10]

A DEGREE OF PROTECTION

The world would be more competitive than cooperative for the Confederacy than its exponents had earlier hoped, and this reality had to be reflected in national planning. In July, in his re-launched periodical, *De Bow's Review*, De Bow predicted Confederate exports would be worth five hundred million dollars. The Confederacy needed to be a naval power in order to protect this overseas commerce. The motives for a strong navy would resemble those needs of a merchant marine that Alfred Thayer Mahan would see as essential in the late nineteenth century, as well as the proslavery and projection of power considerations that historian Matthew Karp argues constituted antebellum "southern navalism." Confederate navalists deemed possession of a fleet of ironclads as essential to combat the Union at sea and to be a great power in the future. Despite the significant obstacles caused by iron shortages at home and difficulties in obtaining supplies through the blockade from Europe, planners were cheered that Navy Secretary Stephen Mallory had made encouraging progress in wartime. The acting British consul from his observations both in Charleston and Wilmington, together with a report made to Congress on naval management, informed British foreign secretary Lord Russell that there was "evidence of the progress towards construction of a national navy."[11]

The frustrations diplomats experienced in their attempts to obtain ironclad vessels from Europe, together with the ever-tightening blockade, meant they became more convinced in 1864 on the vital need for a strong navy in future. Napoleon III's decision to terminate the Confederate shipbuilding program, in order to obtain recognition by the U.S. government—or at least its toleration—of his Mexican puppet regime, was a lesson especially meaningful for the Confederate commissioner in Paris. "When the war shall have ceased," Slidell recommended to Benjamin on June 2, "one of our earliest cares should be to lay the foundation of a respectable navy." Confederates, he continued, had to abandon the "Arcadian dreams of following undisturbed the peaceful pursuits of agriculture." Instead, Slidell concluded, "The condition of national existences now is capacity of each to defend itself and inflict injury on others." Hence in this otherwise anarchic world of competing nation-states, a conservative power would need a strong navy as the necessary counterpoint to the balance of power structure to provide security on land.[12]

Diplomats believed their state had to be a naval power because of geography, territorial ambitions, and strategic considerations. "The Confederate States must have a navy in same proportion to the magnificent sweep of gulf and ocean coast," Hotze insisted on June 23. In Halifax, Nova Scotia, Holcombe added that "in a war like the present our govt. ought never to yield, that the citizens of a belligerent state, with or without a commission may capture enemies property at sea." Therefore, Holze concluded that it was "of the utmost importance that the Confederate

States has a powerful navy." Commercial planners looked forward to a "blue water" offensive strategy overseas to protect and expand markets combined with defense at home and a conservative foreign policy.[13]

The imminence of peace and with its pressing financial liabilities led to planners taking inventories of the nation's assets. Even though the Union had occupied large tracts of the Deep South by 1864 and with the damage inevitably sustained by prolonged storage, they estimated the cotton stored in the Confederacy to be huge, three million bales according to the *Index* on August 25. Given this amount of cotton would be worth as much as six hundred million dollars, this calculation enabled James D. B. De Bow boldly to declare, "We care not what the amount of debt" the government would hold at the war's end. He estimated the debt may be as much as two billion dollars; but according to DeBow, its interest would be easily paid by levying a duty of five cents per pound on exports of cotton. In addition, De Bow expected imports of manufactured goods to be subject to a 20 percent tariff, which would net, together with the cotton duty, the necessary hundred million dollars income to pay off the debt at 5 percent interest per annum. Hotze suggested the cotton store be nationalized and exported to pay off the interest. "Our resources, then, properly husbanded and applied would be virtually inexhaustible," he told Benjamin on January 16. "At the present rate of exportation through the blockade, say 150,000 per annum," he estimated, then "it would take 20 years to export the cotton now in the Confederate States." With effective government regulation, Confederates believed that the "Cotton Standard" would become the Confederacy's own gold standard.[14]

Sound finance mattered; it would determine the future reputation of the Confederacy. John J. McRae, former Mississippi governor, U.S. congressman, and prominent proponent of expansion into the Caribbean, also believed in the importance of financial planning. Acting on the instructions of the new treasury secretary, George Trenholm, McRae served as president of a meeting tasked with setting wartime prices and taming rampant wartime inflation. In September 1864, addressing this convention of the commissioners of appraisement held in Montgomery, McCrae declared that solvency mattered because "the happiness and welfare of our people after the war are too deeply involved." Old arguments about northern financial discrimination in the antebellum United States provided evidence of Confederate financial potential. "Why should our ability to bear this burden be doubted?" McRae asked, "Before this war, it was alleged (and my opinion with great truth) that a sum fully as great as this [estimated interest on the debt] was annually paid in tribute to the northern states. Why should it not be paid with equal ease to our own government?" The doubts had arisen because evidence of Confederate fiscal incompetence about the war, such as rampant inflation and arrears in army pay, had undermined faith in the government's long-term creditworthiness.[15]

Hence the importance of planning for the future in order to convince the people of the government's ability to pay off the debt, even if that also meant amending the vision of free trade based on comparative advantage. After the war, Representative Eli K. Bruce of Kentucky predicted, the Confederacy would run a trade surplus based on exportations of cotton and a more self-sufficient economy. He forecasted that Confederate bonds would appreciate postwar because "the exchange of the world will be necessarily and irrevocably turned in favor of the Confederate States." Foreign investors would then flock in to buy securities and beat up the price of the bonds as "countries must provide these bonds rather than exhaust themselves of their coin." The "excessive exportations" to Europe from the postwar Confederacy, Bruce explained, would "give us control of the coin of the world for all time to come." Rather than planning an economy based on roughly equivalent imports and exports, as they had earlier done, optimists expected to run a trade surplus and hence build up reserves of gold.[16]

Even though imports in the future would be limited in volume by a combination of duties and increased domestic production, planners still expected that their state would rapidly become a central participant in the international economy. Bruce anticipated that the government could "resume specie payments . . . in less than six months after the ratification of a treaty of peace." The reason for this optimism was the belief that, as Hotze observed, "a single year's cotton crop will form the basis of a credit in the foreign specie market." This emphasis on sound finance, in conjunction with robust military performance, would launch the *Sentinel's* vision of the postwar Confederacy, which "must become the wealthiest nation and people."[17]

Economic planners became aware that, as part of being a future great power, the Confederacy needed to be more self-sufficient, less vulnerable to an enemy blockade, and less dependent on the whims of outside markets. In looking to a future of trade surpluses, individuals wanted a partially industrialized, mixed economy in order to limit imports. As "manufactured products of the old government reached two thousand million dollars," De Bow predicted, on that basis the future Confederate industrial sector would be significant in size. "Say ours after peace be half that sum," he ventured, because "who can doubt that they will reach one quarter," for "peace will bring a tenfold increase in our industry." Planners did not expect the Confederacy to industrialize at once during the postwar period. Even with war mobilization, the economy remained predominantly agricultural, and these individuals expected that most of those workers temporarily involved in war industries would revert, temporarily at least, to peacetime agricultural occupations after the war.[18]

Optimists' confidence in this postwar vision of industrialization was sustained by the achievements during the war and how these were conceived of as a prelude for what was to come. "The progress under these difficulties and peculiarities in the Confederacy is therefore gratifying," declared Edward Keatinge and Thomas A. Ball, the engravers and printers of Confederate treasury notes, and they looked forward to "when the clouds of war have dissipated, [and] industry takes its legitimate rank." The foundations for this role of industry were laid in 1864: first, from changes within the Confederacy itself; second, from interaction with other economies, principally Britain; and third, underpinning the above, from growing consciousness of the Industrial Revolution, which had now spread to North America, as part of global change.[19]

There were incremental changes suggesting an incipient Industrial Revolution taking place in the Confederacy that drew notice from commentators. Observers, such as the British consul at Galveston, Arthur J. Lynn, noted the developments that were ongoing with the textile industry in Texas. Confederate appreciation about the importance of Atlanta reflected a growing awareness, as Kenneth Rayner wrote from Raleigh, North Carolina, in July, of "our invaluable foundries, manufactories &c." The old Whig welcomed industrialization as what he regarded as evidence of conservative progress. By January 1864, there was "more abundant production and a far greater prospect of military sufficiency than we have yet enjoyed," a writer for the Richmond Examiner declared in reference to mining across the Confederacy. The journalist added that this plenty was the case "despite paucity of laborers fluctuating prices and temporary occupancy by the enemy of districts with richest deposits."[20]

Despite these advances, Confederate boosters knew about the gap in industrial development between their country and the Union and Britain. This unease meant Thomas W. Bulitt, a Kentucky prisoner of war, began to stress—in his postwar plans that he wrote up in his diary—the importance of a technical education and the need to learn about and implement more advanced industrial practices. Similar thinking may have provided some rationale for congressional proposals at the same time to develop a system of polytechnics. Science subordinated nature to man, Bulitt argued, "rendering possible the grandest schemes for the development of national resources for alleviating the wants & supplying the comforts of life." More than that, science, by "bringing into combination the highest moral powers and physical," "dignify the age & people" as "the central & controlling force in the progressive civilization of modern times." Hence individuals at both state and national levels had to seize the opportunities offered by the Industrial Revolution lest the Confederacy fell further behind.[21]

Manufacturers undertook steps that addressed immediate wartime needs and paved the way for longer-term industrialization. Captain Edward R. Archer's father, Dr. Robert Archer, was a director of the Tredegar Ironworks in Richmond, while the younger Archer had served as an apprentice there before leaving to serve first in the U.S. and then in the Confederate navy. In March, while in Britain for the launch of the Virginia Volunteer Navy, Captain Archer also found time to visit the Cyclops iron and steel Bessemer furnace in Sheffield as the guest of the director, George Wilson. With the valuable information Archer had gathered, and sent as detailed drawings to his father to show him the advanced process of steel manufacture, he predicted there would soon be a "revolution at Tredegar." Tredegar's boss, Joseph Reid Anderson, who had married Archer's sister, wrote to Davis asking that a soldier, James L. Patton, be detached to Tredegar for two years in order that he go to Europe to procure vital supplies. Davis agreed that this matter was of "such importance" to "justify compliance." Confederates also needed to develop an advanced textile industry; a correspondent told Davis on July 5 that he was going to join the cotton trade expert, George McHenry, in Britain to gather intelligence "with a view to the erection of a modern Cotton Mill in the Southern States at the earliest possible period."[22]

Politicians and railroad promoters understood that actions taken now might change the postwar Confederate economy. On January 31, the president of the Alabama Coal Company Railroad, John R. Kenan, wrote to his brother, North Carolinian representative Owen Rand Kenan, from Kenan Plantation near Selma, Alabama, to tell him that his son, John Jr., had entered claims in Tuscaloosa for coal and iron mines. This move was significant because, "Should we be successful in this revolution the mineral lands in Shelby and Bibb county will be immensely valuable and John is securing as much of it as he can." Industrialization would change the economy from the Deep South to the Border South. During the same month in Richmond, the exiled Maryland pamphleteer W. Jefferson Buchanan predicted that with the steady disappearance of slavery from his home state, there would be "room for the new interest of manufacturing," if that state joined the Confederacy. He forecast rapid growth as a result: "In twenty years, Maryland will outstrip the industry and wealth in manufacturers that Massachusetts accumulated for a century."[23]

Optimists placed this accelerating Industrial Revolution in the Confederacy in a wider context, as part of broader hemispheric and global changes, which in turn would determine their and the nation's future. Buchanan stated that "a grand revolution in the industrial system of America" was now underway. From London, Hotze believed that there was a global Industrial Revolution in progress; he noted that "in the past forty years steam electricity mechanism have realized miracles of swiftness, accuracy, saving of labor, and of time—a one hundred fold increasing of man's power to develop the resources of the soil." In Buchanan's case for Maryland to be included in the Confederacy, he argued that there was a vital "need of the South for a manufacturing locale" because industrialization meant "a complete change." For Buchanan, Hotze, and others, the appeal of rapid industrialization driven by the war was that it offered the chance for the nation, as well as the individual, to "make himself over." Even at their most conservative, planners for the future Confederacy still believed they could manage and embrace change.[24]

HOLDING OFF—OR DOING BUSINESS WITH—THE UNION

Ambitious individuals expected peace with the United States by the end of 1864. The last campaign of the war would conclude by the time of the November presidential election. An immediate armistice would swiftly take place once news of Lincoln's expected defeat had reached the front. Topics, such as whether Union troops would voluntarily withdraw from tracts of land in the Confederacy they had occupied, that in hindsight appear completely delusional to historians seemed most important to planners in early 1864. For these journalists and politicians, Federal behavior on those points would determine the future relations between the United States and the Confederacy, even influencing the anticipated level of involvement by the great powers of Europe in North American diplomacy after the war.

If the Union and Confederacy were to peacefully coexist in the future, there had to be no ambiguity about the northern boundary of the Confederacy. Unlike the southern border, whose fluidity reflected Confederate imperial ambitions southward, the frontier with the United States had to be both demarcated and encompass all slave states in the Confederacy, if their citizens so wished in states' conventions. The agreement also had to be thrashed out between the United States and Confederacy. Otherwise, as John Tyler had made clear in the July *De Bow's Review*, any settlement would be akin to those previously proposed by would-be European mediators and that meant the adoption of the concept of *uti possidetis*. Tyler contended that if this principle had been followed, the "Confederacy would be denuded of all the states and territory that the North shall have grasped and now possess." To bring the British and French in now, Tyler concluded, would mean "foreign diplomacy will bind us where the arms of the enemy have placed us." Not only would the Confederacy either become a rump state as a result of such a process or cease to have an independent national existence, but also adopting such a principle to be used in international relations would lead to anarchy.[25]

Civilized nations could not rely on force of arms to determine their territorial limits. Those who planned a viable postwar Confederacy with good relations with Federals hoped that resolutions passed at states' conventions would be the means of recovering occupied lands. Politicians and diplomats who advocated some sort of immediate negotiation with the United States, perhaps seeking to influence the presidential election there, championed this method. "Let all armed force be withdrawn" to initiate the process, Vice President Stephens explained in a speech on March 16, "and let that sovereign will be fairly expressed at the ballot box by the legal voters," and so: "Let each state have and freely exercise the right to determine its own destiny in its own way." Confederates were confident that the result of any such ballot would be the election of states' delegates in their favor. The verdict of the people had to be accepted, whatever the outcome. Therefore, in the event that, even "with this great truth ever before them a majority of her people should prefer despotism to liberty," then, if necessary, permit "a wayward sister [to] depart in peace."[26]

During 1864, planners understood that the performance of Confederate armies in that year's campaigning season would determine the U.S. government's willingness to negotiate. Those individuals—led by Robert E. Lee—and who in any event doubted the viability of peace negotiations with the Federals on the grounds of public opinion in the North, stressed the need to obtain recognition of territorial integrity by victory on the battlefield. "Success in resisting the chief armies of the enemy will enable us more easily to recover the country now occupied by him," the commander of the Army of Northern Virginia told Davis on May 5 at the start of the Overland Campaign, "if indeed he do not voluntarily relinquish it." After all, "federal occupancy is not conquest" and would "disappear like a mist if once his main army were so effectually driven from the field," and the temporary reality of a "precarious military tenure" would be abruptly revealed. Any military victory, even if not leading to a retreat of Union forces, would lead to an acceptance of Confederate moral claim to the territory by U.S. soldiers, which would compel their voluntary evacuation from all the South.[27]

Confederates believed in this fragile Union military occupation of parts of their nation because they insisted that the population remained loyal to the Confederacy. Confederate incursions behind Union military lines appeared to encourage this belief, notwithstanding the earlier disappointments during the autumn of 1862 in both Maryland and Kentucky. By 1864, with increased Union military exactions on the population and emancipation a U.S. government policy wherever Union forces reached, Confederates had become more confident that the inhabitants under Union control would not waver in their long-term commitment to returning to Confederate rule. When William Henry Mayo passed through Leesburg on July 16, as General Jubal Early's Army of the Valley returned from shelling Washington, he was pleased to witness, on his twenty-first birthday, the "cheers and waving of handkerchiefs from pretty ladies." This scene was proof that "this part [of Virginia] is noted for its loyalty to the Southy," Mayo observed, "notwithstanding they are mostly within the Yankee lines."[28]

Moreover, until fall 1864, Confederates assumed that their armies were on the brink of a substantial recovery of territory. This upturn promised to be especially true in the Southwest and resulted according to commentators in the most extensive change in the map of control since the summer of 1862. Even before the defeat of the Union general Nathaniel P. Banks by Confederate general Richard Taylor at Mansfield,

Louisiana, on April 8, Confederates keenly anticipated such successes. On March 21, the New Orleans correspondent of the *Index* looked toward the Southwest for where "a better opportunity for offensive operations will hardly present itself during the year." These actions were intended to ensure that "the navigation of the Mississippi [would be] again closed" to the Union, as Memphis, Vicksburg, Port Hudson, and "even" New Orleans "may be wrested from them for ever." On July 23, Mayo heard rumors in Winchester that Taylor had indeed recaptured New Orleans. Confederates clung onto their hopes of progress in the Southwest until well into the autumn of 1864.[29]

Northern allies would assist in the realization of this ambitious vision. Buoyed by their military effort in the spring and expecting that therefore Lincoln would lose the election, ambitious planners anticipated a powerful conservative party would demand peace and accept separation, as opposed to accept peace and demand reunion. Politicians began to speculate about the implications for the future Confederacy in the wake of an electoral triumph of this peace party in the Union. Once the United States government recognized Confederate peace commissioners and an armistice was established, James L. Orr in the Senate and Henry S. Foote in the House declared on June 2, "it is confidently believed would eventuate in the restoration of peaceful and amicable relations between those now waging war upon each other." Foote's choice of the word "restoration" was ambiguous, but he was not alone in predicting a glorious future as the result of a peace party triumph in the elections, even if, in the summer of 1864, the precise relationship between North and South postwar had to be left vague for the sake of Democrat Party support in the Federal electorate.[30]

In order to boost Peace Democrats, Davis and his supporters resurrected the argument, common in early 1861, that the Union would be better off without the southern states. They argued both North and South would regain in separation the domestic racial and commercial harmony that apparently prevailed during the early republic. On April 28, Hotze argued, "The loss of the southern territory will diminish nothing of splendor of that destiny which the Yankees lay claim . . . nor dim the brightness of their future." To the contrary, there would be a greater prosperity for the Union arising from separation because of the "confinement of their energies to a climate where whites can work without injury and without competition." Separation would rid the Union of slavery and render the wages of free white labor safe from African American competition, which would now be restricted to the Confederacy. With a conservative peace movement in office, "proximity and geography would secure to the north if ever a good understanding should be established a large and profitable trade with the south." The economies of the Union and Confederacy would be closely interconnected, even interdependent. Yet the war party threatened to jeopardize this relationship, "if they risk losing southern trade it is because they resisted southern political severance not because of it." This unnatural outcome would be easily avoided. A Peace Democrat administration "ought not to ask for more," Hotze concluded, with a warning to conservative believers in reunion.[31]

Once the Union agreed to be the first country to recognize Confederate independence, diplomats promised to be magnanimous, for they knew that such a concession would be unwillingly given, the result of domestic contention. "The present state of northern finances, and the fierce and passionate dissensions . . . among the northern people," Benjamin told Slidell on July 12, meant that "the first recognition of the Confederacy will come from our enemies." The State Department considered offering a commercial pact as an incentive to Union peacemakers. Politicians also had to consider both constitutional implications of such concessions and the consequences for their future. Davis insisted there could be no compromise on independence; but as he told Senator Herschel V. Johnson of Georgia, he too wished to support the peace party. Davis added that northerners then "would much more fully realize the blessings of peace, and much more numerously sustain the policy of stopping the war." Considering what terms would be acceptable, Davis vaguely wanted an outcome that reconciled "the peaceful solution of the questions at issue and the future obligations to our States and people."[32]

Davis believed that an offer of eventual closer relations, especially economic ties, would act as a sufficient inducement for the United States government to seek peace. During unofficial Confederate-Union meetings that summer, speculation about the future of the Confederacy and its relations with the Union grew most intense. Two northern clerics, James R. Gilmore and James F. Jaquess, visited Richmond in July; the following month, former Confederate senator Clement C. Clay of Alabama and others met Horace Greeley, editor of the *New York Tribune*, at the Canadian side of the Niagara Falls. In Richmond, Davis told the northern emissaries on July 17, "there are essential differences between the North and the South that will, however the war may end, make them two nations." In part, the deepening conflict was to blame for these

differences, as Davis asked them: "If you enter my house and drive me
out of it, am I not your natural enemy?" Memories would only slowly
fade because the Union was sowing "such bitterness" that "our children
may forget this war, but *we* cannot." To support an eventual reconciliation these visits needed to be repeated, Davis told the clergymen, as
"your coming may lead to a more frequent and more friendly intercourse
between the North and the South." Perhaps a commercial treaty, at most,
could be negotiated between the two.[33]

Ambitious Confederates recognized that a free-trade agreement
would not be enough to provide security from the Union. The Richmond
newspaper closest to the Davis administration hoped that the political
map of North America would be decisively changed in the Confederacy's
favor. The *Sentinel* speculated that the reconstruction of a southern-
dominated Union required the expulsion of New England. At the same
time, advocates of a postwar powerful Confederacy depended for their
vision on the separation of the midwestern states from the rump of the
United States. In both cases, they recognized that as a "consolidated
Government," the Union in 1864 was too powerful to be contained by
even an expansive Confederacy alone. Hence the Union needed to be
broken up.[34]

Some Confederate observers believed that opposition to Lincoln's tyrannical rule and abolitionism was acute in the Midwest and went beyond politics as usual. By the summer of 1864, in the context of military
successes both secured and anticipated and the approaching election,
planners of the Confederacy hoped for the emergence of an allied nation in North America based on a shared value of liberty. Exiled Kentuckians understood the 'liberation' of their own state from the Union as
intimately tied up with issue of Midwest secession. There was a "vigorous and rapidly growing party in the northwest for a separate republic,"
Kentuckian representative Eli Bruce told the House on the June 9 and
10, "which will form a close alliance with the Confederates States to fight
a common foe—the enemy of constitutional government and mankind."
The perceived radicalization of the Lincoln administration, with emancipation and the increasing deployment of African American soldiers, together with the rhetoric accompanying the approach of the presidential
elections, appeared proof of both the parallel failure of democracy and
the imminence of a ruinous race war. Bruce was "willing to visit Canada,"
Richard Hawes, a former governor of Kentucky, told Davis, in part "to
carry out operations" aimed at "electing a Democrat president." Bruce

would also pursue the "most material fruits," meaning encouraging secession of one or more Midwest states, which, Hawes added, were "better
for us."[35]

To Confederate planners, Midwest secession was not only about an
election; it was also a continuation of the revolution that secessionists
had started in 1860. Hotze welcomed the prospect that the Midwest was
finally awakening to a "consideration of its real interests" and the "ab-
surdity of the part it has hitherto played." He claimed that most of the
citizens of Ohio, Illinois, and Indiana have "no interest in subduing or
wasting the South and a very strong interest in resisting and humbling
the East." From a future perspective, Hotze speculated, historians would
see that the election in November "marks a transfer of electoral power
from the older states," providing proof of the "decadence of New England
and aggrandizement of the West." In this context, Hotze's northwestern confederacy would have an additional purpose to weaken the Union
and establish a balance of power involving Canada and Mexico as well as
the Confederacy. Both the Confederacy and Canada would also benefit
by the carrying trade of this landlocked nation. On June 23, the *Index*
argued that the Midwest's "true avenues of its commerce will flow past
Quebec and New Orleans."[36]

Planners knew that economic inducements were not sufficient on
their own to determine outcomes; they hoped that ideological bonds
would assist the Confederacy, as they conceived the new midwestern
confederacy to be an ally to help safeguard republicanism. John Tyler Jr.
wrote that midwesterners "realize they cannot afford the subjugation of
the South," and the "conservative elements fear the permanent subversion
of government and loss of liberty." On June 28, in a pamphlet titled *Rebellion in the North*, an anonymous writer declared that the "time has come
[for Indiana, Ohio and Illinois] to free itself of usurpations and tyranny."
On August 11, Clay told Benjamin that he regarded midwesterners as
"natural allies and as champions of State Rights and of popular liberty."
Deep-seated republicanism, indifference to slavery, and predominance of
economic motives in pursuing the contest meant the Midwest would,
optimists believed, be amenable to negotiation with the Confederacy.[37]

The prospect of a new republic, or at least a serious rebellion against
Lincoln, appeared tantalizingly close to those individuals who wished it
to happen. Proponents insisted one more Confederate military success
in the West would trigger the underground movement to emerge and
change everything. Clay told Benjamin on August 11 that the Midwest

would rise "if our armies occupied any states north of the Ohio for a month or even a week." A day later, Kentuckian Austin H. Price concurred with a similar proviso, suggesting to Davis that the Confederacy "[lend] support" and send troops to Missouri and Kentucky. The following month, with Sherman now in Atlanta, Jacob Thompson—another Niagara Falls attendee—was less ambitious for Confederate arms, but he still believed there was merit in the "application of proper stimulants." "There can be no question that there is a strong revolutionary element in the Northern & Western States, if we can hold our own" on the battlefield. If that military deadlock continued to be sustained, even in the event of Lincoln's reelection, "the violent feeling will blow up."[38]

Nevertheless, a combination of tyranny and apathy might keep the free states united. Planners pondered what further concessions beyond reciprocal trade and appeals to a shared ideology would be necessary to either encourage separatist movements or establish an agreement with the Union that offered protection for Confederates to pursue their ambitions. At the Niagara Falls conference, the unofficial Confederate delegation tried to be as accommodating as possible to perceived Union sensibilities. The Confederate position had to be left in a form that "would be most valuable to the friends of Peace in the North and West," Clay explained to Davis on July 25, for "they hug the idea of reunion would follow peace at no distant period." Contrary to northern press reports, there was no proposal for reunion from the Confederate delegation, Clay reassured Benjamin on August 11, "but I think the South will agree to an armistice of six or more months and to a treaty of amity and commerce." Any consequent treaty between Union and Confederacy would be ambitious in scope and would be achieved by "securing peculiar and exclusive privileges to both sections," which meant the retention of slavery in one and its exclusion in the other. Moreover, the treaty might have military and foreign policy components added later for it held open "possibly to an alliance defensive, or even, for some purposes, both defensive and offensive." These diplomats conceded the balance of power in North America, in order to participate in a joint revolutionary "American Foreign Policy," which aimed at ejecting Europeans and monarchies from Mexico, Canada, and Cuba.[39]

The negotiators at Niagara Falls accepted a qualification on Confederate independence, at least in terms of its external relations, for there would be not just "amity," but an "identical foreign policy." Policymaking would be conducted by a federal institution composed of representatives of the "twin confederacies." The pro–Davis administration *Richmond Sentinel* did not go so far as Clay in looking for an arrangement that promised to be "morally and physically stronger than the old Union"; nevertheless it also commented that provided this supervisory body offered "us something that will preserve equal rights in the Union," it may well be acceptable to Confederates, A new imperialist Union, committed to territorial growth in all directions, offered Confederates a chance to realize many of their ambitions for slavery and commercial expansion. At the same time, any federal government had to be sufficiently weak to preclude any interference with slavery and other Confederate priorities.[40]

The idea of a loose confederation between the North and South had its attractions even for ambitious planners in the late summer of 1864, especially if southerners led it. Some believed northern Democrats wanted southern leadership. On August 30, New York Democrat Samuel J. Anderson told Davis, "the northern mind, as a whole, is in an extremely malleable condition," and with Confederate military successes, "they pant and sigh for the restoration" of the southern leadership of the Union, being fully conscious of how it led the Union before 1860. Anderson believed the Democratic Party's presidential candidate, George B. McClellan, was a doughface who would accept reunion on the basis of southern sectional dominance. Anderson warned it was a fleeting opportunity, and if it was rejected, the Confederates faced a "war with *a united North*. Then would ensue a reign of terror compared with which Lincoln's impressments would be mild and merciful." With Atlanta's fate still in the balance and the Democratic Party convention meeting in Chicago, it seemed that Confederates needed to hold on and wait for President-elect McClellan's proposals.[41]

Some planners advocated a postwar constitutional convention of all states that would result in a new all-American confederation. A new or much amended constitution would provide an orderly way to safeguard Confederate autonomy while, they believed, being also acceptable to many Democrats. After all, a vague pledge to summon a convention had been included in McClellan's election platform. On September 22, the champion of antebellum manifest destiny, John L. O'Sullivan, asked Davis to help him be elected a delegate to a convention McClellan planned to call on his election. "I think such a body could elaborate a new system which, with complete sectional autonomy and substantial independence, would constitute a true compact of federation." Nevertheless, this "system" would amount to a compromise that many Confederates would dislike. On September 12, the former interior secretary in the Buchanan administration and Mississippi political rival of the president, Jacob Thompson, agreed with O'Sullivan; but he also warned Davis, as a result of such negotiations, that the best outcome that could be hoped for was that "we could be one people militarily & as far as practicable commercially." Another opponent of Davis's, representative William W. Boyce of South Carolina, suggested that prior to holding negotiations, Confederates should militarily improve their bargaining position and "fortify if you can by victories." Military successes would help in any negotiation to secure the best future outcome for the Confederacy.[42]

DEFINING THE CONFEDERATE NEGOTIATING PARTNER

As part of their opening gambit in any negotiation with the Union and to provide gateways for the new nation to Pacific markets and northwestern Mexico, Confederate planners continued to assert the inclusion of Indian Territory, Arizona, and New Mexico in the Confederacy. According to historian Michael T. Bernath, geographers John Rice and Miranda Moore sought in their textbook published in 1864 to instill national pride by lauding the Confederate political system, catalog its resources, celebrate wartime achievements, and predict still greater accomplishments to come. They reinforced the plausibility of these expectations by, in Bernath's words, "optimistically including" Missouri, Kentucky, New Mexico, and Arizona within the limits of the Confederacy. Scholars of Confederate printing and publishing note that 1864 was the peak year for the publication of new periodicals and textbooks. Individuals at the time projected these increases to continue into the future. Above all were the huge sales of Augusta Jane Evans's *Macaria*, again published in Richmond during 1864, which conveyed an image of a grand, even imperial, future Confederacy, one well worth incurring sacrifice by men and women in the present.[43]

The strength of Confederate cultural demands for the Southwest coexisted with a suspension of direct governmental—especially military—activity furthering these claims. This shift was consistent with existing practice. Since secession, ambitious Confederate planners had claimed Arizona, New Mexico, and perhaps parts of California, and they also insisted these lands would be taken, not by direct force of arms, but by a combination of commercial penetration and local support. Nevertheless, a pretense of an intention to establish a military presence had been

maintained into 1863; whereas by 1864, elites on the ground had to orig-
inate proposals, argue how they would support the war effort further
east, and demonstrate that they would not require any resources from
the War Department. Lansford W. Hastings, a proponent of westward
and southward migration and Arizona territorial judge, and Colonel
Spruce M. Baird, former attorney general of New Mexico—who had
earlier in March 1862 entertained the soldiers of Sibley's expedition on
his ranch near Albuquerque—lobbied the Richmond government on the
status of Arizona and New Mexico; they wrote to and met Davis, Seddon, and Benjamin. Control of these territories mattered because, as
Baird warned on May 10, New Mexico and Arizona territories in the
hands of the United States would be an irresistible refuge for runaway
slaves and isolate the Confederacy from the Pacific. In May and again
in October, Davis attempted to encourage his subordinates to attend to
this issue. Seddon agreed with the future goals but added that he lacked
the current means to achieve them. At the end of the war, the southwestern territories would somehow revert to the Confederacy as necessary
possessions for the realization of ambitious plans across the Pacific and
Mexico. In the meantime, the government would support its agents on
the ground with words and not resources.[44]

More numerous and closer geographically to the Confederate heart-
land, Native Americans living in Indian Territory offered superior military assistance to the government than did the scattered adventurers
of the Southwest. Furthermore, the inclusion of Indians in the Confederacy's supposedly stable social order presented an opportunity for
planners to maintain a vision of the Confederacy to the world that incorporated subject races in a hierarchy. This nation would, they contended,
offer in the future a stark contrast to the United States where, in
pursuit of the chimera of racial equality, its leaders would end up exter-
minating inferior peoples. The winter and spring witnessed a period of
military crisis of control in the Indian Territory. There was "much discontent in the Indian Department," General Kirby Smith wrote to Davis
on January 20, "from the loss of territory, from a failure to comply with
promises of Arms and supplies, and from a want of confidence and distrust of their commander." In April, the two Arkansas senators warned
that the Union forces under their new commander, James G. Blunt, were
poised to take the offensive, and the government seemed to be on the
verge of surrendering the territory.[45]

Lacking military means, the Davis administration maintained its claim to Indian Territory rhetorically. On George Washington's birthday, February 22, Davis formally wrote to the president of the Council of the Six Confederate Nations, Israel Folsom, telling him, with a continued paternal note, that Native Americans were "especially entitled to [the Confederacy's] fostering care": "Our cause is one and our hearts must be united." On June 28, Davis yielded to the earlier requests made that January by the Cherokee representative in the House, Elias Boudinot, to confirm the Indian Territory as a separate territory from Arkansas, with Douglas H. Cooper appointed as superintendent. The more promising military context that summer was the ideal time for this assertion of Confederate claim to the Indian Territory.[46]

Planners of the future Confederacy believed the inclusion of Native Americans would also bring immediate military rewards. In his report of April 1864, the Confederate commissioner of Indian affairs, Sutton S. Scott, noted that he had visited the territory twice, both "affording encouragement and maintaining fidelity" from Native Americans. He signaled that the government would continue its policy of control by benevolence, noting that it was "important that [the Native Americans] should be dealt with in a spirit of consideration and liberality." The promotion of Stand Watie—Cherokee chief, lawyer, entrepreneur, Boudinot's uncle, and member of the Knights of the Golden Circle—to command the First Indian Brigade on May 6, 1864, appeared proof that "the great body of Indians, notwithstanding their losses, is attached to the Confederacy and confident in its fortunes."[47]

MEXICO AS THE SUBORDINATE PARTNER IN THE CONFEDERACY'S PLANS

The twin objectives of a nation governed with conservative political principles and populated by a hierarchy of races merged at the beginning of 1864 in the State Department's plans for Mexico. On a formal level, as Davis wrote to the Archduke Maximilian on January 7, the Confederate government wished "to establish and cultivate the most friendly relations" with Mexico once the latter was emperor. Privately, as Benjamin told the new Confederate envoy, Brigadier General William Preston, "the future safety of the Mexican Empire is inextricably bound up with the safety and independence of the Confederate States." Confederates planned a future of economic exploitation both indirectly and directly. They believed Mexico to be dependent on the Confederacy and planned for their southern neighbor to be a supporter of an alliance for the conservative cause and, by so doing, shut out any United States influence. Diplomats hoped other Latin American countries would be eager to join such a coalition. In return for these Confederate services, optimistic planners looked for reciprocal benefits from Mexico. Southerners looked forward to easily exploiting the potential wealth of the country. Moreover, the country's access to the Pacific and Mexican Gulf would improve the Confederacy's maritime position and make it invulnerable to future blockades.[48]

Government policy focused on the early agreement of a commercial pact with Mexico. On January 5, the Senate unanimously passed the resolution to send an envoy to Mexico City with the purpose that "reciprocal free trade proposed on the frontier be extended to the ports of the two countries and to articles of growth, produce and manufacture thereof." While the priority was boosting the contraband trade, commentators and politicians also enthused about the long-term opportunities in Mexico, because "the wretchedly abject condition of Mexico during the past forty years" was not necessarily "the standard of [what] it had ... always been and always would be." With the right government, the *Index* stressed, Mexico would be "the richest and most beautiful country on the globe." Its fertility and climate were ideal for cash crops. De Bow agreed that for Confederates, Mexico was "a great theatre of future wealth and commerce." On March 20, Preston requested the long-serving Confederate agent in Monterrey, Mexico, Jose Quintero, to continue his efforts and to "communicate with me regularly with regard to the events and policy of the country, especially the condition of affairs, trade and intercourse on the frontier."[49]

Some planners continued to hope that a convergence in labor systems operating on both sides of the border would foster close future relations between the Confederacy and Mexico. Tyler, writing in *De Bow's Review*, saw great potential in what he regarded as French plans to acquire in Mexico another tropical region. According to the journalist and soldier, Napoleon already introduced a "coolie and modern apprentice system of labor in Algeria." Tyler believed the peon servitude that existed in Mexico would be "easily convertible into slavery." Therefore, he looked forward either way to the establishment of a "permanent labor system" and a pro-slavery alliance with the Confederacy. Neither the French ruler nor his puppet in Mexico had any intention of establishing slavery there, but

Napoleon's obsession in establishing alternative sources of cotton production with contract workers may well have given such an impression to
those individuals who passionately believed that staple crop production
required slave labor.[50]

A more concrete plan to build a Confederate presence in Mexico appeared to gather momentum during 1864. The apparent success of the
plan of William Gwin, the former senator from California, to colonize Sonora offered a chance to both cement a Confederate-Mexican alliance
and perhaps annex the northwest Pacific coast province once the French
departed. Citing Gwin as his source, Preston assured Davis that there
were estimated to be fifteen thousand to twenty thousand "men of southern birth in California who are now restless and persecuted under the
fierce social and political proscriptions of the civil war." With these alleged pro-Confederates too remote to serve the slaveholders' republic directly, the best way to assist would be by moving into Mexico. In addition
to increasing support within Mexico for an alliance with the Confederacy, these Anglo-American individualists championed the international
cause of republican self-government better than the alternative of French
investors representing "corporate wealth and privilege." The challenge for
diplomats and politicians was they had to first secure Mexican friendship and trust in order to attract such settlers. These Californians, Gwin
explained to Preston, "can only be induced . . . to colonize Sonora or emi-
grate to Mexico" on one condition. The California adventurer considered
that the establishment of friendly relations between the Confederacy
and Mexico was indispensable to his plan of settling Sonora. Once the
settlers were there, the future prospects would be bright. Not only would
such immigrants be a lobbying group on behalf of the Confederacy in
Mexico, but they also had experience in mining and possessed the requisite skills in repelling "savage Indian" assaults, which would help develop
this neglected region. Eventually, a colony of settlers would follow the
example of Texas and leave Mexico and join the power to their north.[51]

For those diplomats away from Gwin's influence, however, supporting the territorial integrity of Mexico appeared the wiser course to pursue, especially given their belief that the U.S. government politicians
and agents also championed plans for colonizing their southern neighbor. On January 7, Benjamin warned Preston about a different California intrigue, noting that an unnamed U.S. senator from California
had proposed threatening resolutions in the Senate. "Lower California,
Sonora and Sinaloa," Benjamin explained, "have long been looked upon

by Californians as their easy and assured prey whenever the occasion shall be opportune for seizing these defenseless provinces." Such reports of possible colonization of these provinces by free white California migrants appeared designed to thwart the expansion of slavery and the Confederacy. Hence the initial skepticism Gwin encountered in 1863 when he presented his plan to Davis and Benjamin in Richmond, before he left for Paris.[52]

Slidell, when briefed by Gwin on his plan in Paris, was cautious in his reaction. Even though Gwin had been able to meet both Napoleon and Maximilian repeatedly, and "his scheme has been fully examined and approved," Slidell recommended a policy of wait and see. Gwin's ambitious plan "offers, as I believe, fair chances of success," he told Benjamin on June 2, adding, "If carried out its consequences will be most beneficial" for the Confederacy. Nevertheless, Slidell counseled, "it is better that we should be quite untrammelled as to our future movements in that direction." The commissioner did not want the Davis administration to alienate his Mexican conservative friends whom he had cultivated that winter when they were in Paris.[53]

Besides, pro-Confederate Californians remaining at home would be useful for planners who still had their eye on remaking the political geography of the rest of the United States. "The birth of an independent confederation of the Pacific is only a question of time," Hotze asserted on June 23. "It will take place on the day when it is for the interest of the people of those distant states and territories to cut loose from the political mismanagement and overwhelming indebtedness of the United States." Although not as strategically important as the Midwest, a Pacific confederacy would assist in the establishment of a balance of power on the continent that would offer the Confederacy long-term security from the United States. A Pacific confederacy's commercial importance was obvious to optimists, as "San Francisco will be the New York of the Pacific." Therefore, diplomats preferred that any pro-southern Californians had better remain where they were because these discontented individuals could foment trouble in their home state with their votes and even push for its secession once Lincoln lost—or even won—the presidential election.[54]

Given the increasingly evident determination of Maximilian and Napoleon to put distance between France, Mexico, and the Confederacy, Gwin persuaded Preston to endorse the colonization plan despite the misgivings of his colleagues. On the verge of abandoning his mission after a long sojourn in Cuba, having waited in vain for an invitation to proceed to Mexico City from Maximilian, Preston encountered Gwin—an old friend and former U.S. congressional colleague—passing through Havana on his way from Paris to Mexico. Gwin offered to break through the diplomatic impasse by telling Maximilian about "the importance of establishing a good understanding at the beginning between two adjacent nations." The relationship between the Confederacy and Mexico would be mutually beneficial, "having many vast interests in common and which must hereafter augment with their growing wealth and population." The Kentucky minister plenipotentiary decided not to go home. "It was my intention to recall you," he told his aide-de-camp Captain R. T. Ford, whom he had sent ahead, "but now" he ordered Ford to "remain in Mexico City" until Gwin arrived.[55]

Preston explained to his superiors in Richmond that Gwin's plan now made sense because the new regime of Maximilian was weak. The imperial regime would need more than French assistance if it were to survive in the long term given Union hostility, and only the Confederate government would be in a position to help. Above all, Maximilian required veteran soldiers in his armies, and it was this resource, Hotze was convinced, that in the very near future the Confederacy would possess in abundance. With peace expected daily with the United States, the War Department would soon have a demobilized army on its hands. Some of the veteran soldiers of the Confederate states, Hotze believed, "will prefer a service promising military activity to the tame routine of civilian life." The ultimate outcome would be that the Confederacy and not France would "establish the military power of the young Empire" of Mexico.[56]

Confederate policymakers assumed French support of Maximilian in Mexico to be at best temporary. Preston expected Napoleon to retire in the face of Mexico's domestic problems and his nominee's hesitancy. As early as February 1864, the newly appointed envoy worried about the "disturbed condition" of Mexico in the absence of certainty about Maximilian's intentions and the threat posed by supporters of the ousted liberal Mexican leader Benito Juárez. Moreover, since he became emperor in 1852, Napoleon had used quick foreign policy successes to win prestige and popularity for his regime at home; once his protégé had been triumphantly installed by French troops in Mexico City, Napoleon would

be unlikely to be interested in the longer duration task of nation building; instead he would recall his troops and move on to a new scheme
in another part of the world. After all, the Confederate commissioner in
Paris had witnessed previous changes of mind on the part of the mercu-
rial French ruler. Therefore, as Slidell observed on March 16, a prompt
French exit would mean "Maximilian may be obliged to rely on his own
resources at a much earlier day than he expects."[57]

Confederate interests would be best served by cultivating Mexican
conservatives. Hence Slidell spoke to the Mexicans in Paris who were
in Maximilian's entourage even though he had been denied an audience
with the archduke. He warned them "that without the active friendship
of the South, he [Maximilian] will be entirely powerless to resist northern aggression." Lamar spoke for many on April 14, when he proclaimed
that the imperial regime amounted to a transient "French protectorate in
Mexico whose durability depends on the establishment of the Confederacy." On August 25, Hotze anticipated that "the sooner Napoleon III
bestows on Maximilian the privilege of independent action the faster the
nascent empire will attain the rank and dignity of an independent nation." Hotze hoped that as a result, "Maximilian may well be impressed
with the grandeur of his mission" and therefore not only rise above his
own hesitations and dependency on the French but also become a part of
the Confederate-sponsored balance of power in North America.[58]

Every revelation of Union hostility to Maximilian's regime strengthened the prospect that Maximilian would consent to Mexico being part
of this Confederate-sponsored arrangement. On April 4, Henry Winter Davis's joint resolution condemning the empire had been reported
in the U.S. House of Representatives, and Confederate newspapers
provided extensive coverage of the proceedings; members of the Davis
administration considered this evidence of profound Union antagonism
to the French-backed Mexican government that not even the forensic
skill of Seward could disguise. In a letter to Senator Hunter on April 12,
Littleton D. Q. Washington, a long-serving official in the State Department, stated his belief that the threatening language of the U.S. legislators would help bring the Confederacy, France, and Mexico into close
alliance. Reports crossed the Atlantic. On May 6, Edward Archer wrote
from London—where he was both industrial spy and officer in the fledg-
ing Virginia Volunteer Navy—to his brother Bert that he "looked for
him [Maximilian] to make his first duty the recognition of the south

and that Napoleon III, provoked by the resolution, will follow." Archer therefore concluded, "Maximilian stands more in need of our recognition than we do of him—we know by whose power alone Maximilian can become firmly seated on the throne." The Austrian's stubbornness would fade, and diplomats believed the French and Mexican members of Maximilian's administration recognized this situation and would invite Confederate aid. Slidell cheerfully told Benjamin that Maximilian's chief of army staff, General Woll, "is perfectly capable of appreciating the necessity of the support of the Confederacy to protect the new government against the aggression of the north."[59]

Journalists and diplomats hoped Federal aggression would not only ally the Imperial government of Mexico with the Confederacy but also bring the rest of the administrations in Latin America into a hemispheric league—led by the Confederacy—against the United States. With the archduke's installation by the French as emperor, the State Department's mission to undermine the Union's Monroe Doctrine, with its preference for republican governments and opposition to European intervention in the Western Hemisphere, had apparently succeeded. The Monroe Doctrine "is from this time forth," stated the *Richmond Dispatch*, "an exploded humbug." The world owed the Confederacy "a debt of gratitude" for having "forbidden" the Union from conquering an empire stretching "from the St. Lawrence to Cape Horn."[60]

Opposition to the Monroe Doctrine did not mean that ambitious individuals had either renounced republicanism or their own plans for expansion across Latin America. After all, Confederate foreign policy possessed "no new-born admiration of monarchical institutions" and, led by a president who was "inflexible a believer as ever in the ultimate operations of the self governing system," was committed to allowing "every people to choose its own form of government." Rather, they critiqued the Monroe Doctrine as an ineffective, even counterproductive, means to achieve the goal of hegemony throughout the Americas. Based on their belief in racial distinctions and different rates of progress among peoples, Confederate framers of their country's future foreign policy denied the applicability of republican self-government everywhere. They doubted that "federalism and universal suffrage contain in themselves some hidden virtue capable of redressing evils in national character." It followed that the U.S. policy of the dedication of the Western world to democratic government was seriously flawed. As well as being inappropriate for the racial and social mix of peoples to be found in Latin American nations, they also conceived U.S. promotion of republicanism abroad as a cynical disguise covering the reality of Union imperialism.[61]

Instead of emulating the blundering Federal interference in Latin American countries on behalf of an inappropriate ideology, Confederate diplomats presented an alternative vision of sovereign nations united in self-interest, based on a common desire to resist this ham-fisted U.S. bid for dominance. Confederate policymakers also believed the adoption of monarchical forms of government in Latin America would mean that the nations so administered would be open to more covert Confederate influence. "As a republic she will be at the mercy of the United States," Lamar warned about Mexico, but then added, "as a monarchy she will be our friend and ally." The type of government established there would determine which of the two leading North American powers would prevail in both Mexico and across Latin America. It was in that context that Preston from Havana—as did Slidell in Paris—focused his lobbying not on Maximilian but on prominent Mexican conservatives.[62]

Diplomats presented their Confederate future as the antithesis of the United States. On May 6, Preston wrote to the prominent Mexican conservative, General Juan Nepomuceno Almonte. He argued the United States government's policy toward Latin America was determined "alone by selfish motives." So "even when the just interest of civilization demanded it," Union administrations "forbade all intervention by the powers of Europe in American affairs," and "they behold these republics lapse one after another into anarchy." Preston alleged that successive U.S. administrations exhibited paranoid suspicion of Europeans' motives, seeing behind every debt collection enterprise a scheme to reestablish colonial rule. Preston contended members of the Lincoln administration refused "to incur the slightest risk to remedy their disorders or arrest their ruin" across Latin America. By blocking European aid, Federal policy protected corruption and incompetence in those countries from reform. If left unchecked, not only would the United States government prevent attempts at outside intervention to pacify chaotic republican governments, but it would also actively destabilize remaining conservative regimes. In Mexico, specifically, Preston charged, if the United States "can crush or subdue the Confederacy," then the Lincoln administration would "assist the anarchists to overthrow Maximilian," whereas an independent Confederacy would guarantee the establishment of resilient conservative regimes in Mexico and elsewhere across Latin America with European cooperation.[63]

During his long residence in Havana, Preston also reported to Richmond on the situation in Cuba, Puerto Rico, and Santo Domingo. He concluded that both the future of slavery in these islands and continued Spanish colonial rule depended upon the success of the Confederacy in the war. Diplomats' confidence in the permanence of the Spanish colonial regime and its commitment to slavery had diminished with the revelations of a spreading revolt in Santo Domingo and increasing governmental instability in Madrid. In Havana, Preston observed that the Spanish government in Madrid was "greatly embarrassed with Santo Domingo" and that it was "probable after these years of struggle that Spain will halt in her purpose and abandon the island." The reason for such a policy shift was that "the effort is unpopular and costly in Cuba," and therefore "the new liberal government of Arrozola [sic] in Madrid orders no new troops." Preston dismissed the liberal administration in Madrid's explanation of the retreat; he "doubted the veracity" of "the alleged cause is fear of servile insurrection in Cuba." Yet all was not well on the island. There were divisions among Cubans—"the native Spaniards are almost unanimous in their sympathies for the Confederacy and the creoles generally pro US and advocate gradual emancipation here either from fear of the future or hostility to the Spaniards." Preston agreed with the agent, Charles Helm, that Cuba's fate depended on that of the Confederacy. As Preston wrote in June, "The news of the great struggle between Grant and Lee absorbs all minds here in Havana." Cuba's destiny and survival, as with that of Mexico, depended upon the outcome of the fighting in Virginia and Georgia.[64]

Brazil's slavery system appeared stronger, and politicians and diplomats worried less, although they did fret about Dom Pedro II's apparent inability to resist British and, later, Federal maritime aggression. As elsewhere in Latin America, planners agreed that any backbone on the part of the Brazilian regime in withstanding such outrages against its sovereignty and attempts to undermine slavery would have to rely on the Davis administration's extrication from its war with the Union. The government would then be free to implement a Latin American policy that was proslavery and, in theory, pledged to non-interference in domestic concerns. Politicians and diplomats qualified their policy of non-interference, as they clearly wished the governments of Latin America to tilt in a conservative direction, with government by Hispanic elites, and would even welcome European interventions as long as the latter were geared to such an end and not for the promotion of abolition.

RETAINING A GLOBAL MISSION

The primacy of practical, even Hobbesian, self-interest, which planners anticipated would be the hallmark of Confederate foreign policy, reflected not only an increased sense of their weakness vis-à-vis the armed forces of the Union but also how the dogged defensive nature of the war effort in 1864 influenced the policies of the future nation. Nevertheless, leading Confederates saw themselves as enlightened visionaries, whose ambitions for their nation's future greatness required its government to perform global leadership. They asserted that their Confederacy alone perpetuated the universal values of the American Revolution, which they equated with true conservatism, against those radical ideals of the French Revolution that Confederates now saw reborn in the Union.[65]

This sense of a global mission regained credibility for many individuals in the context of the U.S. presidential election combined with the apparent success of the Confederates' defensive military strategy. In her dedication to the Confederate armies at the beginning of her 1864 novel, *Macaria*, Augusta Jane Evans praised the soldiers who "have delivered the South from despotism, and who have won for generations yet unborn the precious guerdon of constitutional republican liberty." While Evans saw the significance of the struggle in terms of the Confederate future, others recognized its relevance across the world as well. "The Confederate States is fighting the great moral and political battle of this generation," Hotze later wrote, "the battle of established right against popular will—liberty versus democracy—law versus numbers." It was still a harmonious, interdependent world, but with a more Burkean tone. The Confederacy was simply "the representative of all conservatism, vested right, traditional institutions, solemn constitutional compromises," he continued, which had been "determined by inherent rights of the states and explicit provisions of the constitution." Institutions needed to be preserved, and in the Confederacy, the state governments served the same function as the House of Lords and monarchy in Britain, namely managing democracy. Hotze believed that, by protecting slavery, the States were "the checks on which liberty is protected against the populace—the few secured against the uncontrolled and unlimited tyranny of the many." He concluded that the Confederacy fought the war on behalf of global elites and stood for "the case of the educated classes of the world."[66]

Politicians hoped to avoid appearing weak and beleaguered in the face of forces of change, while at the same time fighting for these conservative principles. This meant some rhetorical somersaults had to be accomplished and Burke needed to be supplemented. "Ours is not a revolution," Davis insisted, but at the same time, "upon the success of the Confederacy alone depends the existence of Constitutional liberty in the world." White equality sustained by slavery was only possible in the Confederacy. If the Confederacy failed, Davis therefore warned, "constitutional government political freedom, will fall with it." Such a sentiment imposed a daunting burden of expectations on the future, and for at least one prominent Confederate required an amendment to classical political thought. Lucius Lamar, once the president's protégé in Mississippi politics, who had passionately believed in the connection between "American liberty" and "Southern Institutions," added Hegel's optimistic view of social progress to the supremacy of republican self-government. The German philosopher's influence had left Lamar a believer in the benign application of reason to human problems, by which the greater happiness of the greater number might patiently and gradually be believed. The politician and diplomat perhaps also exhibited the broader influence of the German pietism movement, which emphasized duty and moral purposefulness as the path to utopia, which for Lamar served as a way to chart the Confederate future. He explained the change on the grounds that "our cause rests on higher ground than revolution." Indeed the Confederacy was in "moral transition" into a new era, one in which "a greater capacity of self sacrifice, a higher tone of thought and feeling, a greater earnestness of purpose, purer motives of action, a deeper moral life" of the Confederate people would receive ample recognition in the world. If the people in their future careers lived up to the "high reputation, which our arms have acquired," then the nation would maintain "our present exulted position."[67]

THROUGH THE end of the summer, 1864 had been a year of significant Confederate optimism, albeit one juxtaposed with significant disaffection with the government. As the war had taken on a greater magnitude, so therefore did Confederates' expectations of their future. Optimists portrayed their future nation as a power committed to preserving its economy, society, and revolutionary traditions in the face of a massive assault by the Union. It would still be an expansive and ambitious nation because it was made up of a people of sufficient character, and it had to be a mighty power in order to contain the Union. Diplomats had to seek allies to support its mission of saving the world from what they regarded as a corrupted revolution that seemed poised to spread from the United States. In reconciling these demands, the government claimed to stand for universal conservative values—continuity, peace, and stability—in order to provide a framework for the individual and collective ambitions of its people. To convince overseas countries as well as maintain support, the government undertook to sell the Confederate future both at home and abroad, insisting that it would serve the interests of all.[68]

The stalwart posture of the Confederacy rested on two contingencies: that its military would continue to resist Union attacks; and that Lincoln would not be reelected president of the United States. By the end of November 1864, with the important exception of Lee holding on at Petersburg, these hopes had been dashed. In the face of military disaster in Georgia and Tennessee and political disappointments with the failure of northern Democrats in the elections and the inaction of midwestern secessionists, planners had to confront a new set of circumstances. They had to accept that adverse events had jeopardized their nation's future; in that context, by the end of the year, leaders of the Confederacy began to consider that such a pervading sense of uncertainty might not be a sufficient basis for their ambition.

6

The Sacrifice Cannot Be in Vain

THE FUTURE IN A TRANSFORMED WORLD, NOVEMBER 1864 TO MAY 1865

B Y EARLY 1865, the Confederacy's journalists wrote about how its people had been transformed by the war with implications for the future. On February 13, the Richmond correspondent of the *Index* observed that "four years of war has left its impress not only on the scenery, but in the faces, habits, customs, modes of speech," and even the "very thoughts" of the people. Such changes would have repercussions for the Confederacy's purpose—whether it would turn inward into an isolationist posture or continue existing in and contributing to the world at large. For Secretary of State Judah P. Benjamin, who probably wrote the article, such a context informed his thinking about installing a temporary dictatorship during these months of crisis and considering reforms to, even abolition of, slavery.[1]

FROM NOVEMBER 1864 onward, with the reelection of President Lincoln and the commencement of the unopposed march of Sherman's army out of Atlanta and deeper into Georgia, planners for the future nation had to adjust to the fact that they now expected, at best, a further four years of war. Detached from the need for these plans to be moored in present-day reality, some of these internationalist visions once more anticipated slavery and territorial expansion and global free trade, which resembled the most optimistic predictions made in 1861. Yet at the same time, other Confederates pondered the meaning of their revolution and whether it would be rendered more radical by fighting for so much longer and the need to seek revenge on the various Federals, Europeans, and traitors within who had hitherto thwarted their achievement of independence. A dictatorship, especially a terror, should that be necessary, implied a new beginning, a year zero. Therefore, predictions of what the Confederacy would be after the war became vaguer and fainter over time. Some individuals, who had been keen planners before, ceased to think about the future of the nation as they focused attention on personal and local concerns. They did not consciously stop being Confederates, but in their hierarchy of loyalties, the one owed to the Confederate nation descended in importance.[2]

Nevertheless, some Confederates still sought to think in national terms and at the same time endeavored to be practical about the future. For these individuals, however, what had to be confronted more than ever was the degree of compromise that would be necessary with Federals in order to end the war. Substantial reforms would also be necessary to the Confederacy's economy and society if it was to survive in a tough global environment. Not only would substantial commercial concessions be the minimum needed to placate the Union, but also changes to the agrarian economy and slavery would have to be implemented. Even self-avowed conservatives never considered their political, economic, and social institutions to be fixed. The hallmark of strong and stable societies was their ability to undergo reform. Change had to be gradual and under Confederate auspices, and it was in this context that debates in Congress and the press over the enlistment of enslaved African American males of military age took place. Yet if these planners deemed flexibility a virtue, they also hoped that allies in the Union, the performance of Confederate armies, and the activities of adventurers and agents abroad would help improve the Confederacy's bargaining position in any settlement with the United States.

Confederates believed they would have both independence and cooperation with the Union. Some individuals—president pro tempore of the Senate Robert Hunter, for example—held both opinions at the same time; Hunter reserved the former for public utterances and the latter for private correspondence. Lincoln's policy objectives for reconstruction contradicted these expectations, but Confederate emissaries judged these pronouncements to be for the northern public only and not nonnegotiable. Envoys undoubtedly hoped to be so duped, especially when confronted at home with unpalatable alternatives of a revolutionary terror, an overhaul of national institutions, including slavery, and even taking to the hills in order to fight a guerilla war. It was easier to imagine that large parts of the Confederate mission might be accomplished in association with the United States, including a resumed southern expansion all the way to the isthmus that one day would be the site of the future Panama Canal. A great future would be possible, optimists believed, if Confederates were treated as an equal half of the Union.

"Every Negro, Bond & Free, Is Identified with Us in Soil, Climate & Association"

Most planners still insisted that the Confederacy would, at one point in the future, become sufficiently independent so as to have control over domestic and foreign policies. Slavery would continue. The Confederate economy would remain agricultural and would resume exports. The Confederacy would remain a participant in a continued manifest destiny across the Pacific. Potentially, they would not perform this mission alone: Britons, Frenchmen, Mexicans, and Californians would support this quest, as Confederate merchants would be their allies in preventing a U.S. monopoly in this contest to control the China trade. Chinese commerce was never as prominent for politicians and adventurers than during this bleak period of the history of the Confederacy.

Planners still believed that staple crop production would recover from the damage during the war because, Confederates maintained, African Americans would have a better future in the Confederacy than anywhere else in the world, especially that to be had in the United States. They would want to work as inferior, but protected, participants in a booming, expansive nation. African Americans would occupy "a very different place in the scale of civilization," Hotze insisted on November 10, "than a mere tool of a foreign enemy employed in crimes against common humanity." Furthermore, he considered that slaveholders had trained African Americans to be productive, and "if any population of negroes can make good use of freedom it must assuredly be that of the Confederate States." This belief about African American loyalty to, and enhanced status in, the Confederacy provided the context for the debate over the enlistment of enslaved people as soldiers. "Every negro, bond & free," physician Charles B. Leitner assured Davis on December 31, "is identified with us in soil, climate & association."[3]

In Confederate eyes, evidence existed to support this contention. Those enslaved people who fled had done so on account of lies disseminated by

Federal agents. The fact was that many enslaved people had remained on the plantations, which meant a restoration of slavery was possible. In January 1865, G. L. Strucker, a planter of St. Mary's Parish, Louisiana, told General Joseph L. Brent that a visible deployment of the army in the locality would be sufficient to reestablish the plantation system. "On such places," he explained, "the presence of a strong arm during the planting season would insure bountiful harvests." These planters believed that interest as well as coercion would mean that African Americans would continue to work. "All the influential men that I have met agree that the negroes are better disposed and do more work than they have done since the commencement of the war," Colonel Louis A. Bringier in Le Blanc, Vermillion Parish, Louisiana, told Brent on April 6. "They understand the urgent necessity of making crops, and have gone to work in earnest."[4]

Given that disposition to work, some Confederates considered that the proposal to arm enslaved people would undermine both the economic and social structure of the Confederacy and with that any chance of a prosperous future. "Who would live in such a country as ours without slaves to cultivate it?" Barnwell Rhett asked former South Carolina governor William Aiken in a public letter. He predicted "hideous ruin" for a Confederacy inhabited by four million freed people. On Christmas Day, South Carolina planter William F. Robert bluntly warned Davis that nothing could be worse than arming the enslaved people; "uncontrollable Anarchy" would result.[5]

Perpetuating a hierarchy of races would enable Confederates to dominate the tropics. Some argued that the proposal to arm some individuals did not mean any change in the status of African Americans as members of an inferior race. On December 21, in a letter to Charleston newspaper owner Fred A. Porcher, Benjamin emphasized that it remained the government's "doctrine that the negro is an inferior and unfitted for social or political equality with the white man." War Secretary Seddon agreed in his November report to Congress that although no compunction should be felt in using enslaved men as soldiers, "they are inferior" and "confessedly inferior in all aspects to our white citizens in the qualifications of the soldier." As a result, "it will not do to risk our liberties and safety on the negro while the white man may be called to the sacred duty of defense." While there remained white soldiers, it would be "best to leave subordinate labors of society to the negro."[6]

Optimists believed African Americans accepted this inferiority and would remain loyal to the Confederacy on account of the worse fate that awaited them at the hands of the Union forces. Therefore, according to Seddon on November 4, enslaved people l "are more vitally concerned than us" in the cause of independence. He explained that while "with whites, the future is one of nationality, honor and property"; for African Americans, the "dread issue in no distant future" was "the question of their existence as a race." Seddon believed the very survival of African Americans depended on their protected subordinate condition, which would only be guaranteed by Confederates granting African Americans a defined role in society. By contrast, in an economy in which members of the races had to compete against each over for waged jobs, such as the Union envisaged by Lincoln promised, African Americans would fail and subsequently perish. On March 16, Charles J. Hutson, then in the trenches with the Army of Northern Virginia outside Petersburg, informed his planter father back in South Carolina that the "army is the safest place for negroes now." The only way African Americans could save themselves was by supporting a Confederate military victory.[7]

The Future Economy: Self-Sufficient or Interdependent?

Planners agreed that along with slavery, the Confederacy would remain an agricultural economy in the future. A question they debated was whether the blockade would permanently change it from an interdependent exporting market economy to a self-sufficient closed society. This debate had implications beyond economics and would help determine the place of the Confederacy in the world—whether the slaveholders' republic would be an active participant in international affairs or whether it would retreat into a suspicious, impoverished, isolation.

General John B. Magruder, a senior commander in the Trans-Mississippi Department, ceased his earlier encouragement of the "lucrative" cross-border cotton trade between Texas and Mexico in order to reach former markets in New England. He now recognized there were ethical concerns about persevering with such a commercial policy in a hostile world. The "cotton trade with the enemy should at once be stopped," the general proclaimed to the people of Arkansas on December 6, for "it is contrary to the law especially when carried on by private individuals ... [for] it substitutes the love of money, luxury and convenience for the Roman virtues of patriotism and self denial." The end result, he concluded, was demoralization. With the loss of foreign markets and the financial crisis, which demanded urgent attention but seemed beyond solution, Magruder and others reconsidered what were the resources of the nation and where its strength lay. In such a calculation, radical change in the future would be the inevitable outcome, perhaps making the Confederacy a pastoral small-holding society. On February 15, Augustus W. Ashton, a Methodist minister, in a letter to Davis, recommended voluntary land redistribution, as landowners would willingly give up land to government to pay debt. For the former planters, just two hundred acres would be set-aside "for property owners." Meanwhile, a "small tract" would be awarded by government to each military pensioner and disabled veteran.[8]

The future of the Confederacy would be dramatically different, although an agrarian nation might still be a significant force on the world stage. On January 12, Hotze wrote that the racial and security benefits arising from a focus on subsistence agriculture would offset the loss of wealth from a reduction in the Confederate share of world trade. "The life of commercial powers has generally been short," he reflected, "and [their] influence temporary," whereas "it is by agricultural and military states that empires are founded and systems of civilization spread over the world." A growing commerce had negative consequences, Hotze warned, because "trade and manufactures have a tendency to slowly deteriorate the physical and moral character of a race exclusively devoted to them." In times of crisis it was much better to be an independent farmer. Trade was always at risk from enemy navies, so, "whenever worsted at sea," a commercial power "is deprived of the foundation of its prosperity." By contrast, "an agricultural power" has swifter means of recuperation even when "maybe ravaged, overrun" because "its soil cannot be destroyed ... within 2 years of a retreat of the enemy it may have recovered all its necessary resources." In conjunction with the new phase of the war, the loss of coasts and cities converted Hotze's future vision for the Confederacy into that of a self-sufficient agricultural subsistence economy.[9]

This idea of insulating the nation economically from the world was not shared by all Confederates. Others held that resuming the export of agricultural products, underpinned by free trade, was essential to obtain hard currency and with that power. Confederates' wartime trading with the enemy both obtained vital supplies and demonstrated the persistence of commercial habits. Even Lee supported this endeavor because "the interest and cupidity of individuals will be found far more effectual . . . than the most energetic efforts of regular government agents . . . stimulated only by their desire to do their official duty." His view corresponded with reality on the ground: planting remained a visceral need for Confederates. "Is any one making a crop near Natchez?" Planter Frances E. Sprague asked her daughter in Natchez, Mississippi. "I know if my friends were doing well," she explained, "I could put up with my troubles better." She expected that the "Yankees may take the place before I attempt to work it again," but "I hope in two years time there will be a change for the better." Even the prospect of federal appropriations did not discourage planters from planning to resume cotton production in the near future.[10]

While planters intended to sow another crop, they preferred to have Confederate government support for their efforts. "You can sell *more* cotton if they are going to open the free trade as I hear they are," Abram Archer advised his father on January 24, 1865. Short-term sacrifice would be balanced by the promise of wealth later, which would only come from an unfettered commerce and the Davis administration adopting at least the silver standard in order to encourage overseas trade and investment. The present gloomy situation, Representative Joseph H. Echols of Virginia told the House on January 19, had made it more—not less— necessary that the government give "substantial assurances to our people that we intended to place our currency upon a metallic basis and reorganize our finances upon the intelligent principles of political economy." He echoed the president's earlier arguments for free trade. Export duties were "an annual incubus" on the producer, Echols continued, which "will lessen their production," and "array in perpetual antagonism bondholders and agriculturalists." The government should "lay as few restrictions on trade as possible," he recommended, "and leave it to the operation of its own unchangeable laws."[11]

For the sake of revenue as well as by instinct, many optimists wanted their nation to remain a commercial economy, rather than retreat to a closed, small-holding entity. However, the free trade ideal had to accommodate the reality of the requirement of tariffs to raise revenue in order to satisfy the obligations of future indebtedness. The government's future financial commitments grew remorselessly. By the end of 1864, expectations of the size of the debt swelled dramatically as it would not only include monies owed due to the war, but also compensation payable to the owners of any emancipated enslaved people. On February 8, John H. Stringfellow, who had once been a leader of the proslavery settlers in the Kansas territory, told Davis that an export duty on cotton was needed not only pay down two billion dollars of wartime debt, but also up to as much as four billion dollars owed to slaveholders. The debt burden on the future would triple in size for Confederates.[12]

Therefore, with such huge sums to be paid back by future generations, politicians insisted that Confederates could not afford to turn their backs on the global economy. On January 30, 1865, Representative Daniel C. De Jarnette of Virginia complained to the House about the insularity of agricultural people. Unlike Hotze, this politician did not romanticize a pastoral economy, perhaps because he drew on his experience as a landowner in Caroline County who had engaged in agricultural pursuits before being elected to both the state and U.S. Houses of Representatives in the 1850s. "Nothing is more difficult than to convince them," he argued about farmers and planters, "that agriculture is not the great and absorbing interest that should control the action of governments." Instead, commerce "has been the great archimedian lever which has shaped the world." Far from being a source of moral and physical decline, as asserted by Hotze, trade was essential for future greatness. "The highest hopes and aspirations of all nations have been to possess and control it because they know that no wealth can be acquired [and] no power preserved without it." Only by understanding this maxim, De Jarnette argued, can Confederates "appreciate the nature of this great struggle in which we are now engaged and the effect of its results on the commercial interests of the world." For the master of Spring Grove Manor, the Confederacy would remain a factor in the shaping of the future world economy because it had no choice.[13]

Connecting the Confederacy to the world was more than a state of mind. At the end of 1864, Duff Green, still an energetic and practical adventurer despite his great age, interested himself in the future of commerce on the Pacific Ocean. The urgent question of the era, Green told Davis in December, was which nation would control "the trade of the Pacific." Since the late 1850s, this restless individual had been elaborating schemes to connect the South with the Pacific and thereby aid the region's economic expansion. With the rise of the Union's power and the prospect of a ruinous competition with U.S. merchants, Green hoped that Britain and France might form a commercial alliance with the Confederacy geared to excluding U.S. commerce and "to divide with us ... the occupation of the Pacific States and the control of the trade of the Pacific." Global mastery would depend on domination of the Far East market, De Jarnette agreed a month later, "which ever has been the source of commercial power and wealth in all ages springing as it does from the labor of eight hundred million Asians." California was the ideal base for the Confederacy to participate in this future great game, as it had the "finest deltas, rivers, harbors, climate, productions, mineral wealth ... enough to support two hundred million people." To supply these massive markets both at home and abroad, Confederate colonists planned to be busy superintending settlers "exploiting the rich silver and gold reserves as well as developing the rich pastoral and arable resources" of the Mexican provinces of Sonora, Chihuahua, and Baja California.[14]

De Jarnette and others framed their ambitions within a global context as part of a shift in power from east to west. Arguably this fascination arose at this time due to the final disappointment in the Atlantic Powers and the progressive tightening of the Union's blockade (resulting in the intercepting of one in two vessels); however, the conquest of the West had always been a goal of optimistic ambitious planners and of believers in manifest destiny. When the question of how to implement such plans of territorial growth ceased to have any relevance, providential missions filled the void. It was "no fancy to say to the west the star of empire takes its sway," De Jarnette intoned, as "the march of human events [and] the standards of civilization—move from east to west." He looked forward to "the spectacle of an empire that shall rise on the shores of the Pacific surpassing in grandeur the most opulent nation whereof history has preserved the record." The Virginia politician spoke for many when he argued that the Confederacy would influence the development of this power. "It is part of the wise legislation of our country," De Jarnette declared, "to see that the language of this great empire shall be our language, that its principles shall be our principles, and that the history whereto it shall look back ... should be the history we are making today."[15]

The Radicalization of the Confederate Revolution

Many planners—determined to preserve slavery from both internal and external threats—stressed the centrality of their labor system to the survival of the Confederate revolution. On November 28, Governor Zebulon Vance of North Carolina declared that the "proposition to emancipate them by the Confederate States government ... would stultify us in the eyes of the world and render our whole revolution nugatory." Instead, the revolution would become "a mere objectless waste of human life" because "our independence is chiefly desirable for the preservation of our great political institutions the principal of which is slavery." According to Virginian lawyer John H. Gilmer, the proponents of emancipation were a danger to the republic, as they were a faction of "bad and wickedly ambitious men."[16]

The revolution was about more than safeguarding what many Confederates once regarded as their Fifth Amendment right to protect property vested in enslaved people. Senator Williamson Oldham of Texas understood the need to frame the slavery issue in ideological terms, as he told his colleagues on January 30: it was "an issue vastly more important than any mere question of property." The question was instead "to preserve our freedom and sovereignty without which all else is valueless." Legislators agreed, and the parting message of Congress, issued on March 6, reflected these arguments even as it also noted that the effect of Union depredations "has seriously diminished our agricultural labor." Nevertheless, according to the politicians, the "relationship with the servile race intensified this feeling" of the right to self-government because it "invested love of liberty with sentiment of personal privilege."[17]

Revolutionary sentiment had been heightened by the sense of betrayal Confederates harbored about the failure of European powers to recognize their independence. "If the governments of Europe have not seen fit to recognize us as a free and independent power and welcome us into the family of nations," Gustavus A. Henry of Tennessee told his fellow senators on November 29, "it is their fault not ours." Encouraging revolutionary sentiment abroad would augment commercial pressure as future penalties for aristocratic European administrations. "At some future day when under God's good providence we have earned our title to freemen," De Jarnette expected Confederates would seek revenge. Seddon spoke for many in his report of November 4, when he wrote of the anger in the Davis administration about the "separate and equal place among the nations of the earth which is our birthright and which has been unjustly withheld from us."[18]

The heightened sense of revolution would have implications for future foreign policy. Just a year before, diplomats had presented the Confederacy as a conservative power dedicated to working with other countries; now they celebrated the birth of a popular uprising dedicated to universal objectives. On November 17, Hotze looked back to secession and deemed it "not the work of politicians"; rather it "arose as great revolutions do from the spontaneous impulse of the people." Over the previous three and a half years, this original revolutionary impulse had been intensified by "a war waged against every individual citizen . . . the war is a mortal feud not a national tournament." Finally, the reelection of the tyrant Lincoln would "serve to the South to nerve their arms and quicken their purpose—they are the last hope of true republican liberty." Diplomats regarded their nation as the "champion of the liberty and tranquility of the world."[19]

Reconceiving the Confederate revolution, to make it more akin to its French predecessor as opposed to its American predecessor, offered a way for planners to imagine both a glorious future and a more potent means to defeat the Union. At the end of 1864, former governor of Virginia John Letcher described Confederates as "a people who have sustained a revolution more gigantic in its operation than any that has ever occurred on Earth." William McDonald referred to the revolution as a "commotion," and "a great revolution," one "that is destined to change the direction of human progress, a great tragedy that now fills a continent." At the same time, in Shreveport, Louisiana, Joseph Brent told General Simon B. Buckner that Confederates "have *reached* the advanced stages of the revolution." This development was "a sign that would defeat the enemy . . . a pledge of terrible energy to be manifested."[20]

An evocation of a general will of the people reminiscent of the French Revolution offered a chance to replenish the depleted armies and compel civilians to make further sacrifices for the war effort. "It shall no longer be the momentary occupation of the Confederate States congress and people," Henry told the Senate on November 18, "but the business of their lives to gather together the entire strength of the country in men and material of war and put it forth as with the will of one man." Action on the ground followed the speeches and, as well as violating the sanctity of property, also portended a departure from the market economy. "The compulsory cultivation of a fixed quantity & quality of crops . . . & the . . . impressment of every species of property of the recusant planters" meant to Brent that the stage had been reached when "whatever it may be in politics it is difficult in morals to [reason] why the property as well as for mere persons['] blood should not it alike devoted the cause of independence."[21]

Calls for revolution reopened debates about the Constitution. "In terms of war and invasion, the Constitution is dead," Porcher challenged

Benjamin on December 16; "the safety of the people is the supreme law of the land." Therefore, he argued, the government cannot let a "constitutional scruple" over arming enslaved people stand "in the way of our subjugation." Benjamin "cannot concur" with Porcher's call for the Davis administration's "assumption of powers not [created] in the Constitution." While "alterations" would be necessary, Benjamin conceded, these problems were "best settled by degrees." Benjamin wondered though if the Confederate government should be dissolved for the remainder of the war. "If the constitution is not to be our guide," he admitted, "I would prefer to see it superseded by a revolution which should declare a dictatorship during the war after the manner of Ancient Rome." After the war a constitutional convention would assemble, thus "leaving to the future," Benjamin suggested, "the care of establishing a formal and regular government." The secretary kept his remarks hypothetical and abstract, but the language reflected discussion in Richmond drawing rooms that winter about the possibility of granting emergency powers to Lee.[22]

Reaching the Limits of the Revolution

Opponents mocked the glorious vision presented by these increasingly vociferous radical revolutionaries. "The jewel of state sovereignty is far more valuable than the dominion of power or the wealth of the world," John H. Gilmer wrote on December 28, "in the absence of civil and religious liberty." Foote agreed, while it was also "allowable for said States to confer together in their highest sovereign capacity, in general convention or otherwise . . . for the purpose of imparting to their common agent, the Confederate States Government, such additional powers as may be needed for the efficient prosecution of the pending war for independence." He would not compromise on the erosion of individual liberties. Having nearly fought a duel with John Mitchell of the Richmond Examiner on November 22, Foote made no secret that he was "threatening to leave the Confederacy if Habeas Corpus [is] suspended and martial law declared." Foote quit the Confederacy on January 28. Others continued to deploy Foote's arguments. The writ of habeas corpus was one of the "great bulwarks of freedom . . . as the people of this Confederacy are united in a great struggle for liberty," said Foote's colleague and supporter Representative James T. Leach of North Carolina; "no exigency exists justifying its suspension." Opposition in the House focused on perceived dictatorial tendencies of the Davis administration. "Is the cause worth the sacrifice?"

As legislators stated in their last message to the people, citizens "must constantly keep the end for which we are contending ... the sovereignty of the states and the right of self-government."[23]

The fall of Richmond in early April and the termination of the regular organized government that it represented showed to the president and his supporters the need to radicalize the revolution. If the Confederacy was to continue, its future had to be dedicated entirely to the war. Davis declared in Danville on April 4 the loss of Richmond had certainly inflicted "great moral as well as material injury to our cause." Nevertheless, the setback might be advantageous, as "we have entered into a new phase of the struggle, the memory of which is to endure for all ages and to shed ever increasing luster upon our country." On April 20, then in ignorance of Lee's surrender, Hotze added the Confederacy was now in a position "to replace the failed trial of strength—if a war, the struggle is drawing to a close, if a revolution it has just begun." Confederates should feel liberated not despondent by the end of a conventional war that focused on defending cities with regular armies.[24]

The end of a conventional war meant that any existing institutions of government or peacetime pastimes of the people had to be discarded, and with these went any idea of what the future might bring to individuals, save a need for further sacrifice. On April 19, in Charlotte, Davis stressed the all-encompassing dimensions the struggle had assumed; due to the dispersal of the formal armies, "this has been a war of the people for the people." His wife had seen the need for drastic measures for a while. "Our Constitution is framed for peace," Varina Davis confided to prominent South Carolina planter and politician General John S. Preston on March 31, and was therefore "incompatible with the successful prosecution of a war." After all, "the cohesive power of a strong government is needed," she continued, "when the devastating tendency of misery is at work." To her husband four weeks later, after the fall of Richmond and surrender of the eastern armies, she was blunter. "You have now tried the 'strict construction' fallacy," Varina told Davis on April 28. "If we are to require a constitution, it must be much stretched during our hours of outside pressure if it covers us all." A few Confederates thought about what "stretched" might mean.[25]

The Confederate purpose became in the spring of 1865 what some historians argue it was from the beginning: abstract, ideological, and destructive; in short, it became a cause rather than a nation-building project. Instead of planning and implementing the future by means of practical steps toward achieving prosperity and security in a new nation, Confederates demanded sacrifices that transcended nation building. "The Govt. *must be clothed with the power to command the men and means of the country,*" William T. Sutherlin, the mayor of Lynchburg, Virginia, told Davis on March 14. He justified this call for maximum effort: "Secure for the nation *independence* and the people will *excuse everything;*" but "fail, and they will *excuse nothing.*" On April 30 in Shreveport, Louisiana, Brent diagnosed the twin existential threats to the Confederacy in the Trans-Mississippi Department: "by the want of hope and by the terror of the enemy." In order "to overcome this terror, we should use a greater terror, to dissipate this want of hope, we should develop so formidable an energy as to command it." Therefore, "our authorities must terrorize the country," as "illustrated by the committee of public safety of the French revolution . . . [by the] operation of this gigantic energy & despotic powers we may find the path of safety." If citizens still hoped for a Confederate future, they would "sacrifice their property & even temporarily our civil govt," although Brent also hoped to "avoid the bloody excesses of these great revolutionists" of 1793.[26]

The calculation to be made was what effort Confederates should make for the creation of a "new & regenerating morale." The cost would be huge, Brent insisted; the people had to be capable of "holding our liberty as beyond price" in order to "protract the struggle." Otherwise, if the people were not prepared to meet this test, "nothing adequate to compensate for the sacrifices [of] property & blood will be realized." The immediate future confronting Confederates under these circumstances was bleak; on April 3, cavalryman William L. Wilson, left behind in the chaos of Lee's retreat, wrote in his diary of the women of the house in which he was billeted, "in a few hours at most they will be at the feet of the brutal soldiery" of the Union. On April 27, Hotze believed, with the assassination of Lincoln on April 15, the price had increased: "If the South had been heretofore disposed to accept terms it cannot now and its resentment become more bitter and resistance more desperate."[27]

Yoking the Destiny of the African Race to the Confederacy

Other Confederate planners believed the Confederacy had something practical to offer the world. For example, the debate over enlistment of enslaved people both compelled and offered a chance for those who recognized the urgency of change to reinvent their nation. On January 2, the *Richmond Enquirer* suggested the government needed to modify or even abolish slavery in the context of a relaunched Confederacy with a new "manifesto of objects and purposes" in order to "convince the world that we are fighting for the [self-government] of whites, not the slavery of blacks," and that "the freedom of the negro is not the purpose of the enemy," but rather to secure Confederate "commercial vassalage and dependence." The newspaper regarded the government's decision to contemplate slave enlistment and ultimate emancipation as a chance to clarify the purpose of the Confederacy. Historian Bruce Levine argues that advocates of enlistment of enslaved people thought that freedom for some African Americans would preserve slavery for the vast majority. If the war was not over emancipation but the future of the white race in the South, then slavery might be changed in order to secure the primary objective.[28]

Mississippi correspondents of Davis believed African Americans were loyal and would remain inferior to whites; they accepted that there was little chance that slavery would continue unchanged in the future, given the Union occupation of most of the state. African Americans should remain enslaved if possible, Judge Robert S. Hudson of Edinburg, Mississippi, told Davis, but if some of them could be "put into service and permitted to have all the fruits of their captures in kind & money, then they might face the fire." If enslaved soldiers made money, presumably they would be able to buy their own freedom, and over time, a class of wealthier free African Americans would emerge in the Confederacy as a whole, as had been the case in New Orleans before the war. Earlier the same month, the wealthy Mississippi planter William S. Price assured Davis that enslaved people did not need the incentives of freedom or wages to fight; instead they should be conscripted and trained under experienced overseers to make them fit for army service. Perhaps to Price, as with Strucker, a fellow planter in Louisiana, the army offered the chance to get recalcitrant enslaved people back under effective control and restore order to slavery.[29]

There was general agreement that slavery had to change in order to survive, and change was most acceptable provided slavery continued to underpin notions of white equality. One way this feat would be achieved was by spreading ownership more widely across the white population. On February 3, Representative John DeWitt Clinton Atkins of Tennessee moved in the House that the addition of enslaved men between the ages of seventeen and forty-five to the armies would mean "we should at once put 100,000 slaves in the field." These enslaved soldiers would be federalized and then dispersed among the veterans, thereby solving both arrears in pay and issues of control. In order to "make them effective and to immediately interest all of our soldiers in the institution," Atkins continued, some radical change was needed in ownership. It would therefore be "expedient that the Confederate States government should purchase all the slaves," he concluded, "and give to each white soldier now in the army or who will join the army within three months . . . a slave to be his absolute right and property."[30]

A variant of the Homestead Act would include enslaved people as well as land. The government should "offer to any soldier who was not a slaveholder or landholder," J. W. Ellis of Raleigh, North Carolina, suggested to Davis on January 28, "one slave and fifty acres." Ellis's purpose was to "spread the institution, you make every family interested in the Govt." He argued the government should also declare that "all negroes captured from the enemy shall belong to the captors." Ellis also believed that extending the chance to become a slaveholder to northerners, especially recent immigrants, would encourage desertion from Union ranks.[31]

These new small slaveholders would probably head west and south after the war. Reformers continued to believe that slavery's very survival and development depended on territorial extension southward. "The African will resume his march to the equator," Representative De Jarnette told the House, "there to work out his destiny on the Amazon and La Plata." Therefore, the African race would achieve what the Virginia slaveholder politician assumed would be its destiny. This expansion would be under white slaveholder auspices because "successful agriculture the handmaid of commerce demands the absolute control of labor." Racial coexistence would be preserved by territorial expansion. Hunter also expected the migrating African Americans to remain enslaved people and be accompanied by their white masters as they moved south. The labor of enslaved African Americans was vital for Anglo-Americans to successfully exploit the tropics. As a result, in the future Confederacy, "We shall solve the problem of the extension of the Anglo-Saxon race to the country south of us," he told the crowd of ten thousand gathered in the snow at the First African Methodist Church in Richmond on February 9. The audience had come to hear the senator's remarks on the failure of the Hampton Roads peace conference—he was the only one of the three Confederate commissioners to speak in public—and instead of a post mortem they heard Hunter "show that the white and black races may be extended together."[32]

Proponents argued that arming selected African Americans would both strengthen the depleted armies and constitute another step in the Confederate Christianizing mission to improve the condition of African Americans as a whole. Such a mission had implications for the future nation. Davis conceived the eventual emancipation of the forty thousand men he (or rather Lee) estimated would be needed to plug the gaps in the Army of Northern Virginia as part of a wider Confederate goal. "The stability of our republican institutions," Davis wrote in his message to Congress on November 7, "rest[s] on the actual political equality of all its citizens and includes the fulfillment of a task already which has been so happily begun: improving the condition and Christianizing the Africans." On February 10, 1865, while waiting in Matamoras to return to the Confederacy, the former minister to Mexico, William Preston, assured his son Wick of the continuing importance of this mission. He personally disapproved of slavery, Preston told his son, but for the African Americans, the Kentuckian soldier and diplomat "thought it was right for me to hold, govern, protect ... them according to the best of my ability as it was better for them and indispensable to the harmony and wellbeing of my country." On February 9, Preston's superior, Secretary Benjamin, told the crowd in Richmond—he was on the same panel of speakers as Senator Hunter—that the government "invites the negro to the highest exercise of judgment and will." As a result, the Confederacy in the future will be "ensuring the bestowal of freedom on the most deserving and best able to use it." Benjamin accepted that enlistment would lead to inequality among African Americans, and he looked forward to a caste system across the Confederacy, such as had existed in his native New Orleans before the war.[33]

Other Confederates, even if they accepted the need for reform, had a less exalted view of the outcome of changes to slavery and of their own future ambition. Those that were turning inward had little interest in their own destinies, let alone that of African Americans. Some expected emancipated enslaved people to remain in the Confederacy as sharecroppers. The enslaved soldiers "should also be promised permission to remain at home, after the war," Governor William Smith of Virginia—an enthusiastic advocate of enlistment—told Davis on March 27, but perhaps not permission to a great future. "After independence," John Stringfellow assured Davis on February 8, "landless blacks will still have to labor for whites on terms about as economical as tho' owned by them." Such an arrangement of labor without responsibility seemed the best of all possible worlds for some planters. "I have at last got rid of I hope a great deal of trouble," Frances Sprague told her daughter Margaret Winchester on January 2, "by hiring out this plantation for two years." She wanted the social aspect of slavery preserved while she was glad to be rid of its burdens. "I do not want slavery again," Sprague added on February 24, "but I wish the negroe to be kept in their proper place, we will not have half the care upon our minds we formerly had when they were sick and trying to improve them." This admission was a diminution of the mission of the Confederacy, but one that preserved something of its social and economic structure.[34]

Some of these Confederates renounced responsibility for African Americans and demanded they leave the Confederacy after the war. Charles Leitner told Davis on December 31, although he was convinced of African American loyalty, there must be African American colonization of Africa on independence. Maybe the Union would support these Confederate colonization schemes. The next day, prosperous planter Alexander Fitzpatrick of Nelson County, Virginia, told Davis, the United States government had no interest in destroying the Confederacy and instead sought "above all things the freedom of the negroes." In these circumstances, the government would finally be left alone if it would not only emancipate them but also "hand them over." Fitzpatrick agreed with fellow Virginia James M. Mason, who—concerned about rumors of Confederate emancipation in return for diplomatic recognition—on January 21 warned Benjamin that any increase in "free blacks after the war" would cause "great mischief and inconvenience." Therefore, Fitzpatrick made it a condition that if the Confederacy voluntarily surrendered its slave population, the Union in return had to "colonize them in Liberia or some other place and they would take care of them." The outcome Fitzpatrick sought was that Confederates would in the future live in "peace and sepperation [sic] from the Yankees." Federal race war aims would have been apparently realized along with some sort of Confederate independence.[35]

Fitzpatrick's segregationist vision was unacceptable to many. For most Confederates, slavery still underpinned the economy and social structure of their nation in the last months of the war, and they expected that it would still determine their future after the war. The sense of racial stewardship gave the nation its mission to pursue in the world. The plans for the postwar Confederacy, Hunter expected, involved the coexistence of both races in pursuit of the ambitious objectives of the slaveholders. "The welfare and training of the negro race is a sacred trust peculiarly confided to the South," Hotze wrote on January 26. "To surrender that trust at an hour of peril is to prove herself unworthy of it." Slavery had a dual purpose, providing both a sense of obligation for African American welfare, especially if the enslaved adult males had fled, and a means of production. "I would willingly go with you [to Europe]," Sprague confided to her daughter Winchester on January 2, "but these poor children have no one but me to attend to them or their interest." As well as a matriarchal sense of duty, self-interest mattered, and thus Sprague combined this maternal attitude with that of the marketplace. In the Mississippi Valley under Union control, hired African Americans remained vital as a source of labor on southern plantations, although only if the price was right. Sprague wanted to know the prevailing rates in Natchez, and added on February 24, "I will not give twenty five dollars a month to a negro who will only work about half his time."[36]

THE NEED TO REFORM THE ECONOMY

Planters reluctantly envisaged an economic future other than that of staple crop production, as it suggested a future of small-holding provincialism. Ambitious Confederates instead looked forward to the rapid development of an industrial sector. Given the Confederacy's economic backwardness, the importation of the very latest technology offered the chance to leapfrog a lengthy and expensive phase of industrial development and apprenticeship and to catch up with Britain and the United States. The government pursued this ambition to the end and continued to send agents abroad to learn about advanced industrial practices. "Ordered to sea by his physicians," according to Varina Davis in October 1864, but "much better" once he had successfully run the blockade outside Wilmington and reached Bermuda, the former secretary of war, George Wythe Randolph, combined his health cure in Europe during the following winter with industrial espionage, making visits to Bessemer steel plants in Sheffield, England, and Bordeaux, France, on behalf of the War Department's Nitre and Mining Bureau.[37]

Farmers had hitherto continued planting because they believed in comparative advantage and that they would always be able to import manufactured goods from blockade-runners. Therefore, in early 1865 disaster loomed for advocates of comparative advantage with the imminent effective loss of the last Atlantic port of Wilmington—through which Randolph had earlier passed en route to Europe—as Union forces threatened Fort Fisher. "Our ports are closed," Post Master General John H. Reagan told Davis on April 22, so the government was "unable to arm our people [even] if they were willing to continue." Lee had earlier grasped the consequences of the pending cessation of European imports. The Confederacy needed to industrialize fast, and it was almost too late. The government must support manufacturing, he told Davis on January 18, and should have done so from the beginning. A strict policy of free trade had to be abandoned. Postwar protection for such infant industries was vital in order to wean planters and merchants from the easy money of cotton. Lee continued, "Capitalists [have] been apprehensive that the return of peace would leave them with their means involved in an unprofitable business." He understood the risk-averse mind of the planter and an appreciation of the upfront costs associated with industrialization—the capital expenditure in the plant, for example, had acted as a deterrent from moving to manufacturing from planting.[38]

North Carolina representatives in the House had anticipated Lee in reiterating demands they had long made for government support for enterprises in their state. With an eye on developing the area's iron and coal and with his locality of Greensboro in mind, John Adams Gilmer argued for the "necessity of establishing government works on Deep River, North Carolina." Meanwhile, the most prestigious industrial enterprise in the Confederacy struggled to survive. The director of Tredegar Iron Works, Joseph R. Anderson, requested that his works be taken under government control due to the acute shortage of capital and labor and the need for impressment of supplies. Even though the works ceased production in March on the grounds of insufficient supplies of coal and iron ore, hope continued that this stoppage might be temporary. On April 1, Davis tried to assure Lee about Tredegar, noting that "we will endeavor to keep them at work, though it must be on a reduced scale. There is also difficulty of even getting iron even for shot and shell."[39]

Confederate advocates for a manufacturing sector believed it promised a future of self-sufficiency, although they cautioned that any industrial activity in the Confederacy would be modest in scale. In the future, as Lynchburg engineer Thomas E. McNeill suggested to Davis on February 19, all factories should be "*small*" and removed "to mountainous areas where they could be defended"; with men still fighting in the armies, he added, "women of our country could be collected" easily around them to provide the labor force. An embrace of manufacturing and self-sufficiency signified a nation turning away from the export trade and internationalism in general. On April 20, Hotze claimed that Richmond had only been chosen as capital with European approval in mind; "but that prestige has proved barren and too dearly bought." With the fall of Richmond, the war was now to be waged "more in accordance with the necessities of the country" in mind, as opposed to "the formalities of a rank among nations."[40]

To those optimists used to planning for a slaveholder-led empire with cosmopolitan pretensions, such a disregard of international prestige signified defeat. On January 30, Oldham declared to his fellow senators that the Confederacy's downfall "means the erasing of our name and country from the maps of the world; the conclusion of our history, with no future." The Union's conquest entailed "the destruction of our government," and in its place, Confederates would be "governed by a triumvirate: consisting of the whining canting hypocritical Yankee, the red republican; the infidel German and superior to the trio, the African negro." Hence the unfolding of the nightmare scenario to Oldham: the "provincialization of our states" oppressed by a "brutalized negro soldiery." A more advantageous arrangement within the United States would perhaps enable internationalists to escape this provincial fate.[41]

Accomplishing Objectives with Union Help

The reelection of Lincoln confirmed emancipation and reunion as the main U.S. government policies. Yet if it was given that the war would end this way to the Union president—it was certainly not clear to many Confederates. The calculation that both reunion and emancipation were negotiable applied even—or especially—to those who already conceded that the future development of the Confederacy would depend on a bargain, collaboration, and pact with the Federals. To ready themselves for this process and give themselves the best possible chances for an acceptable outcome, these optimists sought to project an image of continuing Confederate power through their representation of all the slave states and Indian Territory. They also maintained a claim to the Southwest together with a connection to the Mexican empire as ally, colony, and refuge. Moreover, there was always the chance, while Lee and his army were still in the field, that a military success would improve the negotiating position of the slaveholders' republic. This stance—however deluded it appears to historians—seemed to individuals at the time to rest on assumptions that were eminently realistic.

To successfully negotiate with the United States, the Confederate envoys would have to represent the united voice of the whole white South, including the long-occupied Border States. Davis perceived the Confederacy's claim to the Border States as an impassable barrier to negotiations with the Union. "We assert them to be members of the Confederacy," Davis confidently told a delegation of Georgian politicians on November 17, in reference to the status of West Virginia, Kentucky, Missouri, and Tennessee. All hope was gone to seize these states militarily, yet local democracy might come to the Confederacy's aid. "In settling the boundary" of the Confederacy, John Adams Gilmer told the House, "let the states of Missouri and Kentucky determine for themselves by a free and fair vote of their people." Votes for delegates to state conventions would accomplish what Confederate arms had failed to do. These voters, he added, would have to be "bona fide residents in their respective states at the commencement of hostilities."[42]

Moreover, rumors of military successes in November and early December revived, for a time, a de facto as well as de jure Confederate claim to the Border States, especially in public pronouncements. "Our forces have penetrated into central Missouri," Davis announced in his message to Congress on November 7, "affording to our oppressed brethren in that state an opportunity of which many have availed themselves, of striking for liberation from the tyranny to which they have been subjected." He did not expect the state to be conquered by the army of General Sterling Price, but at least additional Missouri exiles would be gathered further south for future incursions. Although during the autumn Price had already been twice defeated and, by November, was in retreat out of the state, this news was not known yet east of the Mississippi. On November 13, the *Augusta Constitutionalist* expressed the confident belief that Price would winter in Missouri. Whatever War Secretary Seddon's private concerns about the future, which would lead to his pressing for a negotiation with the Union and then his resignation in the coming months, he publicly agreed with the prevailing optimism. "Where Union occupation has been lightened in Kentucky and Tennessee," Seddon reported on November 3, "people rally to the Confederacy." In late November and early December, both Davis and General P. G. T. Beauregard expected that General John B. Hood's invasion of Tennessee would force the war back to the Ohio River by cutting Sherman's supply lines. Optimists continued to claim states even when under complete Union control for the foreseeable future, but the chance of a military incursion cheered these hopes.[43]

Native American tribes had to remain a part of this Confederate negotiating entity. In a letter to the president on November 5, Senator Robert W. Johnson of Arkansas recommended the appointment of Alfred B. Greenwood as superintendent of Indian affairs. Johnson cited the need to "protect Indian interests, afford relief to exiled families of allies who are in an extremely destitute state." The result of such an appointment, he stressed, would be to "secure confidence and loyalty and eradicate sentiment for an independent Indian confederation." On January 4, Davis nominated Greenwood as superintendent. In the final days of the Congress, senators continued to debate appointments in the Indian Territory—on February 22, the Senate referred to the Committee on Indian Affairs the nomination made by Seddon's successor, War Secretary John C. Breckinridge, of the veteran official Douglas H. Cooper as superintendent of Indian affairs.[44]

In December, Confederate control over Native Americans and their lands assumed a greater importance to the government as it became part of the latest Davis administration plan to claim New Mexico and Arizona. On December 21, the former governor of Arizona, John R. Baylor, wrote to Seddon with a proposal to form a "formidable alliance . . . with the numerous Indian tribes" in order for him to be able to recruit in California, New Mexico, and Arizona. The purpose of these activities was to recapture Arizona and New Mexico and defend Texas. Despite Baylor's prior record as a persecutor of Native Americans, Samuel B. Callahan and Elias C. Boudinot, the Creek-Seminole and Cherokee delegates to Congress, respectively, endorsed the plan. The plan had other influential supporters. When Seddon forwarded the matter to Davis on December 30, he added that the scheme "was earnestly commended and pressed on my attention by Col. Harrison," the former Texas commissioner to the Indians.[45]

Davis and Seddon agreed on Baylor's plan to reconquer Arizona in principle, but they differed as before about the immediate importance of the Southwest. There were "no resources" to support such a scheme, Seddon insisted to Davis, and he instead recommended "all the Trans Miss Forces at command should be either brought over to this side or used to create diversions in our favor." The president was more en-thusiastic, although he had no intention of overruling his subordinate. Davis hoped that the devolved structure of the Confederate adminis-tration would mean that formal support would be provided by his ad-ministration in the guise of the Trans-Mississippi Department. It was desirable, he agreed with Baylor on January 5, to have friendly relations with the settled Indians and "secure cooperation of nomadic tribes." De-spite the earlier stories of the then governor of Arizona wishing to exter-minate the Apache, Davis now considered Baylor possessed the "peculiar capacity" to be an Indian agent. Even considering the war secretary's own objections, Davis still wanted Seddon to encourage Kirby Smith to sup-port Baylor's venture; if Kirby Smith can spare troops, because "every feasible effort" should be made "to accomplish such an end." Seddon agreed to confer with Baylor and, according to historian Donald Frazier, Baylor was successful with his lobbying in Richmond and on March 25, 1865, was "reinstated as colonel and assigned to raise a command to re-store the empire in the South West."[46]

Meanwhile, congressmen listened to Native American concerns and praised their efforts on the Confederate side in the war. On Decem-ber 29, Boudinot secured unanimous passage of bills "to regulate trade and intercourse with the Indians." Early in January, Thomas B. Hanley of Arkansas, chairman of the House Committee of Indian Affairs, sub-mitted resolutions to that end on the "organization of the Arkansas and Red River superintendancy of Indian Affairs to regulate trade and in-tercourse with the Indians there and to preserve peace on the frontier." These steps coincided with a congressional joint resolution of thanks to Brigadier General Watie and Colonel Gano. William Porcher Miles of South Carolina, chairman of the Military Committee, congratulated Watie and Gano on the "brilliant and successful gains" they and their men had accomplished in the Indian Territory. Miles, who had been in correspondence with Lee since October about drafting enslaved people into the army, welcomed any Native American contribution to the Con-federate war effort. Into February, Congress continued to concern itself with appropriations for Native Americans, even as the larger plan of al-liance and expansion died in the preoccupied hands of Kirby Smith. The government, to the end, maintained its claim to the loyalty of and trade with the Native Americans, even as it ceased to exercise any direct influ-ence on events in the Indian Territory.[47]

The Baylor plan hoped to invoke the supposed loyalties of some Californians to the Confederacy to assist in retaking Arizona and New Mexico. Planners approved of the emphasis on maintaining a route to the Pacific and Mexico, as they believed the Confederacy was the only ally of Mexico. Historians tend to argue that Confederates had subordinated themselves to French ambitions by this time. Instead, members of the State Department believed that French greed had already alienated the Mexicans, and this made the latter susceptible to Confederate overtures. As a result of this circumstance, Slidell told Benjamin that Maximilian regretted his rumored cession of northwestern Mexico to France in lieu of debts, as the emperor "found that such an arrangement would be very distasteful to his new subjects." Most importantly, De Jarnette and others believed that as the French government returned to focus on global rivalry with Britain, "Now Mexico will be left as France found her to be absorbed by contact and association with us."[48]

As part of their long-term confidence in the ultimate integration of Mexico into the Confederacy, ambitious optimists perceived encouraging progress in the immediate plan to exploit Mexican resources. On November 25, 1864, Colonel Calhoun Benham, awaiting embarkation in Wilmington bound for Sonora, had good news to send his fellow Californian Joseph Lancaster Brent, then serving in General Taylor's command in Louisiana. Maximilian had appointed their friend, the former Senator William Gwin, "director in chief of colonization in the departments of Sonora and Chihuahua." This news meant opportunities beckoned once more for colonists. "It is proposed to colonize [the Mexican provinces] with southern people from California," Benham explained; the settlers would engage in "driving back the Apache and then exploiting the rich silver and gold reserves as well as developing the rich pastoral and arable resources of the lands." By February 9, 1865, Hotze reported that alleged progress in the colonization had already been made, as Gwin by then "had established himself at Sonora at the head of a numerous and well equipped body of resolute pioneers." Gwin returned to France that winter and, according to historian Rachel St. John, had proposed an expansion of his original colonization plan to Napoleon III. The propagandist believed that Gwin had the blessing of Mexico City and added that, as a mark of imperial favor, it had been "announced in some Mexican paper that Maximilian had conferred on him the title Duke of Sonora." As a result, Hotze concluded: "It bodes no good to the United States that a bitter enemy is established on their most exposed frontier at the head of a colony of southern refugees and sympathizers."[49]

Connected with these Mexican developments, optimists continued to have faith that the citizens of the states bordering the Pacific coast were tenuous in their loyalty to the Union. Thus the threat posed by Gwin's colony was rendered all the more formidable when, on November 17, Hotze assured his readers of the chance that far western states would secede from the United States. As "California and her Pacific sister states have taken very little part [in the war]," Hotze reasoned, "the connection with the Union [is] so nominal that it might be severed without shock." On account of the war, migrations of supporters, and geopolitics, the planners of the new nation considered Mexico remaining within their sphere of influence; as a result, they continued to believe that they still could pursue extensive ambitions in the west and south.[50]

Together with proof of an independent Confederate foreign policy, Mexico increasingly served another purpose for loyal rebels: as a place of asylum. "Mexico I think will be my next move," Mrs. Stella Bringier told Brent in Shreveport, Louisiana, "for I cannot and will not live under Yankee rule." And others who were more ambitious and less despairing wished to use the southern neighbor as a means to continue the war after the surrender of the Confederate armies east of the Mississippi River. If Confederates "will seek the protectorate of Maximilian," Wade Hampton assured Davis on April 22, "we can still make head against the enemy." Moreover, by that time, many individuals, as historian Daniel Wahlstrom explains, planned to move across the Rio Grande in order to fulfill their various commercial and agricultural ambitions, which they believed would be unrealizable in a post-emancipation South.[51]

Hopes of fulfilling individual ambitions therefore coexisted with U.S. domination of North America. Peace with the Federals, the essential precondition for the realization of these hopes, would have to come at this price. Planners for the future Confederacy believed they had adapted to changing circumstances when they understood that their nation's growth, at least in the Western Hemisphere, would be better achieved in cooperation with, rather than by either flight from or continued resistance to, the Union. Proposals from Confederate politicians and diplomats to form an alliance with the Federals in lieu of reunion had been momentarily quashed by Lincoln's reelection. However, optimism proved more resilient than disappointment in the electoral performance

of the Democratic Party. By the end of 1864, ideas of a looser confederation with northern states in place of reunion revived. Some members of
the House of Representatives advocated these plans for three reasons:
first, these individuals envisioned the outcome as in the best interest of
the Union and acceptable to members of the Lincoln administration;
second, it would be via a constitutional process with a convention of all
the states; and third, for these Confederate politicians, while it was inferior to complete independence, there were compensations. They could
comfort themselves with the encouraging prospects: retention of slavery,
control of the social system of the South, a boost to global republican
self-government, and participation in expansion abroad. From the administration's official perspective, independence was nonnegotiable, yet
Davis accepted that nationhood could be qualified in ways that, over
time, could result in a new American confederation.

In February 1865, Edward Alfred Pollard, a prominent journalist in
Richmond, insisted in a pamphlet that some northerners would agree to
such an alliance, despite Lincoln's firm opposition. He spoke for many
when he assumed Federals suffered from war weariness, worried about
the constant threat of foreign intervention, and opposed fighting for the
freedom of African Americans. He expected an imminent compromise,
in which slavery and self-government, even if the latter fell short of complete independence, would be at least salvaged for Confederates. Pollard
believed this outcome was feasible because Lincoln's policy of reunion
without conditions was tactical and a matter of "preference or desire but
no longer a passion." As a result, the United States government might be
"disposed to accommodate the enemy with certain treaty favors in lieu of
the union."[52]

Pollard considered that the recent Union military successes in Georgia and Tennessee in late 1864 would make northerners paradoxically
more amenable to conceding Confederate independence, as proof now
existed that the United States no longer required southern cotton to be
a great power. With the authority of four months' sojourn in the Union
as a prisoner of war, he observed that "northerners are not fighting for
Union," but instead for the dispensable goals of power and fulfillment
of ambition. U.S. soldiers wanted to cease fighting because, by 1865,
the Union's wartime boom has taken off, and "the development of her
resources and oil and mines" meant the imminent prospect of "fabu-
lous wealth." According to Pollard, northerners had originally opposed

secession as they thought they needed southern money; but after four years of industrial development, the United States had changed. By 1865, it was clear that "even apart from the south, [the Union] has it within herself the elements of a great national existence." The future evangelist for the "Lost Cause" believed that future progress rested on the primacy of industry and materialism among Federals and the "expansion of slavery into a world system" by the Confederacy.[53]

Commentators on potential negotiations assumed the Federals would drive a hard bargain from their present position of strength. On January 29, John Beauchamp Jones, a War Department clerk and diarist in Richmond, worried about an undue capitulation on the part of the Confederate negotiators. He fretted, as the commissioners departed for Hampton Roads, because "we have suffered so much that almost any treaty, granting us independence, will be accepted by the people." Therefore, he warned: "All the commissioners must guard against any appearance of a protectorate on the part of the United States." The writer and bureaucrat accepted that territorial losses and compensation would be the price of independence. Provided "the honor of the southern people be saved," Jones concluded, "they will not haggle about material losses."[54]

As it fitted their economic vision of the Confederacy, politicians hoped that commercial agreements would be prominent in any settlement with the Union and be welcome to northerners. Once independence has been settled, former U.S. congressman Brigadier General Henry W. Hilliard wrote to Davis on February 2, "we might concede much in a commercial way." This Alabama soldier-politician had long argued that the demands of commerce, Christianity, and racial destiny would be met by westward expansion, and to ensure this outcome, the government might propose, he suggested, "a commercial league . . . so as to provide against any restriction upon trade between the two peoples." John A. Gilmer of North Carolina, another former Whig who now sat in the Confederate House of Representatives, agreed with Hilliard. As long as each nation was "perfectly free and independent of the other," Gilmer told the House on February 20, it was possible for the "right of navigation, trade and transit etc. [to be] properly and fairly agreed and settled." The North Carolinian had been prominent in efforts to forge an agreement between the sections in 1861 and now once more emerged as an advocate of compromise. The setbacks of the war demanded what many Confederates reluctantly perceived to be necessary concessions. This "new Union of two sovereign powers," Hotze believed, was nothing more than a "commutation of [a] capital sentence to penal servitude for life," but given the circumstances, such an arrangement was tempting.[55]

Hilliard considered his commercial pact idea to be acceptable to both sides. A weak central government representing the whole of the former United States would be agreeable to all as the alternative to living in what he described as consolidated nation-states with strong federal authorities that turned a people inward and constrained expansion. Hilliard predicted that replacing the strong central government in Richmond with a weaker one in Washington would stimulate westward expansion by settlers. In addressing the Confederate president, the Alabamian tactfully urged the necessity of such a move. There had to be some kind of transnational structure created in order to "reconcile the people of the North to a political separation," Hilliard added to Davis, and "prevent future quarrels." Antebellum debates, together with the contemporary arrangement of the German Confederation based in Frankfurt, provided material to work with on coming up with a proposal. The moment had come to "realize Calhoun's idea of a dual executive," Hilliard continued, perhaps with a "president for each of the great geographical divisions." By mentioning the name of Davis's political mentor, he presumably hoped to make the proposal more palatable to the president.[56]

American politicians in search for solutions to the sectional crisis had long looked to the German Confederation as a possible example to follow. The all-German political assembly in Frankfurt was a suitably toothless federal organization for Confederates to propose as a template. John A. Gilmer of North Carolina followed this German model when he proposed to the House on February 20 that an "American [D]iet be created." The Greensboro politician was not cynical in his approach; during the secession winter he had been a leading southern Unionist—according to historian Dan Crofts he was secretly asked to join the Lincoln cabinet—although he expected the Republicans to make significant concessions in order to keep the South in the nation. Each section would be "at liberty to send delegates, each being its own judge as to number and manner of electing them." Further negotiations would be necessary, Gilmer suggested, as its exact privileges had to be "clearly and definitely defined." However, one matter was nonnegotiable, as with Austria and Prussia in the German Confederation in which each sovereign state had one vote in the Federal Assembly, an absolute veto for each party was crucial. The Diet would have "but two votes," Gilmer insisted, one each and "only binding on the parties when ratified by House, Senate, and President of each."[57]

Another German arrangement—also once supported by Calhoun and then less palatably for Confederates by Stephen Douglas in 1861—presented an example of a possible commercial union that presented Confederate concessions without political complications. Advocates of a version of the German Zollverein, or a customs union encompassing both countries including zero tolls along shared rivers and with a common tariff wall outside, believed the Federals' commercial interests would assist the process of negotiation. The adoption of the Union's tariff by Confederates would, moreover, be a significant opening concession. Even "if it was possible to subjugate us," Jones wrote in his diary on January 29, "it would only be killing the goose that lays the golden egg, for the southern trade would be destroyed." Perceptions of Yankee greed and rational self-interest would propel a mutually advantageous settlement. "It is in the interest of the United States Government to recognize us—on the basis of reciprocal free trade and free navigation of our rivers and harbors," De Jarnette told the House a day later, because it would "give them the advantages the union formerly gave them," and so this "peace proposal" would give the Federals a "result more satisfactory than the subjugation of the South result to the northern mind."[58]

Henry Hotze, from his vantage point as commercial agent in London, believed that taken together these various political and commercial proposals drawn from German practice should be sufficient for the United States government. Northerners "prefer the reality of union to mere name," he insisted on February 2, and hence would be prepared to propose to the South local government on condition of so close an alliance "as to make it a practicable Union of two States" with each just having the "prestige of each material power." A self-governing South would be able to maintain slavery and sufficient armed force to police, but not much more. Although expansionists recognized that Lincoln was opposed to this policy and that the Thirteenth Amendment abolishing slavery had passed the U.S. Congress, neither circumstance would necessarily be an insuperable obstacle to a negotiation, especially if the government conceded some form of reunion.[59]

Senator Gustavus A. Henry, former Whig and governor of Tennessee, who in October 1863 declined to be Confederate attorney general, believed that a constitutional mechanism, an all-state convention, existed as a process to implement their minimum objectives. "We can now say to the enemy . . . that we are sincerely desirous of peace and that the Confederate States are ready and willing to enter negotiations to that end," Henry assured other senators on November 29, 1864, "through a convention of all the states." The experience of his rivalry in Tennessee with Andrew Johnson during the 1850s taught Henry the need to set firm conditions at the outset. The convention would only assemble on the "basis of their separate independence, repudiating reunion or reconstruction."[60]

Congress predicted that a revised constitution with a loose association between North and South would be the outcome of a convention of all the states. War Bureau Chief Kean observed that a convention also appealed to those politicians who opposed the government, "not thinking the matter would be well handled" by Davis and Benjamin. On January 12, the House Committee of Foreign Affairs led by Jehu A. Orr of Mississippi and William Cabell Rives of Virginia resolved—in words drafted by or at least agreed with Vice President Alexander Stephens—that notice be taken of "a just and sound sentiment manifested by a large portion of the United States people since the last session of congress." As a result, there was a shared understanding between Confederates and the 45 percent of Federals who voted Democratic that "all associations of these American states ought to be voluntary and not forcible and . . . an appeal to forum of reason, to see if the matters of controversy can not be properly and justly adjusted by negotiation."[61]

Whether homegrown or copied from overseas examples, such a constitution, Confederates believed, would be the best outcome not only for themselves but also for Federals and the world in general. Therefore, anyone who opposed such a "reasonable" proposal had to be insane. Lincoln's "political ambition," according to Hotze, with the U.S. president's need to recover the lost, lucrative, and unequal commercial antebellum arrangements the North had imposed on the South, "requires the continuation of the war." He argued that such desires were evidence of "surely a madness that seizes at times whole nations as well as individuals." Eventually more northerners would realize that "the prolongation of the war increasingly imperils the cohesion of the United States." In that scenario, providing the Confederate armies kept on fighting, a moment would come when the individual states of the Union faced the unpalatable choices of "prolonged war or satisfactory peace, increased anarchy or orderly redistribution of power." It was nothing more than common sense,

Hotze believed, that these states would choose the wonderful future of an American continent not governed by "one overgrown and overbearing Empire but many powerful prosperous and improving States," whose relations were those of "allies and friends not confederates" and collectively would prove a "blessing to both America and the world."[62]

The commercial, not to mention strategic, benefits to be derived from partnership in the running of an ambitious, "overgrown and overbearing" empire appealed to many individuals, including the president. It was in this context that the veteran Border State Democratic politician Francis P. Blair Sr. contacted Davis on December 30, suggesting a meeting to discuss ideas "that may not only repair all the ruin the war has brought on the Nation, but contribute to promote the welfare of other nations that have suffered from it." Lincoln reluctantly consented to Blair's proposed mission behind the lines on the strict condition that any agreement would be based on reunion and emancipation. Ambitious Confederate observers nevertheless interpreted Blair's visit as an invitation for the Confederacy to become a partner in an alliance devoted to a global cause based on a shared republicanism with little said on reunion and less on emancipation. In January, when he met Davis, Blair explained in more detail an idea of a shared external mission for both North and South in expelling European aristocratic governments from the Western Hemisphere. Reconciliation "must depend he thought on time and events," Blair agreed, and as far as events and accelerating the pace of reconciliation were concerned, "no circumstance would have a greater effect, than to see the arms of our countrymen from the North and the South united in a War on a Foreign Power, assailing principles of government common to both sections and threatening their destruction."[63]

In his account of the meeting, Davis passed over Blair's single nation reference and focused on the opportunity for mutual expansion. The idea of a joint application of the Monroe Doctrine appealed to Davis on the grounds that it met Confederate needs for expansion and, according to one historian, perhaps even his own ambition to be a military dictator. The president considered, in agreement with Hilliard, that such an expansive polity, if it should become a single nation over time, would have a weaker central government, which would be incapable of interference with slavery in the South or at the very least allow southern leaders to order race relations within their states. In order to preserve southern honor, Davis recorded, Blair envisioned an extended southern territory to the Isthmus of Darien (Panama). The president reversed the order of his visitor's proposals conceding that immediate expansion might enable eventual reunion. Projects of southern territorial growth would open "a new channel for bitter waters" and provide "a common effort" between the Union and the Confederacy. Perhaps in the far-off future, Confederates would accept a union as long as Washington was a distant authority and a center of a vast empire. Two days later, Blair reviewed Davis's record of their conversation and noted, as the president intended, that Davis's memorandum "presented the maintenance of the Monroe Doctrine as the main object" of any agreement between Union and Confederacy.[64]

At the same time as these secret discussions in mid-January, Jehu A. Orr made a similarly bold proposal in a secret session at the House. Orr's Committee on Foreign Affairs requested that three "commissioners shall be authorized to bring into view the possibility of cooperation between the Confederate States and United States in maintaining the principles and policy of the Monroe Doctrine in the event of a prompt recognition of the independence of former by the United States Government." Politicians reversed their earlier hostility to the Monroe Doctrine, provided the Confederacy participated in its enforcement. "The Confederate Government and people have as deep an interest in the firm and inflexible maintenance of what is known as the Monroe Doctrine as the United States," Foote had told the House on November 28; therefore if there is an "early recognition of their independence," and "provided ample justice being done them in other respects," then the Confederate government and people "would doubtless recognize it was their true policy to unite [with the United States government] in support of [the Monroe Doctrine]." In the end, the House narrowly defeated Orr's resolution; but, according to historian Steven Woodworth, the debates reflected a public discussion "throughout the Confederacy, [as] politicians, newspapers, and others were taking up the fantasy of a joint war to enforce the Monroe Doctrine." Davis, Orr, Stephens, and Foote did not know this future was a fantasy, and the vice president repeatedly raised the proposal when he, Hunter, and Campbell met Lincoln and Seward at Hampton Roads, Virginia, on February 3. At the same time, as Woodworth adds, "the Mexican chimera must have been more or less universally attractive to people who were grasping at straws that winter."[65]

Supporters of a powerful future Confederacy, whether knowingly "grasping at straws" or not, offered to the Union, in exchange for this territorial expansion, an ideological alliance based on furthering republicanism with additional commercial benefits. The appeal of republicanism in peril seemed especially urgent, given that the war between the two greatest democracies in the world had put the ideal of self-government on the defensive worldwide. Confederates would have disagreed with those later historians who look back at 1865 as a turning point in world history when democracy scored an irreversible global triumph. Instead it has been "a war that has destroyed the influence of our republican system of free government," Williamson Oldham informed the Senate on January 30, "which has re-established and confirmed despotism in Europe and made it exultant, and has rolled back the sun of liberty for a century." In this context, there was support that the Davis administration should combine with the United States to roll back despotism. "Democracy has discovered how few friends it has in Europe amongst the ruling class," a correspondent of the U.S. minister to Denmark, Bradford Wood, observed in a letter published in the *Index*, yet the desperation of the fighting meant, "its strength has been mutually discovered." In the future, the advance of aristocratic government would be rolled back across the world by an alliance between the Union and the Confederacy.[66]

Republican ideology remained central to Confederates' vision of the future. On January 12, Davis vowed to Blair that, rather than ally with European powers, "he would die a freeman in all respects." According to Blair, Davis was "convinced all the Powers of Europe, felt it their interest that our people in this quarrel should exhaust all their energies in destroying each other, and thus make them a prey to the Potentates of Europe who feel that the destruction of our system of Government was necessary to the maintenance of the monarchical principles on which their own were founded." Those planners who supported such a republican alliance also believed that this common purpose would, if not bring friendship, reduce friction between the two neighbors, as their energies would be directed outward rather than against each other. The Union and the Confederacy should agree to "a treaty of mutual defense" with "an alliance offensive and defensive," Hilliard proposed on February 2, "which would wield the military energies of the American people in a way to secure for us perpetual peace." The security of both would benefit. "A common foreign policy with the Union would guard against all destabilizing forces of foreign intrigue," Hotze agreed two weeks later, however "dishonorable for [the Confederacy] to be dragged at the wheels of a foreign policy influenced by the North." As a result, the Confederacy would exhibit "equal carelessness for the good of the wider world" as a complicit Europe. On February 2, Hotze also noted "peace between the two belligerents and war for the rest of the world." In preparation "for such a war," he added, the Union was "now deliberately preparing by abrogation of the Canadian treaties and insults of French Mexican policy and strengthening their naval forces in European waters."[67]

Members of the State Department distrusted Union intentions, but they comforted themselves that their diplomacy would be similarly duplicitous in its dealing with their northern neighbors. They considered that an alliance between the Confederacy and the United States was the greatest fear of Britain, France, and Mexico; this belief gave these diplomats apparent room for maneuver. Optimists expected to realize their ambitions for the Confederacy by being in a position to play off the competing parties for their advantage. These prevailing expectations provided the context of the Duncan Kerner mission sent to Europe by Davis and Benjamin to explore the question of trading slavery for recognition by London and Paris. Politicians, diplomats, and adventurers continued to place their nation's future in a wider trans-Atlantic, even global, context. Britain and France were interested in "preventing a monopoly of the western slope of the American continent by the United States," Duff Green told Davis in late December, and may decide to join with the Confederacy "to divide with us the occupation of the Pacific States and the control of the trade of the Pacific." Rivalry between Britain and France would also help the ambitions of expansionists. France "must hold" a position on the Pacific coast, De Jarnette announced to the House, if that country was to successfully compete with Britain. Therefore, Slidell believed in Mexican compliance, as he told Benjamin on February 7, with the "rumored accession of Sonora etc. to France." Although he was "unable to ascertain the truth of this rumor," he considered it to be "a real case" and a "private arrangement" between the two emperors. The territories were to be granted in lieu of Mexican debt owed to France, and the French, apparently, were keen to conclude the deal on account of the "Sonora gold fields." At the very least, such an issue might make Mexico yearn for an alliance with the Confederacy to prevent further losses to France. Diplomats instinctively or reflexively remained convinced the nation they represented would continue to play an important role in the great power struggle for global mastery.[68]

As LONG as the Army of Northern Virginia remained in the trenches outside Petersburg, there still remained a sufficient basis for some individuals to plan a future Confederacy. Those who did so were fewer in number than earlier in the war, as other priorities, hitherto suppressed, suspended, or discarded, rose to take precedence. The visions were also more abstract and appeared less coherent than before, although the postponement of peace, anticipated closer ties with the Union, and demands of the war gave their tone a more universal, ideological, and even revolutionary flavor. Nevertheless, neither silence nor vagueness implied an abandonment of the national project. Even those who committed themselves to more modest goals for the future—including the redefinition of "independence" to mean the surrender of some powers over foreign and commercial policies to a federal entity—still expected considerable self-government and the preservation of slavery. They also accorded long-term regional, even global, significance to whatever it was they were planning to do.

EPILOGUE

What Are You Going to Do?

W HILE ONGOING military operations, especially those of the Army of Northern Virginia, continued, leading Confederates—whether planters or diplomats—carried on their pursuits. "The planters in this neighborhood are working their fields with the firm determination to make good crops," Colonel Bringier reassured Joseph L. Brent about the situation in Louisiana on April Fool's Day, 1865, and they will proceed with this task "if we will only guarantee *not* to abandon them." On April 20, over in London and still in ignorance of Lee's surrender, Henry Hotze continued to hope, believing that Lee had achieved "the great object of which is to preserve a formidable organized army for future operations."[1]

Back in the Confederacy, such hopes had been undone by the spread of news about events in Virginia. On April 12, H. T. Douglas in Shreveport, Louisiana, announced to Brent: "I hear a rumor of the evacuation of Richmond, I fear its truth. Should it be correct ... I shall regard the cause as entirely hopeless & work as a man leading on in a forlorn hope." By April 30, even the optimistic Brent admitted his fear to Simon B. Buckner that the "torpor and despair" of the citizen would spread to the army.[2]

From the beginning of Lee's ejection from Petersburg, soldiers in his army sensed the sobering significance of the defeat. On April 2, cavalryman William Wilson, already retreating near the Appomattox River when he heard news of the evacuation of Richmond, confessed in his diary that he considered himself "utterly incompetent to grasp the magnitude of the disaster that has befallen the Confederate arms." He could not predict what the future would be when "Virginia the bulwark of the South is lost," and "I have terrible forbodings [*sic*] of the fate of the Army of Northern Virginia now defeated for the first time in its proud career."

Previous setbacks to that army, such as Gettysburg and Antietam, were in a totally different category to the fate that befell the Army of Northern Virginia during its retreat from Petersburg.[3]

Soldiers admitted to stupefaction when they thought about the consequences of the events going on around them. "I am at a loss to know what is to become of us," Douglas confessed to Brent on the "startling intelligence" of Lee's surrender, which reached the Trans-Mississippi Department on April 24, adding, "I am holding my hands, am willing & ready, but can do nothing." He begged Brent: "Can you suggest anything to relieve this terrible suspense[?]" Douglas waited for something to turn up and, at the same time, dreaded that moment when it finally arrived.[4]

The departure of the Confederate government from Richmond led to paralyzing anxiety among politicians. On April 4, Wilson, swept up in the retreat westward from Petersburg, fell in with the secretary of war and was concerned to learn that "[Breckenridge] is as much in ignorance of Lee's whereabouts as any of us . . . the more I see of matters the less hopeful I become." A day later, Davis revealed his own sense of loss of control, when he told Varina that he had "in vain sought to get into communication with Genl. Lee and have postponed writing in the hope that I would soon be able to speak to you with some confidence of the future." Confederate civilians ceased to believe that the president could influence events; on April 7, Varina informed him that among the inhabitants of Charlotte, North Carolina, "numberless surmises are hazarded here as to your future destination and occupation."[5]

There came a point when the question of an individual's future took over from a collective Confederate destiny. On April 8, 1865, Wilson's "thoughts turn homewards"; for twenty-four hours he tried to resist succumbing to this impulse, and even the news of the surrender did not immediately register. Finally, outside Lynchburg on April 9, the cavalryman diarist "tried to familiarize myself with the idea of surrender but at last it came upon me with a staggering force." He looked around for familiar sources—Lee and the corps commanders—for guidance, but "the scepter had departed,—the oracles are dumb." Instead of a disciplined army, all he saw were men "confused, demoralized, unnerved by despair." Underpinning this paralysis was the realization that "each man is master of his own movements," and each now asked himself: "What are you going to do? Is the question that meets you on every side—the answers are various."[6]

Some Confederates believed they would be conscripted into the Union armies in order to fight future U.S. wars of aggression. They considered

this outcome likely from a tyrannical Republican administration that required the perpetuation of military conflict in order to survive. Lincoln's
assassination rendered this northern aggression more palpable and urgent. On April 20, Hotze reckoned that "Seward is ready for a foreign war
as soon as the southern job is finished." That bleak future of a Confederate draft would arise from "the downfall of a power the establishment of
which alone can prevent the most arrogant nation on earth from disturbing the peace and interrupting the commerce of the world." Fighting for
the Union would be worse for the soldiers than before because, according
to Wade Hampton on April 19, when in the foreign wars intended by the
Johnson administration, Confederates would be "under a more rigorous
conscription than has yet to be obtained [and] here shall be forced to fight
by the side of our own negroes & under Yankee officers."[7]

These committed Confederates insisted southern citizens would suffer additional burdens and indignities. In the future, they would face racial equality and amalgamation, and a tyranny under mob rule based on
the majority. On April 19, Hampton predicted that the southern people
"shall have to pay the United States debt and live under a base and vulgar tyranny." A day later, Hotze asked, "What hope of the future when
[northern politicians] behave like vulgar demagogues in accordance with
the sentiments of the people?"[8]

However, for all their vehemence of the denunciations of northerners, Confederates rapidly adjusted themselves to the new conditions.
A few, such as Hampton on April 19, used bleak predictions of the future
in order to argue that it was better for them to fight to the extreme limit
of their country than to reconstruct the Union on any terms. Others
urged immediate planning for future opportunities. On April 27, Hotze
wondered, "Will the South seek conservative allies in [the] North for ultimate revenge?" Most Confederates came around to seeing their future
within the context of reunion because, as Navy Secretary Stephen R.
Mallory informed Davis on April 24, "the Confederacy is conquered."[9]

The terms of the military conventions in Virginia and North Carolina offered hope to Confederates that the terms of reentering the Union
would be generous. On April 22, Attorney General George Davis comforted the president with the hope that the Charlotte military Convention offered the chance to "reenter the old Union upon the same footing
on which they stood before seceding from it." Postmaster General Reagan
was more skeptical when he wrote a detailed memorandum to Davis on
April 22, but nevertheless he proposed that Confederates had to behave

as "if the future shall disclose a disposition (which I fear the chance is remote) on the part of the U.S. people to return to the spirit and meaning of the Constitution."[10]

Reagan believed Federals recognized that they started the war and conducted it viciously and aggressively, leading them to accept war guilt. This sensibility extended to the U.S. government, and such a sense of remorse, together with the difficulty of accomplishing the feat of reunion, would result in relatively generous war terms. He construed a constitutional peace broadly and advised the president to accept the swift disbandment of any military in Confederate government (not state) service and recognize the authority of the United States government as long as both the state governments and rights of property secured by the U.S. constitution remained in existence. The terms Reagan suggested included the "right of self government, political rights, and property, amnesty for past participation." Therefore, there would be no Confederate contribution toward the United States debt, while honoring the Confederate equivalent and "allow us revenues etc., to satisfy our creditors." He realized these conditions constituted a "liberality never before extended from conqueror to conquered." Yet Reagan conceived them as necessary for reunion: if "the object of pacification is to reconcile, then the terms must be based on perfect equity." The U.S. government wanted "to secure reunion under a common government," and this "should rest on the consent and affection of the people." For a union to work, there must "remain no sense of wrong to rankle in the memories and lay foundations for new difficulties leading to new wars." Both self-government and slavery were the de minimis terms if the war was to end and never recur. Reagan was adamant that because "we did not seek this war," Confederates had a right to expect leniency.[11]

Individual acts of surprising mercy by Federal officers contributed to expectations of liberal terms of reunion. On May 12, the British consul in Mobile observed "the terms of surrender and the generous treatment of many persons, who could little expect it, have received from the U.S. army and navy commanders here, is producing a good effect and will go far to alleviate the great depression of the southern people at the sudden termination of all their hopes after such a fearful struggle." On May 30, General Henry A. Wise at Isle of Wight Court House, Virginia, told his wife about the behavior of Captain Allen, the provost marshal, "who was very kind showing me every attention and granting me all the protection I needed for myself, my horse and my effects."[12]

The most important Confederate symbol made a decisive public contribution to ex-Confederate expectations of reunion. Combined with the
publication of his farewell address to the Army of Northern Virginia,
Robert E. Lee's return to his wife's temporary home in Richmond on
April 15 revived morale in the city. He was "received with enthusiasm his
presence encouraged the people to open again their doors and windows
of houses which had remained obscured since the hostile occupation.
Ladies again appeared at windows with tears in their eyes waved handkerchiefs at the General." Meanwhile Lee's restraint helped the process,
"bowing to the throng of people retired in silence," the Richmond-based
journalist for the *Index* declared. On May 11, Hotze's optimism partially
returned when he predicted the military despotism of the occupation of
the South would end "sooner or later for it is not in nature of American
people to endure the military despotism long or patiently." As with Lee,
Hotze looked not to ultimate reconciliation but for the "rise from the
ruins that nationality which even in defeat reaped the moral fruits of
victory." The devastation of defeat was but a passing phase, and a longer-
term moral victory—that of the "Lost Cause"—would eventually occur.[13]

Embracing the "Lost Cause" memory of the Civil War required a
painful readjustment by optimistic planners who had looked forward
to founding a slaveholding empire. Many soldiers and civilians considered themselves bewildered, disappointed, and degraded. Even the most
committed planners accepted that the Confederacy had been militarily
defeated. Yet the habit of demanding to negotiate as an equal with the
Union lingered, and they believed the Confederate government could
obtain better terms from the United States than individual state governors. On April 22, 1865, Judah P. Benjamin tried to get Davis to order a
general surrender of remaining armies because, he explained, that would
enable the "States" and "people" to act collectively and "obtain for them
by a general pacification rights and advantages which they would, in all
probability, be unable to secure by separate action of the different States."
Rather than a heroic failure, the Confederacy remained for the secretary
of state a means to compromise with the United States government.[14]

The "Lost Cause" narrative took time to develop. In April and May of
1865, as the Confederacy collapsed, the past served different purposes to
individuals: it provided hope, while any armies remained in the field; it
cultivated a sense of grievance at the futility of the sacrifices; and, most
important, it bounded former Confederates together in a remembrance
of common suffering. Only the past could offer hope once Lee had been

forced to retreat from Petersburg and Richmond fell. Therefore, at Danville on April 4, Davis challenged his audience in faithful knowledge of the answer: "Who in the light of the past, dare doubt your purpose in the future?" On April 13, Hotze explained his president's rationale: "We have rather to do with the future than the past, using the latter to shed light on the obscurity of the former." Confidence in final victory, explained Hotze, can be sustained because "such a faith is akin to reason and harmonizes with experience while its supreme force lies in the illustration of past deeds."[15]

For many civilians as well as soldiers, waiting for something to turn up and refusing to accept the obvious fact that all was lost, the collapse of the Confederacy left them destitute of resources. Abstract comforts derived from the past provided nothing, and therefore when this ruin came upon them, most had more questions than answers. Stella Bringier in Shreveport asked Brent: "Where can I direct my wandering steps now? & what is there left to hope for? The news from the other side has crushed me. If Lee has surrendered with his army our only safety is in flight . . . no matter whither and try and hold out some hope, if any." She despaired: "What must be the end of all this [?] My head is so confused." Suspended animation also gripped James M. Mason, the commissioner in Europe. He continued to believe the Confederate government somehow still existed, and he wrote from London on May 1, "In the uncertainty of the future, or what may be the views of the government regarding the continuance of commissioners or other agencies abroad, I can only remain where I am and await its orders." Mason considered this conduct to be a great sacrifice, for he would remain at his post "however desirous to be at home . . . [and to] give aid and protection to my (I fear) distressed family."[16]

Mason's willingness to make this sacrifice can be explained by habits of duty, his isolation in London, the silence from Richmond, and his distrust of newspapers quoting northern sources. Nevertheless, his decision to wait and see mirrored a wider reaction back in his native Virginia once news of definitive surrender had spread among the population and with it the prospect of reunion and emancipation. Davis discovered the limits of the sacrifice he was prepared to make amid the confusion of the retreat into North Carolina. On April 23, he could at least see a future, telling Varina, "This is not the fate to which I invited you when the future was rose-colored to us both." The couple had now "to guard against contingencies . . . there may be better things in store for us than are now in view, but my love is all I have to offer and that has the value of a thing long prepossessed and sure not to be lost." On April 28, Varina replied and agreed that the present outcome was "surely not the fate to which you invited me in brighter days"; however, she continued with comforting exaggeration about any deprivation during their early married life, "you must remember that you did not invite me to a great Hero's home, but to that of a plain farmer." The diminished expectations for Davis meant her relative role in his life would increase for "I have shared all your triumphs, been the only beneficiary of them, now I am but claiming the privilege for the first time of being all to you now these pleasures have past for me." Davis's ambition for the Confederacy ended; his family had become his priority now.[17]

Davis and Mason did not submit to the Union as the logical next step, even if their defiance was muted. Others maintained a more un-compromising stance; on April 19, Stella Bringier assured Brent in Shreveport that she "cannot and will not live under Yankee rule." Many Confederates asserted a deep and abiding hatred, as a public letter to William Cabell Rives declared: "We are enemies in war[;] in peace we never can be friends." According to Hotze, any question of resuming al-legiance was null because "the North has destroyed a great republic!"— which meant not only the Confederacy, but also the United States. On April 22, Reagan told Davis, "I do not conceal the danger of trusting the people who drove us to war by their unconstitutional and unjust aggressions and who now add the consciousness of power to their love of dominion and greed of gain." Even outward passivity might hide inward rebellion; at the same time Reagan had communicated his doubts to Davis, Sarah Morgan in Baton Rouge resolved on "behaving like a lady" toward Union soldiers and veterans she encountered, including a former sweetheart. Yet she also resolved to "remain a rebel in heart and soul, and that all my life I may remember the cruel wrongs we have suffered."[18]

For many former Confederates, passivity seemed the best stance to adopt. Emancipation, losses in the war, and the arrival of the Union military together rendered inaction an apparently sensible adjustment to the times. Robert Kean, as a bureau chief in the War Department, had initially followed the flight of the Confederate government into North Carolina; after it broke up, he traveled north to join his relations in Edgefield, outside Charlottesville. He found a process of "quietly submit-ting" prevailing across Albemarle County. Kean explained that this tor-por was not the result of Union oppression but rather its absence. "The people ... waited patiently for the U.S. military authorities to take some order for reorganizing society and establishing a definite basis upon which such reorganization was to proceed," Kean observed, adding "but none such was vouchsafed." He noted that when individuals got together and acted in community meetings, the items on the agendas were additional confessions of helplessness, pleas to the garrisons of Union soldiers stationed in Charlottesville and Palmyra for help as these citizens feared famine. This anxiety was compounded for many individuals by the departure of formerly enslaved people from the farms into the local towns. Kean concluded that "the community is wholly unable to take up the burdens of a vast pauper system," which had arisen, he believed, from emancipation.[19]

The breakdown of the market economy—long disrupted by the war—now appeared to be permanent. In rural areas, subsistence agriculture prevailed; Nelson County, Virginia, neighbors and planters Maria Massie and William D. Cabell bartered for flour and bacon. In the ports, the situation was worse because the Union blockade remained in force until the summer, and until that time, the British consul in Mobile, Alabama, Fred Cridland, noted on April 21, "no foreign or general commerce can be permitted." Any "trade," he continued, had to be "limited to the wants of the army and navy and necessities of the inhabitants within the lines of military occupation." The future of cotton production and export was uncertain, dependent now on African American compliance and Federal policy. Henry Pinckney Walker, the acting consul in Charleston, explained that "the ability of the inhabitants to reproduce their former staples" relied on what powers they would have over formerly enslaved African Americans. In any event it was an open question, he warned his superiors in London, "when" and "whether" the former Confederate states would be "allowed to take their place in the markets of the world or to be reserved to the sole use of the North people and the U.S. Government."[20]

The submission Kean discovered also reflected either the absence or at least compulsory inaction of many of the hitherto leaders of the community, for the Federal authorities sent them to prison or punished them with political disabilities. By late May, in a single cell within the Carroll prison in Washington, General Joseph E. Johnston joined former governors Zebulon B. Vance of North Carolina and John Letcher of Virginia. "Never could hear why I was arrested," Letcher jotted on a scrap of paper, "and do not know to this day."[21]

Some former Confederates adapted swiftly to the new conditions and seemed effortlessly to pick up where they had left off during the war. Captain Edward Archer, who had been present at the surrender of Joseph Johnston in North Carolina, traveled to Richmond immediately after being paroled in early May and by June had returned to work at Tredegar. Family connections helped: not only was his father, Dr. Robert Archer, a director at the ironworks, but he was also brother-in-law to Joseph Anderson, who ran the industrial complex. For Henry A. Wise, his answer was to try to recover his plantation; he told his wife, mentioning the name of the place for the first time since the spring of 1862, "Rolleston had been advertised to be sold, but I am told that now it will not be, and that on paying taxes I may save it perhaps." Adventurers seemed to handle the transition most smoothly. Only a few months before surrender, in December 1864, Duff Green has been discussing transatlantic trade, transcontinental railroads, and the Pacific Ocean trade with Jefferson Davis at the Executive Mansion. In Richmond once more on April 5, he was back there again, seeking a meeting with Lincoln during the latter's visit in order to present a scheme to enable planters in the South to borrow money with their land as collateral in order to bring liquidity into the southern economy and so revive it from collapse.[22]

Green and others hoped to exploit the opportunities to be had now that the South was back within the United States. The final confirmation of fatal tuberculosis in spring 1865 left George W. Randolph stranded in Europe at the time of Appomattox; he had, as he put it, lost his health, fortune, and country. Yet when he wrote from Paris that July to a niece, he sounded like a future booster for the New South, predicting that Virginia "will yet rise to greater power & prosperity than she could have reached under the old regime. The very necessity for increased exertion will nerve the rising generation and give them far more energy and enterprise than we possessed." Randolph argued that the experience of the Civil War had not been wasted. "Adversity either quashes or elevates a people and I trust that we have too much stamina to be crushed." Randolph added, "We old folks [he was forty-seven] have much suffering to encounter but we mustn't discourage you young ones and still your hopes by mourning for the past." Randolph continued to have an undiminished faith in the future, augmented by the salutary experience of the war. A new generation, less compromised by secession and ruined by defeat, would have to take the lead in the future.[23]

Turning to emancipation, Randolph likewise predicted some opportunities amid the disaster for the white South. "Slavery whether good or bad is dead," he told his niece Sarah, and southerners needed to move on. "Let us forget it and not be eternally haunted by its ghost." The status of white southerners as a pariah people in the world was now over, the general believed, and he assured Molly, another niece, that "having been washed clean from your sins you may prepare yourself for your European tour with less trepidation than you would otherwise have felt." He told both nieces that he also expected the migration of African Americans from Virginia. "Free black labor is probably a mere transition to free white labor, at least in Virginia. Now that cuffey is free to go where he likes he will obey the laws of supply & demand and go where his labor will be best paid, and . . . the cotton and sugar and hot sun of the more southern states will eventually draw him out of Virginia." In Randolph's view, white Virginians should simply encourage the operation of classical economics. "Let us ease him off . . . striving to make the best use of him whilst he stays and wishing him a pleasant journey when he goes." So even though the dream of the Confederacy was over, some of the arguments earlier used to justify secession were redeployed to show that Virginia could thrive under reconstruction.[24]

Some of those prominent individuals who had opposed secession in 1861 and kept a low profile during the years of the Confederacy, thinking they would be able to swiftly return to public life after the war, agreed with Randolph on the need for action. Waiting for something to turn up was not only lazy but also dangerous. On May 8, 1865, Alexander Stuart—once President Fillmore's interior secretary—addressed a mass meeting in Staunton, Virginia, where he was joined on the platform by scions of the other great Valley families. In this patriarchal setting, he addressed the power vacuum that seemed so obvious to Kean. Stuart explained the resulting risks of disorder as well as economic hardship arising, which taken together "are calculated to create a sense of insecurity amongst our people." This situation will get worse, he continued, because "it has been suggested that our wisest course is to do nothing, but to await the development of events." Therefore, Stuart concluded, it was time that "we should endeavor, as far as we can, to give shape and direction as to our own destiny." As to what this destiny would be, Stuart did not elaborate, but even self-preservation required a return to planning for the future.[25]

NOTES

Abbreviations

BA   Rare Books Collection, The Boston Athenaeum, Boston, Mass.

CG   *Congressional Globe,* 38th Congress, 2nd Session, December 3, 1860, to March 3, 1861 (Washington, D.C.: John C. Rives, 1860–61).

CJ   The Library of Congress, *Journal of the Congress of the Confederate States of America, 1861–1865,* 7 vols. (Washington, D.C.: GPO, 1904–5).

DBR   *DeBow's Review and Industrial Resources, Statistics, etc. Devoted to Commerce, Agriculture, Manufactures (1853–1864).*

FHS   Filson Historical Society, Louisville, Ky.

GLC   Gilder Lehrman Collection, New-York Historical Society, New York, N.Y.

HL   The Huntington Library, Art Collections, and Botanical Gardens, San Marino, Calif.

JDC   Dunbar Rowland, *Jefferson Davis Constitutionalist: His Letters, Papers, and Speeches,* 10 vols. (Jackson, Miss.: Mississippi Department of Archives and History, 1923).

JDP   Lynda Lasswell Crist, Mary Seaton Dix, and Kenneth H. Williams, eds., *The Papers of Jefferson Davis,* 13 vols. (Baton Rouge: Louisiana State University Press, 2012).

OR   United States Naval War Records Office, *Official Records of the Union and Confederate Navies in the War of the Rebellion,* 30 vols. (Washington, D.C.: GPO, 1894–1922), ser. 1, vol. 3: *Proclamations, Appointments, etc. of President Davis; State Department Correspondence with Diplomatic Agents, etc.* (Washington, D.C.: GPO, 1922).

PRO   Public Record Office at the National Archives, Kew, London, United Kingdom.

SHC   Southern Historical Collection, Wilson Library, University of North Carolina, Chapel Hill.

UT   Dolph Briscoe Center for American History, The University of Texas at Austin.

UVA   Special Collections, University of Virginia, Charlottesville, Va.

VHS   Virginia Historical Society, Richmond, Va.

INTRODUCTION

1. Jefferson Davis, "Message to Congress," April 29, 1861, *JDC*, 5:84; Davis to Anna Ella Carroll, March 1, 1861, *JDP*, 7:64; "Speech in Atlanta," February 16, 1861, *JDP*, 7:44; Davis to James A. Seddon, January 5, 1865, *JDP*, 11:281. At the outbreak of war, Arizona and New Mexico were both in the New Mexico Territory created as part of the Great Compromise of 1850, and under the terms of Popular Sovereignty, settlers had permission to decide upon the slavery issue when they requested statehood (Rufus K. Wyllys, *Arizona: The History of a Frontier State* [Phoenix, Ariz.: Hobson and Herr, 1950], 150).

2. "Joint Resolutions Recognizing the Practical Neutrality of Oregon and California and the Territories of Washington and Nevada," October 1, 1862, *CJ*, 5:469–70; "Majority Report of the Committee of Foreign Affairs," September 19, 1862, *CJ*, 5:404–6.

3. John Letcher, *Governor's Message and Documents* (Richmond, Va.: William F. Ritchie, 1861), xxv; Robert M. T. Hunter, "The Border States—Their Position after Disunion" *DBR* 5, no. 1 (January 1861): 114.

4. *Report of the Select Committee of The Planters' Convention, February 1862* (Memphis, Tenn., 1862), 7.

5. "The Correspondence of the Telegraph: The Cotton Planters' Convention," *Macon Daily Telegraph*, May 23, 1862; Dudley Mann to Judah P. Benjamin, May 5, 1862, *OR*, ser.1, 3:409–11.

6. Robert M. T. Hunter to John Slidell and James M. Mason, September 3, 1861, *OR*, ser.1, 3:269–71.

7. Daniel Coleman De Jarnette, *The Monroe Doctrine: Speech of D. C. DeJarnette of Virginia, in the Confederate House of Representatives, January 30th, 1865, pending Negotiations for Peace* (Richmond, Va., 1865), 6.

8. On alleged Federal, British, and French plans to transport indentured Chinese laborers to work on plantations, see "A Diabolical Scheme," *Richmond Dispatch*, May 1, 1861, and "ART. XI.—Commercial Importance and Future of the South," 7, no. 1 & 2 *DBR* (March 1862): 120. On Russian serf emancipation, see Major John Tyler, "Our Confederate States Foreign and Domestic," 34, no. 1 *DBR* (July and August 1864): 6–7.

9. "Another Mass Meeting in Richmond," *Index* 5, no. 149 (March 2, 1865).

10. Alexander H. Stephens, *The Great Speech Hon. A. H. Stephens, Delivered before the Georgia Legislature, on Wednesday Night, March 16th, to Which Is Added Extracts from Gov. Brown's Message to the Georgia Legislature, 1864,* Confederate Imprints C.I. 2848, VHS; "The Negotiations for Peace," *Index* 5, no. 147 (February 16, 1865): 104; Hilliard to Davis, February 2, 1865, *JDC*, 6:461–62.

11. John Adams Gilmer, "Amendment to Joint Resolution Expressing the Sense of Congress on the Subject of the Late Peace Commission," February 20, 1865, *CJ*, 7:607; L. Q. C. Lamar, *Speech of Hon. L. Q. C. Lamar of Mississippi, on the State of the Country: Delivered in the Athenaeum, Atlanta, Ga., Thursday Evening, April 14, 1864 Reported by A. E. Marshall* (Atlanta: J. J. Toon, 1864).

12. Stephen W. Berry II, *All That Makes a Man: Love and Ambition in the Civil War South* (New York: Oxford University Press, 2003); Peter S. Carmichael, *The Last Generation: Young Virginians in Peace, War, and Reunion* (Chapel Hill: University of North Carolina Press, 2005), 5–18; Richard Carwardine, *Trans-Atlantic Revivalism: Popular Evangelism in Britain and America, 1790–1865* (Westport, Ct.: Greenwood, 1978). On the way southerners aggressively used the federal government to further their agenda before the war, see Matthew Karp, *This Vast Southern Empire: Slaveholders at the Helm of American Foreign Policy* (Cambridge, Mass.: Harvard University Press, 2016).

13. William J. Cooper Jr., *Jefferson Davis, American* (New York: Alfred A. Knopf, 2000), 123–24.

1. What Would an Independent South Mean for the World in 1861?

1. "Debate on the African Slave Trade Resumed," January 25, 1861, in William R. Smith, *The History and Debates of the Convention of the People of Alabama Begun and Held in the City of Montgomery* (1861; reprint, Spartanburg, S.C., 1975), 236–37 (hereafter cited as Smith, *History and Debates*); "The Elections," *Daily True Delta*, October 12, 1860, in Dwight Lowell Drummond, ed., *Southern Editorials on Secession* (New York: Century, 1931), 312 (hereafter cited as Drummond, *Editorials*); Thomas McAdory Owen and Marie Bankhead Owen, *History of Alabama and Dictionary of Alabama Biography*, 4 vols. (Chicago: S. J. Clarke, 1921), 4:1629; Richard Thompson Archer, "Letter to the Editors of The Sun," December 8, 1859, undated note, folder "Politics, Slavery, States' Rights, Secession," box 2E647, Archer Family Papers, UT.

2. Bland, *A Southern Document: To the People of Virginia. The Great Issue! Our Relations to It* (Wytheville, Va.: D. A. St. Clair, 1861), 8; George W. L. Bickley, *Address to the People of the Southern States* (Richmond, Va., 1860), 29. On the Knights of the Golden Circle using extra-political pressure to propel Texas and Virginia toward secession, but at the same time dispensing with their demand for a grand slaveholding empire in the Southern Hemisphere in favor of the protection of southern rights, see David C. Keehn, *Knights of the Golden Circle: Secret Empire, Southern Secession, Civil*

War (Baton Rouge: Louisiana State University Press, 2013); Ollinger Crenshaw, "The Knights of the Golden Circle: The Career of George Bickley," *American Historical Review* 41, no. 1 (October 1941): 23–50. John McCardell argues that Bickley's efforts only received encouragement in Texas; elsewhere in the Deep South expansionist sentiment was replaced by secessionist sentiment, as if these opinions were mutually exclusive (McCardell, *The Idea of a Southern Nation: Southern Nationalists and Southern Nationalism, 1830–1860* [New York: Norton, 1979], 272).

3. *Journal of the State Convention and Ordinances and Resolutions; Adopted January 1861 with an Appendix, Published by Order of the Convention* (Jackson, Miss.: E. Barksdale, 1861); Bland, *Southern Document*, 6, 8; Thornwell, *State of the Country*, 8, 24; Hunter, "Border States—Their Position after Disunion," 114. Expansionists used the same Slave Power arguments as the Republican Party. Eric Foner and Michael F. Holt still dominate the Slave Power debate whether slavery expansion threatened more the economic expansion of free labor or the existence of republicanism. Both agree that the threat of slavery's territorial expansion was vital for the Republican Party message to gain traction in the North; in particular, as Holt notes, against competition from the nativist Know Nothing Party (Eric Foner, *Free Soil, Free Labor, Free Men: The Ideology of the Republican Party before the Civil War* [New York: Oxford University Press, 1970] and Michael F. Holt, *The Political Crisis of the 1850s* [New York: Norton, 1983]).

4. James Henley Thornwell, *The State of the Country: An Article Republished from the Southern Presbyterian Review* (Columbia, S.C., 1860), 7–8; Elizabeth Fox-Genovese and Eugene D. Genovese, *The Mind of the Master Class: History and Faith in the Southern Slaveholders' Worldview* (New York: Cambridge University Press, 2005), 288. The Boston Athenaeum alone has three copies of the Thornwell imprint, which attests to its wide circulation. For the importance of political preaching especially in the Confederacy where clergy had such authority, see Timothy L. Wesley, *The Politics of Faith during the Civil War* (Baton Rouge: Louisiana State University Press, 2013). On the importance of using providence to achieve political goals, see Nicholas Guyatt, *Providence and the Invention of the United States, 1607–1876* (New York: Cambridge University Press, 2007). Guyatt argues that southern slaveholders reconciled slavery and God in a pessimistic understanding of the U.S. future and its redemptive potential, despite describing Thornwell as "probably the most celebrated southern theologian in antebellum era" (Guyatt, *Providence*, 235, 242). Historians have adopted Thornwell to the cause of counterrevolution and pessimism about the future; see Karp, *This Vast Southern Empire*, 158, and Matthew J. Clavin, *Toussaint Louverture and the American Civil War: The Promise and Peril of a Second Haitian Revolution* (Philadelphia: University

of Pennsylvania Press, 2010), 57. At times that may be so, but Thornwell also urged the need for individual achievement and had no wish to die "unknown, unhonored, and unsung, like the wild beasts of the field" (Fox-Genovese and Genovese, *Mind of the Master Class*, 98).

5. Christopher M. Duncan, "Benjamin Morgan Palmer: Southern Presbyterian Divine" (PhD diss., Auburn University, 2008), 4, 70; Benjamin Morgan Palmer, *A Vindication of Secession and the South from the Strictures of Reverend R.J. Breckinridge DD LLD in the Danville Quarterly Review* (Columbia, S.C.: Southern Guardian Press, 1861), 24; George W. L. Bickley, *Address to the People of the Southern States* (Richmond, Va., 1860), 9, 29. Duncan describes the *Review* as one of the premier quarterly religious journals in the United States and with a wide circulation. Guyatt portrays Palmer as arguing that by seceding, the South was abandoning the "folly and impiety" of the U.S. empire; but Guyatt overlooks the pastor's case for a southern empire (Guyatt, *Providence*, 250–51). Historian Robert E. May adds that Bickley, whom he describes as a "charlatan," recently tried to mount a new filibuster raid from Texas into Mexico but was rebuffed by Governor Sam Houston (May, *Slavery, Race, and Conquest in the Tropics: Lincoln, Douglas, and the Future of Latin America* [New York: Cambridge University Press, 2013], 169–74). On filibustering, see Robert E. May, *Manifest Destiny's Underworld: Filibustering in Antebellum America* (Chapel Hill: University of North Carolina Press, 2002).

6. John B. Thrasher, *Slavery, a Divine Institution: A Speech Made before the Breckinridge and Lane Club on November 5, 1860* (Port Gibson, Miss.: Southern Reveille Book and Job Office, 1861), 21. On Thrasher, see also Marion Thrasher, *A History of the Thrasher Family Traced through the Eighteenth and Nineteenth Centuries in England and America* (San Francisco, 1895), 20–21; Fox-Genovese and Genovese, *Mind of the Master Class*, 515–23, and Clavin, *Toussaint Louverture and the American Civil War*, 57–73.

7. Leonidas W. Spratt, *The Philosophy of Secession: A Southern View, Presented in a Letter Addressed to the Hon. Mr. Perkins of Louisiana, in Criticism of the Provisional Constitution Adopted by the Southern Congress at Montgomery, Alabama, February 13, 1861* (n.p., 1861), 3; Benjamin Morgan Palmer, *A Vindication of Secession and the South from the Strictures of Reverend R. J. Breckinridge DD LLD in the Danville Quarterly Review* (Columbia, S.C.: Southern Guardian Press, 1861), 24, 25. On Spratt, see William C. Davis, *Rhett: The Turbulent Life and Times of a Fire-Eater* (Columbia: University of South Carolina Press, 2001), 354–74; William L. Barney, *The Secessionist Impulse: Alabama and Mississippi in 1860* (Princeton, N.J.: Princeton University Press, 1974), 3, 223; Winthrop Jordan, *Tumult and Silence at Second Creek: An Inquiry into a Civil War Slave Conspiracy* (Baton Rouge:

Louisiana State University Press, 1993), 158; Fox-Genovese and Genovese, *Mind of the Master Class*, 616.

8. William H. Holcombe, M.D., *The Alternative: A Separate Nationality, or the Africanization of the South* (New Orleans: Delta Mammoth Job Office, 1860), 6–7; Joseph Eggleston Segar, *Speech of Joseph Segar, Esq., of the York District, Delivered in the House of Delegates of Virginia, March the 30th, 1861, on the Resolutions of the Senate, Directing the Governor of Virginia to Seize, by Military Force, the U.S. Guns at Bellona Arsenal, and on the Secession of Virginia* (Richmond, Va., 1861), 18; John Majeswki, *Modernizing a Slave Economy: The Economic Vision of the Confederate Nation* (Chapel Hill: University of North Carolina Press, 2009), 94.

9. Robert Toombs, "Secession Speech," November 11, 1860, in William W. Freehling and Craig M. Simpson, eds., *Secession Debated: Georgia's Showdown in 1860* (New York: Oxford University Press, 1992), 40. Michael O'Brien, *Intellectual Life and the American South, 1810–1860* (Chapel Hill: University of North Carolina Press, 2010), 221, 226, 235–46; Harriett Martineau, *Illustrations of Political Economy: Selected Tales*, ed. Deborah Anna Logan (Peterborough, Ontario, Canada: Broadview, 2004). Martineau's conclusion about an "absurd position that a definite quantity of territory can maintain an infinite population" resonated with Confederates, but her remedy of birth control would be unnecessary for a nation with limitless territory. See also Becky Allen, "Austerity. Poverty. Food Scarcity. Thomas Malthus, the Great Population Theorist, Is Being Reinvented for Our Times," *CAM [Cambridge Alumni Magazine]* 80 (Lent 2017): 28–31.

10. Bland, *Southern Document*, 6; Hunter, "Border States—Their Position after Disunion," 114; Hunter to James R. Micou, Thomas Croxton, and others, December 10, 1860, in Charles Henry Ambler, ed., *Correspondence of Robert M. T. Hunter, 1826–1876* (New York: Da Capo Press, 1971), 345–47.

11. James P. Holcombe, "Secessionist Speech," Virginia Convention, March 20, 1861, in William W. Freehling and Craig S. Simpson, eds., *Showdown in Virginia: The 1861 Convention and the Fate of Union* (Charlottesville: University of Virginia Press, 2010), 69; Gustave D'Alaux, *Soulouque and His Empire*, trans. and ed., with an introduction, John G. Parkhill (Richmond, Va.: J. W. Randolph, 1861), xiii; William H. Holcombe, M.D., *The Alternative: A Separate Nationality, or The Africanization of the South* (New Orleans: Delta Mammoth Job Office, 1860), 6–7. William Holcombe in an 1858 speech discussed British rule in India at the time of the Sepoy Mutiny and "praised a just and salutary regime that imposed civilized order on a people incapable of self government" (Karp, *This Vast Southern Empire*, 158–63; Holcombe quoted in Fox-Genovese and Genovese, *Mind of the Master Class*, 215–20).

12. "Disunion," *Daily Constitutionalist* (Augusta, Ga.), December 30, 1860, in Drummond, *Editorials*, 384; Lewis Maxwell Stone, "Speech on Reopening the African Slave Trade," January 25, 1861, in Smith, *History and Debates*, 237. The newspaper editor of the *Daily Constitutionalist* likened the spread of slavery to that of cholera epidemics, and "no power can check it but frost."

13. William L. Yancey and William R. Smith of Tuscaloosa, "Speech on Reopening the African Slave Trade," January 25, 1861, in Smith, *History and Debates*, 203–4, 251. For a recent account of the debates conducted both in Congress and in the media over expansion during the Mexican War, see Amy Greenberg, *A Wicked War: Polk, Clay, Lincoln, and the 1846 U.S. Invasion of Mexico* (New York: Alfred A. Knopf, 2012). For Yancey's persistent expansionism, see Eric H. Walther, *William Lowndes Yancey and the Coming of the Civil War* (Chapel Hill: University of North Carolina Press, 2006), 253–73. On the Spanish "Sugar Plantation as Hacienda," see David S. Landes, *The Wealth and Poverty of Nations: Why Some Are So Rich and Some So Poor* (New York: W. W. Norton, 1998), 122–24.

14. "Cuba, the March of Empire and the Course of Trade—A Southern Confederacy," *DBR* 5, no. 1 (January 1861): 30; Zebulon Baird Vance, *To the Citizens of the Eighth Congressional District of North Carolina, February 13, 1861* (Washington, D.C.: H. Polkinhorn, 1861), 5; John C. Calhoun, "A Disquisition on Government," Constitution Society, http://www.constitution.org/jcc/disq_gov.htm, accessed June 4, 2012.

15. Smith, *History and Debates*, 209, 236. During the 1850s, Leonidas Spratt—from his vantage point of the *Charleston Standard* and at commercial conventions—had made the case for reopening the international slave trade as a way to spread the ownership of slaves among white southerners. Cautious conservatives such as William Trescot opposed the resumption of the trade for the same reason, as it diluted the slaveholding class while he contended that no good can come out of the evils of the middle passage (Karp, *This Vast Southern Empire*, 141–48; McCardell, *Idea of a Southern Nation*, 133–40; Fox-Genovese and Genovese, *Mind of the Master Class*, 114, 512–15; May, *Slavery, Race, and Conquest in the Tropics*, 192, 219).

16. James Ferguson Dowdell, "Speech on the African Slave Trade," January 25, 1861, in Smith, *History and Debates*, 257.

17. Leonidas W. Spratt quoted in Daniel Kilbride, "The Old South Confronts the Dilemma of David Livingstone," *Journal of Southern History* 82, no. 4 (November 2016), 797; "The Constitution of the Confederate States," March 15, 1861, printed in the *Charleston Mercury*; "The Provisional Constitution of the Confederate States of America," printed in the *Charleston Mercury*, February 12, 1861; R. Barnwell Rhett, "Amendment of the CS Constitution," February 8, 1861, *CJ*, 1:35. The First Session of the

Confederate Congress met from February 4, 1861, to March 16, 1861, in Montgomery. Eric Walther argues that Spratt had been agitating for the reopening of the Atlantic slave trade since 1853 (Walther, *Yancey and the Coming of the Civil War*, 203–29).

18. Dowdell, "Speech on the African Slave Trade." Leading southerners circulated rumors about schemes of colonization of Latin America. An acquaintance reported to Hunter about a communication between the Prussian minister in Mexico City and the Mexican minister of the interior on January 2, 1861. "History proves the fact among all the people of the new world that civilization and progress have been introduced by the mixture, contact, and commerce of people of different races and origin," the Prussian diplomat told the Mexican politician. "Without colonization, Mexico will expire, no hope remains that she can repeople herself again. Germany can alone resupply Mexico with the agricultural laborers she stands so much in need of" (Mr. Callaghan to R. M. T. Hunter, April 12, 1861, Box 7, folder title "CA," Hunter Correspondence, VHS). Historian Matthew Pratt Guterl's "nightmare from the south" scenario for planters was the rumored plan by Cuban authorities, under pressure from the British, to import unskilled Chinese indentured laborers in place of emancipated enslaved African Americans (Guterl, *American Mediterranean: Southern Slaveholders in the Age of Emancipation* [Cambridge, Mass.: Harvard University Press, 2008]). Karp notes both Thomas S. Bocock and Duff Green, among others, warned that the "imperial powers were planning to export coolie laborers to their moribund West Indian colonies" (Karp, *This Vast Southern Empire*, 153–54).

19. D'Alaux, *Soulouque and His Empire*, v–xiii, xi. On slaveholder nightmares about Haiti, see Clavin, *Toussaint Louverture and the American Civil War*, and Charles Dew, *Apostles of Disunion: Southern Secession Commissioners and the Causes of the Civil War* (Charlottesville: University Press of Virginia, 2001).

20. Senator Hunter of Virginia, "The Border-States—Their Position after Disunion," *DBR* 5, no. 1 (January 1861): 114. Governor Joseph Brown of Georgia added, "the poor would all become tenants, as they are in England, the New England States, and all old countries where slavery does not exist" (Freehling and Simpson, *Secession Debated*, 152, 155).

21. "Cuba, the March of Empire," 30; Karp, *This Vast Southern Empire*, 59–65. Robert E. May shows how an earlier broad-based national vision of the 1840s was subsequently changed into a bid for balance between the sections; how southward expansion became imperative in the 1850s, as westward appeared to be reserved for the North. This motivation for expansion led to the dominant view among historians that secession rendered redundant any need to pursue further territorial growth. May focuses on the provocative antics of filibusters and highlights how they actually retarded expansion

through the discredit they attracted to America's territorial expansion (May, *The Southern Dream of a Caribbean Empire 1854–1861* [Baton Rouge: Louisiana State University Press, 1973] and *Manifest Destiny's Underworld*).

22. "Resolution offered by Mr. Henderson of Macon," January 12, 1861, in Smith, *History and Debates*, 124. It was decided to delay consideration of this matter until the Provisional Congress of the Confederacy gathered the following month. Editor James D. B. De Bow wrote, "The southern States, rounded off with the Indian Territory, will constitute a splendid Empire" ("Cuba, the March of Empire," 30).

23. Robert G. H. Kean to John B. Minor, February 19, 1861, Box 9, Minor and Wilson Family Papers, #3750, UVA; Robert Bunch to Lord John Russell, February 22, 28, 1861, FO 5/780, p. 120, 127, PRO. Cooper contrasted Davis's "forthright" views on Cuban annexation in the 1850s, while being "not so clear" on filibustering. "He did not denounce the 1854 Presidential Proclamation enforcing neutrality laws" and in contrast to his Mississippi senatorial colleague and rival, Albert Gallatin Brown, Davis denounced filibustering in principle during the 1859 state democratic convention. Yet, at the same time, he never criticized Quitman (Cooper, *Jefferson Davis, American*, 112–23, 240–77.) The consul probably had in mind Davis's firm opposition to the expansion of British interests in Central America, which led him to support William Walker in Nicaragua (Clement Eaton, *Jefferson Davis* [New York: Free Press, 1977, 105–6]). Lord John Russell, the British foreign secretary from 1859 to 1865, would in 1861 be ennobled as the first Earl Russell; see John Prest, *Lord John Russell* (Columbia, SC: University of South Carolina Press, 1972).

24. Robert Bunch to Lord John Russell, February 28, March 21, 1861, FO 5/780, pp. 148–49, PRO; Freehling and Simpson, *Secession Debated*, vii–xxi; Robert Toombs, "Speech on the Slavery Question," January 7, 1861, CG, 270; Eaton, *Jefferson Davis*, 105. According to May, Toombs supported Caribbean expansion and sought compromise in December 1860 (*Slavery, Race, and Conquest in the Tropics*, 205, 222–26). McCardell described Yancey as a man of the frontier with regional rather than Union loyalties who reveled in democracy (*Idea of a Southern Nation*, 277–87). See also Walther, *Yancey and the Coming of the Civil War*, 203–74; Karp, *This Vast Southern Empire*, 216–23; Doyle, *Cause of All Nations*, 40–43; Robert Kagan, *Dangerous Nation: America's Foreign Policy from Its Earliest Days to the Dawn of the Twentieth Century* (New York: Alfred A. Knopf, 2006), 241–43.

25. Robert Bunch to Lord John Russell, February 28, March 21, 1861, pp. 148–49; Jefferson Davis, "Speech at Atlanta," February 16, 1861, *JDP*, 7:44.

26. Bunch to Lord Russell, February 28, March 21, 1861, pp. 148–50. Scholars routinely chide Confederates for such delusions commented upon by Bunch, but this sense of centrality to the global economy was integral to

their vision of the future (Frank Lawrence Owsley, *King Cotton Diplomacy: Foreign Relations of the Confederate States of America* [1931; repr. ed. Harriet Chappell Owsley, Chicago: University of Chicago Press, 1959], 1–2). As the Founding Fathers had earlier demonstrated in 1776, those striving to found a new nation are not habitually modest about their importance to the world. Adam Smith recommended to the British government in 1776 the necessity "of preserving the importance and of gratifying the ambition of the leading men of America." He cautioned that those who dominate the Continental Congress "feel in themselves at this moment a degree of importance which, perhaps, the greatest subjects of Europe scarce feel." The colonists were at present "employed in contriving a new form of government for an extensive empire, which, they flatter themselves, will become, and which, indeed, seems very likely to become, one of the greatest and most formidable that ever was in the world" (Adam Smith, *An Inquiry into the Nature and Causes of the Wealth of Nations* [1776], 825).

27. W. H. Chase, "The Secession of the Cotton States: Its Status, Its Advantages, and Its Power," *DBR* 5, no. 1 (January 1861): 93.

28. Chase, "Secession of the Cotton States," 93. On Chase's role in the development of "southern navalism," see Karp, *This Vast Southern Empire*, 35–40.

29. Wendy Hinde, *Richard Cobden: A Victorian Outsider* (New Haven, Conn.: Yale University Press, 1987), 310. See also John Gallagher and Ronald Robinson, "The Imperialism of Free Trade," *Economic History Review* 6, no. 1 (1953): 1–15. ("The dependence of the commercial thrust upon the political arm resulted in a general tendency of British trade to follow the invisible flag of informal empire" [11–12]).

30. Arthur Lynn to Lord John Russell, March 14, 1861, FO 5/788, pp. 292–93, PRO; Thomas Mure to Lord John Russell, December 13, 1860, FO 5/743, p. 64, PRO.

31. Fox-Genovese and Genovese, *Mind of the Master Class*, 636–49; Clingman, "State of the Union," December 4, 1860, CG, 4; Daniel W. Crofts, *Reluctant Confederates: Upper South Unionists in the Secession Crisis* (Chapel Hill: University of North Carolina Press, 1989), 30; Wigfall, "State of the Union," December 11, 1860, CG, 73; William Howard Russell, *My Diary North and South*, ed. Fletcher Pratt (New York: Harper & Brothers, 1954), 63; Majewski, *Modernizing a Slave Economy*, 144. Economic historian Douglass C. North's analysis (table A-VIII) verified Mure's numbers (*Cotton Exports from the United States, 1815–1860* [Englewood Cliffs, N.J.: Prentice-Hall, 1961], 233). See also Walther, *Yancey and the Coming of the Civil War*, 74–92, and McCardell, *Idea of a Southern Nation*, 261.

32. Robert Barnwell Rhett quoted in Robert Bunch to Lord John Russell, December 5, 1860, FO 5/745, p. 234, PRO; Freehling and Simpson, *Secession*

Debated, 130; Clingman, "State of the Union," December 4, 1860, *CG,* 4; W. Davis, *Rhett,* 266–88; Dew, *Apostles of Disunion,* 59–71. Dew concludes his account of Benning's speech with these words: "whilst he may have moved his audience to tears, he did not move Virginia into the Confederate column."

33. Committee on Foreign Affairs, House of Representatives, Congress, Confederate States of America, *The Report of the Committee on Foreign Affairs on the President's Message Relating to the Affairs between the Confederate and the United States* (Montgomery, Ala., 1861), 3–7.

34. W. Smith, *History and Debates,* 190, 191; Robert Ruffin Barrow, *A Miscellaneous Essay on the Political Parties of the Country, the Rise of Abolitionism and the Impolicy of Secession, December 22, 1860* (New Orleans: L. Marchand, 1861), 14. Barrow argued that individual state secession jeopardized this promise; hence he argued for all the southern states to act as a single unit in order to realize his vision. Historian Robert E. Bonner sees continental expansion, as opposed to commercial or slavery expansion, at the heart of the antebellum southern slaveholder's vision of America, and that this ambition lingered into the Confederacy (*Mastering America Southern Slaveholders and the Crisis of American Nationhood* [New York: Cambridge University Press, 2009]).

35. "Quo Tendimus?" (Where we tend), *DBR* 4, no. 4 (October 1860): 441.

36. George W. L. Bickley, *Address to the People of the Southern States* (Richmond, Va., 1860), 9.

37. Lewis Maxwell Stone, "Debate on African Slave Trade Resumed," January 25, 1861, in W. Smith, *History and Debates,* 237; "Southern Patronage to Southern Imports and Domestic Industry," *DBR* 4, no. 4 (October 1860): 494; Guterl, *American Mediterranean;* Karp, *This Vast Southern Empire.* On the French ambitions for a global Latin Empire, see Doyle, *Cause of All Nations,* 106–28. Historians often assume such expansive ambitions were somehow backward in an age of nationalism; for example, Thomas Bender argues that Lincoln's "modern" territorial definition of "nation," which he evolved during the Civil War, contrasted with the South's looser, more archaic, as well as expansive, mentality (Bender *A Nation among Nations,* 150–63).

38. Wigfall, "State of the Union," 73; James H. Hammond, "Speech of Hon. James H. Hammond, of South Carolina, on the Admission of Kansas, under the Lecompton Constitution: Delivered in the Senate of the United States, March 4, 1858," Washington, D.C., March 4, 1858, in *Selections from the Letters and Speeches of the Hon. James H. Hammond,* with an introduction by Clyde N. Wilson (Spartanburg, S.C.: Reprint Co., 1978). Others were more modest in their calculations. In his broadside seeking election to the Virginia Convention, Cornelius Clark Baldwin—skeptical

of expensive projects such as the James River and Kanawha Canal, which went through his land in Rockingham County—regarded "a revenue duty of twenty percent on the two hundred million dollars of southern imports will yield forty million dollars per annum, an abundance of money for the orderly purposes of a plain and frugal government" ("C. C. Baldwin to the Citizens of Rockbridge," January 28, 1861, broadside B 28 [UVA]).

39. Zebulon Baird Vance, *To the Citizens of the Eighth Congressional District of North Carolina, February 13, 1861* (Washington, D.C.: H. Polkinhorn, 1861), 5; Thomas L. Clingman, "Speech on the State of the Union," December 4, 1860, CG, 4–5; Crofts, *Reluctant Confederates,* 34. On the Whig vision, see Michael F. Holt, *The Rise and Fall of the American Whig Party: Jacksonian Politics and the Onset off the Civil War* (New York: Oxford University Press, 1999), and Daniel Walker Howe, *The Political Culture of the American Whigs* (Chicago: University of Chicago Press, 1979).

40. George W. Randolph to Mary (Mollie) Randolph, November 10, 1860, box 10, Edgehill-Randolph Papers, #1397, UVA, and "Secessionist Speech," March 16, 1861, in Freehling and Simpson, *Showdown in Virginia,* 50; Majewski, *Modernizing a Slave Economy,* 3, 126–30; William A. Link, *Roots of Secession: Slavery and Politics in Antebellum Virginia* (Chapel Hill: University of North Carolina Press, 2003), 239; F. N. Boney, *John Letcher of Virginia: The Story of Virginia's Civil War Governor* (Tuscaloosa: University of Alabama Press, 1966), 93. On Randolph's niece's influence on him, see Fox-Genovese and Genovese, *Mind of the Master Class,* 390.

41. Jefferson Davis, "Inaugural Speech," February 18, 1861, *JDP* 7:47; Robert Toombs to William L. Yancey, Ambrose D. Mann, and Pierre A. Rost, March 16, 1861, in James D. Richardson, ed. *The Messages and Papers of Jefferson Davis and the Confederacy, Including Diplomatic Correspondence, 1861–1865,* 2 vols. (1906; repr., New York: Chelsea House, 1966), 2:7. The British were somewhat disappointed; Consul Bunch considered that "it is not all that we have been led to expect, but it is certainly an improvement on the US tariff of 1857 and still more so upon the new [Morrill] tariff of this year." His counterpart in New Orleans, Thomas Mure, estimated the tariffs on average between 10 and 15 percent lower than those of the Union (Robert Bunch to Lord John Russell, March 14, 1861, FO 5/780, p. 142, PRO; Thomas Mure to Lord John Russell, March 18, 1861, FO 5/788, pp. 66–67, PRO). For the tension between the desire for free trade and the need for repatriation of resources, see Nicholas Onuf and Peter Onuf, *Nations, Markets, and War: Modern History and the American Civil War* (Charlottesville: University of Virginia, 2006).

42. Majewski, *Modernizing a Slave Economy,* 138.

43. "The Southern Route across the Atlantic," *DBR* 4, no. 6 (December 1860): 779. DeBow reported that Maury informed the president of the Charleston

Chamber of Commerce on October 20, 1860, "Permit me to call [your] attention . . . to the advantages in winter of the southern route from Europe or the Mediterranean to ports in the United States south of Delaware inclusive." On southern commercial conventions, see also Vicki Vaughan Johnson, *The Men and the Vision of the Southern Commercial Conventions, 1845–1871* (Columbia: University of Missouri Press, 1992). According to Johnson, as a keen advocate of direct trade with South America, Maury had attacked recent commercial conventions for losing their economic focus due to worries about antislavery in the North. He told an audience at a state agricultural bureau meeting in October 1859, "Look to your commercial conventions, and take warning. Keep men from the political commons out of your meetings." Maury, while engaged in his oceanographic pursuits, was also interested in the development of southern commerce. He promoted the opening of the Amazon Valley to free trade, hoping that one effect of such a measure would be to draw the slaves from the United States to Brazil. Although Johnson claims to encompass the war years in her study, in reality the material covered ceases in 1859 and resumes in 1865. Up to 1859, she charts the growth of a commercial convention movement that evolved from small meetings intent on expanding direct trade into large assemblies that delved into most aspects of southern economic life. Johnson identified these individuals as a self-consciously elite group who possessed an enduring faith in southern opportunity.

44. James C. Hunt to William Massie, December 29, 1860, February 15, 1861, Box 2E493, William Massie Papers, UT; Lynn A. Nelson, *Pharsalia: An Environmental Biography of a Southern Plantation, 1780–1880* (Athens: University of Georgia Press, 2010), 110; John Letcher, *Governor's Message and Documents, January 7, 1861* (Richmond, Va.: William F. Ritchie, 1861), xl–xli, folder 389, John Letcher Papers, #L5684 a FA2 VHS; "Cuba, the March of Empire"; Chase, "Secession of the Cotton States," 30, 91. Massie regularly used the canal from Lynchburg to Richmond to transport tobacco and fruit. The prospect that the French might be more interested in the canal as a result of secession alarmed some individuals, however. R. W. Thompson of Washington asked Letcher whether it would be a good idea "at such a time as this to admit French influence into the state." In particular: "Might it not be a bad policy to have the French government directly or indirectly interested in any of our public improvements?" After all, "secession might invite Napoleon III to seek direction over your internal affairs—with a canal to serve him . . . he might make your interests subordinate to his own" (Thompson to Letcher, January 11, 1861 folder 383 "Governor's Correspondence, 1861 January," John Letcher Papers, VHS).

45. John Letcher, *Governor's Message and Documents* (Richmond, Va.: William F. Ritchie, 1861), xxv; Robert M. T. Hunter, "The Border States—Their

Position after Disunion" *DBR* 5, no. 1 (January 1861): 114; Boney, *John Letcher of Virginia*, 97, 98, 103.

46. W. Holcombe, *Alternative*, 11; New Orleans Picayune, *Extracts from the Editorial Columns of the "New Orleans Picayune": Read and Circulate, January, 1861* (New Orleans, 1861), 23; Frank K. to Margaret G. Winchester, November 9, 1860, folder 6, box 2E912 Margaret G. (Sprague) Winchester Papers—Correspondence, Winchester Family Papers, UT; Fox-Genovese and Genovese, *Mind of the Masterclass*, 91; O'Brien, *Intellectual Life*, 115. Clavin argues that Holcombe was urgent for secession on the grounds of the South's risk of becoming another Haiti if slavery was not allowed to expand (Clavin, *Toussaint Louverture and the American Civil War*, 57–73).

47. Erika Pani, "Law, Allegiance, and Sovereignty in Civil War Mexico, 1857–1867," *Journal of the Civil War Era* 7 4 (December 2017), 578; James Henley Thornwell, *The State of the Country: An Article Republished from "The Southern Presbyterian Review"* (Columbia, S.C., 1860), 28–29.

48. Robert M. T. Hunter, "Forts and Arsenals in the States," January 11, 1861, *CG*, 326–32; Muscoe R. H. Garnett, "House Army Bill," January 16, 1861, *CG*, 411–15; Eaton, *Jefferson Davis*, 121; May, *Slavery, Race and Conquest in the Tropics*, 206–26.

49. Karp, *This Vast Southern Empire*, 208; Jabez Lamar Munroe Curry to Robert M. T. Hunter, January 25, 1861, box 7, "Folder CL-Cu," Hunter Correspondence, Hunter Family Papers, H9196aFAZ, VHS; Karp, *This Vast Southern Empire*, 208; Augusta Jane Evans quoted in Fox-Genovese and Genovese, *Mind of the Master Class*, 680–84; McCardell, *Idea of a Southern Nation*, 41, 277; Dew, *Apostles of Disunion*, 51, 59.

50. Jefferson Davis, "Speech at Atlanta," February 16, 1861, *JDP*, 7:43; Jefferson Davis to Anna Ella Carroll, March 1, 1861, *JDP*, 7:65; Jefferson Davis, "Speech to the U.S. Senate," January 10, 1861, *JDP*, 5:29. In Davis's January 1861 farewell address to the United States Senate, there was also an oblique reference to this wish, when he hoped for "peaceful relations," which would be "mutually beneficial" (Jefferson Davis, "Message on the State of the Union," January 10, 1861, *CG*, 310).

51. "The President at Atlanta, from Our Own Correspondent," *Charleston Mercury*, February 21, 1861, accessed through the internet via the *Accessible Archive, The Civil War, Part I: A Newspaper Perspective*, http://www.accessible.com on December 16, 2010.

52. "C. C. Baldwin to the citizens of Rockbridge"; George Wythe Randolph, "Secessionist Speech," Virginia Peace Convention, March 16, 1861, Freehling and Simpson, *Showdown in Virginia*, 50; "Our Washington Correspondent," *Charleston Mercury*, February 25, 1861, accessed through the internet via the Accessible Archive, *The Civil War, Part I: A Newspaper*

Perspective, http://www.accessible.com; Link, *Roots of Secession,* 224–28; Freehling, *Road to Disunion* 2:513. In resolutions on February 25, the Virginia Convention condemned the North for opposing slavery extension into the territories, and on March 9 the majority report contained elements of both the Crittenden Compromise and the Peace Conference (Crofts, *Reluctant Confederates,* 26–28).

53. William Porcher Miles, "Report," March 4, 1861, *CJ,* 1:105; Jefferson Davis, "Message," March 16, *CJ,* 1:151; Robert Toombs, "Resolution," March 4, 1861, *CJ,* 1:105. The Committees on Territories and Indian Affairs were established on February 11, 1861 (*CJ,* 1:44–45). On February 18, 1861, Louis T. Wigfall, in a letter to Jefferson Davis, told the president that U.S. senator Richard W. Johnson of Arkansas had warned him the United States was competing for the loyalty of the Indian tribes (*JDP,* 7:51–52).

54. Robert Hardy Smith, *An Address to the Citizens of Alabama on the Constitution and Laws of the Confederate States of America, by the Hon Robert H. Smith, at Temperance Hall, on the 30th of March, 1861* (Mobile, Ala.: Mobile Daily Register, 1861), 20; "Admission of Northern States into the Southern Confederation," *Charleston Mercury,* March 25, 1861; "Debate on Permanent Constitution," March 6, 1861, *CJ,* 1: 874. For example, South Carolina delegate Robert Barnwell Rhett's amendment to the constitution made the restriction clear: "nor shall any state remain in the Confederacy which does not authorize the institution of slavery within its limits." South Carolinians in particular feared the old tensions would reappear that beset the United States if nonslaveholding states were allowed to join the Confederacy either now or in the future. "In all such territories, as long as it remains in a territorial condition, the institution of negro slavery . . . shall be recognized and protected by Congress and by the territorial government" (Permanent Constitution, Article IV, section 3, part 3, *CJ,* 1:857).

55. R. Smith, *Address to the Citizens of Alabama,* 20.

56. "Speech by Alexander Stephens at the Savannah Athenaeum, March 21, 1861," *Macon Daily Telegraph,* April 4, 1861; McCardell, *Idea of a Southern Nation,* 250–61; Crofts, *Reluctant Confederates,* 216–17; May, *Slavery, Race and Conquest in the Tropics,* 195. McCardell noted though that "even" Stephens supported Quitman's plans.

57. Thomas C. Faulkner, *History of the Revolution in the Southern States: Including the Special Messages of President Buchanan, the Ordinances of Secession of the Six Withdrawing States* (New York: J. W. Trow, 1861), 26; *CJ,* 1:82.

58. "Cuba, the March of Empire," 30; Yancey, "Debate on the Navigation of the Mississippi River," January 24, 1860, in W. Smith, *History and Debates,* 185; "The Southern Congress and Free Trade," *Charleston Mercury,* February 5, 1861; Chase, "Secession of the Cotton States," 93. *De Bow's Review* also extended its membership, for as "to this political and commercial condition,

Canada and the British provinces must come at last; and to this condition Cuba and Mexico would willingly assimilate, either by annexation
to the Southern and Western confederacy, or by the practice of free trade
principles as sovereign and independent nations." Barrow, the brother-in-
law of the submarine pioneer Captain Hunley and a distant cousin of Edmund Ruffin, subsequently supported the Confederacy and financed the
submarine experiments (William Barrow Floyd, *The Barrow Family of Old
Louisiana* [Lexington, Ky.: n.p., 1963], 24–26).

59. Jefferson Davis to President James Buchanan, February 27, 1861, to "all
whom these presents shall concern [in the British government]," March 16,
1861, OR, Ser. 1, 3:94–95; Davis to President James Buchanan, "announcing
mission of Martin G. Crawford, John Forsyth and A. B. Roman," February 27, 1861, OR, Ser. 1, 3:94–95.

2. How War Changed the Future Nation

1. On the enduring narrative of the ditching of expansionist dreams on
the outbreak of war, see May, *Southern Dream of a Caribbean Empire*.
On the exodus to Mexico, see Todd W. Wahlstrom, *The Southern Exodus to Mexico: Migration across the Borderlands after the American Civil
War* (Lincoln: University of Nebraska Press, 2015). On the triumph of
the moderates and the eclipse of the fire-eaters, see Emory M. Thomas, *The
Confederate Nation, 1861–1865* (New York: Harper & Row, 1979), 67–97.

2. Bruce C. Levine, *The Fall of the House of Dixie: How the Civil War Remade
the American South* (New York: Random House, 2013), 86; Paul Quigley,
Shifting Grounds: Nationalism and the American South (New York: Oxford
University Press, 2012), 142.

3. Levine, *Fall of the House of Dixie*, 63; Bonner, *Mastering America*, 217–51.

4. On the military, especially Robert E. Lee and the Army of Northern Virginia, influencing Confederate nationalism, see Gary W. Gallagher, *The
Confederate War* (Cambridge, Mass: Harvard University Press, 1999). On
the war shaping diplomacy, see Howard Jones, *Blue and Gray Diplomacy:
A History of Union and Confederate Foreign Relations* (Chapel Hill: University of North Carolina Press, 2016), 63–65; Thomas, *Confederate Nation*, 67–97, specifically that policies of "loans and paper money backed by
loans presupposed peace."

5. Bonner, *Mastering America*, 217–51; Guterl, *American Mediterranean*, 47–78.

6. On the transience of patriotism, see Paul D. Escott, *After Secession: Jefferson Davis and the Failure of Confederate Nationalism* (Baton Rouge:
Louisiana State University Press, 1978), ix. On the importance of victimhood before, during, and after the war for southerners, see Quigley, *Shifting Grounds*, 9–10, 56–63, 89–90, 125–26, 212–13. On republicanism, see

George C. Rable, *The Confederate Republic: A Revolution against Politics* (Chapel Hill: University of North Carolina Press, 1994), 64–68. On King Cotton, see Frank Lawrence Owsley, *King Cotton Diplomacy* (Chicago: University of Chicago Press, 1959) and Doyle, *Cause of All Nations*, 38–43.

7. Catherine Edmondston, "Diary Entry for April 17, 1861," *Journal of a Secesh Lady: The Diary of Catherine Ann Devereux Edmondston, 1860–1866*, ed. Beth Gilbert Crabtree and James W. Patton (Raleigh: North Carolina Division of Archives and History, 1979), 50; John A. Campbell to Jefferson Davis, April 28, 1861, *JDP*, 7:137; Walther, *William Lowndes Yancey* 179–202, 229–52; Fox-Genovese and Genovese, *Mind of the Master Class*, 142–46.

8. H. Jones, *Blue and Grey*, 1; *Richmond Examiner*, June 18, 1861. On the legacy of the Mexican War and racial arguments against southward expansion see Amy Greenberg, *Wicked War*; Link, *Roots of Secession*, 223, 233; Charles Sellers, *The Market Revolution: Jacksonian America, 1815–1846* (New York: Oxford University Press, 1991), 396–429; Daniel Walker Howe, *What God Hath Wrought: The Transformation of America, 1815–1848* (New York: Oxford University Press, 2004), 744–92; Susan-Mary Grant, *North over South: Northern Nationalism and American Identity in the Antebellum Era* (Lawrence: University Press of Kansas, 2000), 81–110; Fox-Genovese and Genovese, *Mind of the Master Class*, 603. Unitarians, the highest-minded and intellectual group among dissenters, were exceedingly ambitious, attributes that made them not only natural, indeed founding, Whigs but also demanding of their nation; see Miall, "Our Strength Lies in Aggression." "The Nonconformist's Sketchbook" (1842) from Margaret Oliphant, *Phoebe Junior*, ed. Elizabeth Langford (Peterborough, Canada: Broadview, 2002), 434.

9. "On the Cotton Planters Convention," *Macon Daily Telegraph*, April 26, 1861.

10. "Bill Recognizing the Existence of War between the United States and Confederate States," May 3, 1861, *CJ*, 1:176.

11. Committee on Foreign Affairs, *Report of the Committee on Foreign Affairs*, 1. Charles Tyler Botts, *An Address to His Fellow-Citizens, of the State of California* (Sacramento, Calif., 1861), 14; David Alan Johnson, *Founding the Far West: California, Oregon, and Nevada, 1840–1890* (Berkeley: University of California Press, 1992), 114–15.

12. James A. Headley to his father, May 7, 1861, Thomas Henry Hines papers, # A H662 1, FHS; John Letcher, *Message of the Governor of Virginia* (Richmond, Va.: William F. Ritchie, 1861) in FO 5/786, pp. 342, 348–49, (PRO); "William L. Yancey at the Fishmonger's Company on Saturday," *London Globe*, November 12, 1861, in the *Houston Tri-weekly Telegraph*, December 18, 1861, GLC05959.51.011; William N. Bilbo, *The Past, Present, and Future of the Southern Confederacy: An Oration Delivered by Col. W. N. Bilbo, in the City of Nashville, Oct. 12, 1861* (Nashville, Tenn.: J. D. W. Green, 1861), 10–11; *Houston Tri-weekly Telegraph*, December 6,

1861, GLC05959.51.007; William G. Cutler, *History of the State of Kansas, Atchison County* (Chicago: A. T. Andreas, 1883), part 4, http://www.kancoll .org/books/cutler/atchison/atchison-co-p4.html, accessed October 12, 2017. Headley quoted from William Henry Seward's sentence—also used by Wendell Philips in 1861—from his 1858 Irrepressible Conflict speech, "I know, and all the world knows, that revolutions never go backward." Bilbo would later in the war defect to the Union and become a lobbyist. See Andrew Johnson, *The Papers of Andrew Johnson*, vol. 7 (1864–65), ed. LeRoy P. Graf (Knoxville: University of Tennessee Press, 1986), 382.

13. Robert Bunch to Lord John Russell, June 20, 1861, FO 5/780, p. 281, PRO; Bunch to Russell, December 2, 1861, FO 5/781, 414–15, PRO.

14. John M. Morehead to Thomas Ruffin, November 23, 1861, folder 447, series 1.6, box 29, Thomas Ruffin Papers, #641, SHC; Kentucky Confederate Provisional Government, "Proceedings of the Convention Held in Russellville," p. 26, FHS; Fox-Genovese and Genovese, *Mind of the Master Class*, 670. On the damage earlier conflicts had inflicted on slavery, see Alan Taylor, *The Internal Enemy: Slavery and War in Virginia, 1772–1832* (New York, W. W. Norton, 2013). The notion that stronger central governments somehow ameliorated the hardships of slavery by putting a third party between the otherwise brutal exploitation of the enslaved person by the master goes back to Adam Smith and enjoys some favor among more recent historians. However, the subsequent events in Smith's example, the French colony of Haiti, appear to challenge his analysis (see Landes, *Wealth and Poverty*, 116).

15. Anon., *Providential Aspect and Salutary Tendency of the Existing Crisis* (New Orleans: Picayune Office, 1861), clipping on inside cover, 17–19.

16. Anon., *Providential Aspect and Salutary Tendency*, 8, 10, 13, 15, 17–18.

17. Anon., *Providential Aspect and Salutary Tendency*, 7, Bilbo, *Oration*, 3; Karp, *This Vast Southern Empire*, 1–10, 150–54.

18. Jefferson Davis, Message, April 29, 1861, *JDC*, 5:72–84.

19. Bilbo, *Oration*, 15; Convention of Cotton Planters, *Proceedings of the Convention of Cotton Planters, Held in Macon, Ga., July 4, 1861. With a Communication on the Proposed Issue of Treasury Notes by the Confederate Government, by Duff Green, Esq* (Macon, Ga., 1861), 5.

20. Arthur J. Lynn, "Annual Report of Shipping and Navigation, Trade and Commerce," FO 5/788, pp. 349–55, PRO; Hunt and James to William Massie, William Massie Papers, UT; Robert Bunch to Lord John Russell, July 23, 1861, FO 5/781, p. 57, PRO.

21. Thomas Mure to Lord John Russell, July 1, 1861, FO 5/788, p. 167, PRO; Abram Archer to H. J. Hennington, August 7, 1861, box 2E650, folder 1, "immediate family, 1858–1865," Richard Thompson Archer papers, UT; Edmund Molyneux to Earl Russell, December 4, 1861, FO 5/786, p. 497, PRO.

22. P. A. Champomier, *A Statement of the Sugar Crop of Louisiana with an Appendix, 1861–1862* (New Orleans: Cook, Young, 1862), viii; Richard Follett, "Old South, New South: The Strange Career of Pierre Champomier," in Samuel C. Hyde, ed., *The Enigmatic South: Toward Civil War and Its Legacies* (Baton Rouge: Louisiana State University Press, 2014), 153–73.

23. *Providential Aspect and Salutary Tendency of the Existing Crisis* (New Orleans: Picayune Office, 1861), 15; Peter Randolph to Abram Archer, October 18, 1861, box 2E647, folder title "letters received 1861–8 and undated," Richard Thompson Archer Papers, UT.

24. Kentucky Confederate Provisional Government, "Proceedings of the Convention Held in Russellville," p. 64, FHS.

25. George W. Pickens to the South Carolina Legislature, December 1861, GLC09206.01; Russell, *My Diary North and South*, 67–69; Thomas, *Confederate Nation*, 68–71; William H. Freehling, *The Road to Disunion* (New York: Oxford University Press, 2008), 2: 420; Rable, *Confederate Republic*, 149–50.

26. Convention of Cotton Planters, *Proceedings of the Convention of Cotton Planters*, 8, 27; H. K. Burgwyn, *Our Currency: Some of Its Evils and Remedies for Them. By a Citizen of North Carolina* (Raleigh, N.C.: John W. Syme, 1861), 41.

27. Committee on Foreign Affairs, *Report of the Committee on Foreign Affairs*, 3; Convention of Cotton Planters, *Proceedings of the Convention of Cotton Planters* (1861), 5. A member of the Confederate Department of State, perhaps Toombs himself, had twice written by hand "the richer/ much richer by the trade" on the Committee's Report. On Duff Green and trade, see Thomas R. Hietala, *Manifest Design: Anxious Aggrandizement in Late Jacksonian America* (Ithaca, N.Y.: Cornell University Press, 1985), 10–54; Karp, *This Vast Southern Empire*, 127–34. On Green and Calhoun, see Freehling, *Road to Disunion*, 1:382, 385–87; Howe, *What God Hath Wrought*, 331–32, 341; Sellers, *Market Revolution*, 292, 296–97. Duff Green's interests ranged from canals, including the Chesapeake and Ohio Canal, to railroads, in particular the Southern Pacific Railroad; at the time the war began, Green was arranging with the Mexicans to connect Texas to the Pacific coast via railroad. According to Green, other nations were laggards in the race to free trade, even the British had a "system of exorbitant duties," and France had, in signing the 1860 commercial treaty with Britain, only loosened "the rusty sinews of her protective system a hair's breadth."

28. Robert Bunch to Lord John Russell, May 1, 1861, FO 5/780, p. 210, PRO; Committee on Foreign Affairs, *Report of the Committee on Foreign Affairs*, 3; William John Grayson, *Remarks on Mr. Motley's Letter in the London Times on the War in America* (Charleston, S.C.: Evans and Cogswell, 1861),

21–22. Bunch told Russell, "The southern congress met yesterday in Montgomery, it is supposed that the tariff will be soon discussed." On May 22, news of the secret session deliberations reached Bunch with the passage of the tariff effective August 31. Bunch observed of the tariff, "that the chief provisions of this tariff are eminently favorable to British interests as compared with the US tariff cannot be denied" (Bunch to Russell, May 22, 1861 FO 5/780, pp. 253–55, PRO).

29. Thomas Bragg, "Diary," January 14, 1862, p. 98, folder 3, Thomas Bragg Papers, #03304-z, SHC; Burgwyn, *Our Currency*, 45–46.

30. *Macon Daily Telegraph*, October 15, 1861. The Southern Commercial Convention subsumed, for that meeting, the Cotton Planters' Convention. Such meeting mergers had occurred before the war. In terms of attendance comparison, only 62 delegates attended the Vicksburg 1859 convention and 95 the Montgomery 1858 convention. Four hundred delegates represented the highest number since the 804 delegates attended at Knoxville in 1857 (V. Johnson, *Men and the Vision*, 5, 27). An example of an individual with diverse roles was David Hubbard, who was also a member of the Provisional Congress's committee on territories, later first Confederate commissioner of Indian affairs (Thomas McAdory Owen and Marie Bankhead Owen, *History of Alabama and Dictionary of Alabama Biography* [Chicago: S. J. Clark, 1921], 3:854).

31. *Macon Daily Telegraph*, October 15, 1861; Jefferson Davis to R. M. T. Hunter, September 2, 1861, *JDP*, 7:319; McCardell, *Idea of a Southern Nation*, 250, 273, 336; Thomas, *Confederate Nation*, 77–78; Donald S. Frazier, *Blood and Treasure: Confederate Empire in the Southwest* (College Station: Texas A&M University Press. 1995), 61–73.

32. Botts, *Address to His Fellow-Citizens*, 11; By One of the People, *Remarks on the Policy of Prohibiting the Exportation of Cotton* (Charleston, S.C.: Evans & Cogswell, 1861), 11; O'Brien, *Intellectual Life*, 228–31; Fox-Genovese and Genovese, *Mind of the Master Class*, 316–19.

33. Jefferson Davis, April 29, 1861, *JDC*, 5:72; R. M. T. Hunter to James M. Mason, 23 September, 1861, in Richardson, *Messages and Papers*, 2:84–90.

34. *Richmond Dispatch*, May 1, 13, 18, 1861; *Richmond Examiner*, April 23, September 6, 1861; *Richmond Dispatch*, May 13, 1861; *Richmond Examiner*, September 13, 1861. Daniel Kilbride, "The Old South Confronts the Dilemma of David Livingstone," *Journal of Southern History* 82, no. 4 (November 2016): 800–815. On British plans—supported by Lancashire Mill owners—to construct railroads in order to increase cotton exports from India, see Manu Goswani, *Producing India: From Colonial Economy to National Space* (Chicago: University of Chicago Press, 2004), 46–49.

35. "Southern Trade," *DBR*, 5, no. 5 and 6 (May 1861): 567; Robert Toombs to Charles J. Helm, 22 July, 1861, in Richardson, *Messages and Papers*, 2:46–48.

36. "Bill recognizing the existence of war between the United States and Confederate States," May 3, 1861, *CJ*, 1:176; James Mason, "Resolution" and "Amendment," on "a bill to make temp provision for naturalizing as citizens of the Confederacy persons now citizens of Kentucky, Missouri, Maryland, Delaware," July 31, 1861, *CJ*, 1:288, 302. Other bills offered opportunities to reaffirm the enlarged territorial extent of the Confederacy; for example, in the definition of "enemy aliens" and the bill authorizing the establishment of recruiting stations in border slave states. Karp, *This Vast Southern Empire*, 226–29; McCardell, *Idea of a Southern Nation*, 261–73; May, *Slavery, Race and Conquest in the Tropics*, 132–44; Henry Harrison Simms, *The Life of Robert M. T. Hunter: A Study of Sectionalism and Secession* (Richmond, Va.: William Byrd, 1935), 175–81; Link, *Roots of Secession*, 128–29; Crofts, *Reluctant Confederates*, 30–31. The First Battle of Bull Run (Manassas) was fought on July 21, 1861. The forces of Confederate generals Pierre G. T. Beauregard and Joseph E. Johnston defeated the United States Army commanded by General Irvin McDowell. News of the result reached the Confederate Congress, by now in nearby Richmond, the same day, telegraphed from the battlefield by Davis himself, who had "turned up at the moment of victory." "The South erupted in joy over a victory that seemed to prove that one Southron could indeed lick any number of Yankees" (James M. McPherson, *Battle Cry of Freedom: The Civil War Era* [New York: Oxford University Press, 1988], 345–46).

37. R. M. T. Hunter to J. M. Mason, September 23, 1861, in Richardson, *Messages and Papers*, 2:84–90.

38. R. M. T. Hunter to Henry Holze, November 14, 1861, in Robert F. Durden, "The Index: Confederate Newspaper in London, 1862–1865" (MA thesis, Emory University, 1947). For further information on Hotze and the *Index*, see Charles P. Cullop, *Confederate Propaganda in Europe, 1861–1865* (University of Miami, 1969), and Robert E. Bonner, "Slavery, Confederate Diplomacy and the Racialist Mission of Henry Hotze," *Civil War History*, September 2005, 51. Historians continue to argue that Confederates believed they had to have European intervention to avoid losing the Civil War, and hence their diplomacy has to have been incompetent; for a recent reiteration of this theme see Thomas E. Sebrell II, *Persuading John Bull: Union and Confederate Propaganda in Britain, 1860–1865* (London: Lexington Books, 2014), 70.

39. Jefferson Davis, "Message to the Confederate Congress," April 29, 1861, *JDC*, 5:84; Robert Toombs to Yancey et al., May 28, 1861 in Richardson, *Messages and Papers*, 2:31; John A. Campbell to Jefferson Davis, April 28, 1861, *JDP*, 7:137.

40. *Richmond Examiner*, April 16, 1861; Edward Jackson to Jefferson Davis, April 15, 1861, *JDP*, 7:102; John Forsyth to Jefferson Davis, April 4, 1861,

JDP, 7:91; May, *Southern Dream,* 136–62; Walther, *Yancey and the Coming of the Civil War,* 229–53; W. Russell, *My Diary North and South,* 38, III. William Howard Russell dined with Forsyth the day before he wrote to Davis and described the commissioner as "fanatical in his opposition to any suggestion of compromise or reconstruction."

41. Henry A. Wise, Speeches at the Convention, April 15, 16, 1861; Freehling and Simpson, *Showdown in Virginia,* 167–72; Craig M. Simpson *A Good Southerner: The Life of Henry A. Wise of Virginia* (Chapel Hill: University of North Carolina Press, 1985), 244–45; Robert Lewis Dabney, *Letter of the Rev. R. L. Dabney to the Rev. S. J. Prime on the State of the Country, republished from the Central Presbyterian* (Richmond, Va.: Macfarlane and Fergusson, 1861), 12; Fox-Genovese and Genovese, *Mind of the Master Class,* 98 (quote); 481–84; 630–34, 671–72.

42. William Norwood to James Lyons, April 23, 1861, folder 46, box 6, Lyons Family Papers, HL; Jefferson Davis quoted in Robert Bunch to Lord John Russell, July 22, 1861, FO 5/781, p. 41, PRO. Norwood added, "I and all mine are all for the South, if you can send me a letter by private hand, tell me will Washington City be attacked?" According to historian Michael T. Bernath, James Lyons wrote four essays on the "Right and Propriety" of Secession (Bernath, *Confederate Minds: The Struggle for Intellectual Independence in the Civil War South* [Chapel Hill: University of North Carolina Press, 2010], 129).

43. John Letcher, "To Gentlemen," June 6, 1861, folder 387, Governors Correspondence, June–July 1861, Letcher Papers, VHS; Sam Houston, "Position of General Sam Houston," Cedar Point, Texas, September 12, 1861, box 2R48, vol. 16, January 1861–May 1928, Sam Houston Papers, UT; Boney, *John Letcher of Virginia,* 128–35; Karp, *This Vast Southern Empire,* 208; May, *Southern Dream,* 136–62, 190–205; May, *Slavery, Race and Conquest in the Tropics,* 169–75; Frazier, *Blood and Treasure,* 23–34.

44. "Hunt and James" to William Massie, May 11, 1861, general correspondence folder April–May 1861; John Jones to William Massie, June 10, 1861, general correspondence folder June–September 1861, box 2E493, William Massie Papers, UT; W. T. Walthall to the editors of the *Church Journal,* Mobile Ala., May 17, 1861, in Rev. J. J. Nicolson, *Government or No Government: Or the Question of State Allegiance. A Tract for Churchmen* (Mobile, Ala.: Farrow & Dennet, 1861), 7; Thomas McAdory Owen, *A Bibliography of Alabama* (Washington, D.C: U.S. Government Printing Office, 1898), 1225. Both John E. Jones and J[ames] M. Hunt were members of a committee appointed to publish resolutions at a public meeting at Nottoway Court House, April 11 (Virginia Secession Convention). The warehouse of Hunt and James was on the corner of Cary and Virginia Streets (*Richmond City Business Directory* [1860], 8, Library of Virginia, Richmond).

45. Botts, *Address to His Fellow-Citizens*, 12–13. During the summer of 1861 in London, representatives from Britain, France, and Spain agreed to a tripartite alliance in response to the decision by Mexican president Benito Juárez to suspend payment to foreign bondholders of Mexican debt and cease compensation to foreign owners for property damaged in the recent civil war (David F. Krein, *The Last Palmerston Government: Foreign Policy, Domestic Politics, and the Genesis of "Splendid Isolation"* [Ames: Iowa State University Press, 1978], 30–36).

46. Robert Bunch to Lord John Russell, July 22, 1861, FO 5/781, p. 41, PRO.

47. Grayson, *Remarks on Mr. Motley's Letter*, 4; Committee on Foreign Affairs, *Report of the Committee on Foreign Affairs*, 9; Fox-Genovese and Genovese, *Mind of the Master Class*, 30, 501, 684; Karp, *This Vast Southern Empire*, 169–80; McCardell, *Idea of a Southern Nation*, 71; Kilbride, "Old South Confronts the Dilemma of David Livingstone," 799. On opposition in the South to Jay's Treaty, see Howard Jones, *Crucible of Power: A History of American Foreign Relations to 1913* (Lanham, Md.: Rowman & Littlefield 2009), 31–34, 38–44.

48. Bilbo, *Past, Present, and Future of the Southern Confederacy*, 16; Robert Hunter to John Slidell, September 3, 1861, *OR*, Ser 1, 3: 271. On Slidell's negotiations on behalf of President Polk with Mexico, see Greenberg, *Wicked War*, 77–85; on his attempts to waive the neutrality act to support Quitman's activities, see May, *Slavery, Race and Conquest in the Tropics*, 77–85; on final attempts to purchase Cuba, see May, *Slavery, Race, and Conquest in the Tropics*, 159–69; on Slidell's skills as a diplomat, see Doyle, *Cause of All Nations*, 199; W. Russell, *My Diary North and South*, 127, H. Jones, *Blue and Gray Diplomacy*, 131, 153.

49. Lieutenant Colonel Kannady to John Ross, May 15, 1861, GLC00066.128; Ben McCulloch to Albert Pike, June 17, 1861, folder title "correspondence February 6, 1860 to September 27, 1861," Hines, Thomas Henry papers, #A H662 1, FHS; Pike to Benjamin, November 27, 1861, *OR* vol. 8, 697–98, box 2, Robert Douthat Meade Papers, #9989, UVA [collection hereafter cited as Meade Papers]. On November 30, Bragg conceded on Native Americans that "it is important to have them on our side, but they are an inferior race and ought not to come in now without limit to population to entitle them to admission" (Thomas Bragg, "Diary," 72, folder 3, Thomas Bragg Papers, #03304-z, SHC). The priority of Native Americans was protection from the U.S. government, and as long as the Confederacy could provide that protection, they would be loyal allies—evidenced by fighting on the rebel side at the battle of Pea Ridge on March 6–7, 1862; but after that defeat the CSA could not prevent northern invasion of Indian Territory, and the Native Americans lost enthusiasm (Thomas, *Confederate Nation*, 188–89).

50. "Bill to Organize the Territory of Arizona," December 24, 1861, *CJ*, 1:612; Frazier, *Blood and Treasure*, 48–61, 117–28. The military proclamation stated, "to the people of the territory of Arizona: I, John R. Baylor, Lieut. Col. Commanding the Confederate Army in the Territory of New Mexico, hereby take possession of the said Territory in the name of and on behalf of the Confederate States of America" (August 2, 1861, Parrish, *Confederate Imprints*, 1359). The choice of northern boundary recalled both the Crittenden Compromise and the Missouri Compromise line. A member of Sibley's army invading New Mexico noted, "I cannot see what this country is made for if it is not rich in minerals, for there is no soil or water." "Latest accounts of the Pino[s] Alto[s] gold mines are very encouraging . . . new silver mines in the Papago Country [Arizona] have been discovered of exceeding richness, combination of silver, copper and lead" ("Letter from Sibley's Brigade," "Letter from Tuscon," *Houston Tri-Weekly Telegraph*, December 30, 1861, GLC05959.51.013). On Campbell, see S. A. Cunningham, "Last Survivor of the Original Confederate Congress," *Confederate Veteran* 25, no. 2 (February 1917): 54.

51. Ochiltree Amendment, August 7, 1861, *CJ*, 1:325; Frazier, *Blood and Treasure*, 73–101; "Secession in California," *Daily Sun*, Columbus, Georgia, July 11, 1861, GLC05959.03.01. In May 1861, the *Richmond Daily Dispatch* depicted California as another victim of Union avarice; in planning privateer raids against the Union's specie ships sailing with California gold, the pledge was made that the Californians would not be injured "anymore"; their target was the New York merchants; hence presumption of California sympathy and support (*Richmond Dispatch*, May 16, 1861).

52. Parrish, *Confederate Imprints*, 518; *Richmond Examiner*, May 17, 21, October 22, 1861; *Richmond Daily Dispatch*, May 16, 1861.

53. Doyle, *Cause of All Nations*, 120–28.

54. Robert Toombs to John T. Pickett, May 17, 1861, in Richardson, *Messages and Papers*, 2:21–25. For Confederate diplomatic relations with Mexico, see Thomas David Schoonover, *Dollars over Dominion: The Triumph of Liberalism in Mexican–United States Relations, 1861–1867* (Baton Rouge: Louisiana State University Press, 1978), 13–48, 78–101. In assessing American attitudes to the borderlands, John C. A. Stagg argues that policymakers of the Early Republic sought to implement an ideology of American continentalism or a belief that a secure and independent United States should be the successor state to the rival European powers of North America. Robert Bonner extended this argument to the Civil War era (*Mastering America*, 307, 309). But, according to Stagg, this ideal of Madison was undone by the reality on the ground of "ambition, greed, idealism, patriotism, religious chauvinism and racial contempt for local and indigenous populations." See John C. A. Stagg, *Borderlines in Borderlands: James Madison*

and the Spanish-American Frontier, 1776–1821 (New Haven, Conn.: Yale University Press, 2009). For the complexity of the triangular relationship between Americans, Mexicans, and Native Americans, see Brian Delay, *War of a Thousand Deserts: Indian Raids and the U.S.–Mexican War* (New Haven, Conn.: Yale University Press, 2008).

55. Robert Toombs to John T. Pickett, May 17, 1861, in Richardson, *Messages and Papers*, 2:21–25; *Richmond Examiner*, June 18, October 6, 1861. Article XI of the Treaty of Guadeloupe Hidalgo stipulated, "it is solemnly agreed that all such incursions shall be forcibly restrained by the Government of the United States whensoever this may be necessary," Treaty of Guadalupe Hidalgo; February 2, 1848, *Treaties and Conventions between the United States of America and Other Powers since July 4, 1776* (Washington, D.C., 1871) accessed via the Yale Law School library's web page (https://avalon.law.yale.edu/19th_century/guadhida.asp). For a discussion of the racial attitudes between Confederates and Mexicans, see Sarah E. Cornell, "Americans in the U.S. South and Mexico: A Transnational History of Race, Slavery, and Freedom, 1810—1910" (PhD diss., New York University, 2008); on the dissemination of anti-Mexican propaganda during the Mexican War and the reaction against it, especially in the North, see Greenberg, *Wicked War*.

56. *Richmond Examiner*, September 6, October 6, 1861; *Richmond Daily Dispatch*, September 4, 6, 1861.

57. William M. Browne to J. A. Quintero, September 3, 1861, in Richardson, *Messages and Papers*, 2:77–80; Robert Toombs to Quintero, May 22, 1861, *OR*, Ser. 1, 3:217; Owsley, *King Cotton Diplomacy*, 116; Wahlstrom, *Southern Exodus to Mexico*, 5; Doyle, *Cause of All Nations*, 120. For the Corwin mission, see Schoonover, *Dollars over Dominion*, 16–25. These were the provinces of Nuevo Leon, Tamaulipas, and Coahuila; Davis had the week before been alerted to the friendly disposition of the provincial governor (W. W. Kincheloe to Jefferson Davis, August 22, 1861, *JDP*, 7:285).

58. Browne to Quintero, December 9, 1861, *OR*, Ser. 1, 3:308; May, *Southern Dream*, 136–62; Doyle, *Cause of All Nations*, 120; Wahlstrom, *Southern Exodus to Mexico*, 71. On the success of Quintero in identifying such a community of interest with Vidaurri, see Charles M. Hubbard, *The Burden of Confederate Diplomacy* (Knoxville: University of Tennessee Press, 1998), 47 and Thomas, *Confederate Nation*, 185–86.

59. Jefferson Davis, "Message to Congress," April 29, 1861, *JDC*, 5:72; "We Must Develop Southern Industry," *DBR* 5, no. 4 (April 1861): 449.

60. R. M. T. Hunter to Santiago Vidaurri, September 9, *OR*, Ser. 1, 3:255; Robert Toombs to J. A. Quintero, May 22, 1861, 3:217.

61. "Southern Trade," *DBR* 5, no. 5 and 6 (May 1861): 567; *Richmond Examiner*, September 17, 1861; Robert Toombs to Charles J. Helm, July 22, 1861,

in Richardson, *Messages and Papers*, 2:46–48; Robert Hunter to William L. Yancey, Dudley Mann, and Pierre Rost, August 24, 1861, in Richardson, *Messages and Papers*, 2:72–73; Karp, *This Vast Southern Empire*, 186–99. Note the prevalent press belief that Spanish possession of Cuba was dependent on Confederate goodwill and permission. The correspondence possibly implies that Serrano felt he needed Confederate support to bolster his relations with the Court of Spanish Queen Isabella II; certainly, Serrano had a record of intrigue and enemies back in Spain. Significantly, Boswell Bach of New Orleans wrote to Davis on September 19, 1861, suggesting he thank Serrano for his friendly stance and make sure Madrid was informed of his gratitude (*JDP*, 7:345); Thomas Bragg, "Diary," January 14, 1862, p. 103, folder 3, Thomas Bragg Papers, #03304-z, SHC.

62. Hunter to Yancey, Mann, and Rost, August 24, 1861, in Richardson, *Messages and Papers*, 2:72–73; *Richmond Dispatch*, May 6, 1861, box 2, folder title "1861 285 items on index cards," Meade Papers, UVA; Doyle, *Cause of All Nations*, 112–14.

63. Hunter to Yancey, Mann, and Rost, August 24, 1861, in Richardson, *Messages and Papers*, 2:72–73; James M. Mason to Hunter, October 18, 1861, in Richardson, *Messages and Papers*, 2:105; Anon, *Remarks on the Policy of Prohibiting the Exportation of Cotton, by One of the People* (Charleston, S.C.: Evans & Cogswell, 1861), 9–10; Doyle, *Cause of All Nations*, 109–13; Karp, *This Vast Southern Empire*, 182–86; May, *Slavery, Race and Conquest*, 234–42. On Spain's bid to return to the ranks of great powers, see Wayne H. Bowen, *Spain and the American Civil War* (Columbia: University of Missouri Press, 2011), 35–54. Mason's trip was as Confederate emissary to England; accompanying him was John Slidell, emissary to France. At Nassau, they boarded the British mail packet H.M.S. *Trent*. For a recent study of the Trent Crisis, see H. Jones, *Blue and Grey*, 83–113.

64. Charles J. Helm to R. M. T. Hunter, December 12, 1861, *OR*, Ser. 1, 3:309; Robert Toombs to Charles J. Helm, July 22, 1861, in Richardson, *Messages and Papers*, 2:46–48; Charles J. Helm to R. M. T. Hunter, November 9, 1861, in Richardson, *Messages and Papers*, 2:114; *Richmond Examiner*, January 24, 1862. For blockade-running, see Stephen R. Wise, *Lifeline of the Confederacy: Blockade Running during the Civil War* (Columbia: University of South Carolina Press, 1988). Britain, as the colonial power controlling Bahamas and Bermuda, was the power implicated in assisting blockade-running.

3. Self-Sufficiency at Home and Self-Assertion Abroad

1. *Southern Illustrated News*, October 11, December 13, 1862; Thomas, *Confederate Nation*, 145–66; Rable, *Confederate Republic*, 132–53; Levine, *Fall of the House of Dixie*, 109–10; Andrews, *South Reports the Civil War*.

2. On the army, especially Robert E. Lee's Army of Northern Virginia as the symbol of the Confederacy, see G. Gallagher, *Confederate War*, 61–112.

3. Robert Garlick Hill Kean, *Inside the Confederate Government: The Diary of Robert Garlick Hill Kean*, ed. Edward Younger (New York: Oxford University Press, 1957), 55. The *Examiner* spoke for many as it declared "the late reverses will prove the greatest of blessings if they awaken the sense of duty … we must become the arbiters of our national fortunes" (*Richmond Examiner*, March 7, 1862. Kean, diary entry May 3, 1863). Benjamin "is the most unreliable of news reporters, believes anything, and is as sanguine as he is credulous."

4. *Richmond Examiner*, April 4, 1862; Robert Hunter to James M. Mason and John Slidell, February 8, 1862, in Richardson, *Messages and Papers*, 2:174. For the continuing French coal shortage even as the exploitation of the Pas de Calais region enabled a jump in production in the 1850s, see Landes, *Wealth and Poverty*, 203.

5. "Railroads of the Confederacy," *DBR*, 8, no. 1 (May 1862): 95; Robert Rufus Bridgers to Thomas Ruffin, February 17, 1862, Ruffin Papers, SHC; Edmondston, *Journal of a Secesh Lady*, 147.

6. "As to the Future of the South," *Mobile Register* in the *Index* 1, no. 7 (June 16, 1862): 97; Wahlstrom, *Southern Exodus to Mexico*, 5–13.

7. Jefferson Davis, "Inaugural," February 22, 1862, "Speech," January 7, 1863, *JDC*, 5:200, 390.

8. Richardson, *Messages and Papers*, 2:173. Historian Walter Houghton, drawing on Lecky, Mill, and Buckle, wrote about "the new political economy … [that] had taught men an enlightened interest in the prosperity of nations they traded with … and in the enormous value of peace, since the markets of the world were now so interconnected that any derangement in one of them brought evil on all" (Houghton, *Victorian Frame of Mind*, 42).

9. For example, from 1857 European countries negotiated away levies and tolls on international waterways such as the Danube and Rhine rivers; in 1860 France and Britain agreed a to commercial pact, the Cobden-Chevalier treaty, and other bilateral treaties were in the works (see Landes, *Wealth and Poverty*, 200).

10. Robert Hunter to James M. Mason and John Slidell, February 8, 1862, in Richardson, *Messages and Papers*, 2:174; Thomas B. Lewis to Jefferson Davis, January 15, 1862, *JDP*, 8:19; Benjamin Diary (Micfilm # 9989, Meade Papers, UVA); Rachel St. John, "The Unpredictable America of William

Gwin," *Journal of the Civil War Era* 6, no. 1 (March 2016): 56–89; L. Q. C. Lamar to Davis, December 31, 1862, *JDP,* 8:591. Lewis also noted strong Confederate sentiment in Maryland. The *Southern Illustrated News* had declared on November 8, "the natural and commercial position of Vicksburg must inevitably secure to it a splendid and glorious trade, population and wealth. With the Vicksburg, Shreveport and Texas Railroad extending immediately from the opposite bank of the Mississippi through the fruitful and teaming cotton fields of Louisiana to the Texan border, thence to be connected with the great 'Southern Pacific Railroad' to California." On the reality of increasing loyalty of Californians to the Union, see Glenna Matthews, *The Golden State in the Civil War: Thomas Starr King, the Republican Party, and the Birth of Modern California* (New York: Cambridge University Press, 2012).

11. Henry S. Foote, "Joint Resolution," *CJ,* 5:469–70. On Foote's demands for all Mexico during the Mexican War, see McCardell, *Idea of a Southern Nation,* 230–36; Frederick Merk, *Manifest Destiny and Mission in American History: A Reinterpretation* (New York: Random House, 1966), 152, 164; and Holt, *Rise and Fall of the American Whig Party,* 496. On Foote as Unionist, see Davis, *Rhett,* 288, 307.

12. "Article V—Experiences of the Past—Our Guide for the Future," *DBR* 7, no. 1 and 2 (January 1862): 63. The journalist's pseudonym was "Barbarossa"—De Bow described him as of "both political and literary distinction and now in charge of a distinguished corps."

13. "Article XI—Commercial Importance and Future of the South," *DBR* 7, no. 1 and 2 (January 1862): 120.

14. Planters Convention (1862: Memphis, Tenn.), *Report of Select Committee Appointed by the Planters' Convention* (Memphis, Tenn., 1862), 7; J. B. Gladney to Davis, August 7, 1862, *JDP,* 8:327; Hershel V. Johnson to Jefferson Davis, March 26, 1862, *JDP,* 8:118–19; Johnson to Robert Hunter, August 27, 1862, box 9, Hunter Papers, VHS; Quigley, *Shifting Grounds,* 118–19; Merk, *Manifest Destiny,* 152. The Planters' Convention looked forward to "a further dissolution of the old union into grand natural sectional divisions, and each sectional grand division put under its own confederate or general government for the protection of sectional rights." The planters wanted "friendly alliances offensive and defensive with the Confederate States," which would lead to "A union of these grand divisions into one power through friendly treaties for the protection of the whole."

15. Bonner, *Mastering America,* 217–52. From the perspective of the other side, Jennifer Weber argues that "the main spur was the severe military reverses of 1862" in the formation of the Peace Democrat faction (Jennifer L. Weber, *Copperheads: The Rise and Fall of Lincoln's Opponents in the North* [New York: Oxford University Press, 2006]).

16. Jefferson Davis to Robert E. Lee, Braxton Bragg, and Edmund Kirby Smith, September 7, 1862, *JDC*, 5:338; Hershel V. Johnson to Robert Hunter, August 27, 1862, box 9, Hunter Papers, VHS.

17. Henry S. Foote, "Majority Report of the Committee on Foreign Affairs Relating to the True Policy of the War," September 19, 1862, *CJ*, 5:404–6.

18. Foote, "Majority Report of the Committee on Foreign Affairs," 5:404–6; on the relationship between Davis and Foote, see Cooper, *Jefferson Davis, American*, 90–324. Even though he had relocated to Tennessee in 1859, Foote came back to campaign for Douglas in Mississippi in 1860.

19. Ethelbert Barksdale, "Minority Report of the Committee on Foreign Affairs, Relating to the True Policy of the War," September 19, 1862, *CJ*, 5:406–7. James Robert McLean of North Carolina and William R. Smith of Alabama were also signatories to the minority report. In contrast to Foote, Barksdale, along with his brother, U.S. Representative William Barksdale, had been a passionate campaigner for immediate secession in Mississippi. Prominent local newspaper editor and later printer of the secession ordinance written by Lamar, Ethelbert Barksdale had joined the Jackson Minute Men in November 1860, and his antipathy to any northerners was clear from his Christmas 1860 appeal to citizens to leave the Union: "the triumph of Abolitionism, will be the triumph of discontent, riot, bloodshed, atheism, and every manner of foul thing to pervert the understanding and corrupt the hearts of men. It runs riots over the Northern States. Shall we not protect from its leprous embrace this fair land of our inheritance?" (Barney, *Secessionist Impulse*, 206, 225).

20. Braxton Bragg to Jefferson Davis, October 2, 1862, *JDP*, 8:416–20; Braxton Bragg to the Kentuckians, September 14, and Simon B. Buckner, "Address to the Freemen of Kentucky," September 24, 1862, in Hanleiter and Adair, *Southern Confederacy*, 2:203 (October 12, 1862) GLC05959.09.084; Edmund Kirby-Smith, "Kentuckians, I am Authorized by the President, of the Confederacy, to Organize Troops and Issue Commissions," broadside, 1862 (GLC04507.01).

21. L. Q. C. Lamar to Judah P. Benjamin, December 10, 1862 (Micfilm #9989, Meade Papers, UVA); Jefferson Davis to Theophilus Holmes, December 21, 1862, *JDC*, 5:386; Jefferson Davis, "Speech at Jackson," December 26, 1862, *JDP*, 8:577.

22. Robert Hunter to James M. Mason and John Slidell, August 2, 1862, in Richardson, *Messages and Papers*, 2:171–75. The far West was the Pacific coastal states of California and Oregon and Washington Territory.

23. John Ross to Jefferson Davis, May 10, 1862, *JDP*, 8:170; *CJ*, 1:640, 832; 5:11; *CJ*, 2:138; McPherson, *Battle Cry of Freedom*, 404; Hubbard, *Burden of Confederate Diplomacy*, 45–46. On the idea of a distinct, first continental empire based on "genocide" of Native Americans and a second from

the 1890s based on commercial expansion and more global in scope, see Paul A. Kramer, *The Blood of Government: Race, Empire, the United States, and the Philippines* (Chapel Hill: University of North Carolina Press, 2006), 10–11.

24. Albert Pike to Jefferson Davis, June 10, 1862, *JDP,* 8:235; Benjamin Diary, Micform #9989, Meade Papers, UVA; McPherson, *Battle Cry of Freedom,* 404; Hubbard, *Burden of Confederate Diplomacy,* 45–46.

25. Jefferson Davis, "Message to Congress," August 18, 1862, *CJ,* 5:299; *CJ,* 5:502, 527. The process was not without some reservations from representatives; Foote forced Boudinot's qualification to be considered by the Committee on Indian Affairs, and on October 7, Thomas B. Hanley of Arkansas demanded to see a copy of the relevant treaty (*CJ,* 5: 505). Representative John Milton Elliott of Kentucky from the Committee on Indian Affairs reported that Boudinot could fulfill the following functions: "to propose and introduce measures for the benefit of the [Cherokee] nation, and to be heard in regard thereto, and on other questions in which the said nation is particularly interested" (*CJ,* 5:514).

26. "American Indians," *Index* 1, no. 21 (September 18, 1862): 21; Mary Boykin Miller Chesnut, *Mary Chesnut's Civil War,* ed. C. Vann Woodward (New Haven, Conn.: Yale University Press, 1981), 196. Benjamin recorded on August 28, "Accounts from the North report an extensive Indian outbreak in Minnesota" (Benjamin Diary, p. 93, [Micform #9989, Meade Papers, UVA]).

27. Robert Hunter, "Motion on the Bill to Organize Arkansas and Red River Superintendency of Indian Affairs," March 11, 1862, *CJ,* 2:55; Albert Pike to Jefferson Davis, August 25, November 19, 1862, *JDP,* 8:358, 498; Theophilus Holmes to Davis, August 28, 1862, *JDP,* 8:360–62; George W. Randolph to Davis, September 23, 1862, *JDP,* 8:403; Davis to Randolph, November 19, 1862, *JDP,* 8:498; Davis to James A. Seddon, December 6, 1862, *JDP* 8:528; O'Brien, *Intellectual Life and the American South,* 172. In his earlier letter, Pike complained that he had only "accepted command of this department with the stipulation that it would never have been part of trans-Mississippi." By November, he complained the commanders "Holmes and Hindman had produced the result I had long ago predicted" and the Indian Territory "cannot be redeemed." Holmes on August 28 urged Davis to accept Pike's resignation as he "has ruined us the Indian country, and I fear it will be long before we can re-establish the confidence he has destroyed." On December 6, Davis promoted the experienced Douglas H. Cooper as superintendent but then had him complaining as Pike had done before of having to take orders from the Trans-Mississippi Department. There is no evidence that any more Indian delegates took their seats in the Congress in 1862.

28. Frazier, *Blood and Treasure*, 73; Williamson S. Oldham to Jefferson Davis, August 18, 1862, *JDP*, 8:347–48; Davis note, September 3, 1862, *JDP*, 8:376; Davis to George W. Randolph, October 27, 1862, *JDP*, 8:467; Wahlstrom, *Southern Exodus to Mexico*, 71–76. Baylor combined roles of Indian fighter and agent, membership of the Knights of the Golden Circle, farmer, and politician. On Baylor's campaign against the Apache and its consequences, see Frazier, *Blood and Treasure*, 186–208, 291–98.

29. Frazier, *Blood and Treasure*, 18–23, 71, 109–15, 291–98; *CJ*, 1:691, 701; Jefferson Davis to the Senate, March 13, 1862, *CJ*, 2:59.

30. Benjamin Diary, Meade Collection; Judah P. Benjamin to James M. Mason, John Slidell, and Ambrose D. Mann, April 5, 1862, in Richardson, *Messages and Papers*, 2:215; *CJ* 5:204; Peterson T. Richardson to Jefferson Davis, March 3, 1862, *JDP*, 8:83–84; Thomas P. Ochiltree to Davis, April 27, 1862, *JDP*, 8:156; Francis R. Lubbock to Davis, May 1, 1862, *JDP*, 8:158. In the first six months of 1862, there were in both Benjamin's diary and in the papers of Davis regular correspondence and updates on Sibley's campaign in New Mexico. For example, on March 29, news reached Benjamin by means of a dispatch from Houston of the March 23 battle at Fort Craig. They probably preferred to focus on these events rather than the intractable difficulties in Tennessee and Virginia.

31. Jefferson Davis to Henry Hopkins Sibley, June 7, 1862, *JDP*, 8:229; Frazier, *Blood and Treasure*, 48, 73–101. Sibley's expedition was tiny. Flint Whitlock's *Distant Bugles, Distant Drums: The Union Response to the Confederate Invasion of New Mexico* (Boulder: University Press of Colorado, 2006) informs readers at the outset that action in New Mexico was "the second-smallest campaign of the Civil War in terms of number of combatants. No more than 7,000 men total were involved in the four main battles . . . and fewer than 300 were killed in combat."

32. "The Proclamation of Sibley," *Houston Tri-weekly Telegraph*, February 10, 1862. The paper's editor, Edward Cushing, described Sibley "as skillful a diplomatist as well as a gallant warrior" (GLC05959.51.022). The proclamation may have been initially welcomed; many resident Anglos in New Mexico favored the Confederate cause at least until the actual occupation, when economic strain and both political and legal infringements caused defections to the Union side. See Anthony Mora, *Border Dilemmas: Racial and National Uncertainties in New Mexico, 1848–1912* (Durham, N.C.: Duke University Press, 2011), and William S. Kiser, *Turmoil on the Rio Grande: The Territorial History of the Mesilla Valley, 1846–1865* (College Park: Texas A&M University Press, 2011).

33. Peterson T. Richardson to Jefferson Davis, March 3, 1862; Francis R. Lubbock to Davis, May 1, 1862. According to Sibley's ordnance officer Willis L. Robards, who wrote to Davis on December 8, 1862, the New

Mexicans had resented the Texan dominance of Sibley's brigade (Robards to Davis, December 8, 1862, *JDP*, 8:536–37). On Sibley's expedition as a fiasco, see Gary W. Gallagher, "Bold Rebel Venture in the Desert: General Sibley's Southwestern Conquest Fell Far Short of His Boasts," *Civil War Times* 53, no. 2 (2014): 20, and Frazier, *Blood and Treasure*, 259–77. Frazier notes that Sibley dispatched his aide Tom Ochiltree Jr. to Richmond with a letter pleading for reinforcements for the attention of the War Department (Frazier, *Blood and Treasure*, 229).

34. Peter W. Gray to Jefferson Davis, November 20, 1862, *JDP*, 8:499–500; L. Q. C. Lamar to Davis, December 31, 1862, *JDP*, 8:591. Sibley had sent word to Randolph on September 30 that Baylor had resigned his commission and quit Arizona for the East. Thomas Hadley had written to Davis that Baylor could have held Arizona with one regiment (Thomas B. J. Hadley to Davis, October 10, 1862, *JDP*, 8:457). As Davis noted on October 27, the authority given to Baylor was only to raise troops in Arizona, and the withdrawal of Sibley from El Paso made that impossible (Davis note dated October 27, 1862, on Randolph to Sibley, August 21, 1862, *JDP*, 8:466.) Baylor, as well as persecuting Indians, had also championed a trans-Mississippi department. According to Louisiana governor Thomas O. Moore, Baylor had advocated an appointment of a general of the western department "invested with plenary powers." Davis agreed, noting he had "previously concluded to form a Dept.—it is now a necessity" (Moore to Davis, May 4, 1862 and undated Davis note, *JDP*, 8:163). According to Lamar, "reports of [Magruder's] purpose to attack Galveston are rife throughout the state"; for once the rumors, although only about Texas, were accurate, and a day later on January 1, 1863, the city returned to Confederate control. Giraldi argues that Magruder "did made a difference keeping that state and its resources in the Confederacy for two years" when he retook Galveston and Sabine Pass (Lawrence Lee Hewitt and Thomas E. Schott, eds., *Confederate Generals in the Trans-Mississippi*, vol. 2, *Essays on America's Civil War* [Knoxville: University of Tennessee Press, 2015], 95).

35. William M. Browne to Jose A. Quintero, January 14, 1862, in Richardson, *Messages and Papers*, 2:151–52; Santiago Vidaurri to Jefferson Davis, January 25, 1862, *JDP*, 8:28; Judah P. Benjamin to Louis Trezevant Wigfall, February 15, 1862, box 1, folder title "Photostats of primary sources," Meade Papers, UVA. John T. Pickett, writing to Davis from Vera Cruz, agreed that Vidaurri might look favorably on an alliance with the Confederacy (Pickett to Davis, February 22, 1862, *JDP* 8:55).

36. Peter W. Gray, "Amendment of Bill to Prevent the Exportation of Either Cotton or Tobacco of the Present Crop, Except in Certain Cases," April 17, 1862, *CJ*, 5:257–58; Owsley, *King Cotton Diplomacy*, 116; May, *Irony of*

Confederate Diplomacy, 91. May notes Davis declining Vidaurri's wish to join the Confederacy.

37. Judah P. Benjamin to John Slidell, April 8, 1862, in Richardson, *Messages and Papers*, 2:220–23. For the question of broadening the definition of contraband to include reexport through neutral ports including Matamoras, see Stuart L. Bernath, *Squall across the Atlantic: American Civil War Prize Cases and Diplomacy* (Berkeley: University of California Press, 1970), 34–69.

38. Frazier, *Blood and Treasure*, 18–23, 73–101; Christopher G. Memminger to Jefferson Davis, October 22, 1862, enclosing a letter from John B. Magruder, *JDP*, 8:458–59; McCardell, *Idea of a Southern Nation*, 261–73; *Journal of the State Convention and Ordinances and Resolutions Adopted in January 1861 with an Appendix* (Jackson, Miss.: S. Barksdale, 1861); L. Q. C. Lamar to Davis, December 31, 1862, *JDP*, 8:591; Judah P. Benjamin to Captain Alexander M. Jackson, June 30, 1862 (Micfilm #9989, Meade Papers, UVA). Jackson was assistant adjutant general near Dona Ana in New Mexico. Benjamin referred to Hickman as "citizen of the Confederate States, resident at Chihuahua." On March 13, Jackson had been appointed chief justice of Arizona (*CJ*, 2:59).

39. Edward H. Cushing, "Colonel Reilly's Expedition," *Houston Tri-weekly Telegraph*, May 12, 1862, GLC05959.51.036. See also Patrick Kelly, "The North American Crisis of the 1860s," *Journal of the Civil War Era* 2, no. 3 (September 2012): 337–68; Martin Hardwick Hall, "Colonel James Reilly's Diplomatic Mission to Chihuahua and Sonora," *New Mexico Historical Review* 31, no. 3 (July 1956): 232–42; Frazier, *Blood and Treasure*, 128–47, 186–207, 232–58.

40. Edward H. Cushing, "Colonel Reilly's Expedition," *Houston Tri-weekly Telegraph*, May 12, 1862, GLC05959.51.036.; "Escort" of Mesilla, Arizona, "The Confederate Flag Planted by Houstonian on the Waters of the Pacific," *Houston Tri-weekly Telegraph*, May 12, 1862, GLC05959.51.036. The tripartite expedition was agreed to in London at the end of October 1861, forces landed in Vera Cruz from December 1861, and the Spanish and British departed on April 9, 1862 (Doyle, *Cause of All Nations*, 116–28).

41. H. Jones, *Blue and Grey*, 307–8; "Article IV—Shall We Have a Navy! Shall We Pursue the Defensive Policy, or Invade the Enemy's Country?" *DBR* 7, no. 3–4 (March 1862): 211; "Reviews on the Destiny of Mexico," *Index* 2, no. 33 (December 11, 1862): 97.

42. "Letter from Paris, June 18," *Index* 1, no. 8 (June 19, 1862): 113; "Reviews on the Destiny of Mexico," *Index* 2, no. 33 (December 11, 1862): 97. Hotze continued to predict in June, "The South could afford to give a fifth of its army [so 100,000 men] for the pacification of Mexico." What was crucial for the journalist and agent was Mexico would then have a "white government."

43. L.Q. C. Lamar to Jefferson Davis, December 31, 1862, *JDP,* 8:591.

44. Karp, *This Vast Southern Empire,* 32–48; Alfred Thayer Mahan, *The Influence of Sea Power upon History, 1660–1783* (1890; repr., with an introduction by Louis M. Hacker, New York: Hill and Wang, 1957), 5–7.

45. Cotton Planters' Convention, *Report of Select Committee,* 7; Judah P. Benjamin, diary entries, March 8, April 15, 1862, (Micfilm #9989, Meade Papers, UVA); Russell, *My Diary North and South,* diary entry May 9, 1861, 96–97; Thomas, *Confederate Nation,* 78–80; Guterl, *American Mediterranean,* 50–54; Dudley Mann to Benjamin, May 5, 1862, OR, ser. 1, 3:410; Stephen R. Mallory to Jefferson Davis, March 20, 1862, *JDP,* 8:108.

46. Karp, *This Vast Southern Empire,* 202–8; Merk, *Manifest Destiny,* 211; May, *Southern Dream,* 46–76, 163–89, 245–58; Owsley, *King Cotton Diplomacy,* 394; Frank J. Merli, *Great Britain and the Confederate Navy, 1861–1865* (Bloomington: Indiana University Press, 1970), 3–18; Jay Monaghan, *Diplomat in Carpet Slippers: Abraham Lincoln Deals with Foreign Affairs* (Indianapolis: Bobbs-Merrill, 1945), 13, 113.

47. Stephen R. Mallory to Jefferson Davis, February 27, 1862, *JDP,* 8:66; Henry S. Foote of the Committee on Foreign Relations, "Amendment on Bill Introduced by John Perkins of Louisiana to Authorize the President to Send Additional Commissioners to Foreign Nations," *CJ,* 5:43, 65; Mallory to Charles Magill Conrad, March 18, 1862, GLC08155.01; Chesnut, *Mary Chesnut's Civil War,* 313, 331; P. M. Eachin to Thomas David Smith McDowell, March 31, 1862, folder 99, Thomas David Smith McDowell Papers, #460, SHC. The House Committee on Foreign Relations reported that the president "is further authorized and empowered to adopt such measures for the removal of the blockade ports . . . alone or in connection with foreign powers . . . and to pledge such a portion of the proceeds of the sales of cotton and tobacco as he may find expedient." The appropriations bill passed on April 16 with two million dollars "for construction of ironclad vessels in Europe" (*CJ,* 5:247). On September 16, in secret session, the House passed a bill to authorize the issue of Confederate State bonds to meet a contract made by Mallory for six ironclad vessels (*CJ,* 5:386). On September 24, Davis again requested an additional appropriation, which was approved by the Senate (*CJ,* 2:325, 338). On the superiority of American true iron ships over their European ironclad yet wooden-hulled counterparts, see Sebrell, *Persuading John Bull,* 168–70. On the European ironclad fleets, see also Owsley, *King Cotton Diplomacy,* 394–95.

48. "Article IV—Shall We Have a Navy!," 211.

49. "Article IV—Shall We Have a Navy!," 211; John Esten Cooke, *Commercial Enfranchisement of the Confederate States of America, with Original Articles on a New System of Weights and Measures, and New Coins for the Confederate States, by a Virginian* (Richmond, Va.: West & Johnson, 1862),

11; Cooke quoted from early in the war by Paul Christian Anderson, "A Consummation Devoutly to Be Wished For," *Reviews in American History* 33, no. 3 (2005): 370; James Spence to James M. Mason, end April, *OR*, ser. 1, 3:402–3; Mason to Judah P. Benjamin, November 4, 1862, William Shaw Lindsay to Mason, November 3, 1862, *OR*, ser. 1, 3:592–97. Spence considered that "a great desideratum will be a Cunard Line to a southern port—a line of steamers to connect with Europe without the thralldom of the North." Lindsay argued that "for the first few years of your existence as a nation you will require to study the most rigid economy consistent with efficiency" and therefore proposed to get this done by means of the capitalists of other nations. He suggested French government–subsidized steamers "till you desire to subsidize a line of your own" on at least two routes: St Nazaire to New Orleans and Le Havre to Norfolk.

50. "Article II—Southern Society and British Critics," *DBR* 7, no. 3–4 (March 1862): 187.
51. Jefferson Davis to Stephen R. Mallory, October 4, 1862, *JDP*, 8:426; "Article XI—Commercial Importance and Future of the South," *DBR* 7, no. 1–2 (January 1862): 120.
52. Jefferson Davis, "Inaugural," February 22, 1862, *JDC*, 5:200; "Article VIII—The Cotton Interest and Its Relation to the Present Crisis," *DBR* 7, no. 3–4 (March 1862): 279. De Bow was also an early advocate of cotton loan finance, which also drove his argument that the cotton interest must remain productive and spend the quiet time in improvements.
53. "Preamble and Resolutions Adopted by a Meeting of Cotton and Tobacco Planters Held in the City of Richmond," March 3, 1862, *CJ*, 2:30; *Macon Daily Telegraph*, May 23, 1862; Karp, *This Vast Southern Empire*, 239–48; Chesnut, *Mary Chesnut's Civil War*, 138, 154, 194.
54. Robert Bunch to Earl Russell June 17, 1862, FO 5/843, p. 249, PRO.
55. Robert Bunch to Earl Russell, August 14, 1862, FO 5/844, pp. 38–40, PRO; Edmund Molyneux to Earl Russell, December 6, 1862, FO 5/849, pp. 283–84, PRO; Chesnut, *Mary Chesnut's Civil War*, 313–14. In the spring of 1862, Governor Joseph Brown of Georgia recommended a tax of $20 on every bale of cotton grown that year; by November he requested it increase to $100 (Molyneux to Earl Russell, May 10, November 11, 1862, FO 5/849, pp. 219, 244). Designed to encourage planters to shift to provisions crops, such measures could have unintended consequences, as Ann Barnes Archer told her son: as "our funds were not sufficient to meet all the tax now due—we have to plant cotton" (Ann Barnes Archer to Abram Archer, March 31, 1862, folder 3, box 2E649, Archer Papers, UT). International financial implications also became apparent by the fall. On September 18, Mason in London told Benjamin, "money may be commanded here by the obligations for delivery of cotton by the Confederate government . . . every

reason to believe four or five million pounds sterling or more if required could be commanded in this form." On October 28, Slidell confirmed to Benjamin that Erlanger committed to five million pounds (James M. Mason to Judah P. Benjamin, September 18, John Slidell to Benjamin, October 28, 1862, OR, ser. 1, 3:531, 569).

56. Doyle, *Cause of All Nations*, 38–39; Judah P. Benjamin to John Slidell and James M. Mason, December 11, 1862, in Richardson, *Messages and Papers*, 2:369–73. Doyle, however, interprets these different but complimentary goals as evidence of divisions among Confederates. Slidell told the French foreign minister, Eduard Thouvenal, "If peace were now established, it is not extravagant to suppose that the exports of the Confederate States would within a year reach the value of $250 million, with a crop of 4.5 million bales perhaps even 5 million of cotton, most of which would be exported" (Slidell to Eduard Thouvenal, July 21, 1862, in Richardson, *Messages and Papers*, 2:276.) A month later, Hotze predicted: "Cotton production will increase, due to rise in investment and a natural increase in the number of slaves, from 4.7 million bales to 6 million bales in the first year after peace" ("Federal and Confederate Resources," *Index* 1, no. 18 [August 28, 1862]: 273).

57. Majewski, *Modernizing a Slave Economy*, 141–44; "Article IV—Shall We Have a Navy!," 211.

58. Robert Hunter to James M. Mason and John Slidell, February 8, 1862, in Richardson, *Messages and Papers*, 2:172.

59. Pierre Rost to Robert Hunter, March 21, 1862, in Richardson, *Messages and Papers*, 2:204–5; *Southern Illustrated News*, October 4, 1862; "Article X—Abolitionism a Curse to the North and a Blessing to the South," *DBR* 7, no. 3–4 (March 1862): 295; Bowen, *Spain and the American Civil War*, 89; Karp, *This Vast Southern Empire*, 58–65.

60. Karp, *This Vast Southern Empire*, 186–98; William H. Trescot to Judah P. Benjamin, August 5, 1862 (Micfilm #9989, Meade Papers, UVA); Fox-Genovese and Genovese, *Mind of the Master Class*, 220–24; O'Brien, *Intellectual Life and the American South*, 248. On Trescot's hope that the slavery-based economy of the Confederacy might lead to the slaveholder's republic becoming the supplier of rather than competitor to manufacturing countries, see Quigley, *Shifting Grounds*, 55.

61. William H. Trescot to Benjamin, August 5, 1862. Trescot reminded the secretary of state that an earlier variant of the colonization scheme, relative to Africans captured from the illegal African slave trade, had been rejected in 1859 when he had been acting (in the absence of Lewis Cass) secretary of state in the Buchanan administration. M. Bothe, the agent in Washington from the Danish Virgin Islands, forwarded a plan to settle these Africans in the Caribbean colony; moreover, the Dane was "a very respectable and

intelligent man, himself a planter at St. Croix, [who] was very anxious that it be considered." Trescot added that he "had several long conversations with Bothe." Carlyle argued that the adoption of free trade by the British government in 1845, with its removal of imperial preference protecting the sugar plantations of the West Indies, as well as emancipation from 1833, meant the islands were "sinking wholly into ruin" (Thomas Carlyle, "The Nigger Question: Occasional Discourse on the Nigger Question" [1849], in his *Collected and Miscellaneous Essays: Collected and Republished*, 7 vols. [London: Chapman and Hall, 1839–69], 7:80).

62. Carlyle, "The Nigger Question," 7:80; Russell, *My Diary North and South*, 75–79; Judah P. Benjamin to William H. Trescot, August 11, 1862 (Micfilm #9989, Meade Papers, UVA). Trescot had also negotiated with Consul Bunch in Charleston on the Confederacy's commitment to renounce privateering (see Hubbard, *Burden of Confederate Diplomacy*, 51–53, 59).

63. Dudley Mann to Judah P. Benjamin, November 2, 1862, OR, ser. 1, 3:589–90. The Latin American leaders were probably reacting to reports on Lincoln's address on colonization delivered when he met a group of free black leaders at the White House on August 14, 1862 (William E. Gienapp, *The Fiery Trial: The Speeches and Writings of Abraham Lincoln* [New York: Oxford University Press, 2002], 130–34). On Lincoln's interest in colonization, not only of Haiti, but also Panama and the British West Indies, see Sebastian N. Page, "Lincoln and Chiriqui Colonization Revisited," *American Nineteenth Century History* 12, no. 3 (September 2011): 327–46; Philip W. Magness and Sebastian N. Page, *Colonization after Emancipation: Lincoln and the Movement for Black Resettlement* (Columbia: University of Missouri Press, 2011).

64. "Article XI—Commercial Importance and Future of the South," *DBR* 7, no. 1 and 2 (January 1862): 120. On 1850s slaveholder expectations that European empires would be founded on a "coolie apprentice slave labor" model, see Karp, *This Vast Southern Empire*, 150–58. Such contract labor systems developed during the Californian gold rush, preoccupied politicians in secessionist debates, and persisted as solutions for labor shortages post emancipation (see Howe, *What God Hath Wrought*, 820–21; Smith, *History and Debates*, 257; Wahtstom, *The Southern Exodus to Mexico*, 117–27). On southern nightmares about a future of coolies working in Cuba and elsewhere, see Guterl, *American Mediterranean*, 96–101.

65. Dudley Mann to Judah P. Benjamin, June 23, 1862, OR, ser. 1, 3:447–48; "Colonel Reilly's Expedition"; Joseph C. Addington, *Reds, Whites and Blacks, or, the Colors, Dispersion, Language, Sphere and Unity of the Human Race, as Seen in the Lights of Scripture, Science and Observation* (Raleigh, N.C.: Strother & Marcom, 1862), 33; Kramer, *Blood of Government*, 3. On race, expansion, and world mission, also see Reginald Horsman, *Race and*

Manifest Destiny: The Origins of American Racial Anglo-Saxonism (Cambridge, Mass.: Harvard University Press, 1981), 272–98. On scientific racism and the white stewardship of African Americans, see Bonner, "Slavery, Confederate Diplomacy and the Racialist Mission of Henry Hotze." On condemning the North's pseudo-scientific racism in which slaveholders believed whites and blacks could not coexist, see Eugene D. Genovese and Elizabeth Fox-Genovese, *Fatal Self-Deception: Slaveholding Paternalism in the Old South* (New York: Cambridge University Press, 2011), 102. For the contention that Confederates were less racist than northerners, see Stephanie McCurry, *Masters of Small Worlds: Yeoman Households, Gender Relations, and the Political Culture of the Antebellum South Carolina Low Country* (New York: Oxford University Press, 1995), 231–32.

66. *Macon Daily Telegraph*, May 23, 1862.
67. Dudley Mann to Walter P. Benjamin, May 5, 1862, *OR*, ser.1, 3:409.

4. Renewal through Adversity

1. Connecting in turn with events in Mexico, transnational studies have assisted our understanding of a more complex set of processes than a simple story of predatory expansion on the part of the United States. See Gregory P. Downs, "The Mexicanization of American Politics: The United States' Transnational Path from Civil War to Stabilization," *American Historical Review* 117, no. 2 (April 2012): 388–91. Such studies reinforce the Confederate belief that they could still pursue expansion, even from a position of weakness, because they were pulled into it by events and individuals operating in the territories and Mexico.

2. Henry A. Wise to Elizabeth Wise, 13–14, November 1863, folder "Mary Elizabeth (Lyons) Wise, 1862–3," box 2, Henry Alexander Wise (1806–1876) Correspondence, Mss 1 W7547 bFA2, VHS; Elijah H. Gould, *Among the Powers of the Earth: The American Revolution and the Making of a New World Empire*, (Cambridge, Mass.: Harvard University Press, 2012). For the war fracturing and constraining the Confederate nation-building project and political life during 1863, see Thomas, *Confederate Nation*, 190–258; Rable, *Confederate Republic*, 186–235; Levine, *Fall of the House of Dixie*, 147, 163; Bonner, *Mastering America*, 235, 237, 240. Some scholars have also detected development of Confederate nationalism at this time (see Bernath, *Confederate Minds*, 152; Paul Quigley, *Shifting Grounds*, 181–85).

3. Jefferson Davis, Message to the Confederate Congress, December 7, 1863, *JDC*, 6:107; Eldred J. Simkins to Eliza J. Trescot, August 19–20, 1863, SIM 142, box 1 (correspondence 1842–1863), Papers of Eldred J. Simkins, 1842–1977, HL.

4. Joseph L. Brent, "Reflection on the Situation of Public Affairs in the Trans-Mississippi Department," August 27, 1863, Box 1, BT 80, Papers of Joseph Lancaster Brent, HL.

5. Benjamin H. Hill, *Speech of Hon. B. H. Hill Delivered before the Georgia Legislature in Milledgeville, on the Evening of the 11ᵗʰ December, 1862* (Milledgeville, Ga.: R. M. Orme & Son, 1863), 19; *Southern Illustrated News* (Richmond, Va.), August 15, 1863 (UVA); Fox-Genovese and Genovese, *Mind of the Master Class*, 84; Dew, *Apostles of Disunion*, 22–36.

6. "Lincoln Is Made Dictator of the North," *Southern Illustrated News*, March 14, 1863 (UVA); "Speech," *Houston Tri-weekly Telegraph*, August 21, 1863 (GLC05959.51.086); Edmondston, *Journal of a Secesh Lady*, diary entry, July 13, 1863, 430.

7. Calvin Henderson Wiley, *Scriptural Views of National Trials; or, The True Road to the Independence and Peace of the Confederate States of America by Rev. C. H. Wiley* (Greensboro, N.C.: Sterling, Campbell and Albright, 1863), 110; Levine, *Fall of the House of Dixie*, 155; Guyatt, *Providence*, 268–70; O'Brien, *Intellectual Life and the American South*, 81–88.

8. Bernath, *Confederate Minds*, 202–3; Albert Gallatin Brown, *State of the Country: Speech in the Confederate Senate, December 24, 1863* (n.p., 1863), 9; George Anderson Gordon, *What Will He Do with It? An Essay Delivered in the Masonic Hall, Savannah, on Thursday, October 27, 1863, and Again by Special Request, on Monday December 7, 1863, for the Benefit of the Wayside Home in Savannah and Repeated with Slight Variations for Similar Objects in Augusta, Milledgeville, Macon, Atlanta, La Grange & Columbus* (Savannah, Ga.: George N. Nichols, 1863), 8, 23. Winthrop Jordan, *Tumult and Silence at Second Creek*, 60, 67–68; Fox-Genovese and Genovese, *Mind of the Master Class*, 340; McCardell, *Idea of a Southern Nation*, 200, 261, 306; Barney, *Secessionist Impulse*, 7, 10, 121, 127, 183. Brown was also gearing up to support black enlistment (see Bruce Levine, *Confederate Emancipation: Southern Plans to Free and Arm Slaves during the Civil War* [New York: Oxford University Press, 2005], 58).

9. On revolution, see Michael T. Bernath, "The Confederacy as a Moment of Possibility," *Journal of Southern History* 79, no. 2 (May 2013): 299. On race, see Bernath, *Confederate Minds*, 205; Horsman, *Race and Manifest Destiny*, 272–97. On the ironies and problems generated by Confederate efforts to define their crisis in European terms, see Andre M. Fleche, *The Revolution of 186: The American Civil War in the Age of Nationalist Conflict* (Chapel Hill: University of North Carolina Press, 2012). For a contrasting view in which Americans viewed Europe as increasingly distant from what they came to view as their own exceptional republic, see Timothy Mason Roberts, *Distant Revolutions: 1848 and the Challenge to American Exceptionalism* (Charlottesville: University of Virginia Press, 2009).

10. Jefferson Davis, "Richmond Speech," January 5, 1863, *JDP*, 9:11–14.

11. Jefferson Davis, "Speech at Wilmington," November 5, 1863, *JDP*, 10:50; Albert Gallatin Brown, *State of the Country: Speech in the Confederate Senate, December 24, 1863* (n.p., 1863), 9. See also Brown's resulting Senate Resolutions, December 10, 1863, *CJ*, 3:455.

12. Wiley, *Scriptural Views of National Trials*, 7; Bernath, *Confederate Minds*, 239–40; O'Brien, *Intellectual Life and the American South*, 81–88; Judah P. Benjamin to C. C. Clay, January 3, 1863, *OR*, ser. 1, 3:668. Liberal internationalism can be best defined in its mid-nineteenth-century meaning, as following William E. Gladstone's later argument at Midlothian in 1879. First, it was necessary to "foster the strength of the nation and to reserve it for great and worthy occasions fostered by just legislation and economy at home. . . . The result is the growth of the great elements of national power, wealth, which is a physical element, and union and contentment, which are moral elements. . . . To preserve to the nations the blessing of peace especially when we recollect the sacred name we bear as Christians for the Christian nations. . . . To strive to cultivate and maintain, ay to the uttermost, what is called the Concert . . . neutralise and fetter and bind up the selfish aims of every other nation." The foreign policy must follow these maxims: "avoid needless and entangling engagements," hold that "all nations are equal," and let "no one declare a pharisaical superiority." The foreign policy of civilized nations must be inspired, Gladstone concluded, "by the love of freedom" (John Charmley, *Splendid Isolation? Britain, the Balance of Power and the Origins of the First World War, 1874–1914* [London: Hodder and Stroughton, 1989], 172–80).

13. Ann Blackman, *Wild Rose: The True Story of a Civil War Spy* (New York: Random House, 2006), 268–70; A. N. Wilson, *The Victorians* (London: Hutchison, 2002), 247–72. Thomas Carlyle's Macmillan article was entitled "America in a Nutshell" or, to be precise, "Ilias Americana in Nuce." Carlyle's imaginary conversation continued: "PAUL 'Good words, Peter! The risk is my own. . . . Hire you your servants by the month or the day, and get straight to Heaven; leave me to my own method.' PETER 'No I won't. I will beat your brains out first!' (*And is trying dreadfully ever since but cannot yet manage it.*)" (A. N. Wilson, *The Victorians* [London: Hutchison, 2002], 255). Carlyle was more anti-factory system than proslavery; his *Past and Present*, first published in the United States in April 1844, remained the bedrock of critique on industrialized society's treatment of their workers, as Raymond Williams phrased it. Carlyle believed that "a society is more than economic relationships with cash payment the sole nexus" (Raymond Williams, *Culture and Society from Coleridge to Orwell* [London: Hogarth Press, 1990], 71–86).

14. Slidell, "Memorandum," in John Slidell to Judah P. Benjamin, April 20, 1863, *OR*, ser. 1, 3:743–45; Juridicus (pseud), *The Recognition of the Confederate*

States: Considered in a Reply to the Letters of "Historicus" in the London Times (Charleston, S.C.: Evans & Cogswell, 1863), 34. On the Great Awakening's sectional and partisan divide, see Howe, *What God Hath Wrought,* 580–81.

15. Dudley Mann to Judah P. Benjamin, January 5, 1863, in Richardson, *Messages and Papers,* 2:387; Mann to Benjamin, January 16, 1863, in Richardson, *Messages and Papers,* 2:410; Davis, "Message to the Confederate Congress," December 7, 1863, *JDC,* 6:107.

16. Charles Magill Conrad, "Joint Resolution to Provide a Homestead for the Officers and Privates of the Army of the Confederate States," February 2, 1863, *CJ,* 6:62. The Homestead Bill came before the House on February 2 when Conrad introduced a joint resolution to provide a homestead for the officers and privates of the army. He moved to refer this resolution to the Committee on Military Affairs, but William P. Chilton successfully amended Conrad's resolution to instead refer it to a "Special Committee to consist of one member from each State." On April 22, Conrad reported back to the House from the special committee with the recommendation that it pass with an amendment. But the House decided to postpone consideration of any bill (*CJ,* 6:402.)

17. Kenneth Rayner to Thomas Ruffin, March 8, 1863, folder 454, Ruffin Papers, SHC; John Brown Baldwin, *Substance of the Remarks of Mr. Baldwin, of Virginia, on Offering "A Bill to Fund the Currency," House of Representatives, January 16th, 1863* (Richmond, Va.: Macfarlane and Fergusson, 1863), 15–16; William Blair, *Virginia's Private War: Feeding Body and Soul in the Confederacy, 1861–1865* (New York: Oxford University Press, 1998), 21; Chesnut, *Mary Chesnut's Civil War,* July 16, 1861, 21–22, 100. Baldwin would go on to defeat former governor Letcher in the May 1863 elections for congress (Blair, *Virginia's Private War,* 84).

18. Jacob Newton Cardozo, *A Plan for Financial Relief, Addressed to the Legislature of Georgia, and the Confederate States Congress, as Originally Published on the Atlanta Southern Confederacy, by J. N. Cardozo* (Atlanta: J. H. Seals, 1863); Charles Post Culver, *A Scheme for the Relief of the Financial Embarrassments of the Confederate States: Based upon Real Estate* (Richmond Va.: Geo. P. Evans, 1863); Culver, "Letter on the Currency," *Augusta (Ga.) Daily Chronicle & Sentinel,* November 11, 1863 (GLC05959.07.03); John Schley, *Our Position and Our True Policy,* February 2, 1863 (Augusta, Ga, 1863); Chesnut, *Mary Chesnut's Civil War,* 11n5, diary entry for August 25, 1861, 100; Fox-Genovese and Genovese, *Mind of the Master Class,* 316, O'Brien, *Intellectual Life and the American South,* 218–21. There was a tradeoff: if the nation could not afford to pay any of its debt now, its credit would collapse, and that would impair, perhaps fatally, confidence in the Confederate government. At the same time, Confederates argued it was impractical

to raise all the money now when areas were occupied by the enemy and half a million people of slave property were in the possession of the Union. Clearly the models had to estimate an end date for the war; on the whole in 1863 Confederates tended to predict that the war would come to an end in late 1864 after Lincoln lost the election. The exception to this confidence was immediately after the fall of Vicksburg. Cardozo had in his *Notes on Political Economy* (1826) that he found David Ricardo's theory of distribution neglectful of "increased facility of production," which will cause both real wages and profits to rise as wage goods become available more cheaply and as "the old channels of commerce are constantly enlarged" by free trade. He retained his faith in free trade (Henry William Spiegel, *The Growth of Economic Thought* [Durham, N.C.: Duke University Press, 1971, 1983], 364).

19. A. Georgian, *Remarks on a Volunteer Navy by a Georgian* (Atlanta: Intelligencer Steam Power Press, 1864), 4–5. On February 25, 1863, Senator Brown presented the bill (s58) to establish a volunteer navy, it was immediately referred to the Committee on Naval Affairs and passed the Senate on March 30, 1863 (*CJ*, 3: 100–101, 215; 6:275.) On the navy's place in southern life, see Robert Gudmestad, *Steamboats and the Rise of the Cotton Kingdom* (Baton Rouge: Louisiana State University Press, 2011); Matthew Karp, "Slavery and American Sea Power: The Navalist Impulse in the Antebellum South," *Journal of Southern History* 77, no. 2 (May 2011): 283–324; Karp, *This Vast Southern Empire*, 32–49, 199–208.

20. J. A. Seawell to John Letcher, January 12, 1863, folder 410, Letcher Papers, VHS. The Richmond Government focused on the direct naval warfare with the United States; for example, on April 1, 1863, Mallory asked Davis "that measures be immediately adopted for the construction, equipment and delivery to this government in southern Europe of ten ironclad warships of the classes whose drought shall not exceed sixteen feet . . . it affords a fair prospect of success. The amount seem large when the demands of other branches of the public service are considered but the vast importance of building screw ships which may enter the Mississippi is so evident that I do not hesitate to earnestly recommend it" (Stephen R. Mallory to Jefferson Davis, 1 April 1863, GLC08155.02).

21. A. Georgian, *Remarks on a Volunteer Navy*, 13; Edward Stiles to James M. Mason and John Slidell, September 29, 1863, OR, ser. 1, 3:918; Slidell to John H. Reagan, September 29, 1863, OR, ser. 1, 3:919; James A. Seddon to Edward Archer, September 26, 1863, GLC01896.063; Henry Pinckney Walker to Earl Russell, November 26, 1863, FO 5/969, PRO.

22. Schley, *Our Position and Our True Policy*; Bonner, *Mastering America*, 275.

23. Judah P. Benjamin to John Slidell et al., January 15, 1863, in Richardson, *Messages and Papers*, 2:406.

24. Fred J. Cridland to Earl Russell, December 5, 1863, FO 5/908, PRO.
25. *Index* 2, no. 40 (January 29, 1863): 208; "Can India Save Our Cotton Trade?" *Index* 3, vol. 68 (August 13, 1863): 241; *Index* 3, no. 72 (September 10, 1863): 307. Hotze's representation of Samuel Smith's pamphlet was accurate. In the winter of 1862–63, Smith went to India on behalf of the Manchester Chamber of Commerce to test the cotton-growing possibilities there, in view of the depletion of imports from the South owing to the American Civil War. In a communication to the *Times of India* (embodied in a pamphlet published in England), Smith questioned India's fitness to grow cotton (G. Le G. Norgate, "Smith, Samuel [1836–1906]," rev. H. C. G. Matthew, *Oxford Dictionary of National Biography* [New York: Oxford University Press, 2004]).
26. Matthew F. Maury, quoted in "What the North Is Fighting For," *Index* 3, no. 58 (June 4, 1863): 81.
27. "What the North Is Fighting For," 81; "The Confederate Cause in Lancashire," *Index* 3, no. 71 (August, 27, 1863): 293; Judah P. Benjamin to James M. Mason, June 6, 1863, in Richardson, *Messages and Papers*, 2:495–97; Judah P. Benjamin to John Slidell, June 22, 1863, in Richardson, *Messages and Papers*, 2:518–20; Judah P. Benjamin to Senator C. C. Clay, January 3, 1863, *OR*, ser. I, 3:669.
28. British political economist David Ricardo had established that the advantage by which two countries derive from trading with each other results from the more advantageous employment that thence arises of the labor and capital of both countries. The circumstances are such that if each country confines itself to the production of one commodity, there is a greater total return to the labor of both together; and this increase of produce forms the whole of what the two countries taken together gain by trade. For Confederates, this relationship led to the reciprocal obligations that governed foreign relations. See John Stuart Mill, *Essays on Some Unsettled Questions of Political Economy* (London: John W. Parker, 1844).
29. Schley, *Our Position and Our True Policy*, 9–10; Wise to Mary Elizabeth (Lyons) Wise, November 13–14, 1863, Wise Papers, VHS; Henry A. Wise, *The Currency Question. Letter of Gen. Henry A. Wise, to Hon J. E. Holmes, of S.C. Headquarters Sixth Military District, Department S.C., Ga., and Florida, November 11, 1863* (n.p., 1863), 9; W. Jefferson Buchanan, *Maryland's Crisis: A Political Outline* (Richmond, Va.: J. W. Randolph, 1863), 16.
30. Juridicus (pseud), *The Recognition of the Confederate State*, 39; William Graham Swan(n), *Foreign Relations: Speech of Hon. W. G. Swan, of Tennessee, Delivered in the House of Representatives of the Confederate States, February 5, 1863* (Richmond, Va.: Smith, Bailey, 1863), 5; Hubbard, *Burden of Confederate Diplomacy*, 151; Levine, *Confederate Emancipation*, 40–42; Doyle, *Cause of All Nations*, 251–54. First published in letter form in

the *Charleston Courier*, "The Recognition of the Confederate States" was subsequently circulated as a pamphlet and also published in the *Index*. Historicus was a rising and well-connected British Whig politician, the son-in-law of the cabinet minister the Duke of Argyle and future Liberal chancellor of the exchequer, William Vernon Harcourt.

31. Dudley Mann to Judah P. Benjamin, June 25, 1863, in Richardson, *Messages and Papers*, 2: 520–22.

32. Henry S. Foote, "Joint Resolutions on the Pending War and Matters Appertaining Thereto," January 13, 1863, *CJ*, 6:8–20; February 6, 1863, *CJ*, 6: 80–84; April 11, 1863, *CJ*, 6: 331–50; Chesnut, *Mary Chesnut's Civil War*, 295n5; William M. Bobo, *The Confederate by a South Carolinian* (Mobile, Ala.: S. H. Goetzel, 1863), 100; McCardell, *Idea of a Southern Nation*, 250 (quote); Brian D. Schoen, *The Fragile Fabric of Union: Cotton, Federal Politics, and the Global Origins of the Civil War* (Baltimore: Johns Hopkins University Press, 2009), 217. Although Foote, like Boyce, was a harsh critic of Davis's administration, he shared the same national aspirations as the president, and in a letter on August 26 to the *Richmond Whig*, Foote praised Davis's "lofty goals" (*JDP*, 9:356.)

33. Albert Gallatin Brown, *State of the Country: Speech in the Confederate Senate, December 24, 1863* (n.p., 1863), 14–16; Kean, *Inside the Confederate Government*, 135. As Kean noted on January 31, 1864, Brown's conduct had international implications: "There is a very low state of feeling among members of Congress. Many of them do not expect any good results from the next campaign. Their legislation is of the wildest description and, as the London *Times* said of Governor Albert Gallatin Brown's resolutions, sounds like the utterances of despair."

34. William H. Grigsby, *Genealogy of the Grigsby Family* (Chicago: Robert Hall McCormick, 1905), 3, 6–7. Grigsby to John Letcher, April 16, 1863, folder 413, Governor's Correspondence, Letcher Papers, VHS; J. Marshall McCue, *Speech of Mr. McCue, of Augusta, Delivered in the House of Delegates, on the 16th and 17th of October, 1863, on the Bill to Protect Sheep and Increase the Production of Wool* (Richmond, Va.: George P. Evans, 1863), 12; Blair, *Virginia's Private War*, 132–33. Grigsby was a cousin of the historian Hugh Blair Grigsby of Virginia, described by O'Brien in his introduction as a representative of the middle generation in the antebellum South, who were "romantic, more interested in the pleasures of belonging and more sentimental and more nervous about the possibility of failure" (O'Brien, *Intellectual Life and the American South*, 1–18, Fox-Genovese and Genovese, *Mind of the Master Class*, 95).

35. Culver, "Letter on the Currency"; Simms, *Life of Robert M. T. Hunter*, 191–94; Fox-Genovese and Genovese, *Mind of the Master Class*, 596–603; "'Peacemaker,' An Appeal," December 22, 1863, broadside. Robert M. T.

Hunter had a more conventional faith as he told Mary Chesnut on December 17: "The parsons tell us every Sunday that the Lord is on our side. I wish, however, he would show his preference for us a little more plainly than he has been doing lately" (Chesnut, *Mary Chesnut's Civil War*, 505).

36. Bobo, *Confederate by a South Carolinian*, 100; Rable, *Confederate Republic*, 185, 207; Jordan, *Tumult and Silence at Second Creek*, 68–71; Governor John Milton to Jefferson Davis, April 15, 1863, *JDP*, 9:143.

37. Jefferson Davis, "Speech in Richmond," January 5, 1863, *JDP*, 9:12; Kenneth Rayner to Thomas Ruffin, February 16, 1863, folder 453, Ruffin Papers, SHC.

38. A. M. Keiley to Judah P. Benjamin, January 9, 1863, box 1, Meade Papers, UVA; "A Conceivable Calamity," *Index* 3, no. 62 (July 2, 1863): 145. On Keiley's postwar career, see Joseph P. O'Grady, "Anthony M. Keiley (1832–1905): Virginia's Catholic Politician," *Catholic Historical Review*, 54, no. 4 (January 1969): 613–35.

39. Bobo, *Confederate by a South Carolinian*, 100.

40. On the dynamic Mexican situation in the summer and fall of 1863, see Doyle, *Cause of All Nations*, 120–28.

41. On changing racial attitudes to Native Americans by 1850, see Horsman, *Race and Manifest Destiny*, 189–207.

42. Bureau of Indian Affairs, *Report of the Commissioner of Indian Affairs, Confederate States of America, War Dept., Office of Indian Affairs, Richmond, January 12, 1863* (Richmond Va., 1863), 9–11.

43. McCardell, *Idea of a Southern Nation*, 71–85; Doyle, *Cause of All Nations*, 35; Bonner, "Slavery, Confederate Diplomacy and the Racialist Mission of Henry Hotze," 309; "Confederate States Executive Documents," *Index* 2, no. 52 (April 23, 1863): 401; Bureau of Indian Affairs, *Report of the Commissioner of Indian Affairs*, 11.

44. Thomas B. Hanley, "Indian Affairs Committee Resolutions," December 14, 1863, *CJ*, 6: 529.

45. "Letter to Holmes," *Houston Tri-weekly Telegraph*, March 16, 1863 (GLC05959.51.055); Albert Pike, *Address, to the Senators and Representatives of the State of Arkansas in the Congress of the Confederate States* (La., 1863), 8; William P. Chilton, Committee on Commissary and Quartermasters' Departments, "Joint Resolution," April 29, 1863, *CJ*, 6:454; Jefferson Davis, note, March 28, 1863, on John R. Baylor to John R. Magruder, December 29, 1862, *JDP*, 9:117.

46. Frazier, *Blood and Treasure*, 115, 291–97.

47. Malcolm H. MacWillie to Jefferson Davis, March 21, June, 8, 1863, *JDP*, 9:113, 211. MacWillie cited *Uti Possidetis*, Latin for "as you possess under the law."

48. Jefferson Davis note, April 2, 1863, *JDP,* 9:113; Davis note, December 18, 1863, referring to Seddon "for consideration and conference with reference to other papers," *JDP,* 10:112; Frazier, *Blood and Treasure,* 291; Knox County (Ohio) Historical Society, "Lansford Hastings," http://www.knoxhistory .org/index.php/local-history/authors/118-travel/168-lansford-hastings, accessed November 27, 2017. The Donner Pass party used the Hastings Cutoff to reach California. After the war, Hastings went to Brazil to establish a colony for refugees from the Confederacy. He published *The Emigrant's Guide to Brazil* in 1867 and was able to guide one shipload of people to their new homes in South America. He died in 1870 while en route with a second group.

49. "The Southern Press on Mexico," *Index* 3, no. 72 (September 10, 1863): 372; Judah P. Benjamin to John Slidell, February 2, 1863, *OR,* ser. 1, 3:685–86; Judah P. Benjamin to John Slidell, August 4, 1863, in Richardson, *Messages and Papers,* 2:541–43; James M. Mason to Benjamin, September 4, 1863, in Richardson, *Messages and Papers,* 2:557. Mason told Benjamin: "You have not informed us as to the president's policy it may become us to pursue in the event, now at hand, of a monarchy established in Mexico by France. Would it not be well that such policy should be defined and put in possession of [Slidell] and myself?"

50. Sam Houston, "Speech in Galveston," March 18, 1863, printed in the *Texas Republican,* April 4, 1863, box 2R48, vol. 16, January 1861–May 1928, Sam Houston Papers, UT; L. Lowyle to Joseph Lancaster Brent, April 24, 1863, BT 156, box 1, Joseph Lancaster Brent Papers, HL; Andrew Jackson Grayson to Jefferson Davis, August 21, 1863, *JDP,* 9:350. The attitude of grudging acceptance and "making the best of it" summed up the attitude of the Unionist Houston to the Confederacy, although he never ceased to believe secession was a mistake. Grayson, a keen ornithologist, wrote notes on the birdlife in Mazatlan (see Lois Chambers Taylor, "Prior Description of Two Mexican Birds by Andrew Jackson Grayson," *Museum of Vertebrate Zoology* 53 (July 1951), 194–97).

51. John Slidell to Judah P. Benjamin, *OR,* ser. 1, 3:976; José Quintero to Judah P. Benjamin, September 16, 1863, *OR,* ser. 1, 3:899–900; Sam Houston, "Speech in Galveston"; "Letter," March 28, 1863, *Houston Tri-weekly Telegraph,* April 3, 1863 (GLC5950.59.060); Williamson S. Oldham, "Senate Commercial Committee Motion," April 23, 1863, *CJ,* 3:333. Former California senator Dr. William M. Gwin in conversation in Havana with William Preston, minister to Mexico, the following year put the number of willing Confederate migrants at between fifteen and twenty thousand (Preston to Jefferson Davis, June 28, 1864, Letter book of William Preston, Minister to Mexico from the Confederacy, Preston Family Papers—Davie Collection, FHS). Houston praised Oldham's efforts: "your advocacy of

the measure of receiving foreign goods duty free," he wrote in February, "I regard as a piece of pure statesmanship" (*Houston Tri-weekly Telegraph*, May, 11, 1863 [GLC5959.51.070]; Sam Houston to Williamson Oldham, February 24, 1863, box 2R48, vol. 16, January 1861–May 1928, Sam Houston Papers, UT).

52. Hershel V. Johnson to Jefferson Davis, August 6, 1863, *JDP,* 9:321; Alfred G. Haley to Davis, February 21, 1863, *JDP,* 9:71. Haley had also been in contact with the Quartermaster's Department with regard to procuring horses and mules from Mexico (Quartermaster General Abraham C. Myers to Davis, March 4, 1863, *JDP,* 9:89).

53. Anthony M. Keiley to Benjamin, January 9, 1863, box 1, Meade Collection, UVA; Doyle, *Cause of All Nations,* 9–10, 185–205.

54. Historian Jay Sexton argues that the term "Monroe Doctrine" for the first time "became a nationalist symbol, a permanent feature of political and diplomatic landscape, during the Civil War" (Sexton, *The Monroe Doctrine: Empire and Nation in Nineteenth Century America* [New York: Hill and Wang, 2011], 156).

55. "Letter from Paris," *Index* 3, no. 71 (September 3, 1863): 302; Guyatt, *Providence,* 269–71; Wiley, *Scriptural Views of National Trials,* 182–84; Merk, *Manifest Destiny,* 24–60.

56. Instructions quoted in William Preston to General Almonte, June 6, 1864, Letter book of William Preston, Minister to Mexico from the Confederacy, Preston Family Papers—Davie Collection, FHS; Jefferson Davis, "Message to the Confederate Congress," December 7, 1863, *JDC,* 6: 107–8.

57. Judah P. Benjamin to Jefferson Davis, December 28, 1863, GLC069919.01; Senate Executive Session, December 28, 29, 31, 1863, *CJ,* 3:493–94, 508. As Benjamin wrote to Davis, "it has not been usual to keep secret the fact of sending a mission to a foreign country." The Senate was still considering the resolution on appointment and instructions at the end of the year.

58. Instructions quoted in William Preston to General Almonte, June 6, 1864; Malcolm H. MacWillie to Jefferson Davis, June 8, 1863, *JDP,* 9:211; Cameron Erskine Thom to Joseph Pembroke Thom, January 5, 1863, HM 47967, Papers of Cameron Erksine Thom, HL. Cameron Thom wrote from Los Angeles just before departure to fight for the Confederacy in Virginia. He was reacting to news that the Mexican province of "Sonora is professed to be occupied by a French division." Thom asked whether this French move was "because we have a turbulent element here [in southern California]?"

59. McCue, *Speech of Mr. McCue,* 4. McCue sent his speech in pamphlet form to the governor of South Carolina among others. The arming and freeing of slaves was still viewed in government circles as the "ultimate sacrifice of the future for independence." On antebellum and wartime southern

migration plans, see Wahlstrom, *Southern Exodus to Mexico*, 5–13. On Lincoln's colonization plans, see Magness and Page, *Colonization after Emancipation*. On antebellum proslavery foreign policy, see Karp, *This Vast Southern Empire*, 1–9, 226–48.

60. Henry Hotze to Judah P. Benjamin, June 6, 1863, *OR*, ser. 1, 3:784. On southern support for Brazil, especially when Wise was consul, before the war, see Karp, *This Vast Southern Empire*, 72–81. The British gunboat diplomacy of Lord Palmerston had been engaged in stamping out the transatlantic slave trade and was renowned for its heavy-handed treatment of Brazilian shipping in particular. Historians have debated the extent to which such aggression was the result of cultivating public opinion at home or the basis of incipient liberalism (see David F. Krein, *The Last Palmerston Government: Foreign Policy, Domestic Politics, and the Genesis of "Splendid Isolation"* [Ames: Iowa State University Press, 1978]; E. D. Steele, *Palmerston and Liberalism, 1855–1865* [New York: Cambridge University Press, 1991]). After 1859, Palmerston had to share foreign affairs with Lord John Russell, and historians have portrayed him as either a replicate or a restraint on the prime minister's foreign policy (see John Prest, *Lord John Russell* [Columbia, SC: University of South Carolina Press, 1972]; Paul Scherer, *Lord John Russell: A Biography* [Selinsgrove, Pa.: Susquehanna University Press, 1996]).

61. Charles Helm to General Serrano, February 22, 1863, as enclosure in Charles Helm to Judah P. Benjamin, March 3 1863, *OR*, ser. 1, 3:700–701; Bowen, *Spain and the American Civil War*, 99–100. Bowen argues that the fear of the return of slavery boosted support for the rebels in Santo Domingo and helps explain why a major insurrection began there in August 1863. Helm sent minutes of his last meeting with Serrano to Slidell, who told Benjamin of the "emphatic manner in which he declared his hearty sympathies with our cause, and his determination, on his arrival in Spain [as minister of foreign affairs], to exert all his influence in favor of the recognition of the Confederate States" (John Slidell to Judah P. Benjamin, February 6, 1863, in Richardson, *Messages and Papers*, 2:424.) It proved a short-lived wish as Serrano soon fell from power as another victim of the Santo Domingo imbroglio (Slidell to Benjamin, May 28, 1863, in Richardson, *Messages and Papers*, 2: 493).

62. Judah P. Benjamin to John Slidell, May 9, 1863, in Richardson, *Messages and Papers*, 2: 482–85. Benjamin had made the appointment on Slidell's own earlier suggestion: "As Gen. Serrano is now minister of foreign affairs at Madrid, I think it is to be regretted we have not there a diplomatic agent ready to avail himself of his friendly disposition" (Slidell to Benjamin, February 6, 1863 in Richardson, *Messages and Papers*, 2:424). On Spanish ambition, see Bowen, *Spain and the American Civil War*, 34–54.

63. Benjamin to Slidell, May 9, 1863, 2:484; Bowen, *Spain and the American Civil War*, 136. In rejecting the proposal of the Entente Powers, Everett argued that the United States had a special interest in Cuba on account of its proximity, that the United States had already purchased Louisiana and Florida, and that, constitutionally, the government would not renounce annexation as it was not "within the competence of the treaty-making power in 1852 effectually to bind the government in all its branches; and, for all coming time, not to make a similar purchase of Cuba" (Everett to the Comte de Sartiges, December 1, 1852, U.S. Department of State, *Message from the President of the United States: In Answer to a Resolution of the Senate Calling for Information Relative to a Proposed Tripartite Convention on the Subject of Cuba* [1853], state document 13, p. 17).

64. Kenneth Rayner to Thomas Ruffin, December 14, 1863, box 30, folder 458, series 1.6 1862–65, Ruffin Papers, SHC.

5. A CONSERVATIVE FUTURE

1. Historians of Confederate nationalism have moved from the earlier argument of Emory Thomas that 1864 was the time of disintegration of Confederate nationalism. Factors, such as celebration of the Army of Northern Virginia as the symbol of the Confederate nation, proximity of victory, and a feeling of collective victimhood, if anything, strengthened Confederate national identity in 1864. Beyond historians' investigations of the remarkable ambition and activity of Confederate printing presses and literati, Robert Bonner's contention remained unchallenged that the fall of Vicksburg in July 1863, at the latest, saw the final quashing of the last, faint embers of antebellum southern dreams (see Thomas, *Confederate Nation*, 245–77; G. Gallagher, *Confederate* War, 61–112; Levine, *Fall of the House of Dixie*, 229; Quigley, *Shifting Grounds*, 199; Bernath, *Confederate Minds*, 199, 277–80; Coleman Hutchison, *Apples and Ashes Literature, Nationalism and the Confederacy* [Athens: University of Georgia Press, 2012], 69; Robert E. Bonner, *Mastering America*, 286–322).

2. C. A. Bayly, *The Birth of the Modern World, 1780–1914: Global Connections and Comparisons* (Malden, Mass.: Blackwell), 161–64.

3. For Bismarck's assertion of the primacy of national self-interest in the Schleswig-Holstein crisis of 1864 (in which he followed the lead of Napoleon III of France, Prince Felix Schwarzenberg in his direction of Austrian foreign policy, and Foreign Minister Gorchakov of Russia), see Jonathan Steinberg, *Bismarck: A Life* (New York: Oxford University Press, 2011, 210–26).

4. Jefferson Davis, "Speech at Columbus," September 30, 1864, *JDP*, 11:75. Even at this late stage, slaveholders deluded themselves into believing

slavery had a future. For examination of this topic of sincere self-deception, see Levine, *Fall of the House of Dixie*; Genovese and Fox-Genovese, *Fatal Self-Deception*. For the variety of slave resistance, see Vincent Harding, *There Is a River: The Black Struggle for Freedom in America* (New York: Harcourt Brace, 1981), which built on the groundbreaking theory of the General Strike formulated by W. E. B. Du Bois, *Black Reconstruction in America, 1860–1880* (1935; repr. with an introduction by David Levering Lewis, New York: Simon and Schuster, 1992). Historian Steven Hahn argues that because four hundred thousand enslaved people "had rebelled" by the middle of 1864, a return to status quo antebellum was impossible, and a "renegotiation" of master-slave relations would be essential after the war (Hahn, *A Nation under Our Feet: Black Political Struggles in the Rural South from Slavery to the Great Migration* [Cambridge, Mass.: Harvard University Press, 2005], 62–116).

5. Fred J. Cridland to Earl Russell, March 29, 1864, FO 5/970, pp. 176–77, PRO. Cridland alleged that one of the speculators was John H. Dent, brother-in-law to U.S. General Ulysses S. Grant. On Grant's nepotism, see Joan Waugh, *U.S. Grant: American Hero, American Myth* (Chapel Hill: University of North Carolina Press, 2009), 126.

6. "Letter from New Orleans," January 23, 1864, *Index* 4, no. 95 (February 18, 1864): 108; Major John Tyler Jr., "Our Confederate States: Foreign and Domestic," *DBR* 34, no. 1 (July and August 1864): 25; Charles S. Morehead, *Slavery and Lincoln's Emancipation Proclamation*, reviewed in the *Index* 4, no. 98 (March 10, 1864): 145. After traveling and conducting unofficial diplomacy in Europe, Morehead returned to the Confederacy in 1864; on his way home in Havana, he wrote to Davis explaining that his work was written for "British taste. It is useless to argue the abstract question of slavery in Europe, and I have endeavored to present it in a different light" (Charles S. Morehead to Jefferson Davis, April 27, 1864, *JDP*, 10:368).

7. James M. Mason to Judah P. Benjamin, January 25, 1864, *OR*, ser. 1. 3:1007–8; Bonner, *Mastering America*, 190–93; Bonner, "Slavery, Confederate Diplomacy," 309; Karp, *This Vast Southern Empire*, 57–58, 125–26, 134–40, 154–57. Tyler believed the British were just awaiting the suppression of Confederate slavery before they could introduce coolie labor cotton production schemes across their colonies (John Tyler Jr., "Our Confederate States: Foreign and Domestic," *DBR* 34. no. 1 [July and August, 1864]: 6; Judah P. Benjamin to James Spence, January 11, 1864, Box 1, Meade Papers, UVA; Robert E. Lee to Jefferson Davis, July 6, 1864, *JDP*, 10:503).

8. Tyler, "Our Confederate States," 6; "Will Peace Immediately Bring Down the Price of Cotton?" *Index* 4, no. 124 (September 8, 1864): 569; Bonner, "Slavery, Confederate Diplomacy," 297; Schoen, *Fragile Fabric*, 237;

Karp, *This Vast Southern Empire*, 45–48, 154–57; Fox-Genovese and Genovese, *Mind of the Master Class*, 255–70.

9. Jefferson Davis, "Speech in Augusta," 3 October, 1864, *JDC*, 6:358–59, *JDP*, 11:79. See also William Emmett Simms, "Resolutions on the Foreign Commerce Regulations Bill," May 23, 1864, *CJ*, 4:76–77; "Message of Jefferson Davis on the Foreign Commerce Regulation Act of February, 1864," December 20, 1864, *CJ*, 7:368–71.

10. Henry Hotze to Judah P. Benjamin, January 16, 1864, *OR*, ser. 1. 3:1001–4; "Independence and Recognition," *Index* 4, no. 89 (January 7, 1864): 9. For cotton's health as well as commercial benefits, see Landes, *Wealth and Poverty*, 154.

11. "Article IV: The War, Independence, Watchman, What of the Night," *DBR* 34, no. 1 (July 1864): 47–59; Henry Pinckney Walker to Earl Russell, February 22, 1864, FO 5/968, PRO; Mahan, *Influence of Sea Power*, v; Karp, *This Vast Southern Empire*, 32–48, 199–209.

12. Lynn M. Case and Warren F. Spencer, *The United States and France: Civil War Diplomacy* (Philadelphia: University of Pennsylvania Press, 1970), 454–65; John Slidell to Judah P. Benjamin, June 6, 1864, *OR*, ser. 1, 3:1139.

13. "The Confederate Navy," *Index*, 4, no. 113 (June 23, 1864): 395; James P. Holcombe to Judah P. Benjamin, April 1, 1864, *OR*, ser. 1, 3:1073.

14. "Confederate Financial Prospects and Plans," *Index* 4, no. 122 (August 25, 1864): 537; De Bow, "The War of Independence," 34, no. 1 *DBR* (July and August, 1864):47–59. The estimate of the cotton store was probably provided by De Bow, cotton agent until August 5. The British consul in Mobile, Cridland, had earlier estimated the stored cotton to be 4.5 million bales (see Fred Cridland to Earl Russell, December 5, 1863, FO 5/908, PRO). De Bow had also been in Mobile, so possibly he briefed the consul. The phrase "cotton standard," according to Hotze, was Seddon's. Hotze asked that given "the Confederate Government had already undertaken to pay the interest on the part on its domestic funded debt in cotton (the cotton loan), why not extend this expedient to the principal of its future unfunded debt?" (Henry Hotze to Judah P. Benjamin, January 16, 1864, *OR*, ser. 1, 3:1001–3; Jefferson Davis to Zebulon Vance, March 26, 1864, *JDP*, 10:299–301).

15. De Bow, "War of Independence," 47–59; John J. McRae, *Proceedings of a Convention of the Commissioners of Appraisement from the States of Florida, South Carolina, Georgia, Alabama, Mississippi and Tennessee, Meeting in Accordance with instructions from the Hon. Secretary of War, at Montgomery, Alabama, September 20, 1864* (Montgomery, Ala.: Montgomery Advertiser Job and Book Office, 1864), 5. The convention also fixed the debt at two billion dollars and called for Confederates "to replace the gold standard with the cotton standard." Barney, *Secessionist Impulse*, 191–204; May, *Caribbean Dream*, 245–58.

16. Eli M. Bruce, *Remarks of Hon E. M. Bruce, of Kentucky, in the House of Representatives of the Confederate States of America, June 9th and 10th, 1864: On the Financial Policy of the Government,* 1864, Call No. P&W 5202 (BA), 11.

17. Jefferson Davis, "Message to Congress," May 2, 1864, *CJ*, 7:8–11; Bruce, *Remarks of Hon E. M. Bruce,* 11; *The People, [From the Sentinel] To the Congress of the Confederate States.* (Richmond, Va., 1864), 5.; "Foreign Loan," *Index* 4, no. 116 (July 14, 1864): 441.

18. De Bow, "War of Independence," 47–59. De Bow added that during the war "industry has been exerted as it never has been exerted before."

19. Edward Keatinge and Thomas A. Ball, *Remarks on the Manufacture of Bank Notes, and Other Promises to Pay. Addressed to the Bankers of the Southern Confederacy, January 30th 1864* (Columbia, S.C.: F. G. De Fontaine, 1864), 30–31.

20. Arthur J. Lynn to James Murray, October 22, 1864, FO 5/970, p. 50, PRO; Kenneth Rayner to Thomas Ruffin, July 4, 1864, folder 461, Thomas Ruffin Papers, #641, SHC; Howe, *Political Culture of the American Whigs,* 182–83; *Richmond Examiner,* "The Material Resources of the Confederacy," *Index* 4, no. 93 (February 4, 1864): 71. Lynn continued, "there are in the course of construction, two buildings for the manufacture of cotton and woolen cloths; the Confederate authorities have also erected at Marshall in Harrison County works for smelting, casting and rolling iron ... should the state remain free from hostile invasion the people by their industry will soon be able to supply all their necessities." Murray was permanent undersecretary at the Foreign Office in Britain.

21. Thomas Walker Bulitt, entry of March 19, 1864, "Diary, 1862 to 1864," #A B937 FHS. In February, the House considered Senate Bill s198 to establish a Bureau for Polytechnics, but just before recess Representative William Porcher Miles of South Carolina recommended its consideration be postponed. In June, Senator Williamson Oldham introduced another bill, s64, for the same purpose (*CJ*, 4:138, 146, 6:840, 862). Calvin Henderson Wiley's bills to introduce state funding for teacher training (normal) schools and graded (high) schools passed both North Carolina houses in 1864 (Bernath, *Confederate Minds,* 239).

22. Nathan Vernon Madison, *Tredegar Iron Works: Richmond's Foundry on the James* (Charleston, S.C.: History Press, 2015), 83, 133; Edward R. Archer to Dr. Robert Archer, 18 March 1864, and to Frances Archer, 29 March, 1864, "E. R. Archer's letterbook," GLC01896.159; J. R. Anderson to Jefferson Davis, April 30, 1864, *JDP,* 10:375; M. Chadwick to Jefferson Davis, July 5, 1864, *JDP,* 10:501; Bonner, "Slavery, Confederate Diplomacy," 309. For Dr. Robert Archer's connection with Tredegar, see "Tredegar Iron Works Richmond," http://www.the-visitor-center.com/pages/Tredegar -Iron-Works-Richmond/index.htm. For the Wilson brothers, see *Grace's*

Guide to British Industrial History, https://gracesguide.co.uk/George _Wilson, accessed November 23, 2019. According to Archer, Wilson "was in Richmond a few years ago and knew Anderson . . . and saw them at the Tredegar." Chadwick sought exemption for twenty-five thousand bales of cotton to export through Wilmington. McHenry, once a Philadelphia Democrat and now Confederate, was a financial supporter and fellow, along with Henry Hotze, of the center of global scientific racist thought, the Anthropological Society in London (Bonner, "Slavery, Confederate Diplomacy," 301, 309).

23. J. R. Kenan to O. R. Kenan, January 31, 1864, folder 12, series 1, Kenan Family Papers, #4225, SHC; W. Jefferson Buchanan, *Maryland's Hope: Her Trials and Interests in Connection with the War* (Richmond, Va.: West & Johnson, 1864), 52.

24. Buchanan, *Maryland's Hope*, 45; "The Empire of Mexico," *Index* 4, no. 99 (March 17, 1864): 170; Howe, *Political Culture of the American Whigs*, 266.

25. Tyler, "Our Confederate States Foreign and Domestic," 1–33. On empire transcending frontiers, see Charles S. Maier, *Among Empires: American Ascendancy and Its Predecessors* (Cambridge, Mass.: Harvard University Press, 2006), 99–110. On the importance of borders as a definition of independent nationhood where they were contested, see George Nathaniel (Lord) Curzon, *Frontiers: The Romanes Lecture, 1907* (Oxford: Clarendon Press, 1907).

26. Alexander H. Stephens, *The Great Speech of Hon. A. H. Stephens, Delivered before the Georgia Legislature, on Wednesday Night, March 16th, to Which Is Added Extracts from Gov. Brown's Message to the Georgia Legislature* (1864).

27. Robert E. Lee to Jefferson Davis, May 5, 1864, *JDP*, 10:390; "Independence Day," *Index* 4, no. 115 (July 7, 1864): 425; "The War," *Index* 4, no. 116 (July 14, 1864): 441.

28. "Diary Kept by William H. Mayo," 1864–1865, HM 70373, Etha Mayo Woodruff Memorial Collection of Family Papers, HL.

29. "Diary Kept by William H. Mayo"; New Orleans Correspondent, "Confederate Prospects in the South West," *Index* 4, no. 94 (April 21): 247. General Leonidas Polk outlined a similar proposal to Davis on March 21, 1864; Davis passed Polk's plan to Braxton Bragg, who replied a month later, "practicality and policy seem to me doubtful" (*JDP*, 10:288). Taylor wanted to march in force on St. Louis by midsummer (copy of Richard Taylor to Kirby Smith, April 27, 1864, BT 217, Papers of Joseph Lancaster Brent, HL). Confederates relied on more than just rumors of an organized movement against Lincoln. On the extensive political opposition to Republican Party rule in the United States, which reached its apogee in the summer of 1864, see Weber, *Copperheads*. On the more clandestine activities of the Knights of the Golden Circle and other secret societies,

see Mark A. Lause, *A Secret Society History of the Civil War* (Urbana: University of Illinois Press, 2011).

30. Henry S. Foote, "Amendment to the Joint Resolutions on the Subject of Peace," June 2, 1864, *CJ*, 7:150–51. In the Senate, James L. Orr introduced a joint resolution in relation to the opening of negotiations for peace between the Confederacy and the Union on the same day (*CJ*, 4:143).

31. "Southern Independence and Northern Liberty," *Index* 4, no. 105 (April 28, 1864): 266.

32. Judah P. Benjamin to John Slidell, July 12, 1864, *OR*, ser. 1, 3:1172–73; Jefferson Davis to Hershel V. Johnson, September 18, 1864, *JDC*, 6:336.

33. Jefferson Davis, "Interview with Northern Emissaries," July 17, 1864, *JDP*, 10: 533–34. Clay was accompanied by James P. Holcombe, Jacob Thompson, William W. Cleary, George N. Sanders, and Beverley Tucker (with the dollar–gold *JDP*, 10:559).

34. *Richmond Sentinel*, "Terms of Peace," *Index* 4, no. 122 (August 25, 1864): 541.

35. H. V. Johnson to Jefferson Davis, January 4, 1864, *JDP*, 10:152; Leonidas Polk to Jefferson Davis, February 27, 1864, *JDP*, 10:263; J. W. Tucker to Davis, March 14, 1864, *JDC*, 6:204–5; Bruce, *Remarks of Hon E. M. Bruce*, 3; Richard Hawes to Jefferson Davis, July 18, 1864, *JDP*, 10:535. Hawes noted that Bruce "has had an interview with you looking to the best mode of opening communications with those in Kentucky and the North West United States who may have a powerful agency in directing public affairs in that quarter." Hawes mentioned he already had an agent, Cleary, in Canada, the secretary of the Niagara Conference, "who is highly fitted to do what he can to aid our cause in Kentucky"; but he wanted a more prominent personage, such as Bruce or former governor Charles S. Morehead, to go to Canada as well.

36. "The West and the War," *Index* 4, no. 116 (July 14, 1864): 442; "The Growing Power of the West," *Index* 4, no. 126 (September 22, 1864): 601. Hotze was prompted by the publication of letters from Major General Morgan of Ohio and W. M. Anderson calling for an armistice.

37. "Confederate Navy," 395; Tyler, "Our Confederate States Foreign and Domestic," 1–33; Anon., *Rebellion in the North! Extraordinary Disclosures! Vallandigham's Plan to Overthrow the Government! The Peace Party Plot! Full Details of the Organization. Its Declarations, Oaths, Charges, Signs, Signals, Passwords, Grips, &c., &c* (Richmond Va., 1864), foreword; Clement C. Clay to Judah P. Benjamin, August 11, 1864, Bryan Hagan Collection. In the foreword to a series of documents dated June 28, 1864, and allegedly smuggled from the Union, the anonymous writer contended that *Rebellion in the North* was "evidence of strongly prevalent opinion in the North."

38. Clement C. Clay to Judah P. Benjamin, August 11, 1864, Bryan Hagan Collection; Austin H. Price to Jefferson Davis, August 12, 1864, *JDP,* 10:609; Jacob Thompson to Jefferson Davis, September 12, 1864, *JDP,* 11:25–27. Price provided information on "the grand council of leading men from the states of Kentucky, Missouri, Illinois and Indiana" held recently in Chicago and dedicated to "the overthrow of the despotism under which we live." Even after Atlanta fell, Confederates remained confident for some weeks that Sherman's extended supply lines would compel him to undertake a humiliating and dangerous retreat.

39. Clement C. Clay et al. to Jefferson Davis, July 25, 1864, *JDP,* 10:559–61. Clay explained that "our last response is not as pointed as we would have made it in repelling the idea of peace on any terms inconsistent with territorial integrity and with the maintenance of the authority of the States to manage their own social institutions. . . . But it was thought advisable to leave it in a form which, without committing ourselves to the surrender of any right, would be most valuable to the friends of Peace in the North and West" (Clay to Judah P. Benjamin, August 11, 1864).

40. *Richmond Sentinel,* "Terms of Peace," *Index* 4, no. 122 (August 25, 1864): 541; "The Prospect of a Speedy Peace," *Index* 4, no. 121 (August 18, 1864): 521–22.

41. Samuel J. Anderson to Jefferson Davis, August 30, 1864, *JDC,* 6:324–26. As seen below, those Confederates optimistic about McClellan's flexibility with regard to Confederate independence had to swiftly reevaluate their assessment as a result of the Democratic Party convention.

42. John L. O'Sullivan to Jefferson Davis, September 21, 1864, *JDP,* 11:58; Jacob Thompson to Jefferson Davis, September 12, 1864, *JDP* 11:25; William W. Boyce to Jefferson Davis, September 29, 1864, *JDP,* 11:73. Based in London during this time, O'Sullivan wrote pamphlets urging northern Democrats to end the war and the British government to recognize the Confederacy, and to work closely with George McHenry, the northerner O'Sullivan wished to be awarded Confederate citizenship.

43. Bernath, *Confederate Minds,* 202–3; Augusta Jane Evans, *Macaria; or, Altars of Sacrifice,* ed., with an introduction, by Drew Gilpin Faust (1864; rept., Baton Rouge: Louisiana State University Press, 1992). For a discussion of Evans's ambition in writing *Macaria,* see Coleman Hutchison, *Apples and Ashes,* 63–98; Bernath, *Confederate Minds,* 256–67; Fox-Genovese and Genovese, *Mind of the Master Class,* 362, 656–63; Evans, *Macaria,* xiii–xxix.

44. Lansford W. Hastings to Jefferson Davis, January 11, 1864, *JDP,* 10:168; Spruce M. Baird to Jefferson Davis, May 10, 1864, *JDP,* 10:406; Davis to James Seddon, June 6, 1864, Seddon to Davis, June 8, 1864, Davis to Judah P. Benjamin, undated, *JDP,* 10:406; L. W. Hastings to Jefferson Davis, October 17, 1864, *JDP,* 11:111; Frazier, *Blood and Treasure,* 186–207. Davis forwarded Hastings's letter to Seddon on November 7

with the remark:"this subject is known to you and I think has been heretofore presented." Such proposals appealed to Davis as they promised local support. Hastings had a plan to separate California from the Union and unite it with the Confederacy.

45. General Kirby Smith to Jefferson Davis, January 20, 1864, *JDP,* 10:188–90; Charles B. Mitchel and Robert W. Johnson to Jefferson Davis, April 29, 1864, *JDP,* 10:375.

46. Jefferson Davis to Israel Folsom, February 22, 1864, *JDC,* 6:184–86; Elias Boudinot to Jefferson Davis, January 4, 1864, *JDP,* 10:151.

47. Report of Indian Commissioner Sutton S. Scott was included in "The Report of the Secretary of War," April 28, 1864, *Index* 4, no. 121 (August 18, 1864): 516; Elizabeth Brown Pryor, *Six Encounters with Lincoln: A President Confronts Democracy and Its Demons* (New York: Viking, 2017), 154. The Arkansas senators had lobbied for Watie's promotion as it "will also signal appreciation of Indian soldiers." Davis immediately asked Samuel Cooper, "Has a brigade been formed to which Stand Watie could be properly assigned?" (*JDP,* 10:375).

48. Judah P. Benjamin to William Preston, January 7, 1864, *OR,* ser. 1, 3:988–89; Jefferson Davis to the Archduke Maximilian, January 7, *JDP,* 10:158; Benjamin to Preston, January 7, 1864.

49. William Preston to José Quintero, March 20, 1864, and Preston to General Almonte, June 6, 1864, letter book 1864–65, correspondence, Preston Family Papers—Davie Collection, #A/P037d 39, FHS; James L. Orr, "Amendment to Second Resolution Advising That Negotiations Be Entered upon His Imperial Majesty on the Basis Proposed in the Draft of Instructions Accompanying the President's Message," January 5, 1864, *CJ,* 3:515–16; "Mexico in the French Chambers," *Index* 4, no. 93 (February 4, 1864): 74; De Bow, "War of Independence," 47–59; Rose Greenhow to Jefferson Davis, January 2, 1864, *JDP,* 10:143; John Slidell to Judah P. Benjamin, June 2, 1864, *OR,* ser. 1, 3:1139–40.

50. Tyler, "Our Confederate States," 1–33; Case and Spencer, *United States and France,* 604–8.

51. William Preston, "Memorandum," June 26, and William Preston to Jefferson Davis, June 28, 1864, letter book 1864–65, correspondence, Preston Family Papers—Davie Collection, #A/P037d 39, FHS; John Slidell to Judah P. Benjamin, June 2, 1864, *OR,* ser. 1, 3:1139–40. On the devastation of northern Mexico during the first half of the nineteenth century by Native American raids, see Brian Delay, *War of a Thousand Deserts: Indian Raids and the U.S.–Mexican War* (New Haven, Conn.: Yale University Press, 2008).

52. Judah P. Benjamin to William Preston, January 7, 1864. In London, Greenhow noted Gwin was active in his machinations by the beginning of 1864 (Rose Greenhow to Jefferson Davis, January 2, 1864, *JDP,* 10:143).

53. John Slidell to Judah P. Benjamin, June 2, 1864; Greenberg, *Wicked War,* 77–84, 103. A Confederate agent in Mexico City, Captain A. M. T. Beauregard, wrote to Preston on June 18, "the French are or are expected to be in Acapulco en route for the possession of Sonora, said to be threatened by Yankee sympathizers from California" (A. M. T. Beauregard to William Preston, June 18, 1864, 1864–65 letter book, correspondence, Preston Family Papers—Davie Collection, # A\P937d, FHS).

54. "The Confederate Navy," *Index* 4, no. 113 (June 23, 1864): 395.

55. William Preston to Captain R. T. Ford, June 23, August 20, 1864, letter book 1864–65, correspondence, Preston Family Papers—Davie Collection, #A/P037d 39, FHS. Preston told Ford that both Mason and Slidell had advised him to abort his mission, but Preston had been persuaded otherwise by Gwin as the former senator "takes a very different view of matters and regards the impediments as merely temporary."

56. "The Empire of Mexico," *Index* 4, no. 89 (March 17, 1864): 169.

57. William Preston to Judah P. Benjamin, February 13, 1864, letter book 1864–65, correspondence, Preston Family Papers—Davie Collection, #A/P037d 39, FHS; John Slidell to Judah P. Benjamin, March 16, 1864, *OR,* ser. 1, 3:1063–65. Preston later told Benjamin that "a single corps of our army might maintain or destroy his government if deprived of the aid of France." He warned Benjamin that the "adherents of Juarez occupy the northern routes" (William Preston to Judah P Benjamin, April 28, June 2, 1864, letter book 1864–65, correspondence, Preston Family Papers—Davie Collection, #A/P037d 39, FHS). Slidell saw Union opposition and above all the unpopularity of the Mexican project in France as bigger obstacles; the French foreign minister's "great dissatisfaction at the tardiness of the Archduke's movements" did not alleviate these challenges.

58. "The Mexican Policy," *Index* 4, no. 122 (August 25, 1864): 537–38; Lamar, *Speech of Hon. L. Q. C. Lamar of Mississippi,* 10. Slidell spoke to the chief of the Mexican commission sent to Europe to offer Maximilian the throne, Don J. M. Gutierrez de Estrada, and later to Maximilian's army chief of staff, General Adrián Woll (John Slidell to Judah P. Benjamin, April 30, June 2, 1864, *OR,* ser. 1, 3:1108–9, 1140; Judah P. Benjamin to John Slidell, April 23, 1864, *OR,* 1100; Dudley Mann to Judah P. Benjamin, April 4, 15, 1864, *OR,* ser. 1, 3:1076; Henry Hotze to Judah P. Benjamin, April 16, 1864, *OR,* ser. 1, 3:1086–90).

59. Henry Winter Davis, "The Empire of Mexico," in *Speeches and Addresses by Henry Winter Davis* (New York: Harper & Brothers, 1867), 395; L. D. Q. Washington to R. M. T. Hunter, April 12, 1864, box 9, folder v-w, Hunter Family Papers, #H9196aFAZ, VHS; Edward R. Archer to Bert Archer, May 6, 1864 letter book, GLC01896.159; John Slidell to Judah P. Benjamin, April 30, 1864, *OR,* ser. 1, 3:1108–9. The resolution

declared "that the Congress of the United States were unwilling by silence to leave the nations of the world under the impression that they are indifferent spectators of the deplorable events now transpiring in the Republic of Mexico; and that they therefore think fit to declare that it does not accord with the policy of the United States to acknowledge any monarchical government erected on the ruin of any republican government under the auspices of any European power." Edward Archer believed that Maximilian would only accept the crown if Napoleon recognized the Confederacy (Archer, letter to his mother, March 29, 1864, letter book, GLC01896.159).

60. "The Southern Press on the Monroe Doctrine," *Index* 4, no. 107 (May 12, 1864): 295.

61. "Southern Press on the Monroe Doctrine," 295; Dudley Mann to Jefferson Davis, February 29, 1864, *OR*, ser. 1, 3:1042–43; William Preston to Juan Nepomuceno Almonte, June 6, 1864, letter book 1864–65, correspondence, Preston Family Papers—Davie Collection, #A/P037d 39, FHS.

62. Lamar, *Speech of Hon. L. Q. C. Lamar of Mississippi*, 10–11.

63. William Preston to Juan Nepomuceno Almonte, June 6, 1864.

64. William Preston to Judah P. Benjamin, March 4, March 11, 1864, letter book 1864–65, correspondence, Preston Family Papers—Davie Collection, #A/P037d 39, FHS; Charles Helm to Judah P. Benjamin, January 1, 1864, *OR*, ser. 1, 3:987. Lorenzo Arrazola y García's administration lasted only a few months as Spain subsided into chaos (Charles Helm to Judah P. Benjamin, April 14, 1864, *OR*, ser. 1, 3:1085; William Preston to Jefferson Davis, June 2, 1864, letter book 1864–65, correspondence, Preston Family Papers—Davie Collection, #A/P037d 39, FHS). Preston tired of Cuba rapidly and quit at the end of the month for Europe; just before he departed, he wrote to Davis that "Cuba is exceedingly disagreeable . . . the Captain General, though professing sympathy for the Confederacy, is really afraid of the North" (William Preston to Jefferson Davis, June 28, 1864, letter book 1864–65, correspondence, Preston Family Papers—Davie Collection, #A/P037d 39, FHS).

65. See Timo Airaksinen and Martin A. Bertman, *Hobbes: War among Nations* (Aldershot, UK: Avebury, 1989); Edmund Burke, *Reflections on the Revolution in France*, ed. J. G. A. Pocock (Indianapolis: Hackett, 1987); Immanuel Kant, *Kant's Principles of Politics, Including His Essay on Perpetual Peace*, ed. W. Hastle (Edinburgh, UK: T. & T. Clark, 1891).

66. Evans, *Macaria; or, Altars of Sacrifice*, 3; "Our Stake in the War," *Index* 5, no. 182 (March 23, 1865): 186.

67. Jefferson Davis, Speech in Augusta, October 5, 1864, *JDC*, 6:357; Jefferson Davis, "Speech in Augusta," September 22, 1864, *JDP*, 11:60; Quentin Skinner, *Liberty before Liberalism* (New York: Cambridge University

Press, 1998); McCardell, *Idea of a Southern Nation*, 261–73; Fox-Genovese and Genovese, *Mind of the Master Class*, 532; Wilson, *Victorians*, 108–12; Lamar, *Speech of Hon. L. Q. C. Lamar of Mississippi*, 11. James Lyons, in his February 1864 eulogy of representative Muscoe Russell Hunter Garnett, told the House of Representatives that a statesman had to "resist the passion for notoriety, that infirmary of finite minds," and instead focus on "higher and more solid attainments" (James Lyons, "Eulogy on Muscoe Russell Hunter Garnett," February 14, 1864, box 7, folder 22, Lyons Family Papers, HL).

68. For an emphasis on disagreement over the Confederate national vision during this period, see Rable, *Confederate Republic*, 236–76. I would rather stress that at this stage Confederates exhibited a greater degree of consensus on the ends of the Confederate nation, while they bitterly contended about the means.

6. THE SACRIFICE CANNOT BE IN VAIN

1. "Letter from Richmond," *Index* 5, no. 152 (March 23, 1865): 181; "Another Mass Meeting in Richmond," *Index* 5, no. 149 (March 2, 1865): 133.

2. In the final months of the war, Confederates did not behave as if they, as Bruce Levine argues, were "looking to a way to salvage at least something" from the wreckage, after "Sherman broke the power of the secessionist government." Historians tend to identify this period as when Confederates confronted their failure, when they ceased to believe in their government and prepared for the inevitable future of reunion with a substantial downgrading of expectations. Robert Bonner observes that "the crisis faced by the Confederacy in late 1864 changed the old arguments," and "the southern hopes of securing Confederate independence by going around Lincoln and his party vanished." As George Rable contends, Confederates chose not to respond to adverse events in, a reactionary or even counterrevolutionary way, having deemed their revolution a failure. Instead they sought to find a solution in their revolution, sustained by a profound sense of entitlement, which Paul Quigley notes the sufferings inflicted by the war had only intensified. There was no conscious movement to postpone the bid for national independence to a better time and a more protracted method, which Michael Bernath believes was the case for cultural nationalism. There was no moment before surrender when Confederates came to the realization that "racism was far more durable than southern nationhood." Bonner rightly sees this development as a postwar phenomenon (Levine, *Fall of the House of Dixie*, 238, 248, 251; Bonner, *Mastering America*: 286–323; Rable, *Confederate Republic*, 277–98; Quigley, *Shifting Grounds*, 212–13; Bernath, *Confederate Minds*, 268–70). On loyalties, see

Gary W. Gallagher, *Becoming Confederates: Paths to a New National Loyalty* (Athens: University of Georgia Press, 2013).

3. "The Negro in the Southern Armies," *Index* 4, no. 133 (November 10, 1864): 713–14; Charles B. Leitner to Jefferson Davis, December 31, 1864, *JDP,* 11:266.

4. G. L. Strucker to Joseph L. Brent, January 13, 1865, BT 208, Papers of Joseph Lancaster Brent, HL; Louis A. Bringier to Brent, April 6, 1865, BT 89, Papers of Joseph Lancaster Brent, HL. On Confederate plans to free enslaved people, see Levine, *Confederate Emancipation.*

5. Acting Consul Henry Pinckney Walker to Earl Russell, November 19, 1864, FO 5/969, PRO; William F. Robert to Jefferson Davis, December 25, 1864, *JDP,* 11:252. Walker considered that despite his retirement, Rhett's "opinions are nevertheless held in very high esteem and the views brought forth will be embraced by the people of S.C., without any dissent."

6. Fred A. Porcher to Judah P. Benjamin, December 16, Benjamin to Porcher, December 21, 1864, box 1, Meade Papers, UVA; James Seddon, "The Report of the Secretary of War," November 4, 1864, *Index* 4, vol. 136 (December 1, 1864): 766. In his letter of December 16, Porcher called for arming slaves on the grounds that it is better to "anticipate rather than await the decision of events."

7. James Seddon, "Report of the Secretary of War," 766; Henry Pinckney Walker to Earl Russell, February 27, 1865, FO 5/1030, p. 92, PRO; John Beauchamp Jones, *A Rebel War Clerk's Diary at the Confederate States Capital,* 2 vols. (Philadelphia: J. B. Lippincott, 1866), 2:321–23, 449; Charles J. Hutson to Richard W. Hutson, March 16, 1865, GLC08165.69.

8. Patrick J. Kelly, "The North American Crisis of the 1860s," *Journal of the Civil War Era* 2, no. 3 (September 2012): 353; "General Magruder to the People of Arkansas," *Index* 5, no. 147 (February 16, 1865): 109; Augustus W. Ashton to Jefferson Davis, February 15, 1865, *JDP,* 11:402. From Washington County, Va., he met Davis on January 24. According to Kelly, in early 1863 military officials in the Trans-Mississippi Department were especially anxious for the French to occupy Matamoras to guarantee the smooth functioning of the lucrative cotton trade, and accordingly Magruder sent secret agent A. Superviele to Mexico in April.

9. "The Perils of Commercial States," *Index* 5, no. 142 (January 12, 1865): 26. Hotze added a month later that the Confederacy had "no commercial intercourse" remaining with the outside world ("The Negotiations for Peace," *Index* 5, no. 147 [February 16, 1865]: 104). The idea of vigor of a race being enhanced by "primitive" farm work in place of the "advanced" factory showed the influence of Carlyle on Hotze (see also Bonner, "Slavery, Confederate Diplomacy," 298–99; Horsman, *Race and Manifest Destiny,* 168–86; O'Brien, *Intellectual Life and the American South,* 166–72).

10. Robert E. Lee to Jefferson Davis, January 17, 1865, *JDP*, 11:338–39; Frances E. Sprague to Margaret G. Winchester, February 24, 1865 folder 3, correspondence: Margaret G. Sprague Winchester, box 2E913 Frances E. Sprague Papers, Winchester Papers, UT.

11. Abram Archer to Richard T. Archer, January 24, 1865, folder 1, immediate family correspondence, box 2E650, Archer Family Papers, UT; Joseph Hubbard Echols, *Speech of Hon. Joseph H. Echols: The House of Representatives, on January 19, 1865* (Richmond, Va., 1865),

12. John H. Stringfellow to Jefferson Davis, February 8, 1865, *JDP*, 11:391–92; Aaron Sheehan-Dean, *The Civil War: The Final Year Told by Those Who Lived It* (Boone, Iowa: Library of America, 2014), 576.

13. Daniel Coleman De Jarnette, *The Monroe Doctrine: Speech of D. C. DeJarnette, of Virginia, in the Confederate House of Representatives, January 30th, 1865, pending negotiations for peace* (Richmond, Va., 1865), 6, 8.

14. Duff Green to Jefferson Davis, December 29, 1864, *JDP*, 11:259; Pryor, *Six Encounters with Lincoln*, 269–73, 313; De Jarnette, *Monroe Doctrine*, 19. "I have just received yours of this date." Davis replied to Green. "It will give me much pleasure to see you at my residence in the evening." Elizabeth Brown Pryor argues that Green "was rebuffed coldly in Richmond" (Pryor, *Six Encounters with Lincoln*, 312).

15. De Jarnette, *Monroe Doctrine* (BA).

16. "Legislature of North Carolina with Message of Governor," November 28, 1864, in Henry Pinckney Walker to Earl Russell, December 2 1864, FO 5/969, PRO; "Letter from John H. Gilmer to Peter Saunders Esq., a Member of the Virginia Senate, on the Position and Duties of Virginia in the Existing State of Political Matters" (broadside, December 28, 1864).

17. J. Jones, *Rebel War Clerk's Diary*, 2:416; Oldham, *Speech on Texas Resolutions*, 9–10; "Supplement to March 6, 1865 Address of the Confederate Congress to the Country," *Index* 5, 154 (April 6, 1865): 221.

18. Gustavus Adolphus Henry, *Speech of Hon. Gustavus A. Henry, in the Senate of the Confederate States, November 29, 1864* (Richmond, Va., 1864), 2, 3, 5; De Jarnette, *Monroe Doctrine*, 5–6; Seddon, "The Report of the Secretary of War," November 4, 1864, *Index* 4, no. 136 (December 1, 1864): 766.

19. "Reconstruction," *Index* 4, no. 134 (November 17, 1864): 729; "The Negotiations for Peace," *Index* 5, no. 147 (February 16, 1865): 104.

20. John Letcher, "Reflections upon the State of Our Situation of the Country," draft letter to the editor, undated 1864, but almost certainly December, folder 421, John Letcher Papers, VHS; William Naylor McDonald, *The Two Rebellions; or, Treason Unmasked. By a Virginian* (Richmond, Va.: Smith, Bailey, 1865), 6; Joseph L. Brent to Simon A. Buckner, [31 December?] 1864/1865, BT 24, Joseph Lancaster Brent Papers, HL.

21. Gustavus Adolphus Henry, "Resolutions in Congress," November 18, 1864, *Index* 4, no. 137 (December 8, 1864): 781; Joseph L. Brent to Simon A. Buckner, [31 December?] 1864/1865, BT 24, Joseph Lancaster Brent Papers, HL.

22. Fred A. Porcher to Judah P. Benjamin, December 16, Benjamin to Porcher, December 21, 1864, box 1, Meade Papers, UVA. On the dictatorship debate, see Blair, *Virginia's Private War*, 131–33; Levine, *Fall of the House of Dixie*, 156; J. Jones, *Rebel War Clerk's Diary*, 2:364, 368.

23. "Letter from John H. Gilmer to Peter Saunders Esq., a Member of the Virginia Senate, on the Position and Duties of Virginia in the Existing State of Political Matters" (broadside, Richmond, December 28, 1864); Henry S. Foote, "Resolutions," November 30, 1864, *CJ*, 7:312–13; J. Jones, *Rebel War Clerk's Diary*, 2:337, 359; James T. Leach, "Resolutions"; note in *JDP*, 11:467. On Foote's attempt to cross to the Union see Jefferson Davis, "Message," January 13, 1865; John B. Clark, "chairman of Committee of Elections Motion," January 16, 24; John Adams Gilmer of North Carolina, "Minority Report," January 24, 1865, *CJ*, 7:454, 458, 490–91; Leach, "Resolutions," February 15, 1865, *CJ*, 7:582; "Supplement to the March 6 address of the Confederate Congress to the country," *Index* 5, no. 154 (April 6, 1865): 221. Leach described Benjamin's speech as "derogatory to his position as a high public functionary of the Confederate Government, a reflection on the motives of Congress as a deliberative body, and an insult to public opinion."

24. Jefferson Davis, "Address to the Confederate People," April 4, 1865, *JDC*, 6:529–31; "The Fall of Richmond," *Index* 5, no. 156 (April 20, 1865): 248–49.

25. Jefferson Davis, "Speech at Charlotte," April 19, 1865, *JDP*, 11:549–50; Varina Davis to Jefferson Davis, April 28, 1865, *JDP*, 11:569–71.

26. William T. Sutherlin to Jefferson Davis, March 14, 1865, *JDP*, 11:441; Joseph L. Brent to Simon A. Buckner, April 30, 1865, BT 27, Joseph Lancaster Brent Papers, HL. Davis described Sutherlin's letter to an aide as "very spirited."

27. Brent to Buckner, April 30, 1865; William L. Wilson, "Diary of William L. Wilson, B Company, 12th Regiment, Virginia, Cavalry," p. 35, GLC00653.17; "The Assassination of Lincoln," *Index* 5, no. 157 (April 27, 1865): 264.

28. "Extracts from the Southern Papers' Latest Dates," *Index* 5, no. 144 (January 26, 1865): 45–46; for African American enlistment, see Levine, *Confederate Emancipation*.

29. Robert S. Hudson to Jefferson Davis, November 25, 1864, *JDP*, 11:188–89; William S. Price to Davis, November 14, 1864, *JDP*, 11:159. But other planters vehemently opposed blending slavery with army service. Abram Archer complained to his mother, while he was away with his cavalry regiment,

that even to threaten slaves with enlistment undermined discipline: "I am sorry pa threatened Tom with the soldiers as it does more harm than good to do so—and besides this has a bad effect on the others after this if any them show a disposition to misbehave" (Abram Archer to his mother, March 1, 1865, box 2E650, folder 1 immediate family 1858–1865, Richard Thompson Archer Family Papers, UT).

30. John DeWitt Clinton Atkins, "Amendment to Peace Resolution of Samuel J. Gholson of Mississippi," February 3, 1865, *CJ*, 7:535.

31. J. W. Ellis to Davis, January 28, 1865, *JDP*, 11:358. On the concept of a slave South as a "*Herrenvolk* democracy," see George M. Frederickson, *The Black Image in the White Mind: The Debate on Afro-American Character and Destiny, 1817–1914* (New York: Harper and Row, 1971), 61–70. For an argument for white inequality in the South, see McCurry, *Masters of Small Worlds*, 93.

32. De Jarnette, *Monroe Doctrine*, 7–8; "Another Mass Meeting in Richmond," *Index* 5, no. 149 (March 2, 1865): 133.

33. Davis, "Message to Congress," November 7, 1864, *CJ*, 7:254; William Preston to Robert Wickliffe Preston, February 10, 1865, Letter Book of William Preston, 1864–65, #A P937d 37, Preston Family Papers, FHS; "Another Mass Meeting in Richmond," *Index* 5 149 (March 2, 1865): 133. According to the account of the *Richmond Dispatch*, Benjamin's speech was greeted with "rousing cheers."

34. William Smith to Jefferson Davis, March 27, 1865, *JDP*, 11:476; John H. Stringfellow to Davis, February 8, 1865, *JDP*, 11:391–92; Frances E. Sprague to Margaret G. Sprague Winchester, January 2, February, 24, 1865, box 2E913—Frances E. Sprague papers, folder 3 "Correspondence: Margaret G. Sprague Winchester," Winchester Family Papers, UT.

35. Charles Leitner to Jefferson Davis, December 31, 1864, *JDP*, 11:266; Alexander Fitzpatrick to Davis, January 1, 1865, *JDP*, 11:266–67; James M. Mason to Judah P. Benjamin, January 21, 1865, *OR*, ser. 1, 3:1259. On the Kenner Mission, see Doyle, *Cause of All Nations*, 274–80.

36. "The False Road to Recognition," *Index* 5, no. 144 (January 26, 1865): 49; Frances E. Sprague to Margaret G. Sprague Winchester, January 2, February, 24, 1865, box 2E913—Frances E. Sprague papers, folder 3, Correspondence: Margaret G. Sprague Winchester, Winchester Family Papers, UT.

37. George W. Randolph to General Colin L McRae, February 3, 1865, box folder 16, box 1, Papers of Randolph Family of Edgehill, #5533-c, UVA; "List of Expenses due to George W. Randolph from the Nitre and Mining Bureau," folder 9, Dickins and Kirk Families additional papers, #5533–k,j, UVA; Varina Davis to Mary Chesnut, October 8, November 20, 1864, in Chesnut, *Mary Chesnut's Civil War*, 664, 675. On industrial espionage and leapfrog theory, see Landes, *Wealth and Poverty*, 276–91.

38. John H. Reagan to Jefferson Davis, April 22, 1865, *JDP,* 11: 556–57; Robert E. Lee to Davis, January 18, 1865, *JDP,* 11:338–39.

39. John Adams Gilmer, "Resolution for Committee on Ordnance and Ordnance Stores," December 5, 1864, *CJ,* 7:329; Joseph R. Anderson quoted and Jefferson Davis to Robert E. Lee, April 1, 1865, *JDP,* 11:492–94; Nathan Madison, *Tredegar Ironworks: Richmond's Foundry on the James* (Mount Pleasant, S.C.: Arcadia, 2015), 77; Charles B. Dew, *Ironworker to the Confederacy: Joseph R. Anderson and the Tredegar Iron Works* (New Haven, Conn.: Yale University Press, 1966), 285. On November 21, William Russell Smith of North Carolina wanted to know "what legislation is required to prevent the prostration of the industrial interests of the country?" On December 5, Gilmer argued for "the necessity of establishing government works on Deep River, N.C., to secure more effectually the benefits of coal and iron so important to our defense" (*CJ,* 7:289, 312).

40. Thomas E. McNeil to Jefferson Davis, February 19, 1865, *JDP,* 11:412; Henry Pinckney Walker to Earl Russell, February 7, 1865, FO 5/1030, pp. 64–67, PRO; "The Fall of Richmond," *Index* 5, no. 156 (April 20, 1865): 248.

41. Oldham, *Speech on Texas Resolutions,* 12.

42. Jefferson Davis, "Meeting with the Georgia Senators," November 17, 1864, *JDP,* 11:162–65; John Adams Gilmer, "Amendment to the Resolutions of the Committee of Foreign Affairs," in "Congressional Resolutions," *Index* 5, no. 151 (March 16, 1865): 166, and February 20, 1865, *CJ,* 7:607.

43. Jefferson Davis, "Message to Congress," November 7, 1864, *CJ,* 7:249; Kirby Smith to Davis, November 21, 1864, *JDP,* 11:175–78; Kean, *Inside the Confederate Government,* 198; Blair, *Virginia's Private War,* 115–17; Davis to P. G. T. Beauregard, November 30, and Beauregard to Davis, December 6, 1864, *JDP,* 11:194, 206. Price had been defeated at Pilot's Knob on September 26 and Westport on October 23. On both the grandiose objectives and significant numbers of forces engaged in Price's 1864 Missouri campaign, which only became a 'raid' in retrospect, see Mark A. Lause, *Price's Lost Campaign: The 1864 Invasion of Missouri* (Columbia: University of Missouri Press, 2011).

44. Robert W. Johnson to Jefferson Davis, November 5, 1864, *JDP,* 11:138; *CJ,* 4:590.

45. Jefferson Davis to James A. Seddon, January 5, 1865, *JDP,* 11:281. By now a brigadier general, Harrison was also fluent in Choctaw and Creek languages (Thomas W. Cutrer, "Harrison, James Edward," *The Handbook of Texas Online,* https://tshaonline.org/handbook/online/articles/fhaac).

46. Jefferson Davis to James A. Seddon, January 5, 1865, *JDP,* 11:281; Frazier, *Blood and Treasure,* 291–97.

47. Thomas B. Hanley, "Resolutions," January 11, 1865, *CJ,* 7:405; William Porcher Miles, "Joint Resolutions," January 19, 1865, *CJ,* 7:465;

Edmondston, *Journal of a Secesh Lady*, 650–51. Hanley's resolution passed the same day (*CJ,* 7:445). Miles praised "the daring and skill exhibited in the capture of over 250 loaded wagons from the enemy in the Cherokee nation on September 19, 1864, and for other brilliant and successful services in the Indian Territory."

48. Slidell to Benjamin, February 7, 1865, *OR,* ser. 1, 3:1262; De Jarnette, *Monroe Doctrine,* (BA). According to the February 8 *Houston Tri-Weekly Telegraph,* Colonel C. L. Pyron, stationed in San Antonio, Texas, and General Florentino Lopez from across the Rio Grande exchanged messages of goodwill; Pyron said Confederates "frankly offer their friendship," and Lopez on January 10 from Piedras Negras, Coahuila, declared he was a "warm friend to the cause" ("The Mexican Empire and the Confederacy," *Index* 5, no. 151 [March 16, 1865]: 167). Thomas Schoonover argues that while Confederates focused on short-term benefits in their relations with Mexico, the French intervention on behalf of Maximilian aided both the conservative Mexicans and Confederates and weakened liberal and republican institutions everywhere in the New World (Thomas Schoonover, "Napoleon Is Coming! Maximilian Is Coming? The International History of the Civil War in the Caribbean Basin," in Robert E. May, ed., *The Union, the Confederacy and the Atlantic Rim* [West Lafayette, Ind.: Purdue University Press, 1995], pp. 101–30.) On the supposed Confederate "Latin Strategy," see Doyle, *Cause of All Nations,* 8–10.

49. Calhoun Benham to Joseph L. Brent, November 25, 1864, BT 13, Papers of Joseph Lancaster Brent, HL; "The Reported Cession of Mexican Territory," *Index* 5, no. 146 (February 9, 1865): 8; Rachel St. John, "The Unpredictable America of William Gwin," *Journal of the Civil War Era* 6, no. 1 (March 2016): 56–81. Benham added, "I have sanguine hopes as to Sonora. If I did not have faith in your achievement of still higher distinction in the service, I would indulge the hope of seeing you there too." On Maximilian's initial "dalliances" with liberals, see Doyle, *Cause of All Nations,* 299–307. Unknown to Hotze, Gwin had become frustrated with Maximilian's concern—based on his wish to cultivate public support for his regime—that such an infusion of Confederate supporters would become unpopular among native Mexicans.

50. "Reconstruction," *Index* 4, no. 134 (November 17, 1864): 729. On the significant California participation on the Union side in the war, including the seventeen thousand men who volunteered for military service, see Matthews, *Golden State in the Civil War.*

51. Stella Bringier to Joseph L. Brent, April 19, 1865, BT 92, Papers of Joseph Lancaster Brent, HL; Wade Hampton to Jefferson Davis, April 22, 1865, *JDP,* 11:556; Wahstrom, *Southern Exodus to Mexico,* xiii–xiv. According to

Doyle, in Richmond that April "it was known that Maximilian was wel-coming Confederate refugees" (Doyle, *Cause of All Nations*, 288).

52. Edward Alfred Pollard, *A Letter on the State of the War. By One Recently Returned from the Enemy's Country* (Richmond Va., 1865), 2–3; Bonner, "Slavery, Confederate Diplomacy," 312–13.

53. Pollard, *Letter on the State of the War*, 2–3; Fox-Genovese and Genovese, *Mind of the Master Class*, 215–20; Wahlstrom, *Southern Exodus to Mexico*, 117–27.

54. J. Jones, *Rebel War Clerk's Diary*, 2:402.

55. Henry W. Hilliard to Jefferson Davis, February 2, 1865, *JDC*, 6:461–62; John Adams Gilmer, "Amendment to Joint Resolution Expressing the Sense of Congress"; "The Negotiations for Peace," *Index* 5, no. 147 (Febru-ary 16, 1865): 104; Horsman, *Race and Manifest Destiny*, 272–98. Davis's response to Hilliard's letter was guarded, as it risked compromising his pursuit of complete independence, he told his secretary on February 15, "Please acknowledge in terms suited to the known facts."

56. Henry W. Hilliard to Jefferson Davis, February 2, 1865; Fox-Genovese and Genovese, *Mind of the Master Class*, 215–20, 711.

57. John Adams Gilmer, "Amendment to Joint Resolution Expressing the Sense of Congress"; Crofts, *Reluctant Confederates*, xxi, 9, 31, 125; Pryor, *Six Encounters with Lincoln*, 283. As well as looking to the example of the German Diet balancing Austria and Prussia, Gilmer was also drawing on Calhoun's ideas of a dual executive (John C. Calhoun, "A Disquisition on Government," Constitution Society, http://www.constitution.org/jcc /disq_gov.htm). On the German Confederation, see Steinberg, *Bismarck*, 111–13. The German Confederation had a narrower council as well as a general assembly: "an international association of German sovereign pow-ers and free cities to preserve the independence and inviolability of the member states and preserve the inner and outer security of Germany." One caveat: no state could leave (112). As historian A. J. P. Taylor makes clear, with the fall of Metternich and the revolutions in 1848, the Austrian chancellor's system that enabled the operation of the Diet by restrain-ing the competition between Prussia and Austria was "dead" (Taylor, *The Struggle for Mastery in Europe, 1848–1918* [1954; repr., New York: Oxford University Press, 1971], 26).

58. Fox-Genovese and Genovese, *Mind of the Master Class*, 62–69; May, *Slav-ery, Race and Conquest in the Tropics*, 226–29; J. Jones, *Rebel War Clerk's Diary*, 2:402; De Jarnette. *Monroe Doctrine*, 3–4; Landes, *Wealth and Pov-erty*, 246–47; Landes, *The Unbound Prometheus Technological Change and Industrial Development in Western Europe from 1750 to the Present* (New York: Cambridge University Press, 1969), 152–53, 166.

59. "Peace Rumors," *Index* 5, no. 145 (February 2, 1865): 64.

60. Kean, *Inside the Confederate Government,* 106; Henry, *Speech of Hon. Gustavus A. Henry,* 794.

61. Kean, *Inside the Confederate Government,* 203–4; House Committee on Foreign Affairs, "Sundry Resolutions on the Subject of Peace," January 12, 1865, *CJ,* 450–52; Steven E. Woodworth, "The Last Function of Government: Confederate Collapse and Negotiated Peace," in Mark Grimsley and Brooks D. Simpson, eds., *The Collapse of the Confederacy* (Lincoln: University of Nebraska Press, 2001), 28.

62. "Reconstruction," *Index* 4, no. 134 (November 17, 1864): 729.

63. Francis P. Blair Sr. to Jefferson Davis, December 30, 1864, *JDC,* 6:432; Francis P. Blair Sr., "Conversation with Francis Preston Blair," January 12, 1865, *JDP,* 11:316–20. On Blair's mission, see William A. Blair, "Finding the Ending of America's Civil War," *American Historical Review* 120, no. 5 (December 2015): 1759; Woodworth, "Last Function of Government," 27–30; James M. McPherson, "No Peace without Victory, 1861–1865," *American Historical Review* 109, no. 1 (February 2004): 14–15.

64. Jefferson Davis, "Memorandum," January 12, 1865, *JDP,* 11:321; Francis P. Blair Sr., "Second Interview," January 14, 1865, *JDP,* 11:328. Using Jones's diary as a source, McPherson assumes that Davis was cool on the Mexican scheme, whereas that was the attitude of the war department clerk and not the president (McPherson, "No Peace without Victory," 15).

65. Majority Report from Committee of Foreign Affairs, "Sundry Resolutions on the Subject of Peace," January 12, 1865, *CJ,* 7:451–52; Francis P. Blair Sr., "Conversation with Francis Preston Blair," January 12, 1865, *JDP,* 11:316–20; Henry S. Foote, "The Monroe Doctrine Resolution," November 28, 1864, *CJ,* 7:308; Woodworth, "Last Function of Government," 28–32. Woodworth observes that Lincoln "would have none of it" when Stephens tried to "divert the discussion to the proposed Mexico adventure" (Woodworth, "Last Function of Government," 31).

66. Oldham, *Speech on Texas Resolutions,* 11; "Letter of R. C. Midhurst to the Hon. B. R. Wood," *Index* 5, no. 154 (April 6, 1865): 215.

67. Henry W. Hilliard to Jefferson Davis, February 2, 1865; "The Negotiations for Peace," *Index* 5, no. 147 (February 16, 1865): 104; "Peace Rumors," *Index* 5, no. 145 (February 2, 1865): 64; J. Jones, *Rebel War Clerk's Diary,* 2:402.

68. Duff Green to Jefferson Davis, December 29, 1864, *JDP,* 11: 259; De Jarnette, *Monroe Doctrine,* 8; John Slidell to Judah P. Benjamin, February 7, 1865, *OR,* ser. 1, 3:1262; "The Reported Cession of Mexican Territory," *Index* 5, no. 146 (February 9, 1865): 81; Dudley Mann to Davis, December 17, 1864, *JDP,* 11:236. Hotze added that the news had reached New York via telegram from San Francisco. Hotze also picked up the story, which had been reported in a New York newspaper.

Epilogue

1. Louis A. Bringier to Joseph L. Brent, April 1, 1865, BT 98, Joseph Lancaster Brent Papers, HL; "The Fall of Richmond," *Index* 5, no. 156 (April 20, 1865): 249.

2. H. T. Douglas to Joseph L. Brent, April 12, 1865, BT 61, Brent to Simon B. Buckner, 30 April 1865, BT 27, Joseph Lancaster Brent Papers, HL.

3. Wilson, "Diary," entry for Sunday, April 2, 32–33, GLCo 0653.17.

4. H. T. Douglas to Joseph L. Brent, April 24, 1865, BT 109 JLB.

5. Wilson, "Diary," entry, April 4, 1865, 37, GLCo 0653.17; Jefferson Davis to Varina Davis, April 5, 1865, *JDP,* 11:503; Varina to Davis, April 7, 1865, *JDP,* 11:513–14.

6. Wilson, "Diary," entry, April 9, 1865, 77, 86–87, GLCo 0653.17. Wilson continued: "The Proud Army of Northern Virginia with all its glorious history has ceased to exist . . . as an organization she will never more exist to fight the battle of freedom—henceforth and for ever she will only live in the memory of her glorious valor and patriotic devotion."

7. "The Northern Exultation," *Index* 5, no. 156 (April 20, 1865): 250. James M. Mason to Henry Hotze, April 27, 1865, "The Assassination of Lincoln," *Index* 5, no. 157 (April 27, 1865): 264, 268; Wade Hampton to Jefferson Davis, April 19, 1865, *JDP,* 11:548.

8. Wade Hampton to Jefferson Davis, April 19, 1865; "The Northern Exultation," *Index* 5, no. 156 (April 20, 1865): 250.

9. Wade Hampton to Jefferson Davis, April 19, 1865; "The Assassination of Lincoln," *Index* 5, no. 157 (April 27, 1865): 264; Stephen R. Mallory to Davis, April 24, 1865, *JDP,* 11:565.

10. George Davis to Jefferson Davis, *JDC,* 6:577–78, *JDP,* 11:555; John H. Reagan to Davis, April 22, 1865, *JDP,* 11:556–57, *JDC,* 6:580–85.

11. John H. Reagan to Jefferson Davis, April 22, 1865.

12. Fred Cridland to Earl Russell, May 12, 1865 FO 5/1029, 96, PRO; Henry A. Wise to Mary Elizabeth (Lyons) Wise, May 30, 1865, box 2, Henry Alexander Wise Correspondence, Wise Family Papers, Mss 1 W7547 bFA2, VHS.

13. "Notes on the Events of the Week," "Lee's Farewell to His Army," *Index* 5, no. 158 (May 4, 1865): 274, 278; "The Surrender of Joseph E. Johnston," *Index* 5, no. 159 (May 11, 1865): 296.

14. Elizabeth R. Varon, *Appomattox: Victory, Defeat, and Freedom at the End of the Civil War* (New York: Oxford University Press), 2014; Judah P. Benjamin to Jefferson Davis, April 22, 1865, *JDP,* 11:554–55.

15. Jefferson Davis, "Address to the People," Danville, April 4, 1865, *JDC,* 6:529–31; "Four Years of War," *Index* 5, no. 155 (April 13, 1865): 232.

16. Stella Bringier to Joseph L. Brent, April 19, 1865 BT 92, JLB HL; James M. Mason to Judah P. Benjamin, May 1, 1865, *OR,* ser. 1, 3:1277.

17. Jefferson Davis to Varina Davis, April 13, Varina Davis to Jefferson Davis, April 28, 1865, *JDP,* 11:558–60, 569–70. At the time of his second marriage in 1845, Davis was hardly a "plain farmer"; he owned forty enslaved people and lived in the mansion of his brother Joseph (who had one hundred enslaved people as early as 1830) (Cooper, *Davis,* 81, 83–84).

18. Stella Bringier to Joseph L. Brent, April 19, 1865, BT 92, JLB HL; "The Destiny of the South," *Index* 5, no. 155 (April 13, 1865): 230; John H. Reagan to Jefferson Davis, April 22, 1865, *JDP,* 11:556; Sarah Morgan Dawson, *The Civil War Diary of Sarah Morgan,* ed. Charles East (Athens: University of Georgia Press, 1991), 609–11.

19. Kean, *Inside the Confederate Government,* 208–11.

20. William D. Cabell to Maria Massie, April 25, 1865, folder "January to July, 1865," Box 2E495, William Massie Papers, 1748–1919, UT; Fred Cridland to Earl Russell, April 21, 1865 FO 5/1029, p. 95, PRO; Henry Pinckney Walker to Earl Russell, May 3, 1865 FO 5/1030, pp. 143–44, PRO.

21. John Letcher, undated note, folder 432, "impressment and parole, May–July, 1865," Letcher Series 7, John Letcher (1813–1884) Papers, 1770–1970, Mssl L5684a FA2, VHS.

22. Note in Archer Diary, June 1865 VHS; Henry A. Wise to Mary Elizabeth (Lyons) Wise, May 30, 1865, box 2, Henry Alexander Wise Correspondence, Wise Family Papers, Mss 1 W7547 bFA2, VHS; Duff Green to Jefferson Davis, December 29, 1864, and Davis, Note, *JDP,* 11:258; Pryor, *Six Encounters with Lincoln,* 269, 272–73, 312–27.

23. George W. Randolph to Sarah Nicholas Randolph, July 23, 1865, group 8, papers of Jefferson, Randolph, Taylor, Smith & Nicholas families, UVA; Paul M. Gaston, *The New South Creed: A Study in Southern Mythmaking* (New York: Alfred Knopf, 1970); C. Vann Woodward, *The Origins of the New South, 1877–1913* (Baton Rouge: Louisiana State University Press, 1981), ix. Randolph did not draw on the old myth of southern superiority for his New South creed.

24. George W. Randolph to Molly Randolph, June 27, 1865, Folder 101, Box 5, The papers of the Randolph family of Edgehill and Wilson Cary Nicholas, MSS 5533, UVA; GWR to Sarah Nicholas Randolph, July 23, 1865, group 8, papers of Jefferson, Randolph, Taylor, Smith & Nicholas families, UVA.

25. Alexander H. H. Stuart, "Broadside to the People of Augusta Co." Broadsides o.s. 1865: 47, Broadsides, VHS.

INDEX

Unless otherwise stated, the indexed institutions, ideas, or events refer to the Confederacy—for example, commerce, Committee on Territories (House), Congress, foreign policy, House of Representatives, navy, Provisional Congress, Senate, State Department, War Department.